Intellectual Property Law in Tanzania

Intellectual Property Law in Tanzania

Third Edition

Jacob Jaconiah

This book was originally published as a monograph in the International Encyclopaedia of Laws/Intellectual Property Law.

Founding Editor: Roger Blanpain
General Editor: Frank Hendrickx
Volume Editor: Hendrik Vanhees

Wolters Kluwer

Published by:
Kluwer Law International B.V.
PO Box 316
2400 AH Alphen aan den Rijn
The Netherlands
E-mail: lrs-sales@wolterskluwer.com
Website: www.wolterskluwer.com/en/solutions/kluwerlawinternational

Sold and distributed by:
Wolters Kluwer Legal & Regulatory U.S.
7201 McKinney Circle
Frederick, MD 21704
United States of America
E-mail: customer.service@wolterskluwer.com

ISBN 978-94-035-4821-0

e-Book: ISBN 978-94-035-4582-0
web-PDF: ISBN 978-94-035-4343-7

The Author

Dr Jacob Jaconiah holds a doctorate in law from the University of Augsburg (2011). His other academic qualifications include a master's degree of intellectual property law (LLM IP) from the University of Augsburg, Germany awarded under the auspices of the Munich Intellectual Property Law Centre (2005) and a bachelor of laws (LLB) from the University of Dar Es Salaam, Tanzania (2003).

Dr Jaconiah has worked in academic institutions in Tanzania, the Netherlands and Germany; he was a German Academic Exchange Services (DAAD) scholar (2007–2010) and a visiting research fellow at the Max Planck Institute for Innovation and Competition (formerly the Max Planck Institute for Intellectual Property and Competition Law) in Munich (2008–2011), and at the Erasmus University of Rotterdam (2012). Dr Jaconiah has previously worked as a consultant to the Academy of European Law (ERA) in Trier, Germany in relation to the academy's training project that covered staff of the European Union's Office for the Harmonization in the Internal Market (Trade Marks and Designs). He also served as academic tutor at the Munich Intellectual Property Law centre as well as a consultant to the Economic and Social Research Foundation (Tanzania) in relation to the Foundation's Service Delivery Survey project commissioned by the government of the United Republic of Tanzania.

The Author

Table of Contents

List of Abbreviations

ARIPO	African Regional Intellectual Property Organization
BARA	Business Activities Registration Act
BNRA	Business Names Registration Act
BPM	Banjul Protocol on Marks
BPRA	Zanzibar Business and Property Registration Agency
BRELA	Business Registration and Licensing Agency
CAEA	Court of Appeal for East Africa
CCM	Chama Cha Mapinduzi (a ruling party in Tanzania)
CD	Compact Disc
Cf.	Confer
COSOTA	Copyright Society of Tanzania
DVD	Digital Video Disc
E.A.	East African Law Reports
EAC	East African Community
EACJ	East African Court of Justice
EACT 1999	Treaty for the Establishment of East African Community, 1999
GN	Government Notice
HCZ	High Court of Tanzania Zanzibar
HP	Harare Protocol on Patent and Industrial Designs, 1982
i.e.	That is to say
IC	Integrated Circuit
IP	Intellectual Property
IPOZ	Industrial Property Office of Zanzibar
ITC	International Trade Centre
Km^2	Square kilometer
Ltd.	Limited Liability Company
MMA	Merchandise Marks Act, 1963
PBRA	Plant Breeders' Rights Act, 2012
PCT	Patent Cooperation Treaty

List of Abbreviations

PLR	Public Lending Right
RE	Revised Edition
TANU	Tanganyika African National Union
TBS	Tanzania Bureau of Standards
TCPA	Tanzania is the Copyright and Neighbouring Rights Act
TMRs	Trade and Service Marks Regulations
TPA	Tanzania Patents Act
TPO	Tanzania Patent Office
TRIPS	Trade-Related Aspects of Intellectual Property Rights
TSMA	Trade and Service Marks Act of Tanzania
TSMO	Trade and Service Marks Office of Tanzania
TZS	Tanzanian Shilling
UK	United Kingdom
UPOV	International Convention for the Protection of New Varieties of Plants
URL	Uniform Resource Locator (i.e., web address)
WIPO	World Intellectual Property Organization
WTO	World Trade Organization
ZIPA	Zanzibar Industrial Property Act No. 4 of 2008

General Introduction

§1. General Background

I. Geography[1]

1. The United Republic of Tanzania is located in the eastern part of Africa between longitude 29^0 and 41^0 East and latitude 1^0 and 12^0 South. This country belongs to the East African Community (EAC); it is one of the community's founder Partner States. Other EAC founder Partner States are Kenya and Uganda. The Republic of Burundi and the Republic of Rwanda joined the community in 2010, thus making the total of five EAC's Partner States to date.[2]

With its geographical area totalling to 945,000 km^2 (out of which water occupies 62,000 km^2, forest and woodlands occupy 3,350 km^2), the United Republic of Tanzania is the world's Thirty-first largest country. In comparison to other African countries, Tanzania is slightly smaller than Egypt and comparable in size to Nigeria. However, Tanzania is the biggest of the East African countries (i.e., Kenya, Uganda, Burundi and Rwanda). Tanzania also has a spectacular landscape of mainly three physiographic regions namely the islands and the coastal plains to the east; the inland saucer-shaped plateau; and the highlands. The Great Rift Valley that runs from north east of Africa through central Tanzania is another landmark that adds to the scenic view of the country. The Rift Valley runs to south of Tanzania splitting at Lake Nyasa; one branch runs down beyond Lake Nyasa to Mozambique; and another branch to north-west alongside Burundi, Rwanda, Tanzania and western part of Uganda. The valley is dotted with unique lakes, which includes Lakes Rukwa, Tanganyika, Nyasa, Kitangiri, Eyasi and Manyara. The uplands include the famous Kipengere, Udzungwa, Matogoro, Livingstone and the Fipa plateau forming the southern highlands. The Usambara, Pare, Meru, Kilimanjaro, the Ngorongoro Crater and the Oldonyo Lengai, all form the northern highlands. From these highlands and the central saucer plateau flow the drainage system to the Indian Ocean, Atlantic Ocean, Mediterranean Sea and the inland drainage system.

Tanzania is mountainous in the northeast, where Mount Kilimanjaro Africa's highest peak, is situated. To the north and west are the Great Lakes of, respectively, Lake Victoria (Africa's largest lake) and Lake Tanganyika (the continent's deepest lake, known for its unique species of fish); and to the southwest lies Lake Nyasa.

1. Information in this part is reproduced from the website of the government of the United Republic of Tanzania http://www.tanzania.go.tz/home/pages/68 in compliance with the copyright notice.
2. Information on the East African Community is available at http://www.eac.int.

The United Republic of Tanzania contains many large and ecologically significant wildlife parks, including the famous Ngorongoro, Serengeti National Park where the white-bearded wildebeest (Connochaetes taurinus mearnsi) and other bovids participate in a large-scale annual migration in the north, and Selous Game Reserve and Mikumi National Park in the south. Gombe National Park in the west is known as the site of Dr Jane Goodall's studies of chimpanzee behaviour. A recently discovered species of elephant shrew called Grey-faced Sengi was filmed for the first time in 2005, and it was known to live in just two forests in the Udzungwa Mountains. In 2008, it was listed as 'vulnerable' on the 2008 Red List of Threatened Species. Lake Natron in northern Tanzania is the largest breeding site for the threatened Lesser Flamingo, a huge community of which nests in the salt marshes of the lake. Areas of East African mangroves on the coast are also important habitats.

II. Cultural Compositions[3]

2. The United Republic of Tanzania has been described as one of the most diverse countries in Africa and this is reflected in the fact that there are more than 158 local languages spoken in the country. Kiswahili is the national language that is widely spoken while English is the official language of education, administration and business.[4]

Local people are native African 99% of which 95% are Bantu consisting of more than 120 tribes and the remaining 1% consisting of Asians, Europeans and Arabs. Most of the population belongs to Christianity, Muslim and indigenous religions though there is a small number of Hindus and atheists. Generally, Tanzania culture is a product of African, Arab, European and Indian influences. Traditional African values are being consciously adapted to modern life, although at a much slower pace among the Maasai.

III. Political System[5]

3. The shaping of the political system of the United Republic of Tanzania started with the European Colonialists. The eighth century saw the growth of city States along the coast after settlement by Arabs as a nation from Oman. It was seven centuries later in 1499 that the Portuguese navigator Vasco da Gama visited the island

3. Information in this part is reproduced from the website of the government of the United Republic of Tanzania http://www.tanzania.go.tz/home/pages/68 in compliance with the copyright notice.
4. It must not be overemphasized here that within the borders of Tanzania coexist approximately 158 ethnic groups speaking languages representing all four major African language groups. These include Khoisan, or 'click' speaking hunter-gatherers, Nilotic-speaking pastoralists (such as the Maasai), Cushitic speakers and Bantu speakers; the latter predominate in terms of population size. Despite the tremendous cultural and linguistic diversity among Tanzanians, ethnic groups are united by the use of a common language – Kiswahili and a sense of national identity.
5. Information in this part is reproduced from the website of the government of the United Republic of Tanzania http://www.tanzania.go.tz/home/pages/68 in compliance with the copyright notice.

of Zanzibar. Another 100 years later in the sixteenth century, the Portuguese occupied Zanzibar. Their occupation did not last for long as in 1699 the Portuguese were ousted from Zanzibar by Arabs of Oman who had returned to make it their own. So in the eighteenth century the Sultan of Oman reasserted Arab overlordship of the East African coast, which became subordinate to Zanzibar.

By 1840, when Sultan Seyyid bin Sultan moved his capital from Oman to Zanzibar, trade in slaves and ivory flourished. In 1861, the Sultanates of Zanzibar and Oman separated on the death of Seyyid. During the nineteenth century, Europeans started to explore inland, closely followed by Christian missionaries. In 1884, the German Colonization Society began to acquire territory on the mainland in defiance of Zanzibar and 1890 Britain obtained protectorate status over Zanzibar, abolished the slave trade, and recognized German claims to the mainland. German East Africa was formally established as a colony in 1897.

The 1905–1907 Majimaji revolt was brutally suppressed by German troops. World events then took over with the outbreak of the First World War, and far as it was from Europe, German East Africa was not immune from the fighting, though effective fighting was short lived due to the successful 1916 Conquest of German East Africa by the British. In 1919, the League of Nations gave Britain a mandate to administer part of German East Africa, known as Tanganyika. In 1946, Tanganyika became a UN trust territory.

A Legislative Council was set up in 1926; it was enlarged in 1945 and restructured in 1955 to give equal representation to Africans, Asians and Europeans, sitting as thirty 'un-officials' with the thirty-one 'officials'. In 1954, a school teacher, Julius Kambarage Nyerere, founded the Tanganyika African National Union (TANU), which promoted African nationalism and won a large public following campaigning for independence. The colonial authorities responded with constitutional changes increasing the voice of the African population while reserving seats for minority communities.

Elections were held in 1958 and again in 1960. The result was an overwhelming victory for TANU, which was by this time campaigning for independence as well as majority rule. The new government and British government agreed at a constitutional conference in London to full independence for Tanganyika in December 1961. Zanzibar achieved independence in 1963 as a separate and sovereign country, under the al-Busaidy Sultan.

Tanganyika became a republic in December 1962, one year after achieving independence, and the direct presidential election brought TANU's leader, Julius Nyerere, to the presidency. In 1965, the Constitution was changed to establish a one-party system. Meanwhile, in Zanzibar, a revolution had overthrown the Arab Sultan on 12 January 1964. One month after independence the Constitution was abrogated; Abedi Amani Karume was declared the first African President of Peoples' Republic of Zanzibar and the country became a one-party State under the Afro-Shirazi Party.

On 26 April 1964, Tanganyika was amalgamated with Zanzibar to form the United Republic of Tanzania.[6] Following the union between Tanzania and Zanzibar,

6. The United Republic of Tanzania came into existence on 26 Apr. 1964 when the then two independent countries, namely Tanganyika and Zanzibar, merged to form a sovereign, united State. The legal concretization of this merger was realized through an agreement containing the Articles of the Union

Julius Nyerere became the first president and head of state of the United Republic, while Karume served as Nyerere's Vice President. In addition to his new role as a Vice President of the United Republic of Tanzania, Karume continued to serve as a President of Zanzibar. In 1971, Karume was assassinated in Zanzibar and Aboud Jumbe succeeded him as President of Zanzibar and Vice President of Tanzania. The political union between Zanzibar and mainland Tanzania has weathered more than four decades of change. Zanzibar has its own parliament and president.

In an effort to create socially equitable and rapid development, it became an early proponent of African socialism, Ujamaa (roughly meaning Togetherness), launched in 1967 under the banner of Arusha Declaration, with nationalization of banking, finance, industry and large-scale trade, marketing through boards, and the resettlement of peasants in communal villages, Vijiji vya Ujamaa, created out of large estates. In 1977, the two ruling parties; namely, TANU and Afro Shirazi Party, merged to form the Chama Cha Mapinduzi (CCM), which continues to rule the country after consecutive successful elections.

In mid-1970s, the United Republic of Tanzania introduced a one-party system that ended in 1992 following the reintroduction of the multiparty system. The United Republic of Tanzania held the first multiparty general election in 1995. The fifth multiparty elections held in October 2015 brought in His Excellency Dr John Pombe Joseph Magufuli from CCM as the fifth President of the United Republic of Tanzania for a second term.[7] Dr Magufuli passed away in March 2021. Following the demise of Dr Magufuli, his then Vice President Her Excellency Samia Suluhu Hassan became the President of the United Republic of Tanzania.

The President of Tanzania and members of National Assembly are elected together by direct popular vote to serve five-year terms. The president appoints a Prime Minister from among constituent elected MPs to serve as his representative in the assembly, and chooses a cabinet, from among its members. The Constitution also empowers him to nominate ten non-elected members of Parliament, who are also eligible to become cabinet members. The assembly is notable for its emphasis

---

signed by the then presidents of Tanganyika and Zanzibar on 22 Apr. 1964. The Act to ratify the Articles of the Union between the Republic of Tanganyika and the People's Republic of Zanzibar (Act of the Union (Act No. 22/1964)) (hereinafter 'Act of the Union') was enacted by the National Assembly of Tanganyika on 25 Apr. 1964, a day before formal proclamation of the Union. The Articles of the Union were thereafter incorporated in the Constitution of the Republic of Tanganyika thus making this Constitution an interim Constitution of the United Republic of Tanzania, providing for several matters relevant to the Union government (cf. s. 5 of the Act of the Union). The permanent constitution of the United Republic of Tanzania (hereinafter 'the Constitution') was enacted in 1977. Although this constitution governs the Republic of Tanzania including Tanganyika, Zanzibar has its own constitution that governs non-union matters. In addition, Zanzibar has its own president, own semi-autonomous judiciary and own parliament (officially designated as the House of Representatives). The House of Representatives enjoys powers to enact laws that regulate non-union matters. On her part, Tanganyika (or rather, Mainland Tanzania), has no independent government and State organs other than those of the United Republic (Cf. s. 8, Act No. 22/1964 & Art. 4 of the Constitution). To date, the Constitution has been amended severally.

7. Since independence, Tanzania has been ruled by five presidents, namely; the late Mwalimu Julius Kambarage Nyerere (1961–1985), H.E. Al Haj Ali Hassan Mwinyi (1985–1995); H.E. Benjamin William Mkapa (1995–2005); H.E. Jakaya Mrisho Kikwete (2005–2015); H.E. Dr John Pombe Joseph Magfuli (2015–2021). The current President of the United Republic of Tanzania is H.E. Samia Suluhu (2021– to date).

on women's rights – seventy-five of its seats are women-only, divided among political parties based on their electoral performance.

The unicameral National Assembly elected in 2010 had 320 members. These included the Attorney General, five members elected from the Zanzibar House of Representatives to participate in the Parliament, the special women's seats, which were made up of 30% of the seats that a given party had in the House, 189 constituent seats of members of Parliament from the Mainland and 50 seats from Zanzibar. Also in the list are the seats for the ten nominated members of Parliament and five Regional Commissioners. At present, the ruling CCM holds about 75% of the seats in the assembly. Laws passed by the National Assembly are valid for Zanzibar only in specifically designated union matters.

Zanzibar's House of Representatives has jurisdiction over all non-union matters. There are seventy-six members in the House of Representatives in Zanzibar, including fifty elected by the people, ten appointed by the president of Zanzibar, five ex officio members and an attorney general. In May 2002, the government increased the number of special seats allocated to women from ten to fifteen, which increased the number of House of Representatives members to eighty-one. Ostensibly, Zanzibar's House of Representatives can make laws for Zanzibar without the approval of the Union government as long as it does not involve union-designated matters. The terms of office for Zanzibar's president and House of Representatives also are five years.

IV. Population Statistics[8]

4. The current current, unofficial estimation of a number of people living in the United Republic of Tanzania is 62, 958, 104.[9] Over the period from 1967 to 2012, the population of Tanzania has almost increased fourfold. The rate of population growth has varied over this period. The population has grown from 12,313,469 persons in the first post-Independence Census in 1967 to 43,188,000 as of the estimated population 2010. The 2012 Population and Housing Census (PHC) for the United Republic of Tanzania was carried out on the 26 August 2012. This was the fifth Census after the Union of Tanganyika and Zanzibar in 1964. The 2012 Population and Housing Census results show that, Tanzania has a population of 44,928,923 of which 43,625,354 is on Tanzania Mainland and 1,303,569 is in Tanzania Zanzibar.

The number of people per square kilometre of land area, or population density in Tanzania varies considerably from region to region. People are particularly concentrated in Dar Es Salaam Region and Zanzibar Urban West. The other regions of Zanzibar and Mwanza are also relatively densely populated.

More than 80% of the population is rural. The Tanzania population consists of 158 ethnic groups. The population also includes people of Arab, Indian, and Pakistani origin and small European and Chinese communities.

8. Information in this part is reproduced from the website of the government of the United Republic of Tanzania http://www.tanzania.go.tz/home/pages/68 in compliance with the copyright notice.
9. https://worldpopulationreview.com/countries/tanzania-population.

§2. Historical Background

5. The United Republic of Tanzania is a common-law country; it observes a legal system bequeathed to it by the UK – the Tanzania's former colonial master. The court system of Tanzania mainland and Tanzania Zanzibar is hierarchically designed from primary court to the Court of Appeal. In both parts of the Union, there are primary courts, district courts, resident magistrate's courts and the High Court. Further to this, Tanzania Zanzibar has a Kadhi's Court dealing with Islamic law issues.[10] In addition to original jurisdiction, both the High Court of Tanzania Zanzibar (HCZ) and the High Court of Tanzania mainland have revision and appellate jurisdiction over decisions made by subordinate courts. The United Republic of Tanzania has a single Court of Appeal. This court has no original jurisdiction; its powers only entitle it to review and hear appeals against decisions of the HCZ as well as decisions of the High Court of Tanzania mainland. The Court of Appeal of the United Republic of Tanzania sits as a special constitutional court when reviewing constitutional issues.

The proposed new constitution of the United Republic of Tanzania is set out to introduce some new features in the court system.[11] One of the proposals contained in this constitution concerns the establishment of the Supreme Court of the United Republic of Tanzania as the country's highest judicial authority followed in rank by the Court of Appeal of the United Republic. The proposed constitution also renames the High Court as the High Court of the United Republic of Tanzania providing it with jurisdiction to deal with civil and criminal cases concerning the Union Matters and those confined to Tanzania mainland. Meanwhile, the new constitution re-establishes the High Court of Zanzibar and bestows upon it the authority to determine matters relating to Tanzania Island (i.e., Zanzibar).

6. As a result of the British legacy, courts in the United Republic of Tanzania are largely influenced by previous rulings or judgments rather than by statutes. As a matter of principle, stipulation of the statute governs the dispute in issue, whereas statutory interpretation rendered by courts of law serves as guidance as to how the provisions of the statute are to be applied. This necessitates judges and/or magistrates in Tanzania to rely on previous court decisions that address matters that are similar or closely resembling the subject matter of the actual dispute. This implies that although abstract codes or texts provide guidance insofar as application of the Tanzanian law is concerned, judges and/or magistrates in Tanzania find the grounds for their decisions in law reports. These reports contain judgments of cases decided

---

10. Note that Tanzania Zanzibar has a long Islamic tradition and the majority of its inhabitants are Muslims.
11. In the first quarter of 2015, the Constituent Assembly was appointed in line with the Constitutional Review Act, 2011 (Cap. 83) as amended by the Constitutional Review (Amendments) Act, 2012 (Act No. 2 of 2012) to enact the new constitution of the United Republic of Tanzania. For this constitution to acquire a force of law, the government of Tanzania has to conduct a referendum, which will give the citizenry an opportunity to accept or reject the proposed constitution. The date for the referendum is yet to be announced.

in the past. Following the doctrine of *Stare Decisis*[12] that is part and parcel of the core structure of the legal system obtaining in the United Republic of Tanzania, judges and/or magistrates in the country under reference are required to abide by an operative part of a previous judgment – a part that contains precedents (i.e., authoritative part of the judgment). However, Tanzanian judges and/or magistrates are not obliged to observe previous court decisions where the material facts of the previous case are dissimilar to those of the current case. As a matter of principle, a precedent set by a court in Tanzania binds that court and courts that are below it in the judicial hierarchy. Although such a precedent cannot bind on courts that are superior in terms of rank to the court that has set it, it may still be regarded as a persuasive authority.[13]

In addition to the rule requiring subordinate courts in the United Republic of Tanzania to abide by previous decisions of the superior courts in the judicial hierarchy, the freedom of inferior courts to depart from their own decisions is limited except where the decisions are distinguishable by facts. However, the Court of Appeal of the United Republic of Tanzania, being at the apex of the judicial hierarchy, has powers to depart from its own previous decisions.[14] This was not the case before 1977 when the United Republic of Tanzania, the Republic of Kenya and the Republic of Uganda owned a single Court of Appeal for East Africa (CAEA),[15] in which case Tanzania had no own Court of Appeal and the highest court at national level was the High Court. The CAEA formed part of the institutional structure of the then EAC established by the Treaty for East African Cooperation of 1967.[16] This treaty ceased to operate when the community and its institutions including the CAEA became defunct in 1977. However, decisions of CAEA still bind courts in Tanzania to date.

7. In 1999, the EAC was revived through the Treaty for the establishment of East African Community, 1999 (EACT 1999). East African Court of Justice (EACJ) forms part of the organizational structure of the new EAC.[17] This court, which was inaugurated on 30 November 2001, is an international court serving the EAC Partner States; namely, the United Republic of Tanzania, the Republic of Kenya, the Republic of Uganda, the Republic of Burundi and the Republic of Rwanda.[18] The EACJ consists of the first instance division and appellate division.[19] The EACJ's

12. *Stare decisis* is a Latin maxim which means 'stand by the matter decided'. This principle provides certainty, uniformity and predictability and makes for a stable legal environment.
13. By implementing common-law principles in the legal system of the United Republic of Tanzania, the Tanzanian courts enjoy a sufficient degree of flexibilities in dealing with everyday situations as they occur; socio-economic changes, and advances in science necessitate Tanzanian judges and/or magistrates time and again to look outside reported decisions for guidance. This approach is particularly resorted to if the court encounters a case involving previously undetermined novel or first impression issues. Judges in Tanzania enjoy a leeway to look to other jurisdictions or to draw upon past or present judicial experience for analogies to help in deciding cases before them.
14. Cf. *JUWATA v. KIUTA* [1988] TLR 146 at 154.
15. Cf. *Dodhia v. National & Grindlays Bank Ltd. and another* [1970] E.A. 195, at 198–200.
16. Cf. Arts 60 and 61, Treaty for East African Cooperation of 1967.
17. Cf. Art. 23, EACT 1999.
18. 15 Dec. 2015, http://eacj.org/?page_id=19.
19. Cf. Art. 23, EACT 1999.

basic jurisdiction is to interpret and monitor proper implementation of the EACT 1999.[20] In this regard, the EACJ enjoys original, appellate and human rights jurisdiction.[21] Note that the EAC Partner States may conclude a Protocol extending the EACJ's jurisdiction.[22] Given that no regional intellectual property (IP) regime has hitherto been installed in the EAC and the EACJ has not yet defined its jurisdiction in relation to these rights, the extent to which the EACJ can exercise jurisdiction over IP matters is not clear.

8. The United Republic of Tanzania is affiliated with African regional organizations dealing with IP. For instance, the country is one of the founding Member States of the African Regional Intellectual Property Organization (ARIPO). Consequently, the country has become a party to the following regional legal instruments for the regulation of IP: (1) Swakopmund Protocol on the Protection of Traditional Knowledge and Expressions of Folklore within the Framework of the ARIPO[23] of 9 August 2010; (2) Cultural Charter for Africa (19 September 1990); (3) Harare Protocol on Patents and Industrial Designs (HP) within the Framework of the ARIPO (26 February 1986); and (4) Lusaka Agreement on the Creation of the ARIPO) (15 February 1978).

9. The United Republic of Tanzania is party to almost all key international legal instruments concerning protection of IP rights.[24] The list of these instruments and

20. Cf. Art. 27(1), EACT 1999.
21. Cf. Art. 27(2), EACT 1999.
22. *Ibid.*
23. This instrument has not yet come into force for lack of the required number of ratifications and/accession. The United Republic of Tanzania is one of the countries, which has not ratified this piece of legislation.
24. These instruments include the following: (i) Agreement establishing the World Trade Organization (WTO) of 1994 (adopted on 15 Apr. 1994 at Marrakesh Entry into Force on 1 Jan. 1995); (ii) World Trade Organization (WTO) – Agreement on Trade-Related Aspects of Intellectual Property Rights (TRIPS Agreement) (1994); (iii) Convention on Biological Diversity of 1992 (adopted on 5 Jun. 1992 at Rio de Janeiro and entered into force on 29 Dec. 1993); (iv) Paris Convention for the Protection of Industrial Property of 1883 (adopted on 20 Mar. 1883 at Paris and entered into force on 7 Jul. 1884; revised on 14 Dec. 1900 at Brussels and entered into force on 14 Sep. 1902; revised on 2 Jun. 2, 1911 at Washington D.C. and entered into force on 1 May 1913; revised on 6 Nov. 1925 at The Hague and entered into force on 1 Jun. 1928; revised on 2 Jun. 1934 at London and entered into force on 1 Aug. 1938 revised on 31 Oct. 1958 at Lisbon and entered into force on 4 Jan. 962; revised on 14 Jul. 1967 at Stockholm and entered into force on 26 Apr. 1970; amended on 28 Sep. 1979); (v) Nice Agreement Concerning the International Classification of Goods and Services for the purposes of the Registration of Marks of 1957 (adopted on 15 Jun. 1957 at Nice and entered into force on 8 Apr. 1961; revised on 14 Jul. 1967 at Stockholm entered into force on 12 Nov. 1969; revised on 13 May 1977 at Geneva and entered into force on 6 Feb. 1979; and amended on 28 Sep. 1979); (vi) Convention Establishing the World Intellectual Property Organization of 1967 (adopted on 14 Jul. 1967 at Stockholm and entered into force on 26 Apr. 1970, and amended on 28 Sep. 1979); (vii) Patent Cooperation Treaty of 1978 (adopted on 19 Jun. 1970 at Washington D.C. and entered into force on 24 Jan. 1978, as amended on 28 Sep. 1979, and modified on 3 Feb. 1984 and on 3 Oct. 2001); (viii) Convention concerning the Protection of the World Cultural and Natural Heritage of 1972 (Adopted on 16 Nov. 1972 at Paris and entered into force on 17 Dec. 1975); and (ix) International Treaty on Plant Genetic Resources for Food and Agriculture of 2001 (Adopted on 3 Nov. 2001 at Rome and entered into force on 29 Jun. 2004).

the dates on which the instruments concerned entered into force with respect to the United Republic of Tanzania is available at http://www.wipo.int/wipolex/en/.

10. Tanzania has no single, centralized institution dealing with IP matters. These matters are administered through different offices belonging to different ministries of the government of the United Republic of Tanzania. In this regard, industrial property rights are regulated in Tanzania by the Business Registration and Licensing Agency (BRELA) established, under the Ministry of Industry and Trade, to provide services in relation to business name registration, trade and service marks registration, patents, company registration and industrial licensing.[25] BRELA is an administrative support framework that facilitates the administration of four registries; namely, the Registry of Companies (under the Companies Act No. 12 of 2002), business names (under the Business Names Act Cap. 213 of the laws of Tanzania), Trade and Service Marks (under the Trade and Service Marks Act No. 12 of 1986) and Patents (under the Patents Act No. 1 of 1987). Administration of matters pertaining to Copyright and Neighbouring Rights in Tanzania are overseen by the Copyright Society of Tanzania (COSOTA), which is a statutory body set up by the government of Tanzania under the Ministry of Industry and Trade. Section 46 Tanzania Copyright and Neighbouring Rights Act, 1999 (No. 6 of 1999) establishes COSOTA as a collective administrator of the Copyright and neighbouring rights in Tanzania. Finally, protection in Tanzania of legal rights relating to plant varieties is carried out by a government office within the Ministry of agriculture, which serves as the Plant Breeders' Rights Registry[26] and manned by a ministerial appointee designated as registrar.[27]

The office responsible for the administration of IP matters in Tanzania Zanzibar is the Zanzibar Business and Property Registration Agency (BPRA). This is a governmental institution established under the BPRA Act 13 of 2012 to replace the Office of Registrar General of Zanzibar. One of the BPRA departments is responsible for registering IP rights in Zanzibar.[28]

The United Republic of Tanzania has a formalized and institutionalized system that guarantees a certain level of enforcement of IP rights. Institutions that are part of this system include the Fair Competition Commission, the Judiciary, Police, Customs and the Ministry of Agriculture.

11. The United Republic of Tanzania has a legally complicated IP regime. This complication has its source in the Constitution of the United Republic. In its first schedule, the Constitution lists all Union Matters.[29] It is noticeable that IP is not expressly itemized in the schedule as one of the Union Matters. This has provided

25. More information on BRELA is available at http://www.brela-tz.org.
26. Cf. Parts II and X, PBR Act.
27. Cf. s. 4(1), PBR Act.
28. At http://www.bpra.go.tz/index.php/registration/intellectual-property-registration (accessed: 1 Mar. 2022).
29. These matters are as follows: (1) the Constitution of Tanzania and the Government of the United Republic; (2) Foreign Affairs; (3) Defence and Security; (4) Police; (5) Emergency Powers; (6) Citizenship; (7) Immigration; (8) External borrowing and trade; (9) Service in the Government of the United Republic; (10) Income tax payable by individuals and by corporations, customs duty and

room for the existence of two different sets of IP laws in the United Republic of Tanzania, with Mainland Tanzania and Tanzania Zanzibar each having its own IP legislations. Based on the coexistence of IP laws in the United Republic of Tanzania as indicated in the immediately preceding sentence, some commentators have concluded that there exist separate IP protection regimes in mainland Tanzania and Tanzania Zanzibar.[30] While coexistence of IP legislation must be acknowledged, a view supporting existence of two independent IP regimes in the United Republic of Tanzania can hardly be defended. It is logical to argue that the unitary nature of the Union between Tanzania mainland and Tanzania Zanzibar, which has led to the coexistence of IP laws in United Republic of Tanzania, speaks also for existence of a single, intertwined IP regime in this country. In addition to specific constitutional provisions, rules governing comity between nations call for this conclusion as well. Given the status of IP system, which has been internationalized through various international IP treaties such as the Agreement on Trade-Related Aspects of Intellectual Property Rights (TRIPS Agreement) to which Tanzania Zanzibar is not a party, the government of the United Republic is bound by all international IP instruments it ratifies or accedes to and not the government of Tanzania Zanzibar. The latter government would only be accountable to the government of the United Republic if it fails to domesticate international obligations attaching to the United Republic.[31] With this view in mind, the legislative organ of Tanzania Zanzibar would be regarded to abuse its legislative powers,[32] which the Constitution of the United Republic of Tanzania bestows upon it if it enacts an IP law that is not in harmony with a piece of legislation enacted by the Parliament of the United Republic of Tanzania. Thus, it is safe to conclude that IP laws enacted by the House of Representatives (i.e., the legislative organ of Tanzania Zanzibar) are applicable only to the extent necessary to enforce international IP obligations of the United Republic of Tanzania and to the extent those IP laws do not conflict with IP legislations enacted by the Parliament of Tanzania.

---

excise duty on goods manufactured in Tanzania collected by the Customs Department; (11) Harbours, matters relating to air transport, posts and telecommunications; (12) All matters concerning coinage and currency for the purposes of legal tender (including notes), banks (including savings banks) and all banking business; foreign exchange and exchange control; (13) Industrial licensing and statistics; (14) Higher education; (15) Mineral oil resources, including crude oil, other categories of oil or products and natural gas; (16) The National Examinations Council of Tanzania and all matters connected with the function of the Council; (17) Civil aviation; (18) Research; (19) Meteorology; (20) Statistics; (21) The Court of Appeal of the United Republic; and (22) Registration of political parties and other matters related to political parties.

30. Cf. August N. Mrema, *Recent Legislative Changes in Trademark Law in Tanzania* (http://www.mkono.com/pdf/Inta%20paper%202009-Final%20doc.pdf (last accessed: 16 Dec. 2015)).

31. Moreover, when it comes to international applications under the PCT or within the IP scheme operated by the ARIPO, only the United Republic is entitled to be designated as a country where international application for the protection of the IP rights concerned is sought.

32. Article 64 of the Constitution provides for the legislative powers of the Parliament of the United Republic of Tanzania (hereinafter 'the Parliament') and the House of Representatives of Tanzania Zanzibar (hereinafter 'the House of Representatives'). While the parliament has exclusive jurisdiction to legislate on all Union Matters and also on all non-union matters concerning Mainland Tanzania (Cf. Art. 64(1) of the Constitution), the legislative competence of the House of Representatives is only limited to non-union matters affecting Tanzania Zanzibar (Cf. Art. 64(2) of the Constitution).

12. It is important to note that international legal instruments do not automatically form part of the Tanzanian law, unless the legislature of the United Republic of Tanzania takes a relevant implementation step. As a common-law country that cherishes and observes English legal traditions, Tanzania follows a *dualist* approach when it comes to domestication of international treaties, conventions and agreements in the country.[33] This implies that, for these legal instruments to have force of law in Tanzania, it is required that the legislature of the United Republic of Tanzania enacts a piece of legislation giving effect the said category of legal instruments in the national legal system. Moreover, a domestic legislation passed by the legislature to implement international obligation as above must meet certain requirements for its effectiveness. Article 64(5) of the Constitution of the United Republic of Tanzania makes the Constitution supreme over all other laws such that any law that is repugnant to the Constitution becomes null and void to the extent of inconsistence.

The analysis in this monograph is largely based on the texts of national legislation on IP – and where necessary – complemented with slight references to provisions of international Conventions and Treaties. Due to paucity of case law on IP matters in Tanzania, carefully selected judgments and decisions rendered by judicial authorities in foreign jurisdictions have been cited as persuasive authorities in addition to very few domestic courts judgments that have been referred to in this monograph.

33. Cf. Andres Mancayo von Hase, *The Application and Interpretation of the Agreement on Trade-Related Aspects of Intellectual Property Rights*, in *Intellectual Property and International Trade* 83 (Carlos M. Correa & Abdulqawi A. Yusuf eds, Kluwer Law International B.V (The Netherlands) 2d ed. 2008).

Chapter 1. Copyright and Neighbouring Rights

13. The history of the Tanzanian Copyright regime dates back to the third decade of the twentieth century; it is based on the UK Copyright Act of 1911, which was made part of the Copyright law of Tanganyika (i.e., Tanzania mainland) on 1 August 1924.[34] Extension of this Act to the territory of Tanganyika was realized through section 1 of the Copyright Ordinance, Cap. 218 of the laws of Tanganyika. In keeping with the provisions of this section, the Copyright Ordinance was supposed to 'be read and construed as one with the (Imperial) Copyright Act, 1911 … as extended to the territory [of Tanganyika]'.[35] This harmonious co-existence between the former piece of legislation and the latter statute is explained by the position that the extension of British Copyright law to the territory of Tanganyika had its roots in section 25 of the (Imperial) Copyright Act, 1911, which stated as follows:

> This Act except such of the provisions thereof as are expressly restricted to the United Kingdom, shall extend throughout his Majesty's dominions; provided that it shall not extend to a self-governing dominion, unless declared by the Legislature of that dominion to be in force therein either without any modification or additions relating exclusively to procedure and remedies, or necessary to adapt this Act to the circumstances of the dominion, as may be enacted by such legislature.[36]

14. Given its status as a territory, which was dependent on the UK of Great Britain,[37] Tanganyika could not assume international obligations such as ratifying or acceding to any international instruments on its own: once the UK had accepted to be bound by any international treaty, Tanganyika would also be required to observe obligations emanating from the respective treaty. As a result, Tanganyika became a party to the Universal Copyright Convention and to the Berne Convention when the United Kingdom (UK) acceded to these legal instruments in 1957.[38] Note that by virtue of its independence gained on 9 December 1961, Tanzania obtained freedom to pull out from international treaties to which the UK was party. Tanzania exercised this freedom in 1966 when the country divested itself of all British copyright legacies, through the Copyright Act of 1966 enacted by the Legislature of the United Republic of Tanzania. Further to this, the Copyright Act of 1966 disallowed application in Tanzania of the UK Copyright Act of 1911, and repealed and replaced the Copyright Ordinance Cap. 218.

15. The Copyright Act of 1966 was intended to play a special role to further the developmental needs of the then young nation (i.e., Tanzania). It must be recalled that 'On attaining independence, most developing countries [including Tanzania],

---

34. Cf. B.A. Rwezaura, *Legal Protection of Intellectual Property in Tanzania*, 4(1) Les. L.J. 240 (1988).
35. Cf. s. 1, Copyright Ordinance, Cap. 218 of the laws of Tanganyika.
36. Cf. s. 25(i), (Imperial) Copyright Act, 1911. Cf. also s. 31 of the U.K. Copyright Act, 1956.
37. Note that the Treaty of Versailles of 1919 (concluded under the auspices of the League of Nations) gave Britain mandate to administer the territory of Tanganyika. Note further that British administered Tanganyika under the UN Trusteeship from 1947 up to independence in 1961.
38. Cf. B.A. Rwezaura, *Legal Protection of Intellectual Property in Tanzania*, 4(1) Les. L.J. 240 (1988).

[gave] priority to the training of their peoples and to education, in order to compensate for shortage of staff and management personnel that are essential to the design and implementation of developing policies and plans.'[39] Given that Tanzania had few proprietors of literary and artistic works and that these works could not satisfy the national training needs, the country felt that it could not realize its development policies and plans without changing its law on Copyright. Key changes that were brought in by the Copyright Act of 1966 included abolition of the reciprocity rule of Copyright protection, meaning that works published abroad could no longer enjoy protection in Tanzania, unless they were also published in the country. This change served as an assurance that foreign works would be available for exploitation in Tanzania, ostensibly contributing to the developmental and training needs of the country.

Note that after the enactment of the TRIPS Agreement, in 1994,[40] to which Tanzania is a party, there is no reason to worry that the country cannot have access to foreign works whenever such need arises. This is because the Berne Convention for the protection of literary and artistic works (adopted at Paris on 9 September 1886, as revised and amended) has been made part of the TRIPS Agreement.[41] The Berne Convention incorporates provisions, which countries of the Berne Union may invoke to authorize exploitation of certain artistic and literary works in the national interests even when the proprietors of these works are against such exploitation.[42] One of the justifiable forms such authorization may take is a compulsory licence. However, the country issuing a compulsory copyright licence must abide by the three-step test provided for under Article 9(2) Berne Convention. In keeping with this test, the issuance of a compulsory licence must be dictated by 'certain special cases' and an assurance must be given that the compulsory licence issued 'does not conflict with a normal exploitation of the work and does not unreasonably prejudice the legitimate interests of the author'.[43]

16. The Legislature of the United Republic of Tanzania took a bold decision in 1999 to repeal the Copyright Act of 1966 replacing it with the Copyright and Neighbouring Rights Act of 1999. This new Act has modernized the Copyright regime of Tanzania: it implements fully obligations, which the United Republic of Tanzania has to observe by virtue of the country's membership to the TRIPS Agreement and the Berne Union (Convention).

§1. Sources: Legislation

17. The basic law that regulates copyright and related matters in Tanzania is the Copyright and Neighbouring Rights Act, 1999 (No. 6 of 199) (hereinafter TCPA).

---

39. Cf. Henry Olsson, *Role of Copyright and Neighbouring Rights in Development*, 4(1) Les. L.J. 51 (1988).
40. The TRIPS Agreement is set out in Annex 1C to the Marrakesh Agreement establishing the World Trade Organization of 15 Apr. 1994. It entered into force on 1 Jan. 1995.
41. Cf. Art. 9, TRIPS Agreement.
42. Cf. Art. 9(2), Berne Convention.
43. *Ibid.*

Several regulations implement this Act. These are: (i) the Copyright and Neighbouring Rights (Registration of members and their works) Regulations; (ii) 2006 published on 20 October 2006 in the Government Notice (GN) No. 6; (iii) the Copyright (Licensing of Public Performances and Broadcasting) Regulations, 2003 published on 10 October 2003 in the GN No. 328; and (iv) the Copyright and Neighbouring Rights (Protection and Distribution of Sound and Audiovisual Recordings) Regulations, 2006 published on 10 February 2006 in the GN No. 18.

Since 25 July 1994, Tanzania is bound by the Berne Convention for the Protection of literary and Artistic Works of 1886 as revised on 24 July 1971 and amended on 28 September 1979 at Paris.

It is important to note that Tanzania Zanzibar has its own copyright regime, which is established under the Copyright Act, 2003. Application of this Act is generally limited to works that meet qualifying factors such as the requirement that copyright owner be a citizen, resident or otherwise established in Tanzania Zanzibar. Although copyright matters are not itemized in the Constitution of the United Republic of Tanzania as Union Matters, a clear stipulation under the TCPA clarifies that the Copyright law of the United Republic of Tanzania has territorial applications in both Tanzania mainland and Tanzania Zanzibar.

§2. Subject Matter of Protection

I. Different Categories of Protected Works

18. The Tanzanian copyright regime protects literary and artistic works as well as derivative works.[44] Derivative works are works derived from copyrightable literary and artistic works.

A. *Literary and Artistic Works*

19. Section 5(2) TCPA enshrines a long list of some literary and artistic works that qualify for copyright protection in Tanzania. Included in the list are the following: (a) 'Books, pamphlets and other writings, including computer programs'; (b) 'Lectures, addresses, sermons and works of the same nature'; (c) 'Dramatic and dramatico-musical works'; (d) 'Musical works (vocal and instrumental), whether or not they include accompanying words'; (e) 'Choreographic works and pantomimes'; (f) 'Cinematographic works, and other audiovisual works'; (g) 'Works of drawing, painting, architecture, sculpture, engraving, lithography and tapestry'; (h) 'Photographic works including works expressed by processes analogous to photography'; (i) 'Works of applied art, whether handicraft or produced on an industrial scale'; and (j) 'Illustrations, maps, plans, sketches and three-dimensional works relative to geography, topography, architecture or science.'

44. Sections 5 and 6, TCPA.

B. Derivative Works

20. Works derived from copyrightable artistic and literary works are protected in Tanzania as original works.[45] According to the TCPA, derivative works protectable as above include 'translation, adaptations, arrangements and other transformation of literary and artistic works'.[46] Note that copyright protection of derivative works does not prejudice protection under copyright law of the works from which the derivative works are derived.[47] For instance, if B translates a book, authored by A, from English into German, both A and B will enjoy copyright protection in their respective works.

II. Works Excluded from Protection

21. The Copyright law of Tanzania follows the general copyright protection pattern whereby certain works are specifically excluded from protection. For instance, mere ideas and written public documents such as legislative instruments do not enjoy copyright protection. This position accords with the provisions of section 7 of the TCPA, which identify works that are ineligible for protection under the copyright regime of Tanzania. For instance, the section decrees that 'laws and decisions of courts and administrative bodies as well as official translation thereof'[48] are under any circumstances not copyrightable. Exclusion from the realm of copyright protection extends also to 'news of the day published, broadcast or publicly communicated by any other means'.[49] In addition, 'any idea, procedure, method of operation, concept, principle, discovery or mere data, even if expressed, described, explained, illustrated or embodied in a work' whatsoever cannot enjoy copyright protection.[50]

As the foregoing paragraph establishes, mere ideas are not protected under the TCPA. For the purposes of copyright protection in Tanzania, this position paves the way for a distinction to be drawn between an idea and expression of the idea concerned: the latter usually attracts copyright protection, whereas the former does not. The distinction between expression and ideas also occupies a central space in the copyright protection regime established under the Agreement on TRIPS of 1994, to which the United Republic of Tanzania is a party. According to Article 9.2 of the Agreement, 'Copyright protection shall extend to expressions and not to ideas … '

The Case of *Donoghue v. Allied Newspapers Ltd* [1938] 1 Ch 106 elucidates the idea-expression dichotomy in the following manner:

> A person may have a brilliant idea for a story, or for picture, or for a play, and one which appears to him to be original; if he communicates that idea to an author or an artist or a playwright, the production which is the result of the

45. Section 6, TCPA.
46. Section 6(a), TCPA.
47. Section 6(2), TCPA.
48. Cf. s. 7(a), TCPA.
49. Cf. s. 7(b), TCPA.
50. Cf. s. 7(c), TCPA.

> communication of the idea to the author or the artist or the playwright is the copyright of the person who has clothed the idea in form, whether by means of a picture, a play, or a book, and the owner of the idea has no rights in that product.[51]

While one authority argues that the distinction between ideas and expression is very fine as it all depends on the operational meaning one assigns to the term 'idea',[52] it is certainly clear that an expression of an idea – however superb it is – may not be worthy of copyright protection unless it is made in a copyrightable fashion of a literary, dramatic, musical or artistic work. Admittedly though, there is no better summative view on the 'idea-expression dichotomy' at the disposal of this monograph's author than that offered by Lord Hoffman in the UK's House of Lords Judgment in *Designer Guild Limited (Appellants) v. Russell Williams (Textiles) Limited (trading as Washington Dc) (Respondents)* delivered on 23 November 2000,[53] who opines that:

> if one examines the cases in which the distinction between ideas and the expression of ideas has been given effect, I think it will be found that they support two quite distinct propositions. The first is that a copyright work may express certain ideas which are not protected because they have no connection with the literary, dramatic, musical or artistic nature of the work. It is on this ground that, for example, a literary work which describes a system or invention does not entitle the author to claim protection for his system or invention as such. The same is true of an inventive concept expressed in an artistic work. However striking or original it may be, others are (in the absence of patent protection) free to express it in works of their own. The other proposition is that certain ideas expressed by a copyright work may not be protected because, although they are ideas of a literary, dramatic or artistic nature, they are not original, or so commonplace as not to form a substantial part of the work.[54]

III. Special Categories of Works

A. *Computer Software*

22. Computer programs qualify for protection under the Tanzanian copyright law. They are protected as literary works within the ambit of section 5(2)(a) TCPA. The Copyright law of Tanzania applies the term 'Computer' in reference to an 'electronic or similar device having information processing capabilities'; and the term 'Computer Program' as a pointer to a 'set of instruction expressed in words, codes,

51. *Donoghue v. Allied Newspapers Ltd* [1938] 1 Ch 106 at 109.
52. *See* the opinion of Lord *Hailsham of St. Marylebone* in *L.B. (Plastics) Ltd v. Swish Products Ltd.* [1979] R.P.C. 551, 629.
53. At http://www.publications.parliament.uk/pa/ld199900/ldjudgmt/jd001123/design-1.htm.
54. *See* s. 6, para. 3, of Lord Hoffman's opinion.

schemes or in any other form, which is capable when incorporated in a medium that the computer can read, of causing a computer to perform or achieve a particular task or result'.[55]

B. Databases

23. The Copyright Act of Tanzania (TCPA) does not enshrine a provision guaranteeing rights in a database as such; it contains a clear stipulation excluding copyright protection in respect of mere data.[56] However, databases which fulfil stipulated protection criteria enjoy copyright protection. The decisive factor for protection in this regard is the degree of intellectual creativity involved in the selection and arrangement of the contents, which make the database special and original.[57] From their general nature, databases are made of facts. For works based on facts as such to be protected it is necessary that the author's work be a result of independent creation coupled with at least a merest but substantial level of creativity. This position can be buttressed by the case of *Feist Publications, Inc v. Rural Telephone Service Co* [1991] USSC 50, at pp. 344, in which it was held *inter alia* that:

> Since facts do not owe their origin to an act of authorship, they are not original and, thus, are not copyrightable. Although a compilation of facts may possess the requisite originality because the author typically chooses which facts to include, in what order to place them, and how to arrange the data so that readers may use them effectively, copyright protection extends only to those components of the work that are original to the author, not to the facts themselves. This fact/expression dichotomy severely limits the scope of protection in fact-based works.

C. Expressions of Folklore

24. Although the TCPA enshrines a sui generis regime for the protection of expressions of folklore, literary and artistic works inspired by these expressions can also be protected in Tanzania as original copyright works.[58]

As regards the *sui generis* regime, protection of folklore in Tanzania is based on the Copyright Act, 1999[59] and the National Arts Council of Tanzania Act, 1984.

55. Cf. s. 4, TCPA.
56. Cf. s. 7(c), TCPA.
57. Cf. s. 6(1)(b), TCPA.
58. Cf. s. 6(1)(c), TCPA.
59. The Legislature of the United Republic of Tanzania enacted the Copyright and Neighbouring Rights Act of 1999 (Act No. 7 of 1999 of the laws of Tanzania) incorporating in it a section providing for a sui generis regime for the protection of expressions of folklore. In particular, this sui generis regime ensures the continuing customary use, development, exchange and transmission of expressions of folklore by local communities, as well as the customary custodianship of these expressions of folklore in Tanzania. The regime devises some mechanisms for deterring gradual disappearance, erosion, misuse, unlawful exploitation, and misappropriation of expressions of folklore by availing

These pieces of legislation implement in the United Republic of Tanzania some of the obligations emanating from international instruments in force in the United Republic. The pertinent international instruments are as follows: (1) The Convention Establishing the World Intellectual Property Organization (WIPO) of 14 July 1967 in force in Tanzania since 30 December 1983; (2) The Convention Concerning the Protection of the World Cultural and Natural Heritage of 16 November 1972 in force in Tanzania since 2 November 1977; and (3) The Cultural Charter for Africa of 5 July 1977 in force in Tanzania since 19 September 1978. All these international legal documents contain some provisions requiring contracting parties to provide for a national legal framework for the protection of traditional cultural expressions (i.e., folklore).[60]

The term 'expression of folklore' is employed under section 4 TCPA as a reference to 'production consisting of characteristic elements of the traditional artistic heritage developed and maintained over generations by a community or by individuals reflecting the traditional artistic expectations of their community'.[61] The Copyright Act enshrines a non-exhaustive list of expressions of folklore protectable in Tanzania. Included in the list are the following: (1) folk tales, folk poetry, riddles; (2) folk songs and instrumental folk music; (3) folk dances, plays and artistic forms of rituals; (4) folk art, particularly those produced in drawings, painting, carvings, sculpture, pottery, terracotta, mosaic, wood work, metal ware, jewellery, baskets, costumes; and (5) traditional musical instruments.[62]

Section 3 TCPA mainly extends protection to 'expressions of folklore developed and maintained in the United Republic of Tanzania'.[63] Expressions of folklore developed and maintained in a foreign country can only be protected in Tanzania based on the reciprocity principle in accordance with provisions of section 3(6)(b) TCPA. Pursuant to the reciprocity rule, 'expressions of foreign folklore' can be protected in Tanzania only if the 'country of the community from which such expressions have been derived, grants similar protection to expression of folklore developed and maintained in the United Republic of Tanzania'.[64]

As regards its ownership, expression of folklore cannot be owned by a single person: the law vests the right to own expressions of folklore in the whole community

local communities owning expressions of folklore with effective and efficient protection against all acts of misuse, unlawful exploitation or misappropriation of their expressions of folklore. Although it does not claim to be a panacea, the Tanzanian sui generis regime for the protection of expressions of folklore can be commended for having put in place a legal framework precluding the improper grant and exercise of IP rights in expressions of folklore and works and productions derived thereof.

60. An important legal development with respect to protection of expressions of folklore in ARIPO Member States took place in 2010, when ARIPO enacted a legal instrument providing for regional protection of expressions of folklore. This instrument is popularly known as the Swakopmund Protocol on the Protection of Traditional knowledge and Expressions of Folklore of 2010. The United Republic of Tanzania is a member of ARIPO and hence it is required to implement provisions of the Swakopmund Protocol. The protocol clearly outlines obligations to protect expressions of folklore and modalities of such protection, regionally and in ARIPO individual Member States that have accepted to be bound by the protocol.
61. Cf. s. 4, para. 12, TCPA.
62. Cf. s. 24(a)–(e), TCPA.
63. Cf. s. 3(2), TCPA.
64. Cf. s. 3(6)(b), TCPA.

of people of the geographical area where the expression of folklore emanates or is known, observed, preserved and practised.[65]

Exploitation of folklore is subject to certain conditions. Within the ambit of section 25 TCPA, interested persons are allowed to utilize protected expressions of folklore provided that the utilization is not for profit and takes place within the 'traditional or customary context'. Note that under certain circumstances the competent authority is allowed to authorize exploitation of expressions of folklore, which is for profit and made outside the traditional or customary context.[66] The competent authority's authorization within the meaning of the immediately preceding sentence applies to: (1) any application, reproduction and distribution of copies of expressions of folklore; and/or (2) communication to the public, including recitation, performance, broadcasting or distribution by cable, of the expressions of folklore. Note that the 'competent authority' within the ambit of the TCPA is the National Arts Council of Tanzania. The Council is established under section 3 of the National Arts Council of Tanzania Act, 1984.[67] Where exploitation of expressions of folklore is subject to the competent authority's authorization, an individual or a blanket application in this regard has to be made in writing by interested parties.[68] Oral application for the utilization of an expression of folklore is not acceptable. Decisions of the competent authority with respect to applications for authorization to utilize expressions of folklore are reviewable by the supervisory authority. In this regard, the supervisory authority acts as a first appeal instance in relation to decisions of the competent authority.

The law empowers the competent authority to determine fees, which persons interested in utilizing expressions of folklore may be required to pay as a condition for such utilization.[69] In discharging this duty, the competent authority has to act in

65. Cf. s. 27, TCPA.
66. Cf. ss 25 and 28, TCPA.
67. According to its long title, the Revised Edition of this Act (i.e., Cap. 204 [RE 2002]) reconstituted the National Arts Council by amalgamating the National Arts Council and the National Music Council and provided for related matters.
68. Unless the National Arts Council, which is an authority competent within the meaning of s. 28(a) of the Copyright Act to authorize exploitation of folklore, issues permission, criminal liability attaches to a person who 'imports or distributes copies of expressions of folklore derived from the United Republic of Tanzania'. Similar criminal liability attaches to a person who imports or distributes in the united Republic of Tanzania 'copies of translations, adaptations, arrangement or other transformations of expressions of folklore' derived from the United Republic of Tanzania, whereby the said copies are made abroad without authorization of the National Arts Council of Tanzania (s. 42(2), TCPA). A person who exploits expressions of folklore by importing and/or distributing copies as above is, upon conviction, liable 'to a fine not exceeding TZS 10 million or imprisonment for a term not exceeding ten years'. Note that direct utilization of expressions of folklore without authorization of the National Arts Council of Tanzania, whereby the said utilization is not exempted under the general exception outlined, is punishable by a fine of up to TZS 5 million or by imprisonment up to three years. Note further that a person purporting to pursue exploitative acts in relation to expressions of folklore that fall within the ambit of the general exception clause outlined above but, either intentionally or negligently does not confine the said acts within the scope of the said exception is 'liable to a fine not exceeding TZS 3 million or imprisonment for a term not exceeding one year' (s. 42(3) TCPA).
69. According to s. 28(b) TCPA, the fee to be collected by the competent authority must be used to promote or safeguard the national culture.

accordance with the tariff scheme approved by the supervisory authority.[70] In this context, supervisory authority is the minister who, for the material time, is an overseer of copyright and neighbouring rights matters in Tanzania.[71]

Exploitation of expression of folklore made with gainful intent and outside the place where the folklore is known and practised is regarded illicit unless the law specifically exempts such utilization from the requirement of the competent authority's prior authorization. Section 26 TCPA provides for an exception to the authorization requirement stipulated in section 25 TCPA. It enumerates instances of exploitation of expressions of folklore whereby the competent authority's authorization is not required. The exception applies to the following: (1) utilization of expressions of folklore for education purposes; (2) utilization by including in an original work created by a single author or by several authors an illustration based on expressions of folklore;[72] and (3) utilization by 'borrowing expressions of folklore for creating the author's original work(s) inspired by folklore'.[73] Incidental utilization of folklore is also exempted from the requirement to ask for the competent authority's authorization. Instances under which exploitation of expressions of folklore may be regarded incidental, within the ambit of section 26(d), include the following: (1) 'utilization of an expression of folklore that can be seen or heard in the course of the current event[s] for the purposes of reporting on [these] event[s] by means of photography, broadcasting or sound or visual recording, provided that the extent of such utilization is justified for informatory purpose';[74] and (2) 'utilization of objects containing the expression of folklore which are permanently located in a place where they can be viewed by the public, if the utilization consists including their image in a photograph, in a film or in a television broadcasting'.[75]

The law requires a source of folklore to be indicated along with utilization of expressions of folklore, unless the utilization concerned is covered by an exception recognized under the law.[76] In this regard, section 27 TCPA provides as follows:

> In all printed publications, and in connection with any communications to the public, of any identifiable expression of folklore its source shall be indicated in an appropriate manner, by mentioning the community and/or geographic place from where the expression utilized has been derived.

The scope of protection of expressions of folklore is stipulated in section 30 TCPA. The section reinforces that the provisions of sections 24–29 TCPA, which set out the regime for the protection of expressions of folklore in Tanzania cannot be interpreted in a way that contravenes the 'normal use', maintenance and 'development of the expressions concerned'.[77] It is arguable that the stipulation against

---

70. Cf. s. 28(b), TCPA.
71. Cf. s. 4, para. 14 and s. 29(a), TCPA.
72. This exception applies only insofar as the utilization does not deviate from the fair practice (cf. s. 26(b), TCPA).
73. Cf. s. 26(c), TCPA.
74. Cf. s. 26(d)(i), TCPA.
75. Cf. s. 26(d)(ii), TCPA.
76. Cf. exceptions outlined in para. 136 below.
77. Cf. s. 30(1), TCPA.

invoking the provisions of the TCPA[78] to obstruct the normal use of the expressions of folklore is not free from ambiguity, since the TCPA does not define what constitutes 'normal use' within the ambit of section 30 TCPA. However, it may equally be discerned from the communal ownership modality underlying expressions of folklore that the term 'normal use' includes utilization of expressions of folklore by individuals of the community owning the expressions concerned, provided such utilization is undertaken in the geographical area where the respective expressions are maintained. In this regard, activities by individuals or civil society organizations, which seek to preserve or develop expressions of folklore, are fully legal even where they seem to be in contravention of the TCPA's provisions – those which are relevant for the protection of expressions of folklore in particular.[79] In other words, an individual who (or an organization which), for instance, without the competent authority's prior authorization, utilizes expressions of folklore in order to maintain or develop the expressions concerned, should not be prohibited to do so.

The TCPA underscores the position that the folklore protection regime, which sections 24–29 TCPA stipulate, does not exclude other available modalities for the protection of folklore. This conclusion is enshrined in section 30(2) TCPA, which provides as follows:

> The provisions of this part of the Act shall in no way limit or prejudice any protection applicable to expressions of folklore under other Parts of this Act, or the laws protecting industrial property, or any other law or international treaty to which the United Republic of Tanzania is a party, nor shall it in any way prejudice other forms of protection provided for the safeguard and preservation of folklore.

In view of the above provisions, any individual may invoke legal provisions other than those providing for a specific protection of expressions of folklore[80] to monopolize these expressions. One of the examples whereby protection may be sought based on provisions other than those providing for specific protection of expressions of folklore would be copyright protection regime.[81] In this regard, the level of creativity and originality would be a decisive factor warranting protection of expressions of folklore under the copyright regime.[82]

78. That is ss 24–29, TCPA.
79. That is ss 24–29, TCPA.
80. *Ibid.*, providing for a specific protection regime of expressions of folklore.
81. Cf. §2(III)(A) of Ch. 1 of this chapter.
82. Cf. para. 20 above.

§3. CONDITIONS OF PROTECTION

I. Formal Requirements

25. The Copyright law of Tanzania does not require any formalities such as copyright notice or registration as a condition for copyright protection. Only creation of an original literary or artistic work merits automatic copyright protection[83] irrespective of the form, expression and quality of the work. Moreover, the purpose for creating a literary or artistic work is irrelevant to the question whether a particular work deserves copyright protection in the United Republic of Tanzania.[84]

26. The Copyright law of Tanzania establishes legal basis for copyright holders to have their works registered notwithstanding the fact that the law does not formally condition copyright protection on copyright registration or on giving notice of copyright existence. The COSOTA is the main authority vested with powers to register works protected under copyright. The society is a statutory body set up by the government of Tanzania under the Ministry of Industry and Trade. According to section 46 of the TCPA, COSOTA is established to serve as a collective administrator of copyright and neighbouring rights in Tanzania.[85] One of COSOTA's objectives is to register its members and their works. These powers stem from section

83. Cf. s. 5(1), TCPA.

84. Cf. s. 5(2), TCPA.

85. Being a body corporate, COSOTA enjoys perpetual succession and has a common seal; and may by virtue of its legal personality do the following: (1) institute legal proceedings and be sued in court in its own name; (2) acquire (through any lawful means), hold and alienate any corporeal and incorporeal property (cf. s. 48(c)-(e) of the TCPA); and (3) perform any other 'acts or things as bodies corporate may by law do or perform' to the extent permitted by the Copyright Act (cf. s. 46(iii) of the TCPA). In addition to all statutory fees payable to it (cf. s. 49), COSOTA receives subsidy from the government of Tanzania, gets grants and bequests to facilitate the society's activities. The governmental subsidy referred to in the immediately preceding sentence is justifiable since COSOTA functions both as a copyright office and a collecting society. The composition of its membership provided for in para. 1(1) of the sole schedule to the TCPA, reflects the foregoing COSOTA's dual roles. According to the provisions of the said paragraph, membership of the Board of COSOTA consists of the delegates from the following: (a) The Commission of culture; (b) The National Arts Council; (c) The office dealing with industrial property; (d) Film Makers Association; (e) National Museum of Tanzania; (f) Faculty of Law of the University of Dar Es Salaam; (g) The Attorney General's Chambers; (h) The Tanzania Authors Association; (i) The Tanzania Broadcasting Commission; and (j) The Customs Department. Of all the organs from which COSOTA Board members are drawn, only two authorities, namely the film makers association and the Tanzania authors associations are run and managed privately: all the rest are governmental institutions or authorities. However, it is notable under para. 2 of the schedule that up to one-third of the above COSOTA's ex officio Board Members have to be replaced by private stakeholders after every two years. Section 47 TCPA entrusts COSOTA with numerous responsibilities, namely the following: (a) 'to promote and protect the interests of authors, performers, translators, producers of sound recordings, broadcasters, publishers, and, in particular, to collect and distribute any royalties or other remuneration accorded to them in respect of their rights provided for in the [TCPA]'; (b) 'to maintain registers of works, productions and associations of authors, performers, translators, producers of sound recordings, broadcasters and publishers'; (c) 'to search for, identify and publicize the rights of owners and give evidence of the ownership of these where there is dispute or an infringement'; (d) 'to print, publish, issue or circulate any information, report, periodical, books, pamphlet, leaflet or any other material

47(b) TCPA. The section is implemented by the regulations on registration of members and their works (hereinafter 'member registration regulations').[86] Pursuant to these regulations, any person may apply for the membership of COSOTA.[87] Once he pays membership application fees, such a person may be registered and issued with COSOTA's membership certificate.[88] Holders of this certificate are entitled to have their works (protected under the TCAP) registered with COSOTA free of charge.[89] This entitlement is enjoyable as long a member who has paid annual subscription fees[90] declares his work to COSOTA.[91] Registration of a work may be refused if a similar work is already registered in the register or if there is any dispute in relation to the work whose registration is being sought. To clarify these matters, COSOTA has to search the register of the works prior to registering the work concerned.[92]

It falls within COSOTA's mandate to administer collectively all income resulting from commercial utilization of works registered by it.[93] This obligation justifies the powers that COSOTA enjoys under section 48(a) TCPA; which is, 'to determine the minimum rates of royalties to be levied in respect of uses to be made of works registered by it' and to distribute the same to its members.[94]

27. Nevertheless, it is important to reiterate that under the Tanzanian law the existence of copyright as well as claim of right in relation to copyright is independent of whether or not a corresponding right is registered.[95] This position of the Tanzanian law argues well with provisions of the Berne Convention obliging Member States of the Berne Union such as the United Republic of Tanzania to establish a domestic copyright protection regime that does not require compliance with some formalities as a condition for protection. Thus, whether or not a work is registered it receives the same protection standards established under the Copyright law of Tanzania. However, a copyright holder who lets his copyrighted work registered is at advantageous position insofar as enforcement of his copyright is concerned. Extracts from the register of copyrighted works have evidentiary value and may serve as a proof of the copyright ownership in enforcement proceedings. This

---

relating to copyright and rights of performers, producers of recordings and broadcasters'; and (e) 'to advise the minister on all matters under the [TCPA]'.

86. Three regulations implementing the mandates of COSOTA have so far been enacted in line with the provisions of s. 45 TCPA, which stipulates as follows: 'The Minister may make regulations prescribing such matters as are required or permitted by this Act to be prescribed or as necessary or convenient to be prescribed for carrying out or giving effect to the provisions of this Act.' The regulations concerned are: (1) the Copyright and Neighbouring Rights (Registration of members and their works) Regulations, 2006; (2) the Copyright (Licensing of Public Performances and Broadcasting) Regulations, 2003; and (3) the Copyright and Neighbouring Rights (Production and Distribution of Sound Audio-visual Recordings) Regulations, 2006.
87. Cf. para. 3 of member registration regulations.
88. Cf. para. 4 of member registration regulations.
89. Cf. paras 6 and 7 of member registration regulations.
90. Cf. para. 5 of member registration regulations.
91. Cf. para. 6 of member registration regulations.
92. Cf. para. 9 of member registration regulations.
93. Cf. para. 5 of member registration regulations.
94. Cf. s. 47(a), TCPA.
95. Cf. s. 5(1), ZA-CA.

implies that a person whose work is not registered with COSOTA will encounter certain degree of difficulty to prove his copyright ownership and entitlement to sue infringers.

II. Substantive Requirements

A. Fixation Requirement

28. The Copyright law of Tanzania does not require any fixation of a copyrightable work as a condition of copyright protection.[96] This position of the Tanzanian law as regards the fixation requirement is in line with provisions of Article 2(2) of the Berne Convention, which provide as follows: 'It shall, however, be a matter for legislation in the country of the Union to prescribe that works in general or any specified categories of works shall not be protected unless they have been fixed in some material form.'

By not making fixation a mandatory requirement of copyright protection, the Tanzanian legislature has avoided some criticisms which are usually levelled against vesting of rights in copyright proprietors only after the work in which the copyright subsists have been fixed in a tangible medium. Critics of this rule argue *inter alia* that the fixation requirement limits the scope of copyright protection by denying protection to authors of unfixed works. By not insisting on the fixation of copyrightable works, the Tanzanian Copyright law has broadened the scope of copyright protection. Currently therefore, the copyright protection threshold provides a space for copyright protection in Tanzania of unfixed works. Should the unfixed work be fixed or reduced into material form by a person other than the author of unfixed work, the Tanzanian law entitles both the author and the person fixing the work to distinct copyrights. This position of the Tanzanian law implies that, depending on the degree of its originality, an oral speech may be a literary work with copyright arising out of its unrecorded form. However, if the oral speech is recorded, 'even by another, the maker of the speech will be considered its author and may have a copyright in the recorded form. Whether the person recording also has a copyright, solely or jointly, may depend on the form of the record, i.e., whether it is written or is automatically recorded on tape or disk'.[97]

The foregoing position of the Tanzanian law regarding the fixation requirement is also supported by *Adeney* who poses and responds to the question 'whether fixation and authorship are parts of the same creative act in relation to literary, dramatic and musical works' in the following manner:

> The importance of the question is that, if authorship does not entail fixation, it should logically be possible for a person independent of the author to reduce the work to material form for copyright purposes. This would significantly

96. Section 5, TCPA.

97. David Vaver, *Principles of Copyright: Cases and Materials* 25 (WIPO 2002), WIPO Publication No. 844(A/E/F).

expand the range of works protected by copyright and would extend protection to those works which have never been fixed by their authors.[98]

B. Nationality or Habitual Residence of the Author

29. Nationality and habitual residence of the author are central for determining the question whether the author's work deserves protection in Tanzania.[99] In this regard, the TCPA extends copyright protection to works whose authors are nationals of the United Republic of Tanzania. Works of authors who are not nationals of the United Republic of Tanzania but whose habitual residence is in the United Republic of Tanzania are also entitled to copyright protection in Tanzania under the TCPA.

C. Place of Publication of the Work

30. Copyright protection of 'works first published in the United Republic of Tanzania' is not dependent on the nationality and habitual residence requirements explained in paragraph 29 above.[100] The Copyright law of Tanzania guarantees protection of such works even if the work's author is neither a national nor a habitual resident of the United Republic of Tanzania. According to the TCPA, 'Works first published in the United Republic of Tanzania' also means 'works first published abroad but thereafter published in the United Republic of Tanzania within thirty days.'[101]

31. The Copyright law of Tanzania employs reciprocity principle to protect a work published in a foreign country whose author is neither a national nor a habitual resident of the United Republic of Tanzania. The reciprocity principle is reflected in section 3 TCPA. Protected under this section are the following:

> unpublished and works first published in a foreign country of authors of foreign nationality and having their residence in a foreign country, provided that the country where the author has his habitual residence or, in case of published works, the country of their first publication, grants similar protection to nationals or residents of the country of the United Republic of Tanzania for their unpublished works to works first published in the United Republic of Tanzania.[102]

98. Adeney, Elizabeth *Authorship and Fixation in Copyright Law: A Comparative Comment*, 35(2) Melb. U. L. Rev. 23 (2011).
99. Cf. s. 3(1)(a), TCPA.
100. Cf. s. 3(1)(b), TCPA.
101. Cf. s. 4, TCPA.
102. Cf. s. 3(6)(a), TCPA.

D. Place Where Architecture Is Located

32. Works of architecture and artistic works incorporated in a building or in any other structure erected or located in the United Republic of Tanzania enjoy copyright protection under the TCPA.[103]

§4. Ownership

I. The Author

33. Not every person can assume a status of an author under Tanzanian law; the TCPA employs the term 'author' only in relation to 'natural person' who creates an original, copyrightable work.[104] As a result, the TCPA vests copyright ownership in a natural person who has created a work qualifying for protection in Tanzania.[105] There is a rebuttable presumption under Tanzanian law that the bearer of a name under which a copyrightable work is disclosed is the author of that work.[106] However, the fact that an author has used a pen name (pseudonym) in relation to his work is not sufficient grounds to rebut a presumption of authorship if the pen name 'leaves no doubt as to the identity of the author'.[107] Even in the circumstances where the pen name assumed by the author or the anonymous work does not identify the true author, a publishing company, which publishes the author's work cannot claim to be the author of the work notwithstanding the fact that this company customarily steps into the author's shoes insofar as economic and moral rights of the author are concerned. In the circumstances, the publishing company can only enjoy a legal, rebuttable presumption of being a representative of the interests of the pseudonymous or anonymous author in the respective work.[108] In this representative capacity, the company is entitled to enforce moral and economic rights of the author.[109] Note that according to Tanzanian law, the publishing company's entitlement to represent the pseudonymous or anonymous author ceases immediately after the revelation of the author's true identity.[110] The right to enforce moral and economic rights is thereafter controlled by the author himself.[111]

---

103. Cf. s. 3(1)(d), TCPA.
104. Cf. s. 4, para. 2, TCPA.
105. Cf. s. 15(1), TCPA.
106. Cf. s. 15(5), TCPA.
107. *Ibid.*
108. Cf. s. 15(6), TCPA.
109. *Ibid.*
110. *Ibid.*
111. However, a question may arise, in this regard, as to whether after revealing his true identity the author will be bound by the activities (such as licences, assignments and transfers) conducted by the publishing company on his behalf. In the event the company sues copyright infringers and loses the suit, it might similarly be questioned whether the judgment will bind the author upon revealing his true identity. An answer to these questions is not provided for under the Copyright law of Tanzania. A solution to these issues may find legal basis in general principles of laws.

II. Joint Works/Works Created by Several Persons

34. Copyrightable works created by several persons can generally result from joint authorship or co-authorship. The Copyright law of Tanzania employs, in relation to joint copyrightable works, the term 'works of joint authorship'. According to the TCPA, 'works of joint authorship means works created by two or more authors in collaboration, in which the individual contributions are indistinguishable from each other'.[112] This delineation implies that if, for instance, two or more persons write a book jointly they, under Tanzanian law, become joint authors with joint ownership of the copyright in their book.[113] Joint authorship in relation to musical works protected under the copyright of Tanzania may also result from combination of different roles played by the musicians. In one case in which four persons teamed up for a musical performance one of them being responsible for 'voice and piano' and three others being in charge of 'guitar' (the first person), 'bass' (the second person), 'drums' (the third person), were regarded to have made a joint work protectable under the copyright.[114] The ground on which this position is justified is that a musical work performed by more than one person is considered to be the outcome of repeated collaborative trial musical performance process. However, not every contribution to a musical work can entitle the individual contributor to the joint authorship of the musical work concerned. In this regard, the English court has set a persuasive position regarding the standards to be met for an individual contribution to merit copyright protection under joint authorship:

> contribution of the individual band member to the overall work is both significant (in the sense that it is more than merely trivial) and original (in the sense that it is the product of skill and labour in its creation) and the resulting work is recorded (whether in writing or otherwise), that band member is entitled to copyright in the work as one of its joint authors and to any composing royalties that follow. This assumes, of course, that there is no contractual arrangement to the contrary.[115]

35. The distinction between joint authorship and co-authorship is very fine; the TCPA does not address in detail copyrightable works of co-authorship.[116] However, one may cite audiovisual work as an example of a work of co-authorship. Usually, this type of work results from a combination of contributions made by different stakeholders. In this regard, the person authoring the dialogue, the person composing the music accompanying the audiovisual work and the director who exercises actual supervision and whose intellectual contribution to the creation of the work can be appraised become co-authors of the audiovisual work and hence, do enjoy

112. Section 4, para. 26, TCPA.
113. Cf. s. 15(1), TCPA.
114. Cf. *Matthew Fischer v. Gary Brooker & Onward Music Ltd* [2006] EWHC 3239 (Ch).
115. *Ibid.*, para. 46.
116. In a legal parlance, works of joint authorship and works of co-authorship are both treated as collective works. The sole difference between these categories of works is that in relation to the latter it is possible to identify and isolate individual contributions made by the authors. When it comes to the former, this identification and isolation is impossible.

economic rights stemming therefrom. Moreover, different authors of independent, pre-existing copyrightable works that have been incorporated in or adapted for the audiovisual work are also considered co-authors of the audiovisual work concerned.[117]

According to Tanzanian law, persons contributing to the creation of an audiovisual work and the authors whose pre-existing works are incorporated in or adapted for the design of audiovisual work sign a legally enforceable agreement with the producer insofar as regulation of economic rights in the audiovisual work is concerned.[118] Unless it states otherwise, the contract between the producer and co-authors of audiovisual work imply an assignment of the latter's economic rights to the former.[119] This presumption is nevertheless limited to economic rights directly attaching to the audiovisual work only. This limitation essentially means that co-authors of audiovisual works retain under Tanzanian law 'their economic rights in their contributions or pre-existing works' provided that 'those contributions or pre-existing works can be subject of acts covered by their economic rights separately from the audiovisual works'.[120]

III. Works Made for Hire

36. Under Tanzanian law, works made for hire are copyrightable works created pursuant to the contract of service or contract for service. The former category of works made for hire refers to works created by an employee in the course of his employment, whereas the latter relates to copyrightable commissioned works. In relation to a contract of service, authors may create literary or artistic works for a natural or legal person pursuant to contractual obligations of service as employees. A contract of service refers to a legal relationship between employee and employer. According to the TCPA,[121] ownership of a copyrightable work created by an employee in the course of his employment does not belong to the employer: The law presumes that work to have been assigned to the employee's employer. To rebut the presumption of assignment, the employee (author) must prove: (1) that a contract concluded between him and the employer prohibits such an automatic assignment; or (2) that the prevailing circumstances at the time the contract of employment was concluded did not show that customary activities of the employer dictated automatic assignment of the employee's copyright to the employer.[122] Note that since the employee does not execute his contractual obligations independently but relies on equipment, guidance and other facilities provided to him by the employer, the legal presumption of assignment of employee's right can be justified in most cases: given that an employee works on direction of his employer in return of salary, the employer should thus legitimately expect to economically benefit from the copyrightable work the creation of which has been facilitated by his resources.

117. Cf. s. 15(2), TCPA.
118. Cf. s. 15, TCPA.
119. Cf. s. 15(3), TCPA.
120. *Ibid.*
121. Cf. s. 15(4), TCPA.
122. *Ibid.*

37. As regards works to be created following an order placed by a person other than the work's creator, section 23(1) of the TCPA employs the term 'contracts for commissioned works' to refer to contracts for service, which governs creation of this category of works.[123] Under this kind of contracts, the author becomes an independent contractor – a legal status that allows him to execute his contractual obligations independent of the person from whom the work is commissioned. This independence implies that an author of a commissioned work does not formally need resources from the commissioner of the work in order to accomplish his contractual obligations. As a result, the commissioner of the work does not exercise control on how the work is to be performed but expects the final work to be rendered onto him. Note that contracts for commissioned works do not provide for automatic assignment of copyright in the commissioned works as the case is with the contract of service.

38. Tanzanian law provides the creator of a commissioned work with legal safeguards ensuring that the commissioner accepts the commissioned work once it is accomplished. In this regard, the TCPA obliges the commissioner to communicate to the author a notice of acceptance or non-acceptance of the work within two months from the date the latter submits the work to the former.[124] If it appears that this two-month period differs from a period provided for in another specific law, the commissioner may be justified should he observe a time limit set in the legislation specifically addressing commissioned works.[125] Note that a presumption that the work is accepted is normally endorsed in favour of the author if the commissioner does not observe the deadline for communicating a declaration of acceptance of commissioned works.[126]

The commissioner is not obliged to declare acceptance of the commissioned work in every circumstance. For instance, if the author produces a work that does not meet the standards agreed to by the parties, the commissioner is entitled to ask the former to modify the work concerned. The request to this effect is inadmissible, unless it is communicated to the author before expiry of the period within which a declaration of acceptance of the work has to be communicated.[127] Once requested to modify the work, the author of a commissioned work is under obligation to respond to the commissioner's plea; if the author refuses to correct or amend the work, the commissioner may, as of right, terminate the contract for the service in issue. Note that once he terminates the contract for commissioned work, the commissioner is under legal obligation to remunerate the author for the work already accomplished.[128] In the circumstances, the commissioner is not obliged to remunerate the author to the full amount agreed on in the contract for the commissioned work.[129]

123. Cf. Marginal note, s. 23(1), TCPA.
124. Cf. s. 23(1), TCPA.
125. *Ibid.*
126. *Ibid.*
127. Cf. s. 23(2), TCPA.
128. *Ibid.*
129. *Ibid.*

39. It follows that the Tanzanian Copyright law distinguishes authorship of a copyrightable work from ownership of such a work. It is possible under the law authorship of a work protected under a copyright law to be attributed to a person who does not own a corresponding work. A particular scenario of this case relates to commissioned works or works made for hire. Notwithstanding the fact that he is not regarded as an author, the person commissioning the work or the employer (as the case may be) becomes the first owner of the copyright in the work concerned. It is advisable to always determine the question of ownership when it comes to making copyright a subject matter of economic transaction such as in drafting an assignment deed or a licence contract. The ground thereof is that the issue of copyright ownership is not always free from ambiguity. In particular, controversy as regards ownership of works made for hire crops up more often than not. The question regarding ownership of this category of works requires one to figure out the scope of the copyright owner's employment and determine whether or not the work in which a copyright subsists was created within that scope. It may be that the employee creates a copyrightable subject matter in his leisure time, in which case the employee alone will be entitled to the first ownership thereto irrespective of whether or not the leisure time was enjoyed at the premises of the employer of the author.[130]

§5. Transfer

40. As an incorporeal property, copyright protected in the United Republic of Tanzania is capable of being transferred from the owner to another person. Two general modalities of legal transfer of copyright are recognized under the Tanzanian law; namely, permanent and temporary transference of copyright. The former is technically referred to as assignment, whereas the latter is applied as reference to copyright transfer by way of licences. Both general contract law and specific provisions of the Copyright Act govern transfer of authors' rights in copyrightable works.[131]

A central position regarding transfer of copyright distinguishes such a transfer from the transfer of the material in which the copyright subsists. The British Academy for the humanities and social science has clarified this position in the following manner:

> Ownership of documents or other material records of a copyright work – e.g. the manuscript of a novel or a musical work, or the original of a painting – is also separate from the copyright in the work. So if an author gives or sells his or her manuscripts to a library, the gift or sale will not also carry the copyright

130. Cf. Andrew Katz ed., *Introduction to Software Protection under United Kingdom Law*, in *The International Free and Open Source Law Book*; available at http://ifosslawbook.org/uk/.
131. Cf. s. 22, TCPA.

> unless that is specifically included in the transaction. Outright transfers of ownership of copyright are different from licences, under which ownership is retained but the other party is enabled to carry out certain acts which would otherwise infringe copyright.[132]

The foregoing position argues well with the Tanzanian Copyright law; it regulates authors' and performers' rights based on the principle that 'the transfer of ownership of the original or of one or several copies of a work shall not imply the assignment of right in the work'.[133]

I. Assignment of Copyright

41. Three modes of copyright assignment are discernible under the Copyright law of Tanzania. One of these modes is an assignment of copyright that is made *inter vivos* (i.e., between living persons). Where the copyright owner is not alive, an assignment of copyright can be confirmed by a testament or through operation of law.[134] An assignment or – just to put it less technical – permanent transfer of copyright does not affect the duration of the copyright, which continues to be calculated (in the case of literary, dramatic, musical or artistic works) around the original author's lifetime.

A. *Copyright Assignment Made Inter Vivos*

42. The Copyright law of Tanzania bestows upon copyright owners a right to assign all or part of their economic rights in relation to literary and/or artistic, copyrighted work(s).[135] A right to assign a copyright hinges on the fact that copyright is a property that can be sold and bought, hence capable of changing hands by way of transfer in the same manner tangible property does.

As regards copyright assignment *inter vivos*, it is mandatory that the legal transaction thereof be recorded in an assignment deed, otherwise the assignment will be null and void *ab initio*. The basis for this conclusion is the position of the Copyright law of Tanzania, which does not validate an oral assignment contract for enforcement in the United Republic of Tanzania. A specific provision supporting this tenet is section 16(2) of the TCPA: it not only requires any assignment contract of the author's exclusive economic rights to be reduced into writing, but also postulates that this kind of contract must bear at least the assignee's signature. This writing requirement is one of the legal means to ascertain a scope of copyright assignment

---

132. British Academy for the humanities and social sciences, Joint Copyright Guidelines, Part 1 at para. 6 (available at http://www.britac.ac.uk/policy/copyright-guideines/part1.cfm#sec6 (accessed: 27 May 2014)).
133. Section 16(5), TCPA.
134. Cf. s. 15(7), TCPA.
135. Cf. s. 16(1), TCPA.

in case of partial assignment. The absence of a rule under the Copyright law of Tanzania that necessarily requires an assignment of a copyright to cover the whole term of protection of the copyright owner's exclusive rights; or to cover the whole territory of the United Republic of Tanzania, has paved the way for the principle of partial assignment of copyright in Tanzania. Depending on what the assignor and assignee agree on, an assignment agreement may, under the law, relate only to some of (and not all) the exclusive rights enjoyed by the copyright owner. Copyright assignment may also be confined to a specific geographical area as well as to a country other than the United Republic of Tanzania. Hence, a contract of assignment is construed literary and strictly and in any case, its scope cannot transcend what is articulated in it.[136]

B. Testamentary Disposition of Copyright

43. Pursuant to the Copyright law of Tanzania, rights relating to literary and artistic works can be 'inherited according to the general rules of the law of succession'.[137] Testamentary[138] disposition rules of succession detail some of the circumstances under which copyright can be assigned to another person by inheritance. USLEGAL™ refers to the term 'testamentary disposition [of a copyright]' as the disposition or transfer of copyright that takes effect upon the death of the copyright owner making it. The testator retains almost entire control of the copyright until death. In short, it is the gift of property, which takes effect at the time of the death of the person making the disposition. The transfer can be made by deed, by an *inter vivos* transaction, or by will. All instruments employed to actualize testamentary dispositions must conform to the requirements of the statute of wills.[139] Apart from customary and Islamic law, a piece of legislation that governs matters appertaining succession in Tanzania is the Indian Succession Act of 1865 whose application was given force in Tanzania by the Indian Acts (Application) Ordinance, Cap. 2 of the laws of Tanzania.

C. Transfer/Assignment of Copyright by Operation of Law

44. In some situations, assignment of a copyright protected in the United Republic of Tanzania may be decided on the basis of general principles of law. Instances in which this kind of transfer can be said to take effect includes where a copyright passes onto an administrator, receiver or liquidator of a company or a trustee in bankruptcy. Similarly, transfer of copyright by operation of law is said to take place if the transfer is conducted in accordance with the rules on intestate succession upon the death of the copyright owner. According to section 24 of the Indian Succession

136. Cf. s. 16(2) and (3), TCPA.
137. Cf. s. 15(7), TCPA.
138. USLEGAL™, Testamentary Disposition Law & Legal Definition, available at http://definitions.uslegal.com/t/testamentary-disposition/ (accessed: 16 Dec. 2015).
139. *Ibid.*

Act of 1865 whose application in Tanzania was given force by the Indian Acts (Application) Ordinance, Cap. 2 (of the laws of Tanzania), a person is regarded to have died intestate in respect of all property of which he has not made an effective testamentary disposition. Thus, while under the succession law of Tanzania, intestate succession applies to the property of a person who, at the time of his death, has not made a will disposing of his estate, the law also clarifies that any person who dies leaving a will disposing of part of his estate is regarded to have died intestate as regards that part of his estate, which is not disposed of in the will. Given that copyright encompasses a set of economic rights as described below in §6 of this chapter, intestate transmission of copyright may relate to all exclusive economic rights known under the law or just one or a limited number of them depending on whether or not the deceased had indicated in his will a clear intention to dispose of all his exclusive rights.

The copyright law, such as that of Tanzania, does not provide a straightforward answer to several questions concerning intestate disposition of copyright in respect of original published material that a deceased leaves to an archive or other repository such as a library. For instance, 'Ownership of the physical property on which a copyright work was first recorded does not necessarily also carry with it the copyright in such circumstances, nor will the date of the author's death always be known so as to determine precisely when the copyright expires.'[140] Moreover, where the deceased deposited the work in which a copyright subsists in the national archive in Tanzania, such work may not be easily and immediately available to the heirs of the deceased since the Director of the archive will have to take into consideration the conditions (if any) set by the deceased contingent to which the work may be made available to the public[141] – a situation that is likely to complicate and delay determination of issues regarding intestate succession of the copyright.

II. Licences

45. Licensing is one of the legal means employed to extend to third parties powers to enjoy some rights, which they would not otherwise enjoy.[142] In relation to copyright, the authority to permit third parties to use protected works rests with the author and any other person who may lawfully claim to be the copyright owner.[143]

140. British Academy for the humanities and social sciences, Joint Copyright Guidelines, Part 1 at para. 7.2 (available at http://www.britac.ac.uk/policy/copyright-guideines/part1.cfm#sec6).

141. Matters appertaining copyright of works reserved in the archive are regulated in the United Republic of Tanzania under s. 24 of the Records and Archives Management Act, 2002.

142. The term 'licence' may be delineated as an authority to perform something, the performance of which without such an authority would be considered a contravention of the law. Cf. Daniel Greenberg, *Stroud's Judicial Dictionary of Words and Phrases* 1522 (Sweet & Maxwell 7th ed. 2006). *See also* Michael Agnes & David B. Guralnik eds., *Webster's New World College Dictionary* 827 (IDG Books Worldwide, Inc 4th ed. 2001).

143. Cf. s. 17(1), TCPA.

In addition, persons who enjoy a legal mandate to enforce copyright on behalf of the author may also grant a copyright licence.[144] A copyright licence may be non-exclusive or exclusive.[145]

A. *Non-exclusive Licence*

46. It is implied, within the terms underlying non-exclusive copyright licences under Tanzanian law,[146] that the licensing agreement does not prohibit the author and any other persons owning copyright in the licensed work from exploiting the work. In a similar vein, the grant of a non-exclusive copyright licence to one person does not enjoin the licensor from granting further licences to other persons. Thus, the holder of a non-exclusive licence is not only expected to use the licensed work concurrently with other licensees of the same work, but also the licensor.[147]

B. *Exclusive Licence*

47. An exclusive licensee of a copyright protected under Tanzanian law has a legal mandate not only to enjoin third parties, but also the author and other owners of copyright from using the licensed work.[148] In this sense, a contract for an exclusive licence creates legitimate expectations not only that the exclusive licensee will enjoy unhampered exploitation of the licensed work,[149] but also that the creator of the work will receive his due remuneration. These expectations cannot be ensured unless terms and conditions of the exclusive licensing contract are certain.[150] Note that to ensure certainty of contractual terms, the TCPA requires that in addition to employing clear, specific and unambiguous terms,[151] each exclusive licensing agreement be in a written document signed by both parties.[152] Note further that a contract for an exclusive licence, which does not contain a clear stipulation to that effect is presumed to be ambiguous hence, prima facie unenforceable.[153] An uncertain term contained in a licensing contract may nevertheless be clarified in the light of the circumstances prevailed during the conclusion of the said contract. Thus, if the licensee successfully convinces the judicial authority dealing with the matter

144. Cf. §4 of this chapter in relation to categorization of persons who can enforce a copyright in a particular literary or artistic work.
145. Section 17(1), TCPA.
146. Section 17(2), TCPA stipulates these terms.
147. Cf. s. 17(2), TCPA.
148. Cf. s. 17(3), TCPA.
149. This must be viewed from the fact that the licensee enjoys '*locus standi* to sue in his own name for infringement of any exclusive right conferred on him' (cf. s. 17(4), TCPA).
150. Cf. s. 17(4), TCPA.
151. *Ibid.*
152. Cf. s. 17(8), TCPA.
153. Cf. s. 17(4), TCPA.

that the parties intended to conclude an exclusive licensing agreement, then the court must treat the licence as exclusive.[154]

48. An exclusive licensee of a work protected in Tanzania is under obligation to exploit the licensed work. In the event the licensee does not comply with this obligation, the TCPA empowers the copyright owner to revoke the licence. This is particularly the case if the non-exploitation of the work prejudices copyright owner's legitimate interests. The author's right to revoke an exclusive licence cannot be 'waived in advance'.[155] This revocation right is nevertheless exercised subject to the following conditions: (a) the exclusive licensing contract must have stipulated the time when the licensee is required to commence exploitation of the copyrighted work and a period the expiry of which the licensee will be considered as having delayed such exploitation; (b) the commencement time and the grace period within which the exploitation must be commenced should have expired; (c) the commencement grace period should not be less than two years from the date of the conclusion of the exclusive licensing contract, or from the date the work covered by the exclusive licence was supplied to the licensee if the delivery of such work was made subsequently after the conclusion of the licence contract; (d) the author must communicate to the licensee his intention to revoke the licence; (e) the copyright owner may then revoke the licence unless the licensee commences use within a reasonable period after the communication of the revocation notice.[156]

C. Conditions Applying to Both Exclusive and Non-exclusive Licences

49. The Tanzanian Copyright law enumerates some conditions generally applying to both exclusive and non-exclusive licences as hereunder:

(a) Each licensing contract must stipulate the scope and modality of exploiting the licensed rights although an omission in this respect is not a ground for invalidating a licensing contract. Note that the scope and modality of exercising the licensed rights pursuant to a licensing contract, which does not comply with a requirement mentioned in the immediately preceding sentence may be limited to the extent discernible from the circumstances surrounding the conclusion of the contract.[157]
(b) The entitlement to enforce moral rights in Tanzania is vested in authors alone. From a legal point of view, it is thus impossible for the author to divorce himself from his moral rights by way of licence. This is buttressed by a legal position that 'only the economic rights expressly mentioned in the contract shall be considered part of the licence'.[158]

---

154. *Ibid.*
155. Cf. s. 20, TCPA.
156. *Ibid.*
157. Section 17(5), TCPA.
158. Section 17(6), TCPA.

(c) The maximum duration of a copyright licensing contract is fifteen years. Any period beyond this duration is not enforceable under the Tanzanian Copyright Law. While the general fifteen year-duration requirement applies also to assignee, the assignee has no mandate to license the work assigned to him for a duration that goes beyond the period of the assignment.[159]
(d) The licensee has no right to sublicense the work licensed to him without the consent of the owner of the copyright, unless if permitted by a specific provision of the law.[160]

D. *Equitable Remuneration*

50. Tanzanian law on copyright licensing strengthens the position of the author by empowering him to claim equitable remuneration in the event the remuneration initially agreed between him and the licensee turns out to be disproportionate in view of the actual licensee's profit resulting from the exploitation of the licensed work. If for instance *A* licenses his work to *B* on an understanding that exploitation of the work by *B* will yield the amount of EUR 2 million, the law affords *A* an appropriate remedy if contrary to the projected EUR 2 million that formed basis for the conclusion of the licence contract *B* is able to realize EUR 3 million. In the circumstances, the law allows *A* to ask for an amendment of the licensing contract in order to recalculate the licence amount commensurate with the 'equitable share' of the licensee's income made out of the use of the licensed work.[161]

The author's right to equitable remuneration is a fundamental one; it 'may not be waived in advance'.[162] However, this right is subject to the following two main conditions:

(a) right to equitable remuneration must be claimed within two years from the time the licensor learns that the remuneration he received is disproportionate;
(b) the circumstances giving rise to the claim of equitable remuneration must arise within five years from the date of the grant of the licence; thereafter, it is presumed that the licensor received proportionate remuneration.[163]

III. Transfer of Rights in Future Works

51. The Copyright law of Tanzania envisages and provides guidance on circumstance whereby authors and artists may attempt to transfer copyright expected to subsist in works to be created in future. In this regard, the law foresees two scenarios; namely, assignment of rights in a work yet to be created and conclusion of

159. Cf. s. 17(7), TCPA.
160. Cf. s. 18, TCPA.
161. Cf. s. 19, TCPA.
162. *Ibid.*
163. *Ibid.*

contracts granting permission to exploit copyright once a work in which the copyright subsists is created.[164] The TCPA accepts – and extends full force of law to – the enforceability of the contracts covered under the latter scenario, on a condition that the contracts for the grant of rights to exploit copyright in a work yet to be created once the work is created be as specific and unambiguous as possible. Inclusion in the contract of a rather general stipulation entitles each of the parties to a licensing agreement to terminate the licensing contract, with respect to the vaguely stipulated terms, by issuing a six-month notice to the other party. Nevertheless, such termination cannot be admissible if preferred after the fourth year of the period succeeding the date of the conclusion of the licensing agreement.[165] Following the rule allowing conclusion of contracts relating to rights expected to subsist in future yet uncreated copyrightable works, an employee or independent contractor has a right to enter into an agreement that will entitle the employer or the commissioner of the work to any copyright that is expected to arise in future with regard to copyright material created in the course of one's employment or commission, whichever may be the case.

52. The position regulating conclusion of contracts for the grant of rights to exploit copyright expected to subsist in a work to be created differs from that controlling assignment of future yet uncreated works. Authors cannot legally enter into an assignment contract in relation to works to be created subsequent to the conclusion of the assignment agreement.[166] Any assignment of this kind is null and void *ab initio*.[167] While a contract assigning future yet uncreated work may meet most of the elements required of a valid contract, the assignment cannot be regulated based on contract law: The Copyright Act specifically identifies the subject matter as incapable of being assigned. Hence, the general law on contracts cannot override a specific law. The logic behind this limitation may be questioned. At any rate, one may argue that the prohibition is geared to protect both the right holder and a third party seeking to exploit author's economic rights by way of assignment. First, it is difficult to get an exact economic measure of rights in future work due to *inter alia* the likely inflation and deflation. Second, the author may become very famous before the work is created – a factor that would mean that the assignee will be able to benefit from the work more than what was envisaged at the time of the assignment contract.[168] This would disadvantage the author who would not be able to reap the fruits of his fame. Third, the author may lack legal capacity to create the work if the law denying the author that capacity is passed after the assignment contract has been concluded. Fourth, the author should not trade off his right to change conviction: assignment of rights in future works would mean that the author would be bound to create the work even when, due to new orientations conceived by the author after the assignment contract, the creation of that work contravenes the author's morality.

164. Cf. ss 16(4) & 21, TCPA.
165. Cf. s. 21, TCPA.
166. Cf. s. 16(4), TCPA.
167. *Ibid.*
168. But *see* s. 19 TCPA regulating 'disproportionate remuneration'. Authors may invoke the provisions of this section to ask for adjustment of contractual terms.

§6. SCOPE OF EXCLUSIVE RIGHTS

53. According to section 8 TCPA, 'Copyright in a literary and artistic work comprises the exclusive economic and moral rights of the author' specified under the law.[169]

I. Moral Rights

54. The contents of moral rights that authors enjoy in Tanzania range from the right to claim authorship to the right of integrity of works. Insofar as the claim of authorship is concerned, an author has a right to demand that his name be mentioned in relation to his work. This may essentially entail the author insisting that he be mentioned as the author wherever the economic exploitation of his work is perpetuated. However, certain circumstances may render it impossible to mention the author's name, thus disentitling the author to legally claim the mentioning of his name in connection with the exploitation of a literary or artistic work. This may particularly be the case if the author's work is exploited by being included in another work, say 'by means of photography, sound or visual recording, broadcasting or distribution by cable'.[170]

Moral rights entitle the author to object to and to seek relief in connection with third parties' activities that may potentially interfere with the integrity of his work. In this regard, the author has a right to object to any mutilation, distortion, or other alterations of his copyrighted work. In this sense, the right of integrity allows the author to prohibit every activity, which is likely to prejudice his honour or reputation in relation to his copyrighted work.[171]

In a similar vein, the author enjoys, under Tanzanian law, the right of having his work published anonymously or pseudonymously and the right to withdraw his copyrighted work from the public should he change his mind or conviction in relation to the work.

II. Economic Rights

A. Reproduction Right

55. The exclusive right to reproduce a work protected by copyright in Tanzania belongs to the author and his agents. This right entitles the author to prohibit third parties from making 'one or more copies of a work … in any manner or form, including any sound or visual recording or any permanent or temporary storage of the work … in electronic form'.[172]

169. Cf. ss 9–11, TCPA.
170. Section 11(a), TCPA.
171. Cf. s. 11, TCPA.
172. Cf. s. 4, para. 23, TCPA.

B. Performing Right and Broadcasting Rights

56. Authors of works protected in Tanzania exclusively enjoy a right to authorize public performance of their works. Section 4 of the TCPA, circumscribes this right to include the following:

(a) in the case of a work other than an audiovisual work, the recitation, playing, dancing, acting or otherwise performing the work, or the expression of folklore, either directly or by means of any device or process;
(b) in the case of an audiovisual work, the showing of images in sequences and the making of accompanying sounds audible; and
(c) in the case of a sound recording, making the recording sounds audible, in each case at a place or places where persons outside the normal circles of the family and its closest acquaintances are or can be present, irrespective of whether they are or can be present at the same place and time, or at different places and times or both, and where the performance can be perceived without the need for communication to the public.[173]

Similarly, authors enjoy a right to authorize broadcasting of their copyrighted works protected in the United Republic of Tanzania. The TCPA defines the term 'broadcasting' to mean the 'communication of a work, a performance or a sound recording to the public by wireless transmission, including transmission by satellite'.[174]

57. Pursuant to the arrangements under the Copyright law of Tanzania, the COSOTA undertakes to administer collectively rights of copyright proprietors. When it comes to licensing for public performances and inclusion in the broadcasts or radio transmission works in which copyright subsists, the former negotiates on behalf of the latter for the terms on whose basis the licence is to be issued. In this regard, COSOTA's powers are stipulated in the Copyright (Licensing of Public Performances and Broadcasting) Regulations, 2003 (hereinafter 'licensing Regulations').[175] Paragraph 3 of the licensing regulations decrees that 'No person shall hold public performances or broadcasting of a work in which a copyright subsists except under a license issued by [COSOTA].' According to the form available in the first schedule to the licensing regulations, an applicant for a performance or broadcasting licence has to submit his application to COSOTA *inter alia* stating in it the

173. Section 4, para. 20, TCPA.
174. Section 4, para. 3, TCPA.
175. The licensing regulations were published on 10 Oct. 2003 in the Government Notice No. 328. These regulations were promulgated in order to realize the legislative aim enshrined in s. 48(a) TCPA, namely to facilitate COSOTA better discharge its duties. In this regard, the section empowers COSOTA to 'determine the minimum rates of royalties to be levied in respect of uses to be made of works registered by it'.

activities of his establishment[176] and the music device used.[177] Note that the activities of establishment and the music devices used are one of the bases for determining the amount of licence fee COSOTA should charge the applicant or the licensee.[178]

It is noteworthy that COSOTA may refuse to issue a licence for public performances or broadcasting. In case this happens, COSOTA has an obligation to give a reason for its refusal to licence.[179] The appropriate reasons in this regard are not stipulated in the licensing regulations thus affording COSOTA a wide discretion in deciding whether or not to issue a licence.

Once it is issued, the licence for public performances or broadcasting only extends to 'the purpose in respect of which it has been issued' and covers the specific period and premises indicated in it.[180] Thus, a licensee is duty-bound to 'display the licence in a prominent and visible position at or near the main entrance to the premises at which the public performance or broadcasting is to be held'.[181] This allows COSOTA to control whether the performer or the broadcaster has secured a licensee at all, and, if so, whether he abides by the terms of the licence concerned.

58. Apart from the general rule enshrined in paragraph 3 of the licensing regulations, there is no rule requiring foreign bands and groups wishing to perform in Tanzania to apply for a licence to COSOTA. A foreign band or a group desiring to come to Tanzania for the purpose of performing in the country must nevertheless secure, beforehand, a clearance from the government of Tanzania.[182] COSOTA has a duty to facilitate such governmental clearance.[183] However, COSOTA can discharge this duty only if a contract between it and a promoter of the foreign bands or groups is concluded 'within twenty-one days before the band or group actually enters into Tanzania' and the promoter pays to COSOTA the pertinent fee within the same period of time.[184] Note that COSOTA has a standard form contract whose terms the promoter has to agree to as a condition for COSOTA to facilitate performance in Tanzania of a foreign band or group.[185]

59. After collecting performance and licensing fees, COSOTA is required to 'pay royalties or other appropriate remuneration accrued or due, to the person

176. Activities of establishment that are identified under the licence application form are the following: radio station, television station, hotel, inn, motel, rest-house, restaurant, bar, bottle store, supermarket, shop or store, tavern, night club, discotheque, entertainment, saloon, bus and minibus, tax operator and car hire operator (cf. first schedule to the licensing regulations).
177. Some of the music devices that the applicant may identify in his application for a licence as being used in relation to the activities of his establishment are the following: radio, radio cassette, record player, music centre, compact disc, live band and television set (cf. first schedule to the licensing regulations).
178. Cf. the second schedule to the licensing regulations.
179. Cf. para. 5(3) of the licensing regulations.
180. Cf. para. 5(2) of licensing regulations.
181. Cf. para. 6 of licensing regulations.
182. Cf. para. 7(3) of licensing regulations.
183. *Ibid.*
184. Cf. para. 7(2) of the licensing regulations.
185. Cf. para. 7(1) of the licensing regulations.

entitled thereto'.[186] To accomplish this exercise, COSOTA must abide by the distribution rules enshrined in the third schedule to the licensing regulations. According to rule 1 of this schedule, the distribution rules relate to some specified rights assigned to COSOTA, namely the following: (1) the copyrights of national and foreign authors of music, literary and dramatic works for the following types of uses: (a) public performance; (b) broadcasting and recording for the purpose of broadcasting; and (c) commercial lending of video cassettes containing such music; and (2) the rights of the performing artists within Tanzania and the Tanzanian producers of sound recordings for the following types of uses: (a) public performances using records; and (b) broadcasting using records. It is important to note the following:

> where a COSOTA tariff applies to both categories of rights hereinbefore mentioned, the income from royalties based on such tariff shall be distributed in the following manner: (i) 75 per cent for the national and foreign authors of musical, literary and dramatic works, and (ii) 25 per cent for the performing artists and the producers of sound recordings'[187] (cf. rule 1 of the Distribution Rules).

C. Adaptation Right

60. Authors of works protected in Tanzania enjoy an exclusive right to authorize adaptation of their works.[188] The TCPA does not provide for an operational definition of the term 'adaptation'. An attempt to delineate this term may not depart from the fact that 'adaption' in the copyright sense refers to a scenario whereby an existing protected work is modified in order to create another copyrightable work. The term 'adaptation' generally connotes an action of producing a copyrightable work based on another work that is already covered by copyright. For instance, an adaptation of a literary work may include translation of that work. Where the literary work is in a non-dramatic form, making a version of that work in a dramatic form (and vice versa) constitutes adaptation of the work. Similarly, conveying a written story or action solely or mainly by means of pictures is regarded under the law as an adaptation of the literary work. Moreover, arrangement or transcription of a musical work and the reproduction in three dimensions of an artistic work that is in two dimensions amounts to adaptation of the respective works.

It follows from the general principles of copyright law that adaptation right of literary works cannot be asserted for computer programs. This is ascribed to the position that the copyright owner has no entitlement to prohibit persons lawfully holding a copy of the program from decompiling such a program. Although such a decompilation right cannot be waived by a contract, an acceptable compilation must abide by the following requirements: the decompilation must result from a desire to obtain

186. Cf. para. 8 of licensing regulations.
187. Cf. Rule 1 of the Copyright and Neighbouring Rights (Protection and Distribution of Sound and Audio-visual Recordings) Regulations, 2006. These regulations are outlined in Part C below.
188. Cf. s. 9(f), TCPA.

information that is necessary to facilitate an interoperability between the decompiled program and another computer program; the person undertaking the decompilation must prove that he has no access to the information concerning the interoperability; and the resulting program must not be substantially similar to the one that has been decompiled.[189]

D. *Translation Right*

61. According to the TCPA,[190] third parties are not allowed to translate a work protected in Tanzania from one language into the other, unless the work's author permits such an activity. Authors enjoy a right to authorize translation of their copyrighted original works. With respect to his translation, a translator of original work enjoys same rights as those enjoyed by the author of the original work. The level of protection that the Tanzanian law bestows upon translators for their translations is the same as that provided to authors of other forms of adaptations. The Copyright law of Tanzania regards translations as one form of adaptation.

E. *Other Rights*

1. Droit De Suite

62. The Copyright law of Tanzania does not contain a provision on droit de suite. Simply stated, droit de suite means resale royalty right. The aim of this right is to enable artistes or their heirs to receive a royalty for any resale of their works. This right cannot be claimed beyond the term of copyright protection of the artist's work. The implication of this conclusion is that, if the law grants protection to artistic works for duration of the artist's life plus seventy years after the artist's death, resale royalty must also be confined within this duration. This right that was first introduced in France in eighteenth century, is distinct from the first sale doctrine, which only bestows upon artistes an opportunity to determine for the first time when and where to place artistic items on the market and thereafter leaving the artistes unable to claim royalties from the resale of their copyrighted artistic articles.[191]

2. Public Lending Right

63. Public Lending Right (PLR) scheme is not existent in the United Republic of Tanzania. In countries where this scheme is exercised, authors get compensation for the use made of their published works by the public, and hence the scheme is financed from the public fund. Pursuant to this initiative, public libraries get money

189. Cf. Andrew Katz ed., *Introduction to Software Protection under United Kingdom Law*, in *The International Free and Open Source Law Book*; available at http://ifosslawbook.org/uk/.
190. Section 9(1)(e), TCPA.
191. At http://en.wikipedia.org/wiki/Droit_de_suite.

from the government, which they use either to pay authors each time a book is borrowed from a library or pay authors for their books kept in libraries. In some countries PLR is made part of the copyright whereby authors are given exclusive right to authorize public use of their work in libraries, whereas in other countries – where the PLR scheme is operational – PLR is not regarded as exclusive exploitation right but authors' right to payment for the public exploitation of their copyrighted work. Information obtained from a webpage administered by PLR International is very instructive in this regard and hence worthy of quoting:

> The copyright-based approach can be found, for example, in Germany and Austria, where lending is seen as a form of copyright exploitation of authors' works. Authors have the right to license the lending of their works by libraries. Arrangements for licensing and distribution of fees are undertaken by collecting societies on behalf of rights holders. In Austria and Germany authors' organizations negotiate with the federal and provincial governments; in the Netherlands negotiations are directly with the libraries.
>
> PLR as a right to remuneration outside copyright exists in the UK.[192] The 1979 PLR Act gives authors a legal right to receive payment from the government for the lending out of their books by public libraries. This is a right to payment, not an exclusive right allowing authors to prohibit or license the lending of their books. The PLR system is administered by the PLR office which, since October 2013, is part of the British Library.
>
> PLR as part of State support for culture exists mainly in the Scandinavian countries where, for example, payments are made only to authors of books written in a country's native language. This is aimed at minority languages and encouraging the writing of literature in those languages. The effect is to prevent PLR payments in those countries going to writers in more dominant languages such as English.[193]

3. Others

a. Distribution Right

64. As one of the means to enable the author realize economic benefits of his work, the law exclusively reserves to him the right to distribute original or copies of the original to the public. The distribution right as employed in the TCPA extends to scenarios in which the author's work or a copy thereof is 'offered to the general public or any section thereof, mainly through appropriate commercial channels'.[194]

192. For instance for the case of the United Kingdom of Great Britain (UK), the public lending right scheme allows public libraries to pay an author 6 pence each time his book is borrowed (http://www.theguardian.com/politics/2008/feb/02/politicsandthearts.letters).
193. At https://www.plrinternational.com/faqs/faqs.htm#menu.
194. Cf. s. 4, para. 11, TCPA.

b. Rental Right

65. The 'rental right', which the author enjoys in keeping with Tanzanian law, relates to the 'original or a copy of an audiovisual work, a work embodied in a sound recording, a computer program, a database, or a musical work in the form of notation'.[195] This right is not considered waived simply because the author parted with the ownership of the original or a copy of the original work by way of sale or by any other means.[196]

While the rental right in relation to most of the works enumerated in the relevant provision of the TCPA[197] is absolute, rental right in relation to computer program is not. To claim this right for a computer program, the author is required to prove that the program itself is the 'essential object of the rental'.[198] The court in Tanzania has not yet offered any judicial interpretation of the legal scenario whereby a computer program may be regarded 'essential object of the rental' within the meaning of section 9(2) TCPA. This interpretation hiatus may nevertheless be supplemented by a hypothetical case: suppose A authors an electronic book, which can only be read on a computer in which a special reading program has been installed. Assume further that A sells the book to B. In addition, A supplies B with software that will allow the latter access the book on his personal computer. B rents the book (together with the access software) to several people on commercial scale. In the circumstances, A can only claim rental rights in a book but may not claim rental rights in the software that allows access to the book; the software is not the 'essential object of the rental' within the meaning of section 9(2) TCPA.

c. Public Exhibition Right

66. Under Tanzanian law, authors enjoy the exclusive right to control public exhibition of their copyrighted work. According to section 4 TCPA, public exhibition entails 'a showing of the original or copy of the work as follows: (a) directly; (b) by means of a film, television images or otherwise on screen; (c) by means of any other device or process; or (d) in the case of an audiovisual work, the showing of individual images consequentially'.[199] Note that such a showing is not considered public exhibition if made before family members alone. For a showing of the author's work to constitute public exhibition it has to be undertaken for commercial purposes. A showing is presumed to be commercially motivated if perpetuated 'at a place or places where a person outside the normal circle of a family and its closest social acquaintances are or can be present'.[200] Thus, it still constitutes public exhibition irrespective of whether the persons referred to in the immediately preceding sentence 'are or can be present at the same place and time or at different places and/ or times'.[201]

---

195. Section 9(1)(c), TCPA.
196. *Ibid.*
197. *Ibid.*
198. Section 9(2), TCPA.
199. Cf. s. 4, para. 19, TCPA.
200. *Ibid.*
201. *Ibid.*

Tanzanian law puts it tritely that the fact that a work is displayed in a manner that does not constitute a legal act of communicating copyrighted work to the public cannot reverse a finding of public exhibition.[202] Public exhibition also encompasses activities such as the display of a book at a book fair or the launching of a copyrighted work by addressing its contents and displaying the work to the invited persons. These activities are not covered by the statutory definition of the term 'communication to the public' stipulated in the Copyright Act.[203]

§7. Limitations or Exceptions to the Scope of Copyright Protection

67. Exploitation rights that the Copyright law of Tanzanian vests in copyright owners are not absolute rights; they are subject to some limitations or exceptions that are enshrined in section 12 of the TCPA. One may instructively note that limitations or exceptions imposed on the scope of copyright protection are impermissible if they conflict with the normal exploitation of the work concerned or should they prejudice unreasonably the legitimate commercial or personal interests of the owner of copyright subsisting in the work.[204] This stipulation of the Tanzanian law echoes the position endorsed under major international legal instruments on copyright such as the Berne Convention, the TRIPS Agreement and the WIPO Copyright Treaty.[205] Articles 9(1), 13(2) and 10(2) of these international legal instruments respectively, essentially enshrine the popular principle of three-step test[206] that is also incorporated in section 12(2) of the TCPA. Taking the provisions of the TRIPS Agreement as an example, limitation or exception to the scope of exclusive rights of the copyright owner may be permitted only if it is proved – pursuant to the requirements under Article 13 of the TRIPS – that: (1) 'certain special cases' that call for the application of the limitation or exception exist; (2) the exceptions or limitations as applied to certain identified special cases are not likely to 'conflict

---

202. *Ibid.*

203. Section 4 TCPA refers to the term 'communication to the public' as follows:

> the transmission by wire, or without wire, of images or sound, or both, of a work, a performance, a sound recording or a broadcast, in such a way that the images or sounds can be perceived or accessed by persons outside the normal circle of a family and its closest social acquaintances at a place so distant from the place where the transmission, the images or sounds would not be perceivable or accessible and, further, irrespective of whether the persons can receive or access the images or sound at the same place and time, or at different places and/or times individually chosen by them (s. 4, para. 4, TCPA).

204. Cf. s. 12(2), TCPA.

205. Cf. *WIPO*, Implications of the TRIPS Agreement on Treaties Administered by WIPO, WIPO Publication No. 464 (E), 2012 (at http://www.wipo.int/edocs/pubdocs/en/intproperty/464/wipo_pub_464.pdf).

206. The three-step test was devised as a means to create a balance between interests of copyright owners and legitimate interests of third parties in relation to the right to access protected information. For this matter, '[No] advocacy for any copyright exception can be complete without briefly acknowledging at least the realities of the three step test' (cf. Dilan Thampapillai, *Creating an Innovation Exception? Copyright Law as the Infrastructure for Innovation*, 7(1) Scripted 104 at 133 (April 2010)).

with a normal exploitation of the work'; and (3) the limitations or exceptions 'do not unreasonably prejudice the legitimate interests of the right holder'.[207] The three-step procedure stipulated under the TRIPS Agreement is not meant to serve a substantive rule within a domestic jurisdiction. It nevertheless acts as a yardstick against which a national copyright legislation such as the Copyright and Neighbouring Rights Act of Tanzania is to be judged. To put it simply, the three-step test

207. For an extensive description of the three-step test principle *see* P. Bernt Hugenholtz & Ruth L. Okediji, *Conceiving an International Instrument on Limitations and Exceptions to Copyright* (Open Society Institute 6 Mar. 2008), (available at http://www.ivir.nl/publications/hugenholtz/limitations_exceptions_copyright.pdf (last accessed: 27 May 2014)). *See also* Christophe Geige, *The Role of the Three-Steps Test in the Adaptation of the Law of Copyright to the Information Society* (e-Copyright Bulletin January –March 2007). The WTO's interpretation of the TRIPS Agreement's three-step test is contained in the Report of the Panel, US – s. 110(5) Copyright Act, 15 Jun. 2000, WTO Doc. WT/DS/160/R, §§6.33 et seq. In relation to the first condition under Art. 13 of the TRIPS that requires existence of certain special cases, the WTO Panel pointed out that 'there is no need to identify explicitly each and every possible situation to which the exception could apply, provided that the scope of the exception is known and particularized. This guarantees a sufficient degree of legal certainty' (cf. the Report of the Panel, US – s. 110(5) Copyright Act, 15 Jun. 2000, WTO Doc. WT/DS/160/R, (henceforth, the WTO Panel Report), §6.108.). The Panel instructed further that:

> the first condition of Article 13 requires that a limitation or exception in national legislation should be clearly defined and should be narrow in its scope and reach. Whereas, a limitation or exception may be compatible with the first condition even if it pursues a special purpose whose underlying legitimacy in a normative sense cannot be discerned. The wording of Article 13's first condition does not imply passing a judgment on the legitimacy of the exceptions in dispute (cf. *The WTO Panel Report*, §6.112).

This conclusion is in full accord with the position that has been advocated by some commentators that suggest that the three-step test should be applied in reverse the last condition being considered first and hence leaving deliberations on the first step to be undertaken last. Proponents of this position see this approach as the significant means to 'accentuate the normative considerations built into the third (then first) step of the test' Cf. P. Bernt Hugenholtz & Ruth L. Okediji, *Conceiving an International Instrument on Limitations and Exceptions to Copyright*, Open Society Institute, 6 Mar. 2008, at 21, (available at http://www.ivir.nl/publications/hugenholtz/limitations_exceptions_copyright.pdf).

Regarding the second condition of Art. 13 of the TRIPS Agreement, the WTO Panel opined as hereunder:

> it appears that one way of measuring the normative connotation of normal exploitation is to consider, in addition to those forms of exploitation that currently generate significant or tangible revenue, those forms of exploitation which, with a certain degree of likelihood and plausibility, could acquire considerable economic or practical importance (cf. The WTO Panel Report, §6.180).

Deliberating on the third condition of Art. 13 of the TRIPS Agreement, the WTO Panel held the following view:

> a certain amount of 'prejudice' has to be presumed justified as 'not unreasonable'. In our view, prejudice to the legitimate interests of right holders reaches an unreasonable level if an exception or limitation causes or has the potential to cause an unreasonable loss of income to the copyright owner (cf. The WTO Panel Report, §6.229).

'is designed to measure the compliance of a nation's domestic copyright laws against a particular international standard'; it does not 'actually operate as part of domestic legislation'.[208]

Viewed globally, cases in which an exception or limitation to the scope of copyright protection can be permitted under the laws of many jurisdictions include those relating to: (i) fair dealing on the basis of (1) education purpose; (2) copies made for library or archive; (3) exploitation of a work whose author is not known or a work whose protection expired; (4) use of a work for judicial proceedings; (5) reading or recitation of a work in public; (6) private recording as a means of time-shifting; (7) incidental inclusion of a work in another work; and (ii) the principle of copyright exhaustion. A description of these cases in the context of the Tanzanian law on copyright follows herein below.

I. Fair Dealing

68. Section 12 TCPA describes scenarios whereby third parties may exercise exclusive rights of the author irrespective of whether or not the latter has consented. These circumstances revolve around fair dealing[209] in literary and artistic works.[210] As an exception to the general rule that only the author (or the artist) and persons permitted by him may enjoy exclusive rights in a work in which a copyright protected in the United Republic of Tanzania subsists, the fair dealing rule is applicable to: (a) quotations; (b) teachings and or illustrations for teaching purposes; (c) reporting and informing the public of certain events; (d) communicating works already made available to the public; (e) recording by broadcasting organizations; (f) temporary reproduction of copyrighted works; and (g) artistic and architectural works.

---

208. Cf. Dilan Thampapillai, *Creating an Innovation Exception? Copyright Law as the Infrastructure for Innovation*, 7(1) Scripted 104 at 108 (April 2010).

209. The term 'fair dealing' can be described in the following manner:

> to be fair dealing any excerpt or extract made from a copyright work must not be an appropriation of an entire work or of that part which would represent the substance of the author's skill and labour. To do this would be to preclude the need for the original. Thus, to be fair dealing, an unauthorised use sought normally to be of a relatively small part of a work, with use of any more needing permission of the copyright owner. However, as with infringement, a purely quantitative approach would not be taken by the courts, and a number of difficult cases can be easily figured in relation to normal academic research activity.

210. Cf. s. 12, TCPA.

A. Quotations

69. Reasonable quotation[211] of a work protected under the Copyright law of Tanzania is exempted from copyright infringement. Thus, fair dealing defence may successfully be invoked to exonerate from copyright infringement liability a person who, without consent of the copyright holder, includes in his work the latter's copyright protected material. This defence cannot succeed unless the person making quotations sufficiently acknowledges the source of the quoted information by mentioning the name of – and attributing the work to – the author. Moreover, the person making quotations must ensure compatibility of such quotations with the fair practice (i.e., complying with the three-step test for copyright protection). Additionally, the person making quotations must limit such taking of information from another source to the extent justified by the purpose.[212]

B. Teachings and or Illustrations for Teaching Purposes

70. Under Tanzanian law, an author X has no legal powers to prohibit a third party Z from incorporating in his work X's work by means of illustration, provided as follows: (1) Z utilizes X's work for teaching purpose; (2) the illustration does not go beyond this purpose; and (3) Z mentions in his publication the source of the work whose illustration is based as well as X's name.[213]

Based on the fair dealing or fair use defence, third parties may lawfully communicate the 'work broadcast or distributed by cable, or sound or visual recording' for use in educational institutions such as schools, universities and professional training institutions, provided that such communication meets the following conditions: (1) it is for educational purposes; (2) it is compatible with fair practice; and (3) it is the source of the work and the author's name are mentioned in the broadcast, the programme distribution by cable or the recording.[214]

C. Reporting and Informing the Public of Certain Events

71. It is permissive under the Copyright law of Tanzania for persons other than the copyright holder to reproduce and communicate to the public literary works addressing current events such as those relating to 'economic, political or religious topics', which have been published in newspaper or periodicals, or which have been

211. The online Oxford English dictionary refers to the term 'quotation' to mean a 'group of words taken from a text or speech and repeated by someone other than the original author or speaker' http://www.oxforddictionaries.com/definition/english/quotation (accessed: 17 Aug. 2015), whereas another source employs the word 'quotation' as a reference to 'something that is quoted; a passage quoted from a book, speech, etc.' (quotation. Dictionary.com. *Dictionary.com Unabridged*. Random House, Inc. http://dictionary.reference.com/browse/quotation (accessed: 17 Aug. 2015)).
212. Cf. s. 12(2)(b), TCPA.
213. Cf. s. 12(2)(c), TCPA.
214. *Ibid.*

broadcast or distributed by cable.[215] An event can be regarded a current event even if it is not of national or political significance, or even where a lesser degree of importance is attached to it. Thus, it is not foreign for an event that only attracts local interests or interests of few people (such as sporting events that take place in local community) to constitute current event.[216] Whether or not the defence of fair dealing for the purpose of reporting current event can be sustained, the determining factor is the fairness of such reporting; and in particular, the extent to which the interests of the copyright holder are affected by the reporting. An assessment in this regard must take into account: (1) the activity carried on by the reporter; (2) whether the copyright owner and the reporter are in competition; (3) the extent to which the reporter has copied the copyright work; and (4) whether the report could have been made in a manner less intrusive upon the copyright owner's rights. These conditions are not met if the motive for the reporter's report is pure personal financial or other economic benefits. In the light of *The Newspaper Licensing Agency Limited v. Marks & Spencer Plc* case, it is incontestable that:

> 'fair dealing' [as it relates to the reporter's report on current events] is concerned with the genuineness of the intentions and motives of the user of the copyright material to report current events and the extent to which (having fair regard to the interests of the copyright owner) it is fair and reasonable in all the circumstances to make as extensive a use as is in fact made of the copyright material. The question is very much a question of degree and one of fact and impression.[217]

To be permissible, the reproduction and communication of a current event as above must carry with it a sufficient acknowledgment as to the source of the work communicated or reproduced.[218] In these circumstances, the fair dealing exception applies to the extent that no liability for copyright infringement can be imputed to the person reproducing or communicating the work in which a copyright subsists. Nevertheless, this exception does not apply in relation to the work broadcasted or distributed by cable if the broadcast or the cable distribution was accompanied by an express statement excluding the free use thereof.

Pursuant to section 12(5) TCPA, third parties may freely exploit a copyrighted work for informatory purposes if the aim is any of the following: (a) to report 'a current event by means of photography, cinematography'; or (b) to communicate to the public or reproduce for 'making available to the public … any work that can be seen or heard' in the course of such communication or reproduction.

---

215. Cf. s. 12(4), TCPA.
216. Cf. *British Broadcasting Corporation v. British Satellite Broadcasting Ltd* [1992] Ch 141.
217. Cf. *The Newspaper Licensing Agency Limited v. Marks & Spencer Plc* [1999] EWHC Patents 266, para. 17.
218. s. 12(4), TCPA.

D. Communicating Works Already Made Available to the Public

72. In keeping with the provisions of section 12(7) TCPA, 'public libraries, non-commercial documentation centres, scientific institutions and educational establishments' may freely reproduce, 'by photography or sound or video recording, or electronic storage ... literary and artistic works which have already been made available to the public'.[219] Note that for such reproduction to be lawful, the reproduction itself, 'the number of copies made, and the use thereof' must meet the following conditions: (1) be limited to the 'need of the regular activities of the entity reproducing the work'; and (2) 'neither conflict with the normal exploitation of the work nor unreasonably prejudice the legitimate interests of the author'.[220]

Section 12(8) TCPA permits third parties to freely reproduce in the press or to freely communicate to the public the following: (a) any speech, of political nature delivered in the public; (b) any speech delivered during legal proceedings; and (c) any lecture, address, sermon or other work of the same nature delivered in public. Note that the free use of the foregoing works is subject to a number of legal conditions. First, the reproduction and/or the communication to the public should be exclusively for the purpose of current information. Second, the author retains the right to publish a collection of such works. This latter condition may be interpreted to mean that unless the reproduction in the press or the communication to the public of the works mentioned in section 12(8) TCPA is solely for the purpose of current information the third parties must seek authorization from the copyright owner as a condition of undertaking such reproduction and/or communication of the work concerned.

E. Recording by Broadcasting Organizations

73. Pursuant to section 12(9) TCPA, a broadcasting corporation, which fulfils four main conditions may freely record in one or several copies any work in which a copyright subsists. One of the pertinent conditions requires the broadcasting organization to secure first a licence from the copyright owner allowing the former to broadcast the copyrighted work. Thereafter, the organization may freely record the copyrighted work licensed to it; but the recording must be undertaken for the purposes of the organization's own broadcasts only. Moreover, the recording must be done by means of the organization's own facilities. Finally, the broadcasting organization must undertake to destroy all copies it has freely recorded for broadcasting purpose within six months, or within any other later period consented to by the author/copyright owner. Note that the obligation to destroy a recorded copy may be waived under the TCPA particularly if the recording has an exceptional documentary character that justifies preservation of a copy of the record in official archives.[221]

---

219. Cf. s. 12(7), TCPA.
220. *Ibid.*
221. Cf. s. 12(10), TCPA.

F. Temporary Reproduction of Copyrighted Work

74. Within the ambit of section 13 TCPA, temporary reproduction of a work protected under Copyright law of Tanzania is not considered copyright infringement particularly if: (a) such reproduction is made by a third party in the 'process of a transmission of a work or an act of making a stored work perceptible'; (b) by virtue of the consent of the copyright owner or the operation of law, the third party is entitled to undertake the said transmission and the act of making stored work perceptible mentioned in (a) above; and (c) such reproduction is an 'accessory to the transmission or making perceptible that occurs during the normal operation of the equipment used and entails the automatic deletion of the copy without enabling the retrieval of the work for any other purpose than those referred to in (a) and (b) above'.[222] Note that for a reproduction of copyrighted work to be regarded temporary and hence permissible in keeping with section 13 TCPA, it must meet each of the foregoing conditions.

G. Works of Art and of Architecture

75. Within the ambit of section 12(6) TCPA, it is lawful to undertake the following activities without permission of the copyright holder: (a) Reproduction of art and architectural works 'in an audiovisual or video recording'; and (b) Communication to the public of works of art and of architecture reproduced as above. However, the free exploitation of copyrighted works within the meaning of the legal provisions under discussion[223] is subject to the condition that the works of art and of architecture must be: (a) permanently located in a place accessible to the viewing public; or (b) included in the audiovisual work or in the video recording: (i) 'by way of background'; or (ii) 'as incidental to the essential matters represented'.

II. The Principle of Copyright Exhaustion

76. The principle of copyright exhaustion refers to a legal scenario whereby exclusive economic rights of the copyright owner are no longer enforceable simply because the author has already enjoyed the corresponding rights. Of the entire author's economic rights enumerated in section 9(1) TCPA, only two items in the list; namely, the right to authorize distribution of a copyrighted work and the right to authorize importation of the work, are affected by the principle of copyright exhaustion. In relation to distribution right, the law[224] puts it lucidly that once original or a copy of the work is sold the author may not invoke this right to prohibit further distribution of the same copy. However, for the distribution right to be exhausted two main conditions must be fulfilled. First, the law requires the initial

222. Section 13(iii), TCPA.
223. That is s. 12(6), TCPA.
224. That is s. 10(1), TCPA.

sale of the copyrighted work to be done by the author himself or by any other person authorized by the author. Second, the initial sale must take place in the United Republic of Tanzania. This latter condition implies that the Tanzanian copyright regime observes the principle of national copyright exhaustion. The application of this principle strengthens another economic right enjoyed by the author; namely, the right to authorize importation into the United Republic of Tanzania of copies of the author's work in accordance with section 9(1)(j) TCPA. Given that the distribution right under the TCPA lapses only if the work is sold in the United Republic of Tanzania, the principle of national exhaustion may imply the following in relation to both the right to authorize importation and the right to authorize distribution: (a) the author may sell his copyrighted products outside the territory of the United Republic of Tanzania territory without exhausting his distribution right within this territory. The author is thus permitted, under the law, to enjoin third parties from reimporting the same into Tanzania based on his right to authorize distribution; (b) third parties may buy copyrighted work lawfully sold in the United Republic of Tanzania and sell the same in other countries. If the work protected under copyright initially sold in Tanzania and thereafter in a foreign country is reimported into the United Republic Tanzania, the author may neither invoke his distribution right nor his importation right; both rights expire after the first sale in Tanzania of the copyrighted work.

77. The principle of copyright exhaustion as provided for in the TCPA is applied subject to certain exceptions. For instance, the principle is not applicable to rental right since section 10(2) TCPA specifically provides to this effect. The section stipulates that 'the author or any owner of copyright preserves the exclusive rights to authorize the rental of copies of such works after the sale of the copies'. Moreover, the author is entitled to claim moral rights in relation to his copyrighted work irrespective of whether his right to authorize distribution of the work is already exhausted. This position can be deduced from the provisions of sections 16 and 17 TCPA, which although do not refer to moral rights indicate that only economic rights may be a subject of assignment or a licence.

§8. Duration of Protection of Author's Rights

78. Section 14(1) TCPA stipulates a general rule regarding the duration of author's right. It guarantees that the author's economic and moral rights are protectable 'during the life of the author and for fifty years after his death'. The exception to this rule applies with respect to a work of joint authorship, anonymous or pseudonymous work, an audiovisual work and a work of applied art. While the duration of the author's right in a work of joint authorship follows the general rule of the author's life plus fifty years after death, the author whose life is taken into account for the calculation of the duration of the author's economic and moral rights is the last surviving author.[225] Economic and moral rights of authors of unanimous and pseudonymous works are protected for fifty years. This rule ceases to apply in order

225. Cf. s. 14(2), TCPA.

to pave the way for the application of the author's life plus fifty years rule if the true identity of the author of the unanimous or pseudonymous work is later on revealed.[226] Economic and moral rights of authors of an audiovisual work are protected for fifty years only.[227] With regard to unanimous, pseudonymous and audiovisual works, the point of reference for the purpose of calculating duration of protection of the respective economic and moral rights is the date on which the work was either created, first made available to the public or first published: The latest date counts.[228] The duration within which economic and moral rights of authors of works of applied art are protected is twenty-five years from the date the work is created.[229]

According to section 14(6) TCPA, the duration of protection of economic and moral rights of authors as provided above ends at the end of a calendar year in which it would otherwise expire. Thus, if the normal duration of protection ends in February of a particular year, the protection of the economic and moral rights will not terminate in February but at the end of that year.

§9. Neighbouring (Related) Rights

79. Neighbouring rights also known as rights related to copyright or rights neighbouring to copyright, are enshrined in the Copyright law of Tanzania to protect interests of 'three categories of people who are not technically authors: performing artists, producers of phonograms (i.e., sound recordings) and those involved in radio and television broadcasting'.[230] Protection of the rights that these groups of people enjoy in Tanzania is guaranteed subject to the provisions of section 5 TCPA.[231] In essence, the section outlines works in which copyright may subsist. This subjective scope of protection implies that performers, producers of sound recordings and broadcasting organizations are first required to secure a licence from authors and other copyright owners of the work on which the performances, production of sound recordings and broadcastings are respectively based.[232]

226. Cf. s. 14(3), TCPA.
227. Cf. s. 14(4), TCPA.
228. Cf. s. 14(3) and (4), TCPA.
229. Cf. s. 14(5), TCPA.
230. At http://www.esa.int/About_Us/Law_at_ESA/Intellectual_Property_Rights/About_copyright_and_neighbouring_rights (accessed: 19 Aug. 2015).
231. Cf. ss 31(1), 32(1) and 33(1), TCPA.
232. Note that there is no requirement to secure licence if the performers, producer of sound recordings and broadcasting organization own the copyright in the work on which the performance, sound recordings and broadcasts are based.

I. Protection of Performers

80. The TCPA defines the term 'performers' to mean 'actors, singers, musicians, dancers and other persons who act, sing, deliver declaim, play in or otherwise perform literary or artistic works including expressions of folklore, and variety and circus artistes'.[233] Performers do not enjoy a copyright protection *stricto sensu* insofar as their performances are concerned: They only enjoy some rights adjacent to copyright. This is in line with the delineation provided for under section 4 TCPA, which refers to the term 'neighbouring rights' as 'secondary right of copyright to which performers are entitled'.[234]

A. *Performers' Exclusive Economic Rights*

81. Lawful performance entitles its performer to a right to exclude third parties from engaging in some specific acts in relation to the performance. These acts are outlined in section 31(1)(a)–(f) TCPA to include fixing and reproducing the performance, making the performance available to the public, public lending of the performance and authorizing broadcasting of the performance.

1. Fixation and Reproduction Rights

82. Performers enjoy a right to fix or to authorize fixation of their unfixed performances. The term 'fixation' is statutorily defined to mean the 'embodiment of sounds or images or both or representations of sounds or images in a material sufficiently permanent or stable to permit them to be perceived, reproduced or otherwise communicated during a period of more than transitory duration'.[235] In the light of this definition, the fixation right may be interpreted to mean that third parties may not record live performance unless the performer consents to that activity.

83. It falls within the performer's exclusive right to directly or indirectly reproduce the performer's fixed performance irrespective of the manner or form such reproduction takes. As used in this context, the term 'reproduction' may mean the making of one or more copies of the fixed performance.[236] Thus, if the performance is recorded on a Compact Disc (CD) or a Digital Video Disc (DVD) for instance, third parties may not make copies of the CD or DVD concerned for commercial purposes without infringing the performer's reproduction right.

---

233. Section 4, para. 16, TCPA.
234. Section 4, para. 15, TCPA.
235. Section 4, para. 13, TCPA.
236. Cf. s. 4, para. 23, TCPA.

2. Right of Making Available to the Public

84. The right to make his fixed performances available to the public is exclusively enjoyed by the performer.[237] Under the Tanzanian Copyright law, this right has two facets.[238] The first facet relates to the performer's right to be the first to make his fixed performance or copies thereof available to the public. If, for instance, the performances are fixed on a CD or DVD, the performer is said to have enjoyed his right to be the first to make available to the public the very moment he sells the CD or DVD or immediately after parting with the ownership thereof in any manner whatsoever.[239] The second facet of the right of making available to the public is circumscribed by the specific means of making available as opposed to the first act thereof. In this regard, it falls within the performer's exclusive right to make 'available to the public of his fixed performance, by wire or wireless means, in such a way that members of the public may access them from a place or at a time individually chosen by them'.[240] This right would, for instance, be infringed by a person who stores recorded performances on the Internet server enabling the public to link to the server and thus getting access to the recorded performances on their personal computers.

3. Rental to the Public or PLR

85. The TCPA clarifies that as regards fixation of his performance or copies of such fixation, the performer enjoys exclusive right to undertake or authorize 'rental to the public or public lending' regardless of whether he still owns the fixation or the copies thereof.[241] It thus means that this particular right is inexhaustible: The right of first making available to the public by way of sale or by any other means of transfer of ownership is exhausted after the parting with ownership without affecting the PLR.

4. Right to Authorize Broadcasting of the Performance

86. The right to broadcast or authorize broadcasting or any other communication to the public of the performance exclusively rests with the performer. The performer's right in this regard does not extend to a 'rebroadcasting made or authorized by the organization initially broadcasting the performance'.[242] Moreover, the performer enjoys the right to authorize the broadcasting of his performance only if the material on which the performer's fixed performance is based is considered to be one of the works in which a copyright may subsist within the meaning of section 5

237. Other persons would enjoy this right only if authorized by the performer.
238. Cf. s. 31(1)(d) and (e), TCPA.
239. Cf. s. 31(1)(d), TCPA.
240. Cf. s. 31(1)(f), TCPA.
241. Cf. s. 31(1)(e), TCPA.
242. Cf. s. 31(1)(a)(ii), TCPA.

TCPA. In a similar vein, the performer's right of broadcasting or of other communication to the public of his fixation of the performance cannot be enforced against third parties if the fixation of the performance was not undertaken by the performer himself or if was undertaken by a third party who was not authorized by the performer. This limitation to the performer's right does not leave the performer without any other legal remedy as he may still mount some remedial measures (based on his right to fix or authorize fixation of his unfixed performance) against the third party concerned.

B. *Performer's Other Rights*

1. Moral Rights

87. The TCPA bestows upon the performer strong protection of moral rights in relation to his performance.[243] Protection in this respect is independent of the economic rights, which the performer enjoys and cannot be curtailed on the pretext that the performer has already transferred his economic rights therein to a third party. Performers enjoy two sets of moral rights, namely, the right of attribution and the right of integrity of the performances. In relation to the right of attribution, a performer is entitled, 'as regards his live aural performances and performances fixed in phonograms', to demand that he be identified as a performer of the respective performances. Nevertheless, an exception applies to the right of attribution: The performer cannot insist on being identified as such if the performance is utilized in a manner that makes such identification impossible.[244] The right of integrity as a constituent part of moral rights entitles the performer to 'object to any distortion, mutilation or other modification of performances' that would be detrimental to his reputation.[245]

2. Freedom of Contract

88. The TCPA extends to performers freedom to negotiate for favourable contractual terms. In this regard, section 31(4) TCPA clarifies that the legal provisions outlining the scope of the rights, which the performers enjoy shall not be interpreted in a manner that deprives or limits performers from enjoying the maximum possible contractual freedom when it comes to negotiating or setting 'terms and conditions more favourable for them in respect of their performances'.[246]

243. Cf. 31(3), TCPA.
244. *Ibid.*
245. *Ibid.*
246. Cf. 31(4), TCPA.

C. Exceptions to the Performer's Economic Rights

89. The TCPA imposes some limitations to the scope of the economic rights that are customarily vested in the performer. For instance, once the performer permits third parties to incorporate his 'performance in an audiovisual fixation' the performer's economic rights thereof are said to be exhausted.[247]

D. Duration of Protection

90. Performers' rights are protected for fifty years. This duration is calculated from the calendar year following the year in which the performance was fixed in a phonogram. In cases wherein the performance is not fixed in the phonogram, the protection duration runs from the calendar year following the year in which the performance takes place.[248]

II. Protection of Producers of Phonograms

91. The TCPA defines the term 'phonogram' to mean the following:

> any exclusively aural fixation of the sounds of a performance or of other sounds, or of a representation of a sound regardless of the method by which the sounds are fixed on the medium in which the sounds are embodied, and it does not include a fixation of sounds and images, such as the sound track of an audio-visual work.[249]

The TCPA defines the term 'producer of phonograms' to mean 'the person who, or the legal entity which first fixes the sounds of a performance or other sounds'.[250]

A. Rights Enjoyed by a Phonogram Producer

92. The TCPA reserves to the producer of sound recording exclusive authority to carry out or to authorize certain acts in relation to his phonogram.[251] In this regard, the phonogram producer is entitled to control the following: (i) 'direct or indirect reproduction of the sound recording, in any manner or form';[252] (ii) 'the making available to the public by sale or other transfer of ownership, of the original or copies of the sound recording that has not already been subject to a distribution

247. Section 31(2), TCPA.
248. Cf. 31(5), TCPA.
249. Section 4, para. 17, TCPA.
250. Section 4, para. 18, TCPA.
251. Cf. s. 32, TCPA.
252. Cf. s. 32(1)(a), TCPA.

authorized by the producer';[253] (iii) 'rental to the public or public lending of a copy of the sound recording, irrespective of the ownership of the copy rented or lent';[254] and (iv) 'the making available to the public of the sound recording, by way of wireless means, in such a way that members of the public may access from a place or at time individually chosen by them'.[255]

B. *Equitable Remuneration*

93. Section 33 TCPA provides for equitable remuneration payable to phonogram producers and performers by users of sound recordings. To give rise to the claim of equitable remuneration, the producer is required to prove that a sound recording published for commercial purpose and/or a reproduction of the sound recording already published for commercial ends is either publicly performed or used directly for the following: (1) for broadcasting; or (2) for other communication to the public.[256] Publication of the sound recording for commercial purposes within the meaning of the immediately preceding sentence include 'sound recording that have been made available to the public by wire or wireless means in such a way that members of the public may access them from a place and at a time individually chosen by them'.[257]

The law obliges the user of a sound recording, as above, to pay equitable remuneration to the producer of sound recording, who in turn pays the performer the equitable amount he deserves. According to the pertinent rule, the producer is under obligation to pay the performer(s) half of the amount he receives from the user retaining the other half for him. The producer's obligation in this regard, may be waived or modified through an agreement between the producer and the performers.[258]

C. *Duration Within Which Rights Emanating from Sound Recording Are Protected*

94. The exclusive rights of producers of sound recordings enumerated in section 32(1) TCPA, and the right to equitable remuneration enjoyed by both the producer(s) and performer(s) provided for under section 33(2) TCPA are protectable for fifty years. This duration is calculated from the calendar year following the year of the publication of the sound recording. In relation to unpublished sound recordings, the duration is calculated from the date on which the recordings were fixed.[259]

253. Cf. s. 32(1)(b), TCPA.
254. Cf. s. 32(1)(c), TCPA.
255. Cf. s. 32(1)(d), TCPA.
256. Cf. s. 33(1), TCPA.
257. Section 33(4), TCPA.
258. Cf. s. 33(2), TCPA.
259. Cf. ss 32(2) and 33(3), TCPA.

III. Protection of Broadcasting Organizations

95. Broadcasting organizations enjoy several rights in relation to their broadcasts. This is in keeping with the provisions of section 34 TCPA, according to which certain activities in relation to broadcasts may only be undertaken by the broadcasting organization or by a third party who is authorized by the organization. These activities include rebroadcasting, communication to the public, fixation and reproduction of the fixation of the organization's broadcasts.[260] Note that broadcasting organizations may only control exploitation of their broadcasts by third parties in Tanzania for a period of fifty years from a 'year in which the broadcasts take place'.[261]

IV. General Exceptions

96. Section 35 TCPA enshrines a general exception clause limiting the scope of the neighbouring rights that performers, phonogram producers and broadcasting organizations enjoy. The nature and purpose of exploitation of the neighbouring right concerned, determines the question whether such exploitation may be covered under the general exception. For instance, third parties' use of 'short excerpts' for the purpose of imparting to the public some information depicting a picture of what is going on in the society may not be regarded as an infringement of the relevant neighbouring rights.[262] In a similar vein, reproduction of neighbouring rights done as a part of some scientific researches does not constitute an encroachment on the pertinent exclusive rights.[263] This applies also to a reproduction made for the sole purpose of instantaneous teachings, provided that two conditions are fulfilled. First, instantaneous teachings must be done in a manner allowing the teacher and the participants in the teaching session to communicate face-to-face. Second, the reproduction for the instantaneous teaching purpose should not cover 'performances and phonograms which have been published as teaching or instructional materials'.[264] Note that third parties may exploit neighbouring rights without any authorization, if the exploitation concerned would be exempted when undertaken in relation to copyrighted material on which the neighbouring rights are based. This therefore implies that neighbouring rights protected in Tanzania do not grant exclusive rights beyond those provided for by the copyright. Hence, exceptions to the exclusive, author's rights[265] are also applicable to neighbouring rights.[266]

260. Section 34(1), TCPA.
261. Section 34(2), TCPA.
262. Section 35(a), TCPA.
263. Section 35(b), TCPA.
264. Section 35(c), TCPA.
265. These rights and the limitations thereof are outlined above in §6 and §7 of this chapter.
266. Cf. s. 35(d), TCPA.

§10. Infringement and Remedies

97. The TCPA incorporates a general, legal criterion according to which an infringement of a copyright protected in the United Republic of Tanzania is determined: it constitutes copyright infringement if a person other than the copyright owner or a person acting on the owner's authority does or causes any other person to do an act in Tanzania, which the owner has an exclusive right to do or to authorize as per outline offered above in Part §6 of this chapter. Consequently, the TCPA provides for various civil and criminal sanctions against third parties who encroach on copyright and neighbouring rights protected in the United Republic of Tanzania. Generally, the TCPA empowers civil and criminal courts deriving jurisdiction from the Copyright Act or criminal procedure Act to deal with infringement of copyright and/or neighbouring rights so as to preserve interests of the injured party through injunctive reliefs. In particular, these courts enjoy powers to order conservatory and provisional measures that are necessary to halt infringement.[267] In addition to the court's power to issue injunctions, both civil and criminal courts enjoy general jurisdiction to impound the following: (1) copies of copyrighted materials or of sound recordings if the copies are suspected not to have been lawfully made or imported;[268] (2) the packaging of such copies; (3) the implements that could be used for the making of such copies; and (4) accounts, documents or business papers referring to such copies.[269]

I. Civil Sanctions and Remedies

98. Section 36 TCPA empowers a proprietor of copyright and neighbouring rights protected in Tanzania to institute legal proceedings against third parties aiming either to restrain an ongoing and future infringement or to redress some losses emanating from an already perpetuated infringing activity.[270] Proceedings in this respect must be instituted before a competent court in Tanzania. A court that is competent to deal with copyright infringement matters in the United Republic of Tanzania is the District Court that is established under the Magistrates Courts Act, 1984.[271] This court has jurisdiction to award various civil remedies to successful plaintiffs. In particular, the court can issue injunctions and award damages. The court may additionally make the following orders: (1) seizure of infringing items; (2) right of delivery; (3) destruction of infringing copies; (4) destructing or rendering unusable infringer's equipment; and (5) modification of the infringing items. These remedies are discussed below.

267. Cf. s. 43(1), TCPA.
268. Within the ambit of s. 43(1)(b), TCPA, copies are deemed to be made or imported lawfully if the proprietor of the copyright and neighbouring right subsisting in the original copies has himself either copied, imported or authorized the copying and importation of the copies.
269. Cf. s. 43(1), TCPA.
270. Cf. s. 36(1), TCPA.
271. That is Act No. 2 of 1984. Cf. s. 4 para. 7 TCPA defining the term 'court' for the purpose of the administration of copyright and related matters.

A. *Injunctive Reliefs*

99. Proprietors of infringed copyright and neighbouring rights are entitled to a court's order preventing third parties from infringing or from continuing the infringement. When moved in this regard, the court may issue an injunction in order to halt ongoing infringement.[272] From a legal, technical point of view, an injunction is a 'judicial process or order requiring the person to whom it is directed to do a particular act or to refrain from doing a particular act'.[273] An injunction is thus viewed as an authoritative directive or preventive order. Depending on the circumstances of each case, the court's preventive order may either be permanent or temporary. In general, the court grants temporary injunction in interlocutory proceedings to preserve the status quo of the parties. If the infringement suit is finally and conclusively determined, the temporary injunction may either be lifted if the proceedings terminate in the defendant's favour or may be converted into permanent or perpetual injunction if the infringement suit terminates in favour of the plaintiff. Perpetual injunction may carry with it an order requiring the wrongdoer to cease-and-desist, should there be any danger of repetition of the acts of infringement.[274] The necessity of this order is circumscribed by the circumstances surrounding the infringement of the plaintiff's rights. At any rate, the court is likely to issue the cease-and-desist order if the defendant's acts of infringement are intentional or are attributable to negligence.[275]

B. *Damages*

100. The plaintiff in a copyright and neighbouring rights infringement suit may ask a court in the United Republic of Tanzania to order an infringer to make monetary compensation commensurate with the economic loss resulting from the latter's infringing activities.[276] The technical term employed when referring to this kind of compensation is 'damages'. Damages are generally paid under the TCPA to offset an economic or pecuniary loss only. However, section 37(2) TCPA provides for an exception to the foregoing general rule, as 'authors, persons having rights in scientific editions, photographers and performers' may get fiscal compensation for the injury they sustain in relation to their works even where the harm is not of pecuniary nature. This exception does not apply automatically. Its application is subject to two conditions. First, the harm or loss suffered should be ascribed to the defendant's intentional or negligent act. Second, the injury suffered by the plaintiff should be of such a nature and degree that justice would not be done but for the monetary compensation thereof. These conditions apply cumulatively.

The law does not stipulate the specific exclusive rights concerned under section 37(2) TCPA. The TCPA therefore leaves it open for legal analysts to wade through

---

272. Cf. ss 36(1)(a) and 37(1), TCPA.
273. At http://dictionary.reference.com/browse/injunction.
274. Cf. s. 37(1), TCPA.
275. *Ibid.*
276. Cf. s. 36(1)(b), TCPA.

the entire Copyright Act in a bid to identify rights whose infringement may not give rise to pecuniary loss. In this endeavour, one may speculate on moral rights as one of the rights whose infringement does not give rise to monetary loss. However, the position that only economic rights in a protected work are legally assignable[277] negates the foregoing conclusion that places moral rights in the group of rights whose infringement may not give rise to pecuniary loss within the ambit of section 37(2) TCPA. This is buttressed by the position laid down in the TCPA that the right to be indemnified for loss other than pecuniary harm is assignable subject to the condition that a contract to that effect be concluded or a suit asserting the right be instituted prior to the infringement event concerned.[278] By their nature, moral rights are not assignable and hence should not be considered one of the rights referred to in section 37(2) TCPA. This implies therefore that section 37(2) TCPA concerns only exclusive economic rights protected under the Tanzanian Copyright law.

101. Section 40 of the TCPA provides for vicarious liability. Within the ambit of this section, owners of enterprises may be held liable for the infringement of copyright and neighbouring rights committed by employees or agents of the enterprises concerned in the course of their contractual duties. If the owner of the enterprise is found liable under vicarious liability, the proprietor of the infringed IP rights is entitled to any of the civil remedies stipulated under sections 37 and 38 TCPA except damages.[279] Note that it is also possible to secure damages in copyright and neighbouring rights infringement suit based on legal provisions other than those of TCPA.[280]

102. As regards modalities of calculating damages awardable to a successful plaintiff in a suit concerning infringement of copyright and related matters, the TCPA endorses two methods. First, the plaintiff may ask the court to award him damages calculated on the basis of reasonable royalty. This method presupposes that had the infringer asked for a licence to undertake the otherwise infringing activities he would have paid a licence fee (or, in other words, a royalty). In demarcating the amount the infringer should pay, the reasonable royalty test, which places the defendant in the shoes of any reasonable man negotiating a licence agreement with the plaintiff must be applied. Thus, pursuant to this base of damages calculation, the defendant is not expected to pay the plaintiff monetary compensation for the infringement more than the amount the reasonable licensee would pay for the permission allowing him to exploit a work enjoying copyright right and neighbouring rights protection.[281] The second method of calculating damages takes into account

277. Cf. s. 16(3), TCPA.
278. Section 37(3), TCPA.
279. That is to say, the remedies, which the copyright owner may claim against the owner of an enterprises within the meaning s. 40 of the Copyright and Neighbouring Rights Act, which are: (i) injunctive reliefs; (ii) order for the seizure of the infringing items; (iii) order for the delivery of the infringing items; (iv) order for the destruction of infringing copies; (v) order for destructing or rendering unusable infringer's equipment; and (vi) order for the modification of the infringing items.
280. Cf. s. 40, CPA.
281. Cf. s. 41, TCPA.

profits made by the defendant directly ascribable to the infringement.[282] In keeping with this method, the plaintiff is not expected to recover damages more than the defendant's profits made out of the infringing activities.[283] To ensure that he keeps abreast of the infringer's profits, the proprietor of infringed copyright and neighbouring rights is entitled to a court's order requiring the infringer to furnish the former with accounting details reflecting the actual profits made out of the infringement.[284]

103. Note that in addition to damages usually calculated on the basis of the infringer's profits or reasonable royalty as above, the court may invoke its discretionary powers to award exemplary damages,[285] particularly if the court is of the opinion that the infringement prejudices the reputation of the proprietor of the infringed copyright and neighbouring rights.[286]

C. Seizure and Right of Delivery of Infringing Items

104. The plaintiff in a copyright and related rights infringement suit is entitled to have any infringing object and the infringer's receipts resulting from such infringement seized.[287] This remedy is of paramount importance; the plaintiff may rely on the seized items to prove the magnitude of the infringement.

105. It is also possible, under Tanzanian Copyright law, for the plaintiff to demand that the infringing copies and equipment be wholly or partially delivered to him. Note that the court can issue an order to this effect only if the plaintiff undertakes to pay the infringer an equitable compensation commensurate with the cost the latter incurred in producing the infringing items.[288]

106. The TCPA bestows upon the proprietor of infringed copyright and neighbouring rights a right to move the court to issue an order allowing the plaintiff to destroy all infringing copies that have been unlawfully manufactured or unlawfully distributed or which are intended for unlawful distribution in the United Republic of Tanzania.[289] However, instead of ordering destruction of the copies as above, the victim of copyright and neighbouring rights infringement is entitled to ask the court to order the infringer to modify the appearance of the infringing copies. This remedy is claimable as of right only if the effect of the modification does not go beyond making the otherwise infringing work not to infringe on the rights concerned.[290]

---

282. Cf. s. 36(b), TCPA.
283. It is questionable, and the court in Tanzania has not yet given any guidance, as to whether the defendant's profit includes the overhead costs or whether these costs are excluded.
284. Section 37(1), TCPA.
285. That is punitive damages.
286. Cf. s. 36(2), TCPA.
287. Section 36(2), TCPA.
288. Section 39, TCPA.
289. Section 38(1), TCPA.
290. Section 38(3), TCPA.

107. Similarly, copyright proprietors are entitled to a court's order allowing them to render unusable equipment that have been or may be used to produce infringing copies.[291] If it is technically impossible to execute this order, the plaintiff is then entitled to an order to destroy the equipment concerned. Note that the order to render unusable or to destroy the equipment as above can be issued only if the equipment concerned is 'destined exclusively for the unlawful production of copies'.[292] Hence, the infringing equipment cannot be destroyed or rendered unusable if such equipment is capable of performing any other lawful function.

108. The Copyright law of Tanzania clarifies that the court has no powers to order destruction of infringing copies, of the infringer's equipment (or the rendering of the infringing equipment unusable) and modification to the infringing work in line with the provisions of section 38(1)–(3) of the TCPA, unless the ownership of the copies and the work concerned has been determined first.[293]

109. Under certain circumstances, the plaintiff in a copyright and neighbouring rights infringement suit cannot be entitled to the grant of injunctive reliefs and to the court's order of destruction, or of rendering unusable, or of delivering the infringing material.[294] This is particularly the case if the infringer proves to the satisfaction of the court that the infringement was neither intentional nor a result of his negligent conduct.[295] In the circumstances, the court may order the infringer to pay the injured party some monetary compensation in lieu of destructing, delivering or rendering unusable the infringing material, or observing an injunction.[296] Note that in order to be allowed to pay this financial indemnification, it must be proved that: (i) remedies other than monetary indemnification 'would produce serious and disproportionate injury' to the infringer; and that (ii) the injured party is, according to the circumstances surrounding the infringement in issue, presumed to be ready to accept the monetary indemnification whose amount is determinable on the basis of reasonable royalty.[297] Once he accepts monetary indemnification, an injured party is presumed to have issued a licence to the would be infringer to utilize the initially infringed work.[298] This presumption does not extend to customary rights, which the proprietor of a right protected under the TCPA enjoys with respect to his work even after issuing third parties with the licence to utilize the work.[299]

291. The typical examples of these equipment include 'moulds, plates, engraving stones, blocks, stencils and negatives' (cf. s. 38(2), TCPA).
292. Section 38(2), TCPA.
293. Section 38(4), TCPA.
294. These remedies are stipulated under the provisions of ss 37, 38 and 39 TCPA.
295. Cf. s. 41, TCPA.
296. *Ibid.*
297. *Ibid.*
298. *Ibid.*
299. *Ibid.*

II. Criminal Liability for Copyright Infringement

110. In addition to civil sanctions outlined in section 36 TCPA, any person who intentionally infringes or causes to be infringed any copyright and neighbouring rights protected in the United Republic of Tanzania may face criminal charges and upon conviction, shall, depending on whether he is a first-time or hardcore offender, be subjected to a fine or imprisonment or both fine and imprisonment.[300] Whereas first-time offender is subjected to a fine the amount of which should not exceed Tanzanian Shilling (TZS) 5 million, hardcore offender is subjected to a fine of any amount that does not exceed TZS 10 million.[301] Insofar as imprisonment terms are concerned, the court has the discretion to imprison the first-time offender for any term up to thirty-six months, whereas this discretion in relation to a hardcore offender extends up to five years imprisonment term.[302]

111. To be successful in a criminal case concerning infringement of copyright and neighbouring rights in Tanzania, the prosecution side must, in addition to proving the accused person's intent to commit an offence, show that the alleged infringement was perpetuated on a 'commercial basis'.[303]

112. Any criminal offence in relation to copyright and neighbouring rights infringement whose penalty is not specifically provided for under the TCPA is punishable by the following: (a) a fine not exceeding TZS 4 million for the infringer's first offence; (b) a fine of up to TZS 8 million for each subsequent offence committed by the infringer; (c) an imprisonment term of up to 'three years for the first offence'; and (d) an imprisonment term of up to 'two years for each subsequent offence'.[304]

113. The TCPA imposes criminal liability of a fine up to TZS 5 million or an imprisonment term of up to three years to the following: (i) a person who, not being an agent of performers 'gives authorization on behalf of performers', and any other person who accepts the said authorization knowing the false pretence of the person purporting to act on behalf of performers;[305] and (ii) a person who, having reproduced lawfully copies of phonograms protected under section 33 of the Copyright Act does not apply to the said copies or their containers a notice indicating that the phonograms are protected.[306]

300. Cf. s. 42(1), TCPA.
301. *Ibid.*
302. *Ibid.*
303. *Ibid.*
304. Cf. s. 42(9), TCPA.
305. Cf. s. 42(7), TCPA.
306. Cf. s. 42(8), TCPA.

III. Technical Means of Copyright Protection and Rights Management Information

A. Technical Means of Protection

114. The TCPA does not stipulate against (but condones) employing lawful technical measures to deter third parties from accessing literary, artistic and derivative works protected in Tanzania. In keeping with the permitted technical measures, the TCPA allows proprietors of copyright and neighbouring rights to apply in relation to their works special devices that would render reproduction and/or copying of the protected works impossible; or that would impair a copy of the reproduced protected material; as well as encryption that would deny third parties reception of broadcasts.[307] Note that manufacturers, importers and any persons otherwise trading in any devices or technology 'specifically designed' or that may be specifically 'adapted' to bypass any of the technical measures mentioned in the immediately preceding sentence, are put in the same class of infringers of copyright and neighbouring rights and are consequently subjected to the respective civil remedies and criminal sanctions outlined above in §10 of this chapter.[308]

B. Rights Management Information

115. Rights management information is one of the legal means to protect artistic, literary and derivative works in the United Republic of Tanzania. Section 4 TCPA defines the term 'rights management information' as follows:

> Any information which identifies the author, the work, the performer, the performance of the performer, the producer of the sound recording, the broadcast, or the owner of any right under [the TPCA], or information about the terms and conditions of use of the work, the performance, the sound recording or the broadcast, and any numbers or codes that represent such information, when any of these items of information is attached to a copy of work, fixed performance, a sound recording or a fixed broadcast, or appears in connection with the broadcasting, communication to the public or making available to the public of a work, a fixed performance, a sound recording or a broadcast.[309]

The TCPA regards 'the removal or alteration of any electronic rights management information without authority' as an infringement of copyright and neighbouring rights protected in Tanzania.[310] This infringement is also imputed to the person who distributes, broadcasts, communicates or makes available to the public 'works,

307. Cf. s. 44(1)(i) and (ii), TCPA.
308. Cf. s. 44(1)(i) and (ii) and 44(2), TCPA.
309. Section 4, para. 27, Act No. 7/1999.
310. Section 44(1)(iii), Act No. 7/1999.

performances, sound recordings or broadcast' in respect of which 'electronic rights management information has been removed or altered'.[311]

The TCPA postulates that the tempering with electronic rights management information and the economic exploitation of works whose electronic rights management information has been removed attracts civil remedies and criminal sanctions.[312] An infringer who is liable for disregarding rights management information can exonerate himself from the liability if he proves to the satisfaction of the court that: (i) the removal or alteration of the rights management information was authorized by the owner of the protected rights; or (ii) he has been authorized by the owner of the respective rights to distribute, broadcast, communicate or make available to the public 'works, performances, sound recordings or broadcast' notwithstanding the fact that the electronic rights management information had been removed or altered; or (iii) he did not and he could not reasonably be expected to know that the electronic rights management information has been removed or altered.[313]

IV. Use of Labels to Curb Infringement

116. To ensure that production and publication in or importation into the United Republic of Tanzania sound and audiovisual recordings, does not infringe upon any rights protected under the TCPA, an adhesive label known as HAKIGRAM, which is delivered exclusively by the COSOTA, has been devised.[314] It is a requirement under the law that this label be affixed to each and every sound recording or audiovisual recording, which is a subject of distribution or offer or exposal (in any manner whatsoever) to 'the public for distribution by way of sale, hire, rental or otherwise within the United Republic'. As a result, sound and audiovisual recordings that do not bear HAKIGRAM as above may be seized either by COSOTA, police authorities or customs department. The seizure does not go beyond sixty days: Within this period the authority that has seized the recordings hears and determines any objection levelled against the seizure. Should the authority be convinced that the seized items do not infringe a copyright, it will release the same to the owner. Otherwise, the items are destroyed by COSOTA in collaboration with the customs authorities and the Police Department. Similar action is also undertaken if the owner does not demand the return of the seized items within sixty days after the seizure.

311. Section 44(1)(iv), Act No. 7/1999.
312. Cf. s. 44(1)(iii) and (iv) and 44(2), TCPA.
313. Cf. s. 44(1)(iii) and (iv), TCPA.
314. The Copyright and Neighbouring Rights (Protection and Distribution of Sound and Audiovisual Recordings) Regulations, published on 10 Feb. 2006 in the Government Notice No. 18.

Chapter 2. Patents

§1. Sources: Legislation

117. Patents governance in Tanzania is not a union matter. Neither the Constitution of the United Republic of Tanzania nor any other piece of legislation bestows upon a single government entity powers to oversee registration and protection of patents across the whole territory of Tanzania. These powers are respectfully shared by both governments of Tanzania Zanzibar and the United Republic of Tanzania. The Zanzibar Industrial Property Act No. 4 of 2008 (ZIPA) serves as a legal basis for the grant and administration of rights appertaining patents in Tanzania Zanzibar. The government of the United Republic of Tanzania draws its powers to control issuance and protection of patents in mainland Tanzania from the Patents Act No. 1 of 1987 enacted by the legislature of the United Republic. This latter piece of legislation is implemented by the Patents Regulations published in the GN No. 190 of 1994.[315]

By virtue of the country's membership to the ARIPO, the Protocol on Patent and Industrial Designs within the Framework of ARIPO (the Harare Protocol), 1982 to which the United Republic of Tanzania is a signatory,[316] facilitates patents protection in both Tanzania mainland and Tanzania Zanzibar.[317]

At the international level, the United Republic of Tanzania is, since 16 June 1963, bound by the Paris Convention of 20 March 1883 as last revised in 1967. Moreover, Tanzania is bound by patent principles laid down in the TRIPS Agreement;[318] as well as those covered under the Patent Cooperation Treaty (PCT) of 1970.[319]

Legal provisions contained in both Patents Act No. 7 of 1987 (applicable in Tanzania mainland) and the ZIPA are substantially similar. Thus, the discourse in this chapter basically takes into account provisions of the former Act. Where necessary, a slight reference to contents of the latter legislation is made in this chapter.

315. The patent protection schemes obtaining in Tanzania Zanzibar and Tanzania mainland may be regarded distinct from one another due to jurisdictional limitations, which the Zanzibar Industrial Property Act, 2008 and the Patents Act (of Tanzania), 1987 establish. When it comes to international system of patent registration and protection established under various regional and international legal instruments in force in Tanzania, such scepticism cannot hold water: the whole United Republic of Tanzania is entitled to be designated as a single territory where international patent protection is sought.

316. The Harare Protocol is in force in Tanzania since 1 Sep. 1999.

317. Cf. the Lusaka Agreement on the creation of an Industrial Property Organization for English-Speaking Africa of December 1976, as amended by the administrative council of ARIPO on 10 Dec. 1982, 12 Dec. 1986 and 27 Nov. 1996, and as amended by the Council of Ministers on 13 Aug. 2004. The Lusaka agreements empowers ARIPO to enact some protocols that are necessary to define the functions and powers of ARIPO in specific fields of IP rights. Thus, ARIPO's competence in relation to issues pertaining to patents and designs are defined by the Harare Protocol, 1982.

318. This Agreement was adopted at Marrakesh on 14 Apr. 1994 and came into force on 1 Jan. 1995.

319. The PCT is in force in Tanzania since 14 Sep. 1999.

§2. Patentable Subject Matter

118. The patent regime established under the Patents Act No. 1 of 1987 of the Tanzania Patents Act (TPA or Act No. 1/1987) aims to protect scientific inventions. The term 'invention' is employed in the Act as a reference to a 'solution to a specific problem in the field of technology'.[320] Upon application, an inventor whose invention fulfils the requirement of the foregoing definition may be issued with a patent.[321] The term patent is usually applied in legal context as a reference to two concepts, namely, the 'exclusive right granted by a government to an inventor to manufacture, use, or sell an invention for a certain number of years' and 'an invention or process protected by this right'.[322] Another source refers to the term 'patent' as a 'document, issued, upon application, by a government office (or regional office) acting for several countries'.[323]

It is instructive to note that not all inventions can qualify for protection under the Patent Law of Tanzania. The TPA outlines at least five categories of inventions that may not be considered for protection.[324] These are: (1) discoveries, and scientific and mathematical theories; (2) plant or animal varieties or essentially biological processes for the production of plant or animals, other than microbiological and the products of such processes; (3) schemes, rules or methods for doing business, performing purely mental acts or games; (4) methods for the treatment of the human or animal body by surgery or therapy, as well as diagnostic methods;[325] and (5) mere presentation of information.

119. An invention that is recognized as such under the TPA is a patentable subject matter irrespective of whether the technological solution provided by such invention relates to a product or to a process.[326] In other words, both product patents and process patents are registrable and hence protectable under the patent law of Tanzania.

§3. Conditions of Patentability

120. An invention must fulfil some conditions appertain to novelty, inventive step and industrial application so as to merit protection in the United Republic of Tanzania.[327] An outline of these conditions follows hereinafter.

---

320. Cf. s. 7(1), Act No. 1/1987.
321. The term 'patent' generally means a 'title issued to protect invention' (s. 2, ZIPA).
322. URL: patent. Dictionary.com. Collins English Dictionary – Complete & Unabridged 10th Edition. HarperCollins Publishers. http://dictionary.reference.com/browse/patent.
323. Cf. Ch. 2 p. 17, WIPO Handbook (2004).
324. Cf. s. 7(2), TPA.
325. However, this restriction does not apply to the products for use in any of those methods (cf. s. 7(2)(d), Act No. 1/1987).
326. Cf. s. 7(1), Act No. 1/1987.
327. Cf. s. 8, Act No. 1/1987 and s. 4, ZIPA.

I. Novelty and Inventive Step

121. The question whether or not a particular invention passes the novelty and inventive step tests is determined on the basis of the state of prior art. Insofar as the Tanzanian law is concerned, every information regarding an invention disclosed to the public in any part of the world forms part of the prior art irrespective of the modality of such disclosure.[328] In this sense, information communicated to the public in a written form including drawings and accompanying illustrations affects patentability of an invention in Tanzania in the same way information disclosed orally, or disclosed through use or the exhibition of the invention does.[329]

A. Novelty

122. In consonance with a well-established principle of patent law, an invention fulfils the patentability requirement if it is new. Newness of an invention is a fact that is determined by a patent examiner's negative findings on a question whether the invention concerned is 'anticipated by prior art'.[330] An invention is said to be anticipated by prior art if a single piece of prior art reveals each and every element of the claimed invention. Generally, information constituting prior art can vitiate novelty of an invention only if its disclosure to the public is actuated prior to the date of the patent application or the date on which the patent applicant claims priority right[331] in relation to his invention.[332]

The Tanzanian law provides for some exceptional circumstances pursuant to which the novelty of an invention may be confirmed notwithstanding existence of any of the above novelty-vitiating factors. The fact that an invention, which is a subject of patent application was displayed 'at an official or officially recognized international exhibition' prior to the date of patent application may not destroy the novelty of such an invention provided that the patent application for the invention concerned is filed within six months from the date of the display.[333] Similarly, disclosure of the invention made in consequence of an 'evident abuse in relation to the applicant or his predecessor in title'[334] does not destroy novelty of an invention, unless the person entitled to file a patent application does not do so within six months – a period which is counted from the date such an evident abuse was perpetuated. The terminology 'evident abuse in relation to applicant or his predecessor' may be clarified as a reference to *inter alia* the circumstances whereby a disclosure of an invention is made by third parties without any authority of the

328. Cf. s. 9(2), Act No. 1/1987 and s. 4(2), ZIPA.
329. *Ibid.*
330. Cf. s. 9(1), Act No. 1/1987.
331. Priority right is described in part 4(I)(C)(2) below.
332. Cf. s. 9(2)(a), Act No. 1/1987.
333. Cf. s. 9(3)(i), Act No. 1/1987.
334. Cf. s. 9(3)(ii), Act No. 1/1987.

owner of the invention or his predecessor in title. This may particularly be the case if a person who is not entitled to file a patent application does so and thereby disclosing the invention to the public.[335]

B. Inventive Step

123. An invention, which meets the novelty requirements outlined above, may nevertheless not be patented if it lacks an inventive step. An invention does not meet the patentability requirement of inventive step if, in the light of the available prior art, it is categorized as an obvious invention.[336] Obviousness of an invention signifies the fact that had any person skilled in the art[337] put together several pieces of information available in the prior art, he would have made the same invention as the one whose patent is claimed in Tanzania.

II. Industrial Applicability

124. As a matter of legal rules, an invention, which is not capable of being applied industrially cannot be patented under the patent law of Tanzania.[338] According to section 11 TPA, an invention has the capability of being applied industrially 'if according to its nature, it can be made or used, in the technological sense, in any kind of industry, including agriculture, fishery and services'. In other words, industrial applicability of an invention refers to the utility of the invention. Thus, the requirement that a patentable invention must be capable of being applied industrially reinforces the rational basis for protecting inventions under the patent regime; the claimed invention must be beneficial to society by being useful in trade or industry. Additionally, the requirement of invention's industrial application reinforces the position that a patentable invention must be capable of producing a technical effect, which is capable of consistent repetition. It is, however, not necessary that the invention be an industrial or commercial success though this would serve to confirm its utility value.

125. Based on public interests, the Tanzanian legislature may decide to prohibit exploitation of certain inventions by enacting a law to that effect. Such prohibition of exploitation cannot be overcome on the grounds that the inventions in issue meet the patentability requirements of novelty, inventive step and industrial applicability. In this regard, it is important to note that inclusion in a patent law of a clause prohibiting exploitation of an invention does not justify denial of a patent thereof.[339]

335. Cf. s. 15, Act No. 1/1987.
336. Cf. s. 10, Act No. 1/1987.
337. A person skilled in the art is a technician of average skill in the art relevant to invention as opposed to a leading expert in the field concerned.
338. Cf. s. 8, Act No. 1/1987.
339. However, when the sole ground for limiting such exploitation is *ordre public* or morality, it is unlikely that a patent with regard to such an invention can be granted (Cf. s. 12, Act No. 1/1987).

This implies that the patents law of Tanzania distinguishes existence of patent from the exercise of the exclusive rights stemming thereof.[340]

126. Moreover, the patent law of Tanzania clarifies that an Act of Parliament may temporarily prohibit the grant of patent in respect of an invention that otherwise fulfils all patentability requirements including those relating to novelty, inventive step and industrial applicability. This legal scenario is particularly imminent if the products resulting from or connected with the invention are statutorily excluded from patentable subject matter.[341]

§4. Formalities

127. The general overseers of industrial property matters in the United Republic of Tanzania are respectively the BRELA[342] and the Office of the Registrar General of Zanzibar.[343] BRELA is thus a general administrator of the Patents Act of Tanzania (i.e., Act No. 1/1987), whereas the Registrar General of Zanzibar administers the ZIPA. Both the foregoing pieces of legislation provide for the establishment of the office of a registrar of patents, which is constituted by a registrar of patents appointed by the President of the United Republic of Tanzania and the President of the Revolutionary Government of Zanzibar respectively.[344] Other statutory officers within the patents offices in the United Republic of Tanzania include deputy registrar(s) who are appointed by the minister responsible for matters relating to patents. In addition to officers appointed as above, the office of the patent office may as well employ skilled persons to serve as patent examiners. The patents offices in the United Republic of Tanzania are responsible for the administration of the patents registry and for the performance of any other duties, which the law assigns to the

340. By drawing such a distinction the legislature implicitly endorses the following conclusions: (i) securing patent protection does not mean an automatic right to exploit a corresponding invention: the patentee is duty-bound to observe existing rules and regulations governing exploitation of his invention; (ii) the law prohibiting exploitation of a particular invention may be amended at any time if the circumstances that led to the enactment of that particular law change and thus allowing the patentee to exploit an invention, which could otherwise not be legally exploited prior to the amendment of the said law; and (iii) an existing invention (including an invention the exploitation of which is prohibited by law) may form a basis for further inventions (including those whose exploitation is not prohibited under the law).

341. Section 13 of the TPA is more elaborate on this point. It provides that:

> Inventions which concern certain kinds of products, or processes for the manufacture of such products, may, by statutory instrument be excluded from patentability for a period not exceeding ten years. Any exclusion as aforesaid may by statutory instrument be extended for further periods, each such period not exceeding ten years.

342. The agency is established under the Government Executive Agencies Act No. 30 of 1997 and formally launched on 3 Dec. 1999.

343. This office discharges its duties under the auspices of the office of the Attorney General of Zanzibar.

344. Cf. ss 4 & 115 of Act No. 1/1987 and ZIPA respectively. Note that such presidential appointment does not become effective, unless a notice thereof is published in Government Gazette.

registrar's office. Apart from receiving and processing patent applications, the registrar or/and assistant registrar have additional duty to maintain a Register of patents. To discharge some of its obligations appertaining administration of patent matters,[345] the office of the registrar of patents is *inter alia* required to include in the register information on granted patents, licences, ownership of patents and other particulars concerning transmission, assignments of patents and so on. Persons who need this information have a right to consult the register and, upon payment of a relevant fee, take extracts from it.[346]

I. National Applications

128. The question whether or not a patent applicant has a legal capacity to make an admissible application precedes other patent application-related issues. An application for the issuance of a patent in Tanzania has to be made to the registrar by a person who has a right to a patent[347] residing in the United Republic of Tanzania. A foreigner with no commercial establishment and residential address in Tanzania who wishes to apply for the grant of a patent can only do so through an agent duly qualified to represent clients before the patent offices in the United Republic of Tanzania. The applicant's agent must be duly appointed. To effect such an appointment, it suffices if the request for the grant of the patent designates the agent as such or if the agent submits to the registrar a power of attorney bearing the applicant's signature.[348]

A. *Some Selected Application Rules*

1. The Request

129. The inventor or any person that legally steps into the inventor's shoes enjoys powers to initiate a process that may lead to a legal protection of an invention through a patent. It is thus a requirement under the law that an applicant for a patent should submit a request to the registrar of patents including in it particulars

345. According to s. 5 of the TPA, the:

> Functions of the Patents Office shall be– (a) to grant patents under this Act; (b) to promote inventiveness among nationals of the United Republic; (c) to establish and operate a patent documentation centre for the purpose of dissemination of information on patents; (d) to collaborate with other bodies whether local or international whose functions relate to patents matters; (e) to provide information on patented technology so as to facilitate transfer and acquisition of technology by the United Republic; (f) to perform such other functions as are necessary for the furtherance of the objects of this Act. See also s. 115(1) of ZIPA.

346. Cf. s. 6, Act No. 1/1987.
347. Right to the patent are enjoyed by the inventor and any other person who can prove by sworn evidence that he has a right to the patent (cf. ss 14 and 18(2)(b), Act No. 1/1987).
348. Cf. s. 18(1), Act No. 1/1987.

on his identity, in addition to a statement that specifically shows that he desires to get a patent for his invention.[349] The application requirements in relation to the patent request are not met by just mentioning the name of the applicant: the applicant must also state in his request whether he is the inventor or just an agent of the inventor. Additionally, the patent request must clearly make a reference to the invention for which the applicant wishes to claim exclusive patent rights.[350]

2. Description, Claims, Drawings and an Abstract

130. In addition to a patent request, it is a requirement under the law that an application for the grant of a patent be accompanied with other particulars describing the invention. Similarly, a patent application must contain an identification of specific claim(s), some drawing(s) (if any), and an abstract.[351]

131. Description of the invention serves as a focal reference point by patent examiners when assessing patentability of an invention. Based on the description, the patent office is able to determine the question whether or not the patent request relates to a patentable invention that is capable of being carried out. The necessity of the applicant's description to clearly disclose the invention so as to enable persons skilled in the art properly evaluate and carry out the invention arises.[352] Note that the inventor is presumed to know everything concerning the invention including the best mode for carrying out the invention. He is, therefore, duty-bound to specify this mode in the description.[353] Where drawings are necessary to enable a person skilled in the art understand the invention, the applicant is allowed to include them in his application. However, hanging drawings, which are not supported by the description are legally valueless and prima facie not acceptable under the patent law of Tanzania.[354]

132. Claims are an important part of an application for the grant of a patent; they delineate the scope of the patent by indicating the matter for which the patent is sought.[355] Thus, the terms of the claims determine the scope of the protection of the patent.[356] Due to their significance, the patent law of Tanzania requires claims in a

349. Cf. s. 18(1)(a)(i), Act No. 1/1987.
350. Cf. s. 18(2)(a), Act No. 1/1987.
351. Cf. s. 18(1)(a)(ii)–(v), Act No. 1/1987.
352. Cf. ss 18(3) and 34(2)(i), Act No. 1/1987.
353. *Ibid.*
354. Cf. s. 18(3), Act No. 1/1987.
355. Cf. s. 18(4), Act No. 1/1987.
356. Cf. s. 36, Act No. 1/1987.

patent application to be unambiguously and concisely stated.[357] In case of ambiguity as to their scope, 'the description and the drawing included in the patent may be used to interpret the claims'.[358] Claims should therefore not transcend the content of the description.[359]

133. Although the law requires that an abstract be included in the patent application, the abstract only serves as technical information and is normally not considered when determining the scope of the claimed patent.[360]

3. Priority Right

134. The TPA does not delineate the term 'priority right' but, makes reference to the Paris Convention[361] as a guiding instrument insofar as priority right is concerned.[362] Article 4 of the Paris Convention circumscribes the right of priority in relation to an application for the grant of a patent as precedence of one patent application over another. The article empowers an applicant for the patent registration or his successor in title, to enjoy the right of priority within one year – a period which is counted after the day on which the applicant makes a regular national filing[363] of a patent application in one of the countries which are bound by, or observe, the principles laid down in the Paris Convention.[364] The effect of the right of priority is to enable the applicant or his successor in title to file a patent application in a country or countries of the Paris Union claiming the date on which similar application was made by him in another country belonging to the Union. In accordance with this, the Convention puts it lucidly that 'any subsequent filing' made by a person entitled to the right of priority cannot be nullified based on any actions perpetuated by third parties such as 'another filing, the publication or exploitation of the invention' since these actions cannot give rise to any legally acknowledgeable 'third-party right or any right of personal possession'.[365]

135. Drawing on the Paris Convention, the patents law of Tanzania acknowledges that one or more earlier national, regional or international applications may form the basis for the claim of priority right.[366] Being an optional right, priority

357. Cf. s. 18(4), Act No. 1/1987.
358. Cf. s. 36, Act No. 1/1987.
359. Cf. s. 18(4), Act No. 1/1987.
360. Cf. s. 18(5), Act No. 1/1987.
361. That is The Paris Convention for the Protection of Industrial Property of 20 Mar. 1883 and any revisions thereof to which Tanzania is or may become a party (cf. s. 2, para. 6, Act No. 1/1987).
362. Cf. s. 21(1), Act No. 1/1987.
363. That is a filing which, according to rules stipulated under the national legislation, bilateral or multilateral treaties, is sufficient to establish a date on which the application is lodged in the country concerned irrespective of whether the patent registration is granted or not (cf. Art. 4A of the Paris Convention).
364. According to Art. 1 of the Paris Convention, the countries to which the Convention applies constitute a Union for the Protection of industrial property.
365. Cf. Art. 4B, Paris Convention.
366. Cf. s. 21(1), Act No. 1/1987.

right is not enjoyable automatically but the beneficiary of this right has to specifically claim it by including in his application for patent registration a declaration indicating that the applicant wants to invoke his right of priority.[367] Note that the patent registrar may require the applicant whose application contains a declaration of priority right to produce documentary evidence supporting the declaration such as a copy of the earlier application issued and certified by the national authority with which the application was filed.[368] Should the earlier application be an international application filed under the PCT, evidence of this application can be accepted by the registrar only if it is issued and certified by the International Bureau established under the Treaty.[369] The registrar can exercise his right of calling upon the applicant to produce the above-mentioned documentary evidence only after the expiry of three months from the filing date of the application containing the declaration of priority right.[370]

136. Failure to produce documentary evidence as detailed in the immediately preceding paragraph implies that the declaration of priority right has to be disregarded.[371] The fact that a claim of the right of priority is unsuccessful does not mean that the application for the grant of patent is automatically disregarded: the registrar will proceed processing the application in the same manner as any other application, which does not claim priority right, but which makes reference to another corresponding foreign patent application and/or patent grant is treated.[372] For instance, for the purposes of determining the inventive step and novelty of the invention claimed in the application whereby the said invention corresponds with the subject matter of a foreign patent application or a patent grant, the registrar is especially entitled to ask the patent applicant to furnish him with information identifying the foreign application or patent or any other foreign title of protection.[373] The required information includes the following:

(a) date and number of the foreign application;[374]
(b) documents evidencing communications between the applicant and the foreign office regarding search results and examination of the application corresponding with the subject matter of the patent application in Tanzania;[375]
(c) documents evidencing communications between the applicant and the foreign office regarding search results and examination of any foreign application other than the one mentioned in (b) above;[376]

367. *Ibid.*
368. Cf. s. 21(2), Act No. 1/1987.
369. *Ibid.*
370. *Ibid.*
371. Cf. s. 21(3), Act No. 1/1987.
372. Cf. s. 22, Act No. 1/1987.
373. Cf. s. 22(1) and 22(4), Act No. 1/1987.
374. Cf. s. 22(1), Act No. 1/1987.
375. Cf. s. 22(2)(a)(i), Act No. 1/1987.
376. Cf. s. 22(3), Act No. 1/1987.

(d) 'a copy of the patent or other title of protection granted on the foreign application';[377]
(e) copies of the final ruling rejecting the grant of the patent by the foreign office in relation to invention that corresponds with the subject matter of the patent application in Tanzania;[378] and
(f) copies of the ruling nullifying the applicant's foreign patent or any other foreign title of protection corresponding to the subject matter of the applicant's application pending before the Tanzania Patent Office (TPO).[379]

The applicant for a patent protection in Tanzania has the right to submit comments clarifying the above-enumerated information.[380]

4. Establishment of a Filing Date

137. One of the routine works of the registrar of patents is to assign a filing date to each patent application that meets the legal conditions for being assigned such a date. The law empowers the registrar to record as a filing date the date on which he receives a complete application for the patent grant. To be complete, the relevant documents containing the application have to depict the 'name of the applicant', as well as sections, which prima facie appear to be a description and a claim.[381] Thus, a date of submission of an incomplete patent application cannot be treated as a filing date but that on which the applicant files some corrections thereof or additions complementing the application.

138. Within the ambit of the law, the Tanzanian registrar of patents may ask the applicant to make some corrections to his patent application. Sometimes, the applicant may decide on his own initiatives to correct the application.[382] Both two scenarios have a significant impact on a filing date to be assigned to a patent application. The application whose correction is made pursuant to the registrar's call is assigned as its filing date the date on which the correction is received by the Patent Office.[383] In a similar vein, an application whose correction is made on the applicant's own initiatives is assigned as its filing date the date on which the correction is received provided that such correction is submitted within thirty days counted from the day the initial application was received at the Patent Office.[384]

139. The applicant has a right to make some additions, which are necessary to enable a filing date to be assigned to the application. For instance, an applicant who refers to some drawings but does not include them in the application is allowed to

377. Cf. s. 22(2)(a)(ii), Act No. 1/1987.
378. *Ibid.*
379. Cf. s. 22(3), Act No. 1/1987.
380. Cf. s. 22(5), Act No. 1/1987.
381. Cf. s. 25(1)(a), Act No. 1/1987.
382. Cf. s. 25(1)(b) and (e), Act No. 1/1987.
383. Cf. s. 25(1)(c), Act No. 1/1987.
384. Cf. s. 25(1)(e), Act No. 1/1987.

submit to the Patent Office the missing drawings.[385] The applicant may do so either on his own motion or upon being asked by the registrar.[386] However, the TPA sets thirty days from the day of the receipt of the application for the grant of patent as a deadline within which the drawings have to reach the registrar's office.[387] It is noteworthy that the day on which the registrar receives the additional documents (such as drawings) complementing the application is recorded as a filing date of the respective patent application.[388]

140. Failure to comply with the registrar's call to correct the particulars of the application signifies that the applicant's application cannot be assigned a filing date. It is commonplace within the ambit of the law that an application, which does not have a filing date is as good as the one which has never been submitted to the registrar.[389]

B. Examination of Patent Applications

141. Within ambit of its mandate, the office responsible for the administration of patents in Tanzania has an obligation to ensure that it accepts only applications for a patent grant, which does not contain any defects. The office achieves this end by examining the particulars of each patent application. In this regard, the examination is conducted with a view to finding out whether any of the following defects apply to the application concerned:

(a) the request does not meet the stipulation under section 18(2) TPA;
(b) the application's particulars such as 'the description, the claims' and the drawings, if any, do not meet the required physical specifications;
(c) there is no abstract in the application;
(d) the applicant disregarded the request made by the registrar inviting the former, pursuant to section 22 TPA, to furnish the latter with information on corresponding foreign applications and grants; and
(e) the application fees have not been paid.[390]

142. If upon examining a patent application it turns out in his view that the application contains some defects, the registrar enjoys some powers to call upon the applicant to adjust the problematic aspects of his application.[391] Once such a call is made, the applicant has no option other than to amend his patent application as

385. Cf. s. 25(1)(d) and (e), Act No. 1/1987.
386. *Ibid.*
387. *Ibid.*
388. *Ibid.*
389. Cf. s. 25(1)(c), Act No. 1/1987.
390. According to s. 23 of the Patents Act, unless the relevant fees stipulated under the regulations are paid, a patent cannot be registered.
391. An applicant for patent registration may be permitted to amend his application on a condition that such an amendment be confined to matters or issues that feature in the original application (cf. s. 20, Act No. 1/1987). Similarly, the applicant possesses a right to withdraw his application for the

directed: failure to comply with directives from the patent office of Tanzania is normally greeted with the registrar's decision to reject the application.[392]

143. The patent office must examine applications for the grant of a patent for compliance with the unity of invention.[393] An application for the grant of a patent meets the requirements of unity of invention if it is confined either to a single invention alone or to multiple inventions which, by virtue of their linkage, imparts in the mind of persons skilled in the art a single, general inventive idea.[394]

144. An applicant whose application does not fulfil the requirements of unity of invention may nevertheless be given an opportunity to restructure his application, either by restricting the very same application or by dividing the application into several independent applications.[395] The applications so divided are technically known as divisional applications.[396] The applicant's failure to seize this opportunity will entitle the registrar to reject the application concerned.[397]

145. An act of dividing an application into several divisional applications as explained above is a type of amendment that is allowed under section 20(2). Therefore, it follows that the divisional application endorsed under the Patents Act is that which does not deviate from the information disclosed in the initial application.[398]

146. The examination for compliance with unity of invention is not needed if the patent application concerned 'is to be the subject of an international-type search under section 26' of the patent law of Tanzania.[399] It then becomes the duty of an international searching authority to examine the application for compliance with the

patent registration. This right can be exercised at any time but not after the 'the grant of a patent or the notification of rejection of the application or of refusal to grant the patent' (cf. s. 24, Act No. 1/1987).

392. Cf. s. 25(3)(b), Act No. 1/1987.
393. Cf. ss 19 and 25(4), Act No. 1/1987.
394. Section 19, Act No. 1/1987.
395. Cf. s. 25(4)(b), Act No. 1/1987.
396. *Ibid.*
397. Cf. s. 25(4)(c), Act No. 1/1987.
398. Cf. s. 20(2), Act No. 1/1987.
399. The registrar of patents manning the Tanzanian Patent Office has powers to direct that an application, which conforms to the requirement of the law be the subject of an international search. By giving the registrar such powers, the Tanzanian legislature has taken an advantage of Art. 15(5)(b) PCT, which provides for an option for a national law of a country belonging to the Patent Cooperation Union to permit the national patent office of such a country 'to subject any national application filed with it to an international-type search'. This position is further confirmed under s. 26 TPA, which requires the international search to be conducted in line with the stipulations of the PCT. The PCT mandates an international searching authority to carry out international search (cf. Arts 16(1) and 15(5)(c), PCT). This authority may be either a national patent office of a country belonging to the Union or 'an intergovernmental organization, such as the International Patent Institute' entrusted *inter alia* with a duty to establish 'documentary search reports on prior art with respect to inventions which are the subject of applications'. The PCT basically empowers the assembly of the Patent Cooperation Union to appoint a single national office or intergovernmental organization to serve as international searching authority for the Union. For such an appointment to be lawful, it is vital that the assembly secures, in advance, the 'consent of the national office or

unity of invention.[400] Even where this authority considers that the application does not comply with the unity of invention, it may nevertheless carry out an international search in relation to the first or main claim.[401] The search in respect of other remaining claims will be conducted only upon the applicant's positive response to the invitation by the authority requiring the former to pay search fees thereof.[402]

147. An inference can be drawn from section 27 TPA that a patent registration may generally be granted in Tanzania without the corresponding application having been examined as to substance, provided that the respective application is found in order as to form. In some specified cases, such registration is nevertheless granted only after the application has been examined as to its substance. In this regard, the law[403] clarifies the following: 'The minister may … direct that applications for patents relating to a specified technical field shall be the subject of examination as to substance.' It falls within the registrar's powers to determine whether or not 'the

intergovernmental organization to be appointed'. It is noteworthy that the PCT also envisages circumstances whereby no single international searching authority has been established thus paving a way for the existence of more than one authority: in the circumstances, each national office will have a right to 'specify the International Searching Authority or Authorities competent for the searching of … applications filed with such office'. Tanzanian law makes it clear that if the registrar directs an international search to be carried out with respect to a particular application, the search process can commence only after the applicant has paid the relevant search fees (cf. s. 26, Act No. 1/1987). Failure to pay the fees means that the registrar will have no option other than to enforce the law, which requires him to reject the application concerned. It must be noted that the aim of an international search is 'to discover relevant prior art' which may include documents published elsewhere. In consonance with this objective, Tanzanian law empowers the registrar to require the patent applicant to submit to him copies of all documents cited in the international search report as relevant prior art. Should the applicant fail to produce the said copies within the specified deadline, his application will be rejected. International search has to be made 'on the basis of the claims, with due regard to the description and the drawings (if any)' (cf. Art. 15, PCT). Thus, if on the face value of the information given in the application it is discovered that the subject matter of the application is not one of those in respect of which meaningful international search may be conducted, the international searching authority will abstain from carrying out the search and consequently report that fact to the national office (cf. Art. 17, PCT). This may be the case in numerous circumstances such as where: (a) the invention as a whole or one or more claims may not fall in the field of technology; and if it does, it may not fulfil the conditions for novelty as required by the law (cf. s. 26, Act No. 1/1987); (b) the application particulars such as the claims, description and the drawings (where applicable) may partly or wholly not comply with the stipulation of the law, in which case an international search report will either not be produced or be produced only in respect of those claims complying with the law; (c) the application may not comply with the requirements of unity of invention. Communication of the foregoing factors by the international searching authority generally entitles the TPO registrar to reject the application concerned. Before endorsing such rejection, the registrar is nevertheless duty-bound to afford the applicant an opportunity to justify why he thinks that the subject matter of his application relates with the field of technology, and hence patentable. Should the reason for rejection be the novelty issue, lack of unity of invention or problems associated with the drafting of the claims, description or any supporting drawings, such rejection may be justified only if the applicant fails to either convince the registrar that the issues raised by the international searching authority with respect to his application are without any merit or amend the respective defective part of the application. Cf. s. 25(4)(4), Act No. 1/1987.

400. Cf. §4(II)(B) of this chapter.
401. Cf. Art. 17(3)(a), PCT.
402. *Ibid.*
403. That is s. 27(1), Act No. 1/1987.

subject matter of an invention for which a patent is sought' is covered by the minister's specifications.[404] In case of affirmative findings, the registrar is then required to cause substantive examination of the patent application concerned to be carried out.[405]

148. The general aim of the substantive examination is to establish whether the subject matter of the application meets the legal requirements for the grant of a patent.[406] Thus, in accordance with the patent law of Tanzania,[407] the substantive examination must particularly respond to the following questions:

(1) whether the claimed invention meets the patentability conditions of being new, of involving an inventive step and of being industrially applicable; or
(2) whether the claimed invention is not temporarily excluded from protection within the meaning of section 13 TPA; or
(3) whether exploitation of the claimed invention is prohibited based on public order or morality, hence a ground for the rejection of patent grant under section 12 TPA; or
(4) whether the application contains sufficient disclosure of the invention so as to enable a person skilled in the art carry out the invention as required by section 18(3) TPA; or
(5) whether the claims meet the clarity, conciseness and preciseness requirements enshrined in section 18(4) TPA.

149. While the registrar's office is entitled to carry out substantive examination, the law provides the registrar with an option to ask an independent authority to conduct a 'preliminary examination as to the patentability of the claimed invention' in line with the guidelines enumerated in the immediately preceding paragraph.[408] The authority works on the basis of the records it receives from the registrar's office, namely, the 'application together with all relevant documents'.[409]

150. After conducting the preliminary examination, the independent authority has to prepare a report containing its findings and submit the same to both the registrar and the applicant.[410] If, based on the conclusions contained in the report, the registrar thinks that the response to any of the patentability guiding questions enumerated in paragraph 183 below is not in the affirmative, he shall forthwith communicate this fact to the applicant.[411] In such communication, the registrar will require the applicant to give his opinion with respect to the negative findings of the authority and consequently amend his application should this be the necessary

404. Section 27(2), Act No. 1/1987.
405. *Ibid.*
406. *Ibid.*
407. Cf. s. 27, Act No. 1/1987.
408. Cf. s. 27(3)(a), Act No. 1/1987.
409. *Ibid.*
410. *Ibid.*
411. Cf. s. 27(4), Act No. 1/1987.

means to cure the defect(s) spotted in the application.[412] If the registrar still holds the view that any of the examinable conditions[413] are not satisfied notwithstanding the foregoing opinion and amendment, he shall refuse to issue a patent and communicate this refusal to the applicant.[414]

C. Grant, Registration and Publication of Patent

151. The outcomes of a patent examination must generally lead to two alternative events; namely, refusal to issue the applicant with a patent, and the decision to grant a successful applicant with a patent. Pursuant to provisions of the patent law of Tanzania, the registrar of patents is under obligation to grant and issue a patent to an applicant who is entitled to such a patent.[415] Circumstances under which the patent applicant is regarded unsuccessful, hence not entitled to a patent include if the application encounters a rejection on the basis of: (1) some grounds contained in the international search reports made by the international search authority; or (2) for not being found in order as to form. . It is noteworthy that no patent can validly be granted to an applicant who – prior to receiving an official notification on the outcomes of his patent application – decides to withdraw the application.[416]

152. In order to safeguard rights and obligations relating to patents granted and protected in Tanzania, the law charges the patents registrar with a duty to register all patents entering into the register maintained by the registrar of patents all details concerning any patent granted in Tanzania.[417] In addition to the names of the inventor and/or the patent applicant and the title of the invention, the patent details that may be put in the patents register may include specification of the invention, claims and an abstract depicting the invention in a nutshell. The law additionally requires the registrar to publish any granted patent as soon as practicable.[418] The registration and publication requirements of any granted patent(s) serve as safeguards for legitimate expectations of third parties who, by perusing the register and publications, should be able to inform themselves as to the following: (1) whether the registered and/published patent infringes on their protected IP rights and accordingly institute legal action challenging the validity of the patent concerned; and (2) whether their activities infringe or are likely to infringe on the rights of the patent holder and limit their activities accordingly.

---

412. *Ibid.*
413. These conditions relate to the questions enumerated in para. 183 below.
414. Cf. s. 27(5), Act No. 1/1987.
415. Cf. s. 28(1), Act No. 1/1987.
416. Cf. s. 24, Act No. 1/1987, which provides as follows: 'At any time before the grant of a patent or the notification of rejection of the application or of refusal to grant a patent, the person who has made an application for registration of a patent may withdraw the application.'
417. Cf. s. 28(2) and (6), Act No. 1/1987.
418. Cf. s. 28(3) and (6), Act No. 1/1987.

D. Appeals Against Registrar's Decisions

153. According to the Tanzanian law, most of the decisions of the registrar of patents may be challenged before the High Court of Tanzania by way of appeal.[419] Appealable decisions are those on the following aspects: (1) patent application's filing date; (2) rejection of an application for the grant of a patent; (3) treating the patent application as if it has not been filed; (4) considering any of the claims to be withdrawn; and (5) refusal to grant a patent.[420]

II. International Patent Applications and Role of the TPO

154. The government of the United Republic of Tanzania recognizes the international system of patent registration established under the PCT of 1970 (as amended and revised from time to time); the country acceded to the Treaty on 14 June 1999. The PCT is an administrative treaty that provides for a legal avenue through which one may get a single patent application processed for protection in more than one PCT signatory country. The PCT provides for two different routes through which applicants may submit international applications; namely, filing patent applications either directly with the PCT central Bureau or through the receiving office. The central Bureau is administered by WIPO whereas the National IP offices such as the Tanzanian Patents Office (TPO) act as receiving offices.

155. The patent law of Tanzania employs the term 'international application' as a reference to an 'international application filed in accordance with the PCT and the regulations established thereunder'.[421] Thus, the TPO is required to discharge its duties in relation to international applications in accordance with the provisions of the Tanzanian patent law[422] and of the Patents Cooperation Treaty.[423] In case of conflicts, provisions of the latter take supremacy over those of the former.[424]

156. The Tanzanian law[425] confirms that the terms 'Receiving Office',[426] 'designated office',[427] 'elected office'[428] as used under the TPA, have similar delineations as those given to identical terms within the ambit of the Patents Cooperation Treaty.

419. Cf. ss 29 and 2 (para. 2), Act No. 1/1987.
420. Cf. s. 29, Act No. 1/1987.
421. Cf. s. 30(1), Act No. 1/1987.
422. That is the Patents Act and any Regulations pertaining thereto (Cf. s. 30(3), Act No. 1/1987).
423. As well as 'the regulations thereunder and the administrative instructions' (Cf. s. 30(3), Act No. 1/1987).
424. Cf. s. 31(3), Act No. 1/1987.
425. Section 30(2), Act No. 1/1987.
426. That is the 'national office or the intergovernmental organization with which the international application has been filed' (Art. 2(xv) of the Patent Cooperation Treaty).
427. That is the 'national office of or acting for the State designated by the applicant' (Art. 2(xiii) of the Patent Cooperation Treaty).

157. The linkage between the two laws manifested in the immediately preceding paragraph, establishes beyond a shadow of doubt the position that the TPO acts in the capacity of a receiving office if an 'international application is filed with it' provided that the applicant is a 'national or resident' of the United Republic of Tanzania.[429] Moreover, the country's patents office serves in the capacity of a 'designated office or an elected office' if an international applicant designates Tanzania for the patent protection or elects Tanzania as a country where international preliminary examination of his application/invention is to be conducted.[430]

158. The scheme of international application for the grant of patents, which the PCT establishes provides for a possibility to secure patent protection of a single invention in Tanzania and in any other countries belonging to the Patent Cooperation Union. This is achievable through a single application filed with a receiving office such as the Tanzanian Patents Office (should the office serve as a receiving office).[431] In his application, the international applicant is required to designate Tanzania (if the Tanzanian Patents Office does not act as a receiving but as a designated office) and/or any other countries in which he desires to secure protection of his invention.[432]

A. *TPO as a Receiving Office*

159. One of the tasks, which the TPO performs in relation to international applications filed with it, is to assign filing dates thereto. The law recognizes the date of receipt of a complete international application as the application's filing date. In this sense, an incomplete international application gets as its filing date the date on which the receiving office receives the missing application details.[433] According to Article 11(1) of the PCT, an international application is complete if it meets the following conditions:

- the applicant does not obviously lack, for reasons of residence or nationality, the right to file an international application with the TPO;
- the international application is in the prescribed language; and
- the international application contains at least the following elements: (a) an indication that it is intended as an international application, (b) the designation of at least one Contracting State, (c) the name of the applicant as, prescribed, (d) a part which on the face of it appears to be a description, (e) a part which on the face of it appears to be a claim or claims.

---

428. That is the 'national office of or acting for the State elected under the applicant' where he wants preliminary examination of his invention to be carried out (Art. 2(xiv) of the Patent Cooperation Treaty).
429. Cf. s. 31(1), Act No. 1/1987.
430. Cf. s. 31(2), Act No. 1/1987.
431. Cf. Art. 10, PCT.
432. *Ibid.*
433. Cf. Art. 11(2), PCT.

If the TPO is of the opinion that an international application is incomplete, the procedure under the national law for amending and submitting information complementing the national application for the purpose of establishing a national filing date[434] will be observed in relation to international applications as well.

B. TPO as a Designated Office

160. In addition to being treated as 'equivalent to a regular national filing within the meaning of the Paris Convention for the Protection of Industrial Property',[435] once international application designating the United Republic of Tanzania is accepted and assigned a filing date, it acquires a status of a 'regular national application' in Tanzania[436] and in any other designated State 'as of the international filing date, which date shall be considered to be the actual filing date' in Tanzania and in any other designated States.[437] In the circumstances, the examination procedure that is done in relation to national patent applications made to the TPO applies *mutatis mutandis* to international application designating the United Republic of Tanzania.

C. TPO as an Elected Office

161. Tanzania is bound by Chapter II of the PCT dealing with international preliminary examination.[438] The chapter outlines the procedure, which an international applicant who has designated Tanzania may follow in order to have a preliminary examination of his international application carried out with respect to Tanzania and a report thereof communicated to the TPO for consideration whilst determining the question whether the subject of the said international application qualifies for the grant of patent in Tanzania. Nevertheless, the preliminary examination report with respect to Tanzania cannot be prepared, unless the applicant does the following: (1) names the TPO as the designated office; (2) elects the TPO for purposes of international preliminary examination;[439] and (3) sends a demand for international preliminary examination to the international authority responsible for such examination[440] with respect to Tanzania.

162. According to Article 33(1) PCT, the 'objective of international preliminary examination is to formulate a preliminary and non-binding opinion on the questions whether the claimed invention appears to be novel, to involve an inventive step (i.e., to be non-obvious), and to be industrially applicable'. However, the international

434. Cf. §4(II)(A)(1) of this chapter. *See also* Art. 11(2), PCT.
435. Cf. Arts 4 and 11(4), the Paris Convention and the PCT respectively.
436. If the applicant designates Tanzania in his application.
437. Cf. Art. 11(3), PCT.
438. Cf. s. 31(2), Act No. 1/1987.
439. Cf. Art. 31(4)(a), PCT.
440. Cf. Arts 31(6)(a) and 32(1), PCT.

preliminary examining authority must abstain from including in its report a 'statement on the question of whether the claimed invention is or seems to be patentable' according to Tanzanian law.[441] This is because determination of the question of patentability of an invention, which is a subject of international application designating Tanzania is done by the TPO.[442] The international preliminary examination report may nevertheless guide the TPO in its conclusions on patentability questions. This is particularly the case should questions concerning unity of invention and defective applications arise.[443]

163. When the issue of lack of unity of invention is raised by the international examining authority, the patents law of Tanzania requires the TPO to act on such issue.[444] In this regard, one may need to note Article 34(3)(a) PCT. This legal provision provides an international applicant with an option to restrict his claims as a means of complying with the unity of invention. In lieu of restricting the claims, the foregoing PCT's provision provides room for the applicant to pay additional fees for any claim that the examining authority treats as independent. The applicant does all this on the invitation of the international examining authority.

If the applicant does not comply with the authority's foregoing invitation, some of the unrestricted claims in respect of which no examination fees have been paid may be considered withdrawn leaving the international preliminary examination report being produced with respect to the claim that the preliminary examining authority considers to be the main invention.[445] Where this is the case, the registrar manning the TPO will not examine the claims that are not covered by the report within the context of the immediately preceding sentence, but consider them as having been withdrawn by the applicant.[446] To prevent such consideration from being endorsed by the registrar, the applicant has to do either of the following: (1) pay the special fee for all claims not covered by the international examination report; or (2) satisfies the registrar that the invitation by the international examining authority requiring him to restrict his claims is not justified.[447]

164. The fact that some defects are available in an international application may cause the international preliminary examining authority to abstain from conducting preliminary examination with respect to the whole application or part of it. The PCT sanctions such abstinence with respect to the whole application if, for instance, the authority finds that the subject matter of international application is not an invention within the meaning of patent law.[448] Sometimes, vaguely formulated applications may make it impossible for the authority to formulate any opinion on the patentability issues. This may lead to the situation whereby no preliminary examination report may be produced or be produced with respect to limited number of

441. Cf. Art. 35(2), PCT.
442. Cf. Art. 33(5), PCT.
443. Cf. s. 32(2)(b), Act No. 1/1987.
444. Cf. s. 32(2), Act No. 1/1987.
445. Section 32(2)(b) and Art. 34(3)(a) and (c), Act No. 1/1987 and PCT respectively.
446. Cf. s. 32(2)(b), Act No. 1/1987. *See also* Art. 34(3)(b), PCT.
447. Section 32(2)(b), Act No. 1/1987.
448. Cf. Art. 34(4)(a)(i); PCT.

claims.[449] In such circumstances, the Tanzanian registrar is empowered to consider any claims in respect of which no preliminary examination was conducted by the authority as withdrawn. To hold otherwise, the registrar will need some convincing arguments from the applicant proving that the defects raised by the preliminary examining authority are not available in the applicant's international application.[450] In a similar vein, should the international preliminary examination report reveal that the invention, which is a subject matter of the international application, is not novel and hence not patentable under the patent law of Tanzania, the registrar is required not to grant a patent. This is particularly the case if the applicant either fails to convince the registrar that his invention meets the novelty requirements, or if he does not amend the claims whereby this initiative would remove the patentability hindrance in issue.[451] A similar position as the foregoing applies also when the registrar responds to an international search report, which ostensibly shows that the international applicant's invention does not meet the requirements for novelty.[452]

D. TPO's Functions in Response to International Search Reports

165. Pursuant to Article 15(1) PCT, it is obligatory for each international application to be the subject of international search. Section 32 TPA implements Article 15(1) PCT by requiring the registrar to work on search reports produced by the international search authority. In case the international search authority fails to produce a search report, but gives the reasons thereof, the registrar has also to address those reasons when determining patentability issues.[453] Thus, following the production of the international search report or failure to produce such a report, the law empowers the registrar to reject an international application in the same manner a national application is rejected following such report or failure to produce the report.[454]

Where the international search authority produces a search report in respect of limited number of claims, the registrar has a right to regard other claims not covered by the search report as withdrawn unless the applicant convinces him otherwise.[455] If the failure to produce such a report in respect of some claims is attributable to the applicant's failure to pay additional fees provided for under Article 17(3) PCT, the registrar is justified to consider those claims withdrawn, unless the applicant does either of the following: (i) pays the required fees; or (ii) convinces the registrar that by inviting the applicant to pay the fees, the international searching authority erred in law.[456]

---

449. Cf. Art. 34(4), PCT.
450. Cf. s. 32(2)(C), Act No. 1/1987. *See also* Arts 34(4) and 35(2), PCT.
451. Cf. s. 32(3), Act No. 1/1987.
452. *Ibid.*
453. Cf. Art. 17(2), PCT.
454. Conditions for the rejection of a national application based on the international search report are outlined in §4 of this chapter.
455. Cf. s. 32(1)(a), Act No. 1/1987.
456. Cf. s. 32(1)(b), Act No. 1/1987.

III. Regional Applications

166. The ARIPO, which was founded in 1976, is one of the institutions providing regional patent services in Africa. The United Republic of Tanzania has a right to join ARIPO by virtue of its membership with the African Union. The country exercised this right on 12 October 1983 when it became party to the Lusaka agreement on the creation of ARIPO.[457] According to Article III of the Agreement, ARIPO aims *inter alia* to 'establish such common services or organs as may be necessary or desirable for the coordination, harmonization and development of intellectual property activities' affecting its members.[458] With respect to patents, this objective is implemented by the HP within the framework of the ARIPO[459] and the Protocol's implementing Regulations.[460] Tanzania became party to the Harare Protocol (hereinafter 'HP') on 1 September 1999. The country is therefore bound by this protocol.

167. Section 1 HP empowers ARIPO to grant patents on behalf of contracting States. This has to be done in accordance with the provisions of the HP.

The patent system established under the HP permits a patent applicant to submit his application either directly to ARIPO or to the patent office of an ARIPO member such as the Tanzanian Patents Office (TPO).[461] Representation before ARIPO is not required if the applicant resides in one of the ARIPO's Member States. Legal representation becomes mandatory if the applicant wishes to submit an application before a national patents office of a country of which he is not a national and cannot prove any connection with the country either through commercial establishment or habitual residence.[462]

168. The power to grant ARIPO patents is vested in ARIPO.[463] For this reason, when the national office such as the TPO receives a regional patent application it acts as an intermediary: TPO is therefore required to transmit the same to ARIPO head office within a month counted from the date the application was received at the TPO.[464] The application is, however, presumed to have been received by ARIPO the same day it was received at the TPO.[465]

---

457. Agreement on the creation of the ARIPO (as adopted by the Diplomatic Conference for the adoption of an Agreement on the Creation of an Industrial Property Organization for English-Speaking Africa at Lusaka (Zambia) on 9 Dec. 1976, and amended by the Administrative Council of ARIPO on 10 Dec. 1982, 12 Dec. 1986 and 27 Nov. 1996, and as amended by the Council of Ministers on 13 Aug. 2004) [As in force from 13 Nov. 2004].
458. Article III(c), Lusaka Agreement.
459. Adopted on 10 Dec. 1982, at Harare (Zimbabwe), and amended by the Administrative Council of ARIPO on 11 Dec. 1987, 27 Apr. 1994, 28 Nov. 1997, 26 May 1998, 26 Nov. 1999, 30 Nov. 2001, 21 Nov. 2003, and 24 Nov. 2006.
460. Text entered into force on 25 Apr. 1984, and amended by the Administrative Council of ARIPO on 27 Apr. 1994, 27 Nov. 1998, 24 Nov. 2000, 21 Nov. 2003 and 24 Nov. 2006.
461. Cf. s. 2(1), HP.
462. Cf. s. 2(4), HP.
463. Cf. s. 3(2)(b) and 3(7), HP.
464. Cf. s. 2(5), HP.
465. Cf. s. 2(2), HP.

169. The procedure leading to the grant of ARIPO patents requires ARIPO to examine patent applications for compliance with the formal[466] and substantive[467] requirements and, upon positive findings, forward the applications to all contracting States designated therein.[468] Should the TPO be one of the designated offices, it will be under obligation to examine an ARIPO application with a view to determining whether the invention, which is the subject matter of the application qualifies for the patent protection in Tanzania by virtue of the provisions of the TPA and/or the HP and communicate its findings thereof to ARIPO.[469] In case of the TPO's positive findings, and also in case six months lapse before TPO communicates its findings as above, ARIPO is mandated to declare that the ARIPO patent protection is effective in the United Republic of Tanzania as well as in any other designated ARIPO Member State, which is presumed under the law to have directly[470] or constructively[471] given ARIPO green light to grant patent protection of a subject matter of the patent application concerned.

If an ARIPO application does not qualify for patent protection in Tanzania, TPO is required to communicate this fact to ARIPO within six months of the receipt of the application from ARIPO.[472] After such communication, the applicant gets three months within which he may exercise his optional right to ask ARIPO that his application be treated as national patent application in any ARIPO contracting State designated in the application.[473] Should Tanzania be one of the designated contracting States, provisions of the TPA apply exclusively to ARIPO patent application treated as a national application.[474]

170. Section 3*bis* HP links ARIPO and its Member States with the system of international patent application introduced under the PCT.

An international application designating at least one ARIPO Member State such as Tanzania, which is bound by both the HP and PCT, tantamount to an application for the grant of a patent under the HP if the applicant's clear desire is to process his international application with the assistance of ARIPO.[475] In addition to the HP and its implementing regulations, the PCT provisions must be applied in relation to the

466. Cf. s. 3(2)(a), HP. According to s. 3(1), HP, an ARIPO patent application is said to meet formal requirements if it does the following: (i) identifies the applicant; (ii) contains a description of the invention, one or more claims, some drawings (if any), and an abstract; (iii) designates one or more countries where patent protection is desired; and (iv) the prescribed fees are paid.
467. Cf. s. 3(3), HP. Examinable substantive criteria are outlined in s. 3(10), HP. These are the novelty, inventive step (non-obviousness) and industrial applicability requirements.
468. Cf. s. 3(2), HP.
469. Cf. s. 3(6), HP.
470. That is if the country has examined the application and confirms that the invention, which is a subject matter of the application can be protected in the country concerned.
471. That is, when a period of six months elapses before the country concerned submits to ARIPO the results of its examination reports, in which event a presumption that the patent under application has been accepted for protection in the pertinent country.
472. Cf. s. 3(6), HP.
473. Cf. s. 3(8), HP.
474. Cf. s. 3(8), HP.
475. Cf. s. 3*bis*(2), HP.

international application mentioned in the immediately preceding sentence. In the event of any conflicts between these pieces of legislation, the PCT becomes the controlling law.[476]

171. ARIPO is therefore empowered to perform different functions usually performable by national patent office of PCT contracting parties.[477] In this regard, ARIPO may serve as a receiving, designated and elected office. The sole condition for ARIPO to act as a receiving office on behalf of the United Republic of Tanzania is that the international application must be filed with ARIPO by a Tanzanian national or resident.[478] Because Tanzania is a party to both HP and PCT, ARIPO may act as a designated office in relation to applications designating Tanzania for the patent grant under PCT.[479] Moreover, ARIPO may act as an elected office in relation to international applications in which Tanzania is elected for the purpose of international preliminary examination.[480]

172. It must be noted that ARIPO enjoys less powers in relation to international application when compared with the powers it enjoys in relation to regional patent applications governed by the HP. For instance, ARIPO does not examine international applications for compliance with the formal requirements and does not enjoy a right to assign a filing date to international applications, since section 3*bis*(6) HP specifically excludes application of sections 2 and 3(2) HP in relation to international applications.[481] By excluding application of sections 2 and 3(2) HP, section 3*bis*(6) HP may be interpreted to mean that the normal requirements under the PCT for assigning filing dates to international applications and for assessing international applications for compliance with formal requirements apply to international applications under ARIPO patent system as well.[482]

§5. Ownership and Transfer

I. Ownership

173. The patent law of Tanzania clarifies that ownership of a patent resulting from an invention made by a sole inventor belongs to the inventor alone,[483] whereas ownership of a patented invention made by two or more inventors jointly belongs to the joint inventors.[484] When it comes to a patent of an invention realized by an

476. *Ibid.*
477. Cf. §4(III) of this chapter.
478. Cf. s. 3*bis*(3), HP and Art. 2(xv), PCT.
479. Cf. s. 3*bis*(4), HP and Art. 2(xiii), PCT.
480. Cf. s. 3*bis*(5), HP and Arts 2(xiv) and 31(4), PCT.
481. Section 2 HP serves as ARIPO basis for assigning a filing date to a regional patent application, whereas, s. 3(2) HP allows ARIPO to refuse regional patent applications for non-compliance with the formal requirements stipulated in the section.
482. For these requirements, cf. para. 166 above.
483. Cf. s. 14(1), Act No. 1/1987.
484. Cf. s. 14(2), Act No. 1/1987.

employee in the course of his employment, ownership of such a patent belongs generally to the employer.[485] This is particularly the case if the environment within which the employee works enabled him to realize the patented invention solely on the basis of the data and/or any other means accessible by him through his employment. As a result, the law regards an employee as a patent owner if the patented invention is attributable to his inventive activity.[486] The law provides further that ownership in Tanzania of a patent that is based on an 'invention made in execution of a commission' belongs to the person who has commissioned the work.[487]

II. Transfer

174. Transfer of ownership of a patent application as well as a granted patent is legally possible under the patent law of Tanzania. By providing that a 'right to a patent may be assigned, or transferred by succession', section 14(4)(a) TPA can be interpreted to mean that ownership of an application for the grant of patent and a patent (if already granted) may change hands. While section 40 TPA confirms the foregoing position, it further requires 'contracts assigning applications or patents' to be 'in writing and signed by the parties thereto' as a condition for validity.[488] The TPA also provides for the transfer of an application or of a patent under joint ownership. In this regard, section 41 TPA allows any of the joint owners to separately transfer their respective shares in the application or patent. This is nevertheless legally impossible if a prior agreement concluded between the joint owners prohibits the separate transfer of shares.[489] The court in Tanzania is not under an obligation to regard 'documents evidencing the change in ownership' as admissible evidence in relation to a 'title of any person to an application or a patent', if the ownership transfer has not been registered in the register of patents.[490]

In view of the foregoing explanation, it is no doubt true that the patent law of Tanzania recognizes two types of patent transfer; namely, transfer through a licence and transfer through assignment of patent rights. An outline of these transfer modalities is provided below.

A. Licensing

175. The patent law of Tanzania uses the term 'licence' as a reference to a temporary transfer of the right to exploit a patented invention: through a licence third parties are allowed to carry out activities that would otherwise constitute an infringement of a patent and be sanctioned by the patentee. Two terminologies;

485. Cf. s. 16(1), Act No. 1/1987.
486. Cf. s. 16(2), Act No. 1/1987.
487. Cf. s. 16(1), Act No. 1/1987.
488. Cf. s. 40, Act No. 1/1987.
489. Cf. s. 41, Act No. 1/1987.
490. Cf. s. 40(3), Act No. 1/1987.

namely, the licensor and licensee are commonly referred to in any licensing contract. According to the patent law of Tanzania,[491] 'licensor' and 'licensee' are parties to a licensing agreement whereby the former possess and/or owns the invention and undertakes to grant the latter permission to exploit the invention concerned. A licence is usually granted over a mutually agreed period of time, on stipulated terms and conditions, in exchange of remuneration in the form of royalties, and under the guarantee of immunity from infringement suits from the patentee.

The licensor's powers to issue a licence may stem either from his application for the grant of a patent pending before the TPO or on the basis of a patent already issued to him. Where the invention to be exploited under a licence is still a subject of a pending patent application, which has been lodged jointly by two or more persons, the powers to licence the invention belongs to the patent applicants jointly. Similar position applies as well in relation to a patent granted to two or more persons jointly, in which case all patentees exercise the right to licence the patent jointly.[492]

176. The patent law of Tanzania regards as invalid and hence unenforceable a licence agreement, which is not reduced into a written form. The same rule applies as well to a licence contract, which – although it is in a written form – does not bear signatures of both the licensor and the licensee.[493] Moreover, the patent law in force in Tanzania requires (as a validation condition) that 'all licence contracts, including modifications thereof' be submitted to the TPO for registration in the register of patents.[494] This requirement is accomplished by way of petition whereby any party to the licence agreement enjoys the right to petition the registrar of patents for registration of the licence contract.[495] Until such time a licence contract is registered and a certificate thereof is issued pursuant to section 49(1) TPA, the contract may not be considered a legally enforceable document. Note that the petition for registration of licence contract is 'subject to payment of a prescribed fee' and must be made in some prescribed forms.[496] Failure by the petitioner to comply with these two requirements will entitle the registrar to refuse to register the licence contract.[497] Moreover, the registrar has no option other than to refuse to register a licence contract, if such a contract refers to some terms contradicting a clear stipulation of the law such as those stipulated under section 48 TPA. This section incorporates some terms the inclusion of which in any licence contract is prohibited.[498] However, the

491. Section 42(2), Act No. 1/1987.
492. Cf. s. 41, Act No. 1/1987.
493. Cf. s. 46, Act No. 1/1987.
494. Cf. s. 47(1), Act No. 1/1987.
495. Cf. s. 47(2), Act No. 1/1987.
496. Cf. s. 47(3) and (4), Act No. 1/1987.
497. Cf. s. 47(6), Act No. 1/1987.
498. According to s. 48, the registrar may, with the approval of and after consultation with other competent government authorities, refuse to register a licence contract if the effect of its terms is as follows: (a) to permit or require the importation of technology from abroad when substantially similar or equivalent technology may be obtained on the same or more favourable conditions without importation from abroad; (b) to require payment of a price, royalty or other consideration, which is disproportionate to the value of the technology to which the contract relates; (c) to require the licensee to acquire any materials from the licensor or from sources designated or approved by him,

power of the registrar to refuse registration of a licence contract is subject to certain obligations. For instance, the registrar is duty-bound to 'notify the petitioner of the defects precluding petition or of terms or defects precluding registration of the licence contract within ninety days from the date of the petition'.[499] If the registrar does not comply with this requirement, a legal presumption will be endorsed that the registrar has registered the licence contract. Similar presumption is endorsed if the registrar, having complied with the ninety-days requirement within which to notify the petitioner as above, does not notify the petitioner of his (the registrar's) refusal to register the licence contract within subsequent ninety days.[500] Moreover, the registrar is required, prior to refusing registration of a licence contract, to notify the petitioner of his intention and afford both the licensor and the licensee an opportunity to: (a) 'submit any observations'; (b) 'correct any defect in the petition'; (c) 'amend any term, or to correct any defect, in the licence contract that has been declared by the registrar to be a term or defect precluding registration'.[501] The parties to a licence contract must make use of the foregoing opportunity within forty-five days following notification of the registrar's intention to refuse registration.

Once the registrar properly decides to refuse registration of a licence contract, the contract becomes void[502] and no appeal against the registrar's decision may be entertained by the High Court of Tanzania. Only registrar's decisions improperly

---

unless it is otherwise impossible, for all practical purposes, to ensure the quality of the products to be produced; (d) to prohibit the licensee from acquiring, or to restrict his acquisition of, any materials from any source, unless it is otherwise impossible, for all practical purposes, to ensure the quality of the products to be produced; (e) to prohibit the licensee from using, or to restrict his use of any materials, which are not supplied by the licensor or by sources designated or approved by him, unless it is otherwise impossible, for all practical purposes, to ensure the quality of the products to be produced; (f) to require the licensee to sell products produced by him under the contract exclusively or principally to persons designated by the licensor; (g) to require the licensee to make available to the licensor without appropriate consideration any improvements made by the licensee with respect to the technology to which the contract relates; (h) to limit the volume of the products produced by the licensee with the help of the technology to which the contract relates; (i) to prohibit or restrict the export of the products produced by the licensee; (j) to require the licensee to employ on permanent basis persons designated by the licensor; (k) to impose restrictions on research or technological development carried out by the licensee; (l) to prohibit or restrict the use by the licensee of any technology other than the technology to which the contract relates; (m) to extend the coverage of the contract to technology not required for the use of the technology, which is the main subject of the contract and to require consideration for such additional technology; (n) to fix prices for the sale or resale of the products produced by the licensee with the help of the technology to which the contract relates; (o) to exempt the licensor from any liability consequent upon any defect inherent in the technology to which the contract relates or to restrict such liability; (p) to prohibit or restrict the use by the licensee, after the expiration of the contract, of the technology acquired as a result of the contract, subject, however, to any right of the licensor under the patent; (q) to require the disputes arising from the interpretation or performance of the contract to be governed by the law other than the law of the United Republic or that such disputes be brought before courts located in a country other than the United Republic; (r) to establish the duration of the contract for the period, which is unreasonably long in relation to the economic function of the contract, provided that any period, which does not exceed the duration of the patent to which the contract relates shall not be regarded as reasonably long.

499. Cf. s. 49(2)(i), Act No. 1/1987.
500. Cf. s. 49(2)(ii), Act No. 1/1987.
501. Cf. s. 47(7), Act No. 1/1987.
502. Cf. s. 47(8), Act No. 1/1987.

refusing registration of licence contract may be appealed against, and in particular when: (1) the 'decision for refusal contains no statement of the reasons for refusal'; (2) 'none of the reasons for refusal specified in the decision is a valid reason' under the patent law or 'was rightly applied to the petition or to the licence contract'; and (3) the 'procedure applied by the registrar was irregular and prejudicial to the rights of the petitioner'.[503]

The patent law of Tanzania enshrines a formula on whose basis the date on which registration of licence contract takes effect is determined. The law regards the date of conclusion of a licence contract as an effective date of the registration of such a contract, provided that the petition for the registration is submitted to the registrar within sixty days from the conclusion of the contract. If this sixty-day requirement is not complied with, then the law regards the date of the petition as the effective date of the registration of the licence contract.[504]

Registration of a licence contract is primarily evidenced by some particulars that are entered in the register of patents and the registration certificate, which is normally issued to successful petitioners. Both registration and certificate must state names of both licensor and licensee; the date of registration and of the petition; and the registration number. All these particulars have to be published in the *Gazette*.[505]

Particulars contained in the registration of licence contract are not available to third persons as of right. This is buttressed by section 50 TPA,[506] which presumes any licence contract to be a confidential document. Parties to a licence contract may nevertheless dispense with this presumption of confidentiality by jointly permitting access to the licence contract by third persons. The parties then become duty-bound to determine the extent to which third persons may access information contained in the licence contract.[507]

The expiry date of a licence contract is, under normal circumstances, determined by a stipulation of the said contract. However, contrary to the expectations of both the licensor and licensee, the licence contract may terminate by operation of law prior to the expiry of its duration. This may particularly happen if: the application for the grant of patent is withdrawn or is finally rejected; the 'grant of a patent is finally refused'; the 'patent is finally declared invalid'.[508] If the licence contract terminates prematurely as above, the law affords the licensee an opportunity to ask the High Court of Tanzania to make some orders remedying any consequential economic losses the licensee may have suffered. In this regard, the law provides as follows:

> court may make any order that it deems reasonable under the circumstances for the repayment of the royalties, or the return of any other consideration, paid or

---

503. Cf. s. 51, Act No. 1/1987.
504. Cf. s. 49(3)(a), Act No. 1/1987.
505. Cf. s. 49(4), Act No. 1/1987.
506. Act No. 1/1987.
507. Cf. s. 50, Act No. 1/1987.
508. Cf. s. 45, Act No. 1/1987.

> given under the said contract, directly relating to any such application [if the basis for the license contract was an application for the grant of a patent pending before the TPO] or patent.[509]

It is instructive to note that a licensee of a patent protected in Tanzania derives from a licence contract a general right to exercise all the exclusive rights customarily exercisable by the licensor in and throughout the United Republic of Tanzania. The licensor may nevertheless limit the terms of the licence contract to some exclusive rights; or to specific part of the United Republic of Tanzania; or to certain duration.[510] In general, the licensee does not enjoy an automatic right to grant permission to third parties to exercise exclusive rights covered by the licence contract.[511] This right is normally enjoyed by the licensor.[512] The law, however, allows the inclusion of a stipulation in the licence contract, which prohibits the licensor from granting further licences or which allows the licensee to sublicense the exclusive rights and vice versa.[513] Thus, the patent law of Tanzania recognizes two categories of licences; namely, exclusive and non-exclusive licences.

1. Exclusive Licence

177. The patent law of Tanzania refers to an exclusive licence contract as a binding agreement that incorporates a clause stipulating expressly that the permission granted to exploit a patented invention is exclusive. The licensee then becomes an exclusive licensee – a status by virtue of which he enjoys the general right to exploit all the exclusive patent rights,[514] which the licensing agreement covers. The law puts it lucidly that upon granting an exclusive licence, the licensor does not enjoy the right to grant further licences to third parties and cannot exploit the invention with respect to the exclusive rights covered under the exclusive licence. If he wants to exercise these rights, the exclusive licence contract should specifically contain a stipulation to that effect.

2. Non-exclusive Licence

178. The TPA refers to a non-exclusive licence in connection with a right of the 'owner of a patent [to] request the registrar to make an entry in the register to the effect that licences under the patent are to be available as of right'.[515] If such entry is made in the register of patents and published in the patents journal,[516] any third

509. *Ibid.*
510. Cf. s. 43(1), Act No. 1/1987.
511. Cf. s. 43(2), Act No. 1/1987.
512. Cf. s. 44(1), Act No. 1/1987.
513. Cf. ss 43(2) and 44(1), Act No. 1/1987.
514. These rights are described in §6 of this chapter.
515. Cf. 60(1), Act No. 1/1987.
516. Cf. 60(4), Act No. 1/1987.

person may, as of right, 'require the owner of the patent to grant him a non-exclusive licence under the patent'.[517] In case no agreement is reached between the licensor and the person asking for the grant of a non-exclusive licence, the High Court of Tanzania may, if moved, fix the terms of the non-exclusive licence sought. In the event the court fixes the terms of the licence contract as above, the licensee or the owner of the patent may, if aggrieved by such fixation, request the High Court to vary those terms should new facts justifying such variation crop up.[518] One of such facts would be the revelation of the fact that the 'patentee has granted contractual licences on more favourable terms'.[519]

It is no doubt true that it is to the advantage of the owner of the patent if his request to have a statement that the licences in relation to his patent are available as of right entered in the patents register receives the registrar's positive response. Once such entry is made, the patentee enjoys freedom to license the invention to more than one person and hence a prospect of some increased royalties. However, the exercise of patentee's freedom as in the immediately preceding sentence is not without bounds. The patent law of Tanzania envisages circumstances whereby the patentee's decision to issue licences to more than one person may jeopardize legitimate expectations of interested parties such as the existing licensees of the same patent. Thus, the registrar of patents is required to notify all interested parties of the fact that the patentee has requested to have a statement allowing him to grant further licences entered in the register of patents.[520] Once such notification is made as above, any licensee may seize an opportunity to object to such entry – the main acceptable grounds for such objection being that the owner of the patent is not allowed under an existing licence contract to grant further licences.[521]

B. Assignments

179. By providing that the 'right to a patent may be assigned, or transferred by succession', the patent law of Tanzania clearly shows that ownership of an application for the grant of patent and a patent (if already granted) may change hands by way of assignment.[522] By assignment, the patent holder divests himself of the entire exclusive rights over the patented invention and vests these in the assignee. Thus, assignment of patent constitutes a total transmission of patent ownership. However, the TPA further provides that for an assignment to be recognized it ought to be registered in the Register of patents.[523]

517. Cf. 60(5), Act No. 1/1987.
518. Cf. s. 60(8), Act No. 1/1987.
519. Cf. s. 58(2), Act No. 1/1987.
520. Cf. s. 60(2), Act No. 1/1987.
521. Cf. s. 60(3), Act No. 1/1987.
522. Cf. s. 14, Act No. 1/1987.
523. Cf. s. 40, Act No. 1/1987.

§6. Scope of Exclusive Rights

180. Section 35 TPA provides for an exhaustive list of some rights that are exclusively enjoyable by the owner of a patent. In relation to a patented product, the section specifically entrusts with the patentee the right to make, import, offer for sale, sell and use the product.[524] In addition, a product patent confers on the patentee exclusive right to stock such product for the purposes of offering it for sale, selling or using it.[525] When it comes to a process patent, the right to use the process belongs exclusively to the patentee.[526] Moreover, a product resulting directly from a patented process confers on the patentee similar rights as those enjoyable in relation to a product patent.[527]

§7. Limitations and Exceptions to the Scope of Patent Protection

181. Exclusive rights that the patent law of Tanzania confers on the patentee are not absolute rights; their exploitation is subject to some limitations and exceptions.[528] Within the ambit of the law, the rights under the patents may not be enforced as follows: (a) against the use of a patented invention for scientific research; (b) if the patentee has exhausted his patent rights; (c) if the patent dispute is in relation to specified property of foreign countries, which enters the United Republic of Tanzania accidentally or temporarily; (d) after the expiry of the term of patent protection; (e) if a compulsory licence is lawfully granted; and (f) if the government wants to exploit the invention through State organs. These limitations and exceptions are expounded below.

I. Use of Patented Invention for Scientific Research

182. The drafters of the patent law of Tanzania designed it in a manner limiting the powers of the patentee to invoke his exclusive patent rights where exploitation of the pertinent rights would stand against the furtherance of technological innovations and scientific research in the United Republic of Tanzania. Thus, the rights under the patent do not empower the patentee to invoke those rights in relation to acts other than those done for industrial or commercial purposes.[529] The law does not, for instance, consider a third person who conducts some scientific research using a patented product or process as infringing the rights under the patent since the law of Tanzania does not classify scientific research as industrial or commercial activity.[530]

---

524. Cf. s. 35(a)(i), Act No. 1/1987.
525. Cf. s. 35(a)(ii), Act No. 1/1987.
526. Cf. s. 35(b)(i), Act No. 1/1987.
527. Cf. s. 35(b)(ii), Act No. 1/1987.
528. Cf. s. 37, Act No. 1/1987.
529. Cf. s. 37(1), Act No. 1/1987.
530. *Ibid.*

II. The Tenet of Exhaustion

183. According to the TPA, the principle of exhaustion of patent rights serves as a limitation to the exclusive use of patent rights that the owner of the patent is entitled to. This principle is enshrined in section 37(2) TPA. The section clarifies that the 'rights under the patent' do not 'extend to acts in respect of articles which have been put on the market in the United Republic [of Tanzania] by the owner of the patent or with his express consent'.

III. Specified Property of Other Countries

184. A patent does not confer on its owner or possessor a right to enforce his exclusive rights in relation to his patented articles used on 'aircraft, land vehicles or vessels of other countries, which temporarily or accidentally enter the United Republic' of Tanzania.[531]

IV. Compulsory Licence

185. Compulsory licence as one of the means through which rights under the patent are limited,[532] is normally issued against the will of the owner of a patent. Issuance of such a licence must therefore be legally justified. To secure a compulsory licence, the applicant has to petition the High Court of Tanzania, which is empowered under the law to decide whether or not the aspirant deserves a compulsory licence. The High Court can grant a compulsory licence only if the applicant satisfactorily proves: (1) that having asked the patentee to grant him a contractual licence, the patentee was unwilling to enter into such a contract, and a reasonable time within which the patentee must have responded to the applicant's request has expired; and (2) that upon being granted the compulsory licence, he will undertake to work the invention to a level that is enough to offset the 'deficiencies or to satisfy the requirements which gave rise to his request'.[533]

186. Prior to the grant of a compulsory licence, the High Court of Tanzania has to undertake some extensive deliberations on the applicant's request.[534] During these deliberations, the registrar manning the TPO has a right to appear before the High Court personally or through representation.[535] If the court decides in favour of the application for compulsory licence it will grant the licence and fix the terms that will govern such a licence. In fixing these terms the court is required to take into account 'any terms agreed by the parties'. Once the court fixes the compulsory

531. Cf. s. 37(3), Act No. 1/1987.
532. Cf. s. 37(5), Act No. 1/1987.
533. Cf. s. 55, Act No. 1/1987.
534. Cf. s. 56(1), Act No. 1/1987.
535. Cf. s. 56(3), Act No. 1/1987.

licence terms, the parties are bound by these terms as if they themselves have fixed the terms pursuant to a normal contractual licence outlined above in §7 of this chapter.[536]

The freedom of the High Court of Tanzania to fix the compulsory licence terms as above is limited by the stipulation of the law;[537] and in particular the terms must ensure that the parties enjoy the following rights: (1) the right of the licensee to exercise all exclusive patent rights[538] except the right of importation. However, if the compulsory licence is made in respect of the products declared by the minister to be of vital importance within the meaning of section 54 TPA, the successful applicant must be allowed to enjoy all exclusive patent rights stipulated under section 35 TPA including the right of importation;[539] (2) the right to grant further licence must generally be exercised by the licensor: the terms must ensure that the licensee exercises this right only upon the consent of the owner of the patent;[540] (3) both the licensee and licensor must be allowed to exploit the invention. In other words, a compulsory licence must be non-exclusive;[541] and (4) the owner of the patent must be guaranteed payment of equitable remuneration 'with due regard to all the circumstances of the case'.[542]

While the TPA enshrines a provision permitting transfer of a compulsory licence, such permission is subject to the condition that the compulsory licence be transferred together with the industrial undertaking in which the relevant invention is used.[543] To be valid, the High Court of Tanzania must consent to the transfer of any compulsory licence.[544]

187. Under certain circumstances, the owner of a patent may be justified to ask the High Court of Tanzania to cancel a compulsory licence. This is particularly the case if the licensee fails to comply with the stipulation of the licence contract, and/or if the compulsory licence can no longer be justified especially if the circumstances that gave rise to the licence do not exist anymore.[545] If a compulsory licence is cancelled, the rights of the licensee are generally determined by the terms of the licence contract. However, if the cancellation of the licence is attributable to the change of circumstances that gave rise to such a licence, the licensee must be given a reasonable time within which to stop exploiting the patent, especially if the licensee immediately stopped 'working the invention he would suffer substantial damage'.[546]

When the reason for cancelling a compulsory licence is the licensee's failure to work the patent to a degree that is enough to offset the circumstances that gave rise

536. Cf. s. 56(1), Act No. 1/1987.
537. Cf. s. 56, Act No. 1/1987.
538. These rights are outlined in §6 of this chapter.
539. Cf. s. 56(2)(a), Act No. 1/1987.
540. Cf. s. 56(2)(b), Act No. 1/1987.
541. Cf. s. 56(2)(c), Act No. 1/1987.
542. Cf. s. 56(2)(d), Act No. 1/1987.
543. Cf. s. 57, Act No. 1/1987.
544. *Ibid.*
545. Cf. s. 58(1)(a), Act No. 1/1987.
546. *Ibid.*

to the issuance of such a licence, both the registrar manning the TPO and the owner of the patent enjoy the right to ask the High Court of Tanzania to cancel the licence. If the cancellation proceedings are instituted by the registrar, the court must grant the cancellation order.[547] In case the owner of the patent puts into machinery the cancellation proceedings, the court is not obliged to issue a cancellation order.[548]

188. It is important to note that the High Court of Tanzania has some powers to vary the terms of a compulsory licence. The court does not exercise these powers *suo motu*; it has to be moved by the owner of the patent or by the licensee.[549] The petitioner must generally prove to the satisfaction of the court the existence of new facts justifying variation of the terms of a compulsory licence. For instance, the owner of a patent may argue that he 'has granted contractual licences on more favourable terms'.[550]

189. The High Court of Tanzania is obliged to communicate to the registrar of patents any decisions it takes in relation to a licence contract, such as the grant and cancellation of a licence as well as variation of the terms of such a licence. Upon such communication, the registrar must register the facts contained in the communication. No fee is required for such registration.[551]

190. Compulsory licence is generally granted under the patent law of Tanzania: (a) for reasons of non-working of the invention and similar reasons; (b) in order to offset the barrier against exploitation of invention caused by interdependence of patents; or (c) in respect of patented products, which are of vital importance.[552]

A. Non-working of the Patent and Similar Reasons

191. The Tanzanian law grants patents subject to a number of obligations, one of which the duty imposed on the patentee to ensure that the invention to which the patent relates is worked in the United Republic of Tanzania. In case of non-working of the patent without any reasonable cause, the patentee will risk his patent being revoked. Section 38(3) TPA clarifies the term 'non-working of the patent' antithetically. It provides that 'a patented invention is worked if the patented product is effectively made, or if the patented process is effectively used in the United Republic [of Tanzania] on a scale which is reasonable in the circumstances and importation shall not constitute working'.

Compulsory licences for non-working of the patent and for similar reasons stipulated in the relevant provisions of the law may be granted under section 52 TPA.

547. Cf. s. 58(1)(b), Act No. 1/1987.
548. *Ibid.*
549. Cf. s. 58(2), Act No. 1/1987.
550. *Ibid.*
551. Cf. s. 59, Act No. 1/1987.
552. Cf. s. 37(5), Act No. 1/1987. Cf. also Part XI TPA.

The TPA stipulates that any person may institute legal proceedings against the patentee before the High Court of Tanzania requesting the court to grant him a compulsory licence in respect of the invention owned by the former. Such a request may also be made by any person in the course of a suit instituted against him by the owner of the patent in relation to the patent. The court cannot consider such a request, unless it is made at any time after four years from the filing date of the application for the grant of the patent. If the patent is already granted, such a request must be made at a time not lesser than three years following such grant. Pursuant to this formula, if a patent is issued three years after the date of application, the four-year period following the application does not count anymore and hence the request for the issuance of a compulsory licence under section 52 TPA can only be considered by the court if made at any time after six years counted from the date of the application for the grant of the said patent.[553]

192. The request for compulsory licence under section 52 TPA may succeed only if the applicant supports his application with any of the following grounds: (i) 'that the patented invention, being capable of being worked in the United Republic [of Tanzania], has not been so worked'; (ii) 'that the existing degree of working of the patented invention in the United Republic [of Tanzania] does not meet in reasonable terms the demand for the patented product [or for product obtained directly by means of a patented process][554] on the domestic market or for the purposes of exportation'; (iii) 'that the working of the patented invention in the United Republic [of Tanzania] is being hindered or prevented by the importation of the patented product [or the product obtained directly by means of a patented process]';[555] and (iv) 'that, by reason of the refusal of the owner of the patent to grant licences on reasonable terms, the establishment or development of industrial or commercial activities in the United Republic [of Tanzania], or the possibilities of exportation from the United Republic [of Tanzania], are unfairly and substantially prejudiced'.[556]

193. It is noteworthy that section 52(2) TPA permits the owner of the patent to dispute the grounds that the applicant puts forth to support his application for the issuance of the compulsory licence. If the owner is successful in this endeavour, the court cannot issue a compulsory licence.

B. Interdependence of Patents

194. A patent may be granted in respect of an invention the exploitation of which may infringe on a prior existing patent. This is particularly the case if the earlier patent (i.e., the patent granted on earlier application) and the later patent (i.e.,

553. Cf. s. 52(1), Act No. 1/1987.
554. Cf. s. 52(1)(b), Act No. 1/1987.
555. *Ibid.*
556. Cf. s. 52(1)(i)–(iv), Act No. 1/1987.

the patent granted on a later application) are interdependent.[557] In this regard, the later patent cannot be exploited without infringing on the earlier patent. Where this is the case, the owner of a later patent may seek compulsory licence through two options; namely to exploit his invention and await an infringement suit to be instituted against him by the owner of the earlier patent and/or a representative of the owner and, in course of the proceedings, ask the court to grant him a compulsory licence; or to institute some legal proceedings against the owner of the patent specifically requesting the court to grant a compulsory licence.[558] The request for compulsory licence on grounds of interdependence may be made before the court in Tanzania at any time.[559]

195. It is important to note that the court cannot issue a compulsory licence with respect to the earlier patent: (a) if such a licence is not necessary for the working of the later patent; (b) if the later invention does not serve 'industrial purposes different from those served' by the earlier patent; (c) if the later patent is not in respect of an invention considered to be of 'substantial technical progress' in relation to the invention, which is a subject of the earlier patent.[560] Where the earlier and later inventions serve substantially similar purposes, the TPA clarifies that compulsory licence may be granted in respect of the earlier patent only if the owner of the earlier patent is also given an option to apply for a compulsory licence in respect of the later patent.[561]

C. Products of Vital Importance

196. The minister responsible for matters relating to patents is empowered to specify that certain kind of products are of vital importance for the defence or economy of the country or for public health and declare the availability of compulsory licences in respect of the patent for these products or in respect of the patented process for the manufacture of these products. The specification and the declaration are made in a ministerial order, which has to be published in the *Gazette* for its enforceability.[562]

197. Judicial enforcement of the foregoing ministerial order rests with the High Court of Tanzania. The court exercises this power in the course of 'proceedings instituted against or by the owner of the patent' whereby the court is requested to issue a compulsory licence in respect of the product or process referred to in the ministerial order.[563] This request can only be made before the court at any time after the grant of a patent.[564]

557. Cf. s. 53(3), Act No. 1/1987.
558. Cf. s. 53(1), Act No. 1/1987.
559. *Ibid.*
560. *Ibid.*
561. Cf. s. 53(2), Act No. 1/1987.
562. Cf. s. 54(1), Act No. 1/1987.
563. Cf. s. 53(2), Act No. 1/1987.
564. *Ibid.*

V. State Exploitation of Patented Invention

198. Any of the exclusive rights to which the owner of a patent is entitled by virtue of any stipulation under the patent law of Tanzania may, without the owner's permission, be exercised by an agency of the government or by any person appointed by the minister responsible for matters relating to patents.[565] This may happen if the patented invention concerned is classified as of a 'vital public interest' the furtherance of which requires exploitation of the invention by the government agency and/or third person(s). Section 61(1) TPA regards 'national security, health or the development of vital sectors of the public economy' as some of the matters that are of vital public interests.

The decision whether the invention should be exploited as above must be made by the minister upon consultation with the registrar, and after a hearing arranged by the minister to which the patentee and licensee(s) (if any) must be given an opportunity to appear.[566]

199. Enforcement of the foregoing minister's decision is subject to the right of equitable remuneration that the owner of the patented invention enjoys. The amount of this remuneration is fixed by the registrar of patents who is required to take into account 'all the circumstances' while determining the remuneration.[567] The owner of the patent has a right to appeal against the registrar's decision in relation to the remuneration fixed. If lodged, such an appeal cannot have any suspensive effects on the minister's decision explained above.[568]

VI. The Term of a Patent

200. The owner or possessor of a patent right cannot enforce his exclusive rights against third parties beyond the duration within which his exclusive rights are protected.[569] The time span of a patent protected under the patent law of Tanzania is outlined below in §8 of this chapter.

§8. Duration of Protection: Maintaining and Termination of Patent Protection

I. Term of Patent Protection

201. Subject to certain conditions such as renewal of the initial term of protection and payment of annual fees, an invention protected under the TPA enjoys a total

565. Cf. s. 61(1), Act No. 1/1987.
566. Cf. s. 61(2), Act No. 1/1987.
567. Cf. s. 61(3), Act No. 1/1987.
568. Cf. s. 61(4), Act No. 1/1987.
569. Cf. s. 37(4), Act No. 1/1987.

of twenty years of protection.[570] The initial term of patent protection is ten years counted after the filing date of the application for the patent.[571] This term can, upon a request of the owner of the patent and/or licensee(s) (if any), be extended for two further terms of five years each.[572] To be admissible, the application for the extension of the protection term must be made within a period of twelve months and not less than a month preceding expiration of the term of protection sought to be extended.[573] Moreover, the request for extension must be accompanied by a prescribed fee.[574]

202. To be successful, the applicant for extension of the patent protection term must satisfy the registrar of patents either that 'the invention which is the subject of the said patent is being worked in the United Republic (of Tanzania)' or that some reasonable justifications for failing to work the invention exist.[575]

203. Upon receiving a request for extension of a patent protection term, the registrar of patents is required to grant or to reject the request within six months. If the registrar does not act on the request within this period, he will be deemed to have extended the term of protection of the invention concerned.[576]

204. Both the patent owner and the licensee have right to appeal to the High Court of Tanzania against the registrar's refusal to grant the request for extension of the patent protection term.[577]

II. Maintenance of Patents

205. To maintain protection of an invention, an annual fee must be paid in advance to the registrar of patents starting with the second year after the date of the filing of an application for patent protection.[578] This period can be extended by six months provided that in addition to annual maintenance fee a prescribed surcharge is paid.[579]

In case of non-payment of annual maintenance fee within the stipulated period, the application for patent protection is deemed to have been withdrawn and – in case of an already issued patent – the granted patent to have lapsed.[580] Nevertheless, this

570. Cf. ss 38 and 39, Act No. 1/1987.
571. Cf. s. 38(1), Act No. 1/1987.
572. Cf. s. 38(2)(a) and (b), Act No. 1/1987.
573. *Ibid.*
574. *Ibid.*
575. *Ibid.*
576. Cf. s. 38(2) and (b), Act No. 1/1987.
577. *Ibid.*
578. Cf. s. 39(a), Act No. 1/1987.
579. Cf. s. 39(2), Act No. 1/1987.
580. Cf. s. 39(3), Act No. 1/1987.

assumption does not apply to international applications; especially if the PCT allows a different period within which annual maintenance fee should be paid.[581]

206. The law obliges the registrar of patents to restore protection of an application that has been deemed to have been withdrawn and a patent, which has been deemed to have lapsed. In particular, this happens if any interested person, upon payment of some prescribed fees, submits to the registrar a request for such restoration and satisfies the Registrar that the failure to pay maintenance annual fee within a prescribed time was not intentional and that 'all annual fees due have already been paid'.[582] Any interested person may appeal to the High Court of Tanzania against any decision to restore or to refuse restoration of protection of an invention.[583]

207. The owner of the patent cannot, after restoration of protection, claim any remedy in respect of any acts, which would be deemed as patent infringement but for the lapse of the protection of the invention. This applies in respect of acts committed in the interval between the lapse and restoration of protection[584] as well as acts perpetuated 'after the date of the order for restoration in relation to articles imported in the United Republic (of Tanzania), or manufactured therein, after the lapse of the patent and before the date of the order for restoration'.[585]

III. Termination of Protection

A. *Surrender of a Patent*

208. It is not a contravention of the law in the event one surrenders his tangible or intangible property. This is also true in relation to patent rights; the patent law of Tanzania does not stipulate against alienation of patent rights by way of surrender: it rather allows the owner to surrender his patent either wholly or in part. A provision of the law refers to partial surrender of a patent as a surrender that is directed to one or more but not all claims, which are the subject of the patent protection.[586] To be effective, a patentee has to play an active role to initiate the process leading to surrender of patent rights. He is thus required to communicate to the registrar of patents a notice of his intention to surrender the patent. The surrender of a patent

581. *Ibid. See also* s. 31(3), Act No. 1/1987.
582. Cf. s. 39(4)(a) and (b), Act No. 1/1987.
583. Cf. s. 39(4)(c), Act No. 1/1987.
584. Cf. s. 39(5)(i), Act No. 1/1987.
585. Cf. s. 39(5)(ii), Act No. 1/1987.
586. Cf. s. 62(1) and (2), Act No. 1/1987.

takes immediate effect following its publication by the registrar of patents.[587] Prior to such publication, the registrar has to record the surrender in the register of patents.[588]

209. Licensees whose licence contract is recorded in the register of patents have a right to block any surrender of a patent. This right may nevertheless be waived by a stipulation to this effect contained in the licence agreement. Where the licensee's right to object to the surrender is not waived as in the immediately preceding sentence, the registrar of patents cannot register a surrender of a patent unless it is accompanied by the licensee's consensual declaration thereto.[589]

B. Invalidation and Revocation

210. Powers to revoke a patent protected in Tanzania lies, in the first place, with the High Court of Tanzania. Revocation is endorsed following successful invalidation proceedings. In this regard, the TPA provides any interested party with a leeway to institute invalidation proceedings against the owner of a patent.[590] Likewise, a person against whom a patent owner institutes infringement proceedings may, in the course of those proceedings, plead a plea of non-infringement and ask the court to invalidate the patent concerned.[591]

211. Licensees under the patent and any other persons who have the right to the patent which is sought to be invalidated are entitled to take part in the invalidation proceedings.[592] The High Court of Tanzania is therefore obliged to inform them of the invalidation request that it has received and afford them an opportunity to appear before it during the proceedings.[593] Licensees may, nevertheless, not enjoy this entitlement if an express clause enshrined in the licence contract indicates that they have waived the right to appear before the High Court of Tanzania during the invalidation proceedings.[594]

212. According to section 63(2) TPA, a patent protected in Tanzania may be invalidated in any of the following situations: (1) the subject matter of the invention protected under the patent is not a patentable subject matter within the meaning of section 7 TPA, or it was not new on the filing date of the application for the patent within the meaning of section 8 TPA, or it did not involve an inventive step within the meaning of section 10 TPA, or it cannot be applied industrially in accordance

587. It is through such publication interested parties get knowledge of the intended surrender and thereby grab an opportunity to oppose the surrender (in case this action is needed) by lodging a notice of opposition to the registrar of patents.
588. Cf. s. 62(3), Act No. 1/1987.
589. Cf. s. 62(4), Act No. 1/1987.
590. Cf. s. 63(1), Act No. 1/1987.
591. *Ibid.*
592. Cf. s. 63(5) and (6), Act No. 1/1987.
593. *Ibid.*
594. Cf. s. 63(5), Act No. 1/1987.

with section 11 TPA;[595] (2) the public order or morality prohibits the exploitation of the invention under the patent within the meaning of section 12 TPA;[596] (3) the patented products are, or the patented process is, statutorily excluded from patentability in accordance with the provisions of section 13 PTA;[597] (4) the invention under the patent was not sufficiently described in line with the requirements under section 18(3) TPA, and/or the claims were not framed well enough to depict the scope of the patent granted as required under section 18(4) TPA; and [598] (5) 'the person to whom the patent was granted had no right to the patent' and 'the patent has not been assigned to a person who has the right to the patent' in accordance with section 15 TPA.[599]

If any of the foregoing grounds for invalidating a patent applies 'only to some of the claims or to some parts of a claim', the invalidation order of the court shall only affect 'such claims or parts of a claim'.[600]

213. Upon issuing an order invalidating a patent, the High Court must, after the expiry of the statutory period within which an aggrieved party may appeal against the order, communicate such order to the registrar of patents. Following such communication, the Registrar is obliged to register the order in the register of patents and publish the same immediately.[601]

214. An 'invalidated patent, or claim or part of a claim is regarded as null and void' *ab initio*; i.e., the invention under the patent to which the invalidation order applies is considered to have not enjoyed any protection under the TPA from the date of the grant of the purported patent.[602]

§9. Infringement and Remedies

215. According to section 65 TPA, an infringement of a patent is constituted by a third person performing any of the exclusive rights described above in §6 of this chapter without authorization of the owner of the patent.[603] A third person may nevertheless avoid liability for patent infringement if his unauthorized acts fall within the limitations and exceptions to the scope of patent protection outlined above in §7 of this chapter.[604]

595. Cf. s. 62(2)(a), Act No. 1/1987.
596. *Ibid.*
597. *Ibid.*
598. Cf. s. 62(2)(c), Act No. 1/1987.
599. Cf. s. 62(2)(d), Act No. 1/1987.
600. Cf. s. 62(3), Act No. 1/1987.
601. Cf. s. 64(2), Act No. 1/1987.
602. Cf. s. 64(1), Act No. 1/1987.
603. Cf. s. 65, Act No. 1/1987.
604. *Ibid.*

216. The law allows the owner of a patent to institute legal action against any actual or perceived infringement of his patent.[605] The owner is therefore entitled to request the High Court of Tanzania to grant him some relief such as the following: (1) an injunction to prevent infringement where infringement is imminent, or to prohibit the continuation of the infringement once infringement has started; (2) damages; and (3) any other remedy provided for in the civil law.[606]

The owner of an international application in which Tanzania is designated is also entitled to the above-mentioned relief 'in respect of acts committed before the grant of the patent but after the date of international publication',[607] provided that the publication was made in English language.[608] Even where the publication was effected in a language other than English, the owner enjoys the same relief if he furnishes the infringer with an English translation of the international publication; and only from the date the infringer receives the translation.[609]

217. Where an alleged patent infringement is in respect of one or more exclusive patent rights in respect of which the owner of the patent has granted an exclusive licence, the exclusive licensee has the right to seek the help of the court to stop such infringement. To achieve this, the exclusive licensee has to send a registered mail to the owner of the patent informing him of the infringement and asking him to sue the infringer for the relief that the exclusive licensee specifies in his letter.[610] If the owner acts on the licensee's request, the licensee has the right to join the infringement proceedings as the second plaintiff. In the event the owner of the patent does not take any legal action against the infringer within three months after the receipt of the licensee's request, the law allows the licensee to institute the said proceedings in his own name.[611] Before instituting such proceedings, the law obliges the licensee to issue notice to the owner of the patent of his intention to sue the infringer.[612] The owner of the patent may join, as a second plaintiff, the proceedings instituted by the licensee.[613]

It is instructive to note that if the licensee 'shows that immediate action is necessary to avoid substantial damage', he may request the court to 'grant an appropriate injunction to prevent infringement or prohibit its continuation' even before the expiry of the three-month period within which the owner of the patent is required to act on the licensee's request to institute legal proceedings against infringer(s) of the patent.[614]

218. Any third person who is in doubt as to whether his activities constitute an infringement of a patent, or who has some other legitimate interests, may ask the

605. Cf. s. 66, Act No. 1/1987.
606. *Ibid.*
607. Publication of international applications is regulated under Art. 21 PCT.
608. Cf. s. 33(1), Act No. 1/1987.
609. Cf. s. 33(2), Act No. 1/1987.
610. Cf. s. 71(1), Act No. 1/1987.
611. Cf. s. 71(2), Act No. 1/1987.
612. *Ibid.*
613. *Ibid.*
614. Cf. s. 71(3), Act No. 1/1987.

High Court of Tanzania to declare that his activities do not constitute infringement of the patent. During the declaratory proceedings, the owner of the patent and the licensees under the patent enjoy the right to appear before the court as defendants.[615] The request for such declaration cannot be granted if the following conditions are met: (1) 'the acts to which the request relates are already the subject of infringement proceedings';[616] or (2) 'if the person making the request is unable to prove that he has previously demanded from the owner of the patent a written acknowledgement of the lawfulness of the acts referred to and that the owner of the patent has refused such demand or has failed to reply within a reasonable time'.[617]

219. A patent owner who threatens a third person exploiting the patent with an infringement suit may be ordered to stop the threats. To achieve this, the third person facing the threats must be able to prove that the 'acts performed or to be performed do not constitute infringement of the patent' and ask the High Court of Tanzania 'to grant an injunction' prohibiting the patent owner's threats.[618] In case financial loss ensues from such threats, the third person is as well entitled to ask the court to redress the loss by awarding him some damages.[619] The TPA, however, insists that the 'mere notification of the existence of a patent shall not constitute threats' of infringement suit.[620]

220. Under certain circumstances, the patent law of Tanzania provides for criminal liability for patent infringement. In this regard, an intentional patent infringement is a criminal offence. This offence is punishable by a fine up to TZS 1,00,000 or a three-year imprisonment term or 'to both such fine and imprisonment'.[621] Habitual, criminal patent infringers may, upon conviction, be imprisoned for a six-year term or be fined up to TZS 200,000 or face both the fine and imprisonment.[622] The TPA regards a person as a habitual infringer if he had faced criminal conviction for the patent infringement within five years preceding a repeated criminal patent infringement allegations levelled against him.[623]

615. Cf. s. 67(1), Act No. 1/1987.
616. Cf. s. 67(2)(i), Act No. 1/1987.
617. Cf. s. 67(2)(ii), Act No. 1/1987.
618. Cf. s. 68(1), Act No. 1/1987.
619. *Ibid.*
620. Cf. s. 68(2), Act No. 1/1987.
621. Cf. s. 69(1), Act No. 1/1987.
622. Cf. s. 69(2), Act No. 1/1987.
623. Cf. s. 69(3), Act No. 1/1987.

Chapter 3. Utility Certificates

§1. Sources: Legislation

221. The Patents Act No. 1/1987 of Tanzania provides, in its part XVI, for protection of inventions through utility certificates. Unless stated otherwise in this part of the Act, issuance of utility certificates and the procedure for applying for these certificates are governed by the same rules relating to patents as enshrined in the patent law of Tanzania.[624] Similarly, Chapter II of the ZIPA is solely devoted to the protection of utility models in Tanzania Zanzibar.

It is indisputable that the United Republic of Tanzania has made tremendous efforts to align its IP protection regime with the protection regime run under the auspices of the African Intellectual Property Organization (ARIPO) – an organization, which is a creation of the Lusaka Agreement.[625] The Lusaka Agreement empowers ARIPO to enact some protocols that are necessary to define the functions and powers of this organization in specific fields of IP rights. For instance, ARIPO's powers in relation to protection of utility models are circumscribed by the *Harare Protocol on Patents and Industrial Designs* of 10 December 1982 as last amended and revised on 25 November 2013. The United Republic of Tanzania is a party to the Harare Protocol; the protocol entered into force with respect to Tanzania on 1 September 1999. In addition to the provisions relating to patents and industrial designs contained in it, the Harare Protocol enshrines as well provisions on the protection of Utility Models.[626]

Tanzania is, since 16 June 1963, bound by the Paris Convention of 20 March 1883 as last revised in 1967. As a country that follows the *dualist* approach when it comes to the domestication of international law in the United Republic of Tanzania, the municipal pieces of legislation on utility models protection enacted by the legislature of Tanzania reflect to a sufficient (if not full) degree the utility models protection regime, which Paris Convention establishes.[627]

624. Cf. s. 72(1), Act No. 1/1987.
625. That is, The Lusaka Agreement on the creation of an Industrial Property Organization for English-Speaking African countries of December 1976, as amended by the administrative council of ARIPO on 10 Dec. 1982, 12 Dec. 1986 and 27 Nov. 1996, and as amended by the Council of Ministers on 13 Aug. 2004.
626. Cf. s. 3*ter*, Harare Protocol.
627. Cf. Andres Mancayo von Hase, *The Application and Interpretation of the Agreement on Trade-Related Aspects of Intellectual Property Rights*, in *Intellectual Property and International Trade* 83 (Carlos M. Correa & Abdulqawi A. Yusuf eds, 2d ed., Kluwer Law International B.V 2008).

§2. The Protection under Utility Certificate

222. To qualify for protection under utility certificate, an invention must be new and capable of being applied industrially[628] irrespective of whether or not the invention meets the threshold for inventive step required as a condition for patent protection.[629] While the patent law applicable in mainland Tanzania completely dispenses with the requirement of inventive step thus providing for a possibility of extending monopoly to inventions that are obvious by way of utility certificates, this is not the case under the ZIPA. Although inventive step is one of the preconditions for protecting utility models in Tanzania Zanzibar under the ZIPA, the degree of inventiveness applicable to utility models differs from that which the law requires for the purpose of patent protection.[630] Exclusion of inventive step from the requirements for the issuance of utility certificates connotes that the obviousness test as applied in the context of patent law does not apply in relation to the grant of protection under utility certificates. In this sense, a utility certificate can be issued even for an invention, which was obvious[631] to a person highly skilled in the art on the filing date of the application, or if the application claims priority, on the date of such priority.[632]

223. Substantive examination, which section 27 TPA stipulates, is not required in relation to applications for utility certificate.[633] Therefore, inventions protectable in Tanzania under utility certificates are only examined for compliance with the formal requirements.

224. The law clarifies that if two persons make same invention independent of each other and apply for protection of the same under utility certificate, the person whose application has the earliest filing date or, if priority is claimed, the earliest validly claimed priority date, and leads to the grant of a utility certificate shall have the right to the utility certificate.[634]

628. Cf. s. 73(1)(a), Act No. 1/1987.
629. Cf. s. 73(1)(b), Act No. 1/1987.
630. Section 17(3) of the ZIPA provides that a 'utility model shall be considered as involving a sufficiently inventive step if, having regard to the differences and similarities between the claimed utility model and the prior art … the utility model does not result in a common manner from the prior art relevant to a person having ordinary skill in the art'. Whereas, s. 4(3) of ZIPA delineates the term inventive step in relation to patent law in the following manner: an 'invention shall be considered as involving an inventive step if, having regard to the differences and similarities between the claimed invention and the prior art … , the claimed invention as a whole would not have been obvious to a person highly skilled in the art or when the method or claimed product are not disclosed in any single piece or any combination of pieces of prior art at the filing date or, … , at priority date of the claimed invention'.
631. It must be noted that obviousness of an invention within the meaning of patent law is a barrier to patent protection. Obviousness is determined in the light of available pieces of prior art the combination of which by a skilled person constitutes the claimed invention (cf. ss 9(2)(a) and 10, Act No. 1/1987).
632. Cf. s. 73(1)(b), Act No. 1/1987 read together with s. 10 TPA.
633. Cf. s. 73(2), Act No. 1/1987.
634. Cf. s. 72(2)(i), Act No. 1/1987.

225. Once issued, a utility certificate has to be registered in the relevant part of the register of patents.[635]

226. The patents law of Tanzania envisages circumstances whereby a utility certificate and a patent may be interdependent.[636] Such interdependence may necessitate compulsory cross-licensing of the patent and/or the utility certificate concerned.[637]

227. The duration of validity of utility certificate with respect to Tanzania mainland is seven years non-renewable term.[638] Utility certificates issued under ZIPA are valid for a non-renewable maximum term of ten years.[639]

228. A utility certificate may be invalidated by the High Court of Tanzania if any of the following grounds apply to it: (1) that the invention with respect to which a utility certificate applies was not new, or the invention under the certificate cannot be applied industrially, or the public order or morality prohibits exploitation of the invention, or the products or process to which the invention relates is statutorily excluded from protection; (2) that the invention under the utility certificate was not sufficiently disclosed to enable persons skilled in the art carry out the invention; (3) that the claims of the invention under the utility certificate are not clear and concise, and hence do not sufficiently define the subject matter of invention; (4) 'that any drawings which is necessary for the understanding of the invention has not been furnished'; or (5) that the person to whom the utility certificate was granted had no entitlement to the certificate and has not yet assigned the same to the person who has the right to it.[640]

229. In addition to civil liability provided for in the Patents Act, an infringer of a right protected under the utility certificate may also face criminal prosecution following same principles governing criminal liability for patent infringement.[641] However, the doubled penalty given to habitual criminal infringers of patent rights is not applicable to criminal infringement of utility certificates.[642]

§3. Conversion of Patent Applications or Applications for Utility Certificates

230. Conversion of an application for a patent into an application for a utility certificate is allowed under the TPA. Likewise, an application initially submitted for a utility certificate may be converted into an application for a patent. The converted

---

635. Cf. s. 73(3), Act No. 1/1987.
636. Cf. s. 72(2)(ii), Act No. 1/1987.
637. Cf. s. 53, Act No. 1/1987.
638. Cf. s. 73(4), Act No. 1/1987.
639. Cf. s. 24, ZIPA.
640. Cf. s. 73(5), Act No. 1/1987.
641. Cf. s. 69, Act No. 1/1987.
642. Cf. s. 73(6), Act No. 1/1987.

application retains as its filing date the date of the initial application. Note that conversion of applications as above is acceptable only if it is done (once) at any time before the grant of a patent/utility certificate or notification of rejection of the application thereof or of refusal to grant a patent/utility certificate; and if the prescribed fee is paid.[643]

643. Cf. s. 74, Act No. 1/1987.

Chapter 4. Trade Names

§1. Sources: Legislation

231. By virtue of its Membership to the World Trade Organization (WTO) and the Paris Union for the protection of industrial property (henceforth, the Paris Union), the United Republic of Tanzania has an inherent obligation to establish a legal regime for the domestic protection of trade names. Article 8 of the Paris Convention for the Protection of Industrial Property of 1967 (henceforth, the Paris Convention) provides for guidance on the modality of trade names protection. Obligations obtaining under Article 8 of the Paris Convention bind on WTO Member States such as Tanzania through Article 2.1 of the TRIPS Agreement.[644]

The legal framework for trade names protection in Tanzania is mainly based on the Registration of Business Names Registration Act (BNRA), Chapter 213 of the laws of Tanzania. This piece of legislation, which generally provides for the registration of business names for both natural and legal persons operating in the United Republic of Tanzania, outlines some qualifications to be met by aspiring business name registrants, registrable names and the conditions the breach of which attracts criminal liability.

Business Activities Registration Act, 2007 (No. 14/2007) (BARA) establishes a central registry, which is controlled by the Business Registration and Licensing Authority (BRELA) of Tanzania.[645] The registry is linked with the registries of business names and companies registration. The Companies Act, 2002 (No. 12/2002) is another piece of legislation with relevance to the protection of trade names. The extent to which the BARA and the Companies Act enhance trade names protection in Tanzania is explored in the next sections of this chapter.

Other pieces of legislation that provide for some sort of trade names protection in Tanzania are: (1) the Merchandise Marks Act, 1963 (No. 20/1963 of the laws of Tanzania) (MMA); and (2) the Protection of New Plant Varieties (Plant Breeder's Rights) Act, 2002 (No. 22/2002) (henceforth, PBRA). The former Act does not provide for trade names registration, but protects a trade name against falsification and misuse by third parties when describing or labelling their products.[646] On its part, the latter piece of legislation contains a provision allowing a breeder of a new plant variety to identify a denomination that is essentially applied as a trade name for that variety.[647]

Moreover, the ZIPA, 2008 that came into force in September 2008 addresses some issues concerning trade names protection in Tanzania Zanzibar.

644. Cf. *United States – Section 211 Omnibus Appropriation Act of 1998*. Report of the Appellate Body, WT/DS176/AB/R (WTO 2002), at para. 341.
645. Cf. s. 6, BARA.
646. Cf. ss 2 & 3, MMA.
647. Cf. s. 23, PBRA.

§2. THE PROTECTION OF TRADE NAMES

232. The general obligation to protect trade names is founded in Article 8 of the Paris Convention, which decrees that a 'trade name shall be protected in all countries of the Union without the obligation of filing or registration, whether or not it forms part of a trademark'.[648] In addition to being a party to the TRIPS Agreement and thus obligated by Article 2.1 of the Agreement to observe provisions of Article 8 of the Paris Convention, the United Republic of Tanzania is also a member of the Paris Union.

The following sections explore the country's domestic legislation and legal infrastructure that are relevant for the protection of trade names.

I. Business Names (Registration) Act

233. The BNRA,[649] which establishes a legal regime for the protection of business names in the United Republic of Tanzania, is administered by the BRELA. As an Executive Agency of the Government of Tanzania, BRELA is under the control of a chief executive officer who doubles as Chief Registrar of business activities and business names registration in Tanzania.

The term 'trade name' – which is the central theme of this chapter – does not textually appear in the BNRA. This begs the question whether BNRA protects trade names. From a semantic point of view, the term 'business name' which the BNRA addresses is a synonym of the term 'trade name'. Some commentators see no differences between business names and trade names. They argue that 'trade name' is an old term, which is now used interchangeably with the term 'business name'. Accordingly, they regard the term 'business name' as the newest and most correct term.[650] A reading of the operational definition of the term 'business name' provided for under the BNRA buttresses this position by suggesting that the term is actually used interchangeably with the term 'trade name'. Section 2 of the BNRA defines the term 'business name' to mean the 'name or style under which any business is carried on, whether in partnership or otherwise', whereby the contextual application of the term 'business' includes a reference to 'profession'.

234. The BNRA enshrines a provision requiring every firm, individual persons as well as corporations carrying on business in Tanzania to register its/his business

648. The wording of Art. 8 of the Paris Convention alone does not enable one to discern the scope of trade names protection, which the Convention provides for. However, when Art. 8 is read together with Arts 2 and 3 of the Paris Convention and the TRIPS Agreement respectively, it becomes clear that the scope of Art. 8 of the Paris Convention is to be determined based on the principle of national treatment (cf. *United States – Section 211 Omnibus Appropriation Act of 1998*. Report of the Appellate Body, WT/DS176/AB/R (WTO 2002), at paras 238–243).
649. Cap. 213 of the laws of Tanzania (henceforth, the BNRA).
650. Cf. http://www.smh.com.au/small-business/resources/whats-the-difference-between-a-business-name-a-trading-name-and-a-legal-name-20140522-38s6g.html#ixzz3hyol2BPE (accessed: 1 May 2022).

name with BRELA. This stipulation applies to a business name that does not consist of a true corporation name, true surnames of the firm's partners or of the shareholders of an incorporated company participating in the firm's partnership or of the sole trader to be registered. However, the directive under discussion does not apply to a business name that is composed of one's own true surname or which consists of a true surname together with true initials or forenames.[651] Although the BNRA does not state it explicitly, the implication of this position is that the Tanzanian law does not oblige a person conducting business in Tanzania using his name as business name to register that name. the corollary of this argument is that individuals enjoy a right to trade in their own names without observing any formalities such as having their names registered.

Where registration of a business name is a precondition for its continued use in Tanzania in relation to a particular business, the BNRA stipulates the procedure for such registration. The law places the obligation to apply for registration of a business name to both business operators who commence business in a period of more than two months counted from the date the BNRA was enacted and those whose business became operational before the BNRA's enactment. Whereas application for registration in respect of the former has to be made within a maximum of twenty-eight days following the first use of the business name, the law stipulates the maximum of three-month period counted from the date on which the BNRA was passed as a period within which an application for a business name registration in relation to the latter has to be submitted to BRELA. This latter period applies also to a business name of a business that was commenced within two months period succeeding the date of the passing of the BNRA.[652]

As regards the contents of an application for registration of a business name, the BNRA requires an applicant to prepare and submit to BRELA a statement of description on the type of business, the physical address of the main or other location of the business, and the very business name sought to be registered. In case of a commercial establishment that operates its business under more than one business name, each of the names has to be included in the 'statement required (under the BNRA to be communicated to BRELA) for the purpose of business name registration'.[653] In addition to these particulars, an admissible application for a business name registration has to bear a signature of the applicant or executive personnel representing a legal person.[654]

In certain circumstances, the registrar is entitled to decide that a particular business name cannot be registered. The registrar's decision to reject an application for business name registration must be justified on any of the following grounds: (1) that the business name is 'identical with or similar' to that of another existing business name registered under the BNRA, or under the Companies Act (Cap. 212 of the laws of Tanzania), or under the Cooperative Societies Act (Cap. 211 of the laws of Tanzania); (2) that the business name 'includes the words "building society" or

651. Cf. s. 4, BNRA.
652. Cf. s. 8, BNRA.
653. The applicant for a trade name registration has to fill these particulars in forms number 3 (in case the applicant is an individual), number 2 (for persons applying as partners) and number 8 (for corporations).
654. Cf. ss 6 & 7, BNRA.

"Cooperative" or their equivalent in any other language or their abbreviation thereof'; these words are only used in connection with societies registrable under the Societies Act, 2002 (Cap. 327) and the Cooperative Societies Act (Cap. 211 of the laws of Tanzania); (3) that the business name contains a word that is regarded by the registrar to be 'likely to mislead the public as to nationality, race or religion of the persons by whom the business is wholly or mainly owned or controlled'; and (4) that the business name suggests presidential or governmental patronage.[655]

BRELA is duty-bound to clear for registration all applications for business name registration that comply with the registration conditions.[656] A certificate of registration issued by the registrar serves as an evidence of one's business name registration. A right to be issued with a certificate of registration can be claimed within twenty-eight days following the registrar's decision to declare that the name is registrable.[657] It is noteworthy under the law, that such a certificate has unlimited period of validity. However, cases of discontinued use of the business name or of non-compliance with the conditions for using the business name under the certificate may lead to deregistration of the name concerned. One of these conditions is the one requiring the certificate holder to display the certificate or a certified copy thereof in a place where it can easily be viewed by the members of the public particularly clients visiting the certificate holder's place of business.[658]

II. Protection under Other Pieces of Legislation

235. The BARA, 2007 (No. 14/2007) protects trade names in two ways, namely, by obliging applicants for business activities registration to state to BRELA the name of a business they plan to undertake[659] and by requiring business operators to depict a certificate of business activities registration in a conspicuous area in the place in which the business is carried on.[660] Whereas the former obligation allows BRELA to search in the business activities and business names registries to see whether the name under which the business activity is proposed to be registered is already registered by someone else, the latter requirement ensures not only that a business holder complied with the BARA provisions pursuant to which any business operational in the United Republic of Tanzania has to be registered, but also helps the public to get knowledge of the business name and be able to enforce their rights in case the business owner appropriated a business name that belongs to another person.

236. The Companies Act, 2002 (No. 12/2002) strengthens the trade names protection regime obtaining in Tanzania. Section 30 of the Act bestows upon a person

655. Cf. s. 9, BNRA.
656. However, s. 10 of the BNRA provides that the 'registration of a firm, individual or corporation … shall not be construed as authorising the use of a business name if apart from such registration the use thereof could be prohibited'.
657. Cf. s. 9, BNRA.
658. Cf. ss 19 & 20, BNRA.
659. Cf. s. 13, BARA.
660. Cf. s. 17, BARA.

aspiring to register a company a right to apply to the Registrar of companies for reservation of a trade name of his company. Where such an application is granted, the reservation becomes valid for a maximum period of sixty days. Other people are allowed to adopt this name for their companies once the reservation expires, unless the applicant completes registration of the company within the reservation period.

237. The Plant Breeder's Rights Act, 2012 (No. 9/2012) (henceforth, PBRA) adds value to the legal protection of trade names in Tanzania. The obligation to assign a name or a denomination to a new plant variety sought to be registered is an indispensable *sine qua non* under this law. The name that designates the variety – and which can only be used in relation to a plant variety upon approval thereof by the registrar of plant breeders' rights – has to be proposed at the time of making an application for the grant of plant breeders' rights and the registration of the new plant variety. As a measure of trade name protection, the PBRA prohibits reference to a registered plant variety by a name other than the one the registrar has approved.[661]

238. The MMA (No. 20/1963 of the laws of Tanzania) deals with labelling, trade descriptions and other modalities of marking of goods. In a manner that constitutes trade names protection, the MMA categorizes the application of false trade descriptions as an illegal act. Within the ambit of this law, a trade name can be used as a trade description. Section 2 of the MMA defines the term 'trade description' as any 'description, statement, or other indication' with direct or indirect reference *inter alia* to characteristics, standards or origin of goods. Since a trade name serves to distinguish one commercial establishment from the other, there exists a possibility of a trade name becoming a brand name of the respective commercial establishment. Where this is a case, it is not unlikely that the brand name may serve as a source-identifier reflecting standards and quality of the products marketed by the said commercial establishment such that if third parties use the trade name in relation to products of different quality and standards from a different commercial establishment such use would be regarded false trade description[662] and hence outlawed under the law.

239. The ZIPA, 2008 contains legal provisions on trade names protection. As opposed to the Tanzania mainland's pieces of legislation – whose trade names protection regime does not extend to the territory of Tanzania Zanzibar – ZIPA provides for a specific delineation of the term 'trade name'. According to section 2 of ZIPA, a 'name or designation' that identifies and distinguishes an enterprise qualifies as a trade name. In a manner that seems to be wholesale implementation of Article 8 of the Paris Convention, ZIPA does not condition protection of trade names in Tanzania Zanzibar on registration.

661. Cf. s. 20, PBRA.
662. The MMA defines the term 'false trade description' to be a 'trade description which is false or misleading in a material respect as regards the goods to which it is applied ... ' (s. 2(1), para. 3, MMA).

Chapter 5. Industrial Designs

§1. Sources: Legislation

240. There is no independent regime for the protection of industrial designs in Tanzania mainland. The current regime in this part of the United Republic of Tanzania – which is dependent on the UK of Great Britain design protection framework – is contained in Part XVII of the Patents (Registration) Act Chapter 217 of the Revised Edition (R.E.) of the laws of Tanzania of 2002. This piece of legislation provides for protection in Tanzania only in respect of industrial designs that are already registered and protected in the UK. Protection of designs in Tanzania Zanzibar is claimed based on Chapter III of the ZIPA.

The Berne Convention for the Protection of Literary and Artistic Works[663] of 1886 (as amended and revised from time to time) (henceforth, the Berne Convention)[664] provides for the protection of both artistic and industrial designs. Hence, this Convention constitutes a source of Tanzanian law on designs protection not only on the basis of the fact that Tanzania is a Member of the Berne Union,[665] but also due to the reason that Article 9 of the Agreement on TRIPS Agreement incorporates in the Agreement provisions of Articles 1–21 of the Berne Convention.[666] Even if it were not for Tanzania's accession to the Berne Convention, the fact that the United Republic of Tanzania is bound by the TRIPS Agreement translates into the obligation on the part of Tanzania to abide by the provisions of both the foregoing Convention and Agreement. Additionally, the country tacitly accepts to be guided by the provisions of the Paris Convention for the Protection of Industrial Property insofar as the regulation of industrial design matters is concerned.[667]

---

663. Adopted on 9 Sep. 1886 at Berne, entered into force on 4 Dec. 1887; completed on 4 May 1896 at Paris, entered into force on 9 Dec. 1897; revised on 13 Nov. 1908 at Berlin, entered into force on 9 Sep. 1910; completed on 20 Mar. 1914 at Berne, entered into force on 20 Apr. 1915; revised on 2 Jun. 1928 at Rome, entered into force on 1 Aug. 1931; revised on 26 Jun. 1948 at Brussels, entered into force on 1 Aug. 1951; Revised on 14 Jul. 1967 at Stockholm, entered into force on 29 Jan. 1970; revised on 24 Jul. 1971 at Paris, entered into force on 10 Oct. 1974; amended on 28 Sep. 1979.
664. With respect to the United Republic of Tanzania, the Berne convention entered into force on 25 Jul. 1994. (cf. http://www.wipo.int/wipolex/en/results.jsp?countries=TZ&cat_id=11 (accessed: 2 May 2022)).
665. The countries to which this Convention applies constitute a Union for the protection of the rights of authors in their literary and artistic works (Art. 1 of the Berne Convention).
666. The TRIPS Agreement became effective in relation to the United Republic of Tanzania on 1 Jan. 1995.
667. The Paris Convention has been in force with respect to Tanzania since 16 Jun. 1963.

The HP within the Framework of the ARIPO,[668] 1982 to which the United Republic of Tanzania is a signatory[669] provides for the protection of industrial designs in ARIPO Member States such as Tanzania. Any design registered under the protocol, in respect of which Tanzania is a designated State, has the same effect in Tanzania as a design granted under the industrial designs law of Tanzania, unless the Tanzanian authorities object to such a design having effect in Tanzania.

§2. Subject Matter of Protection

241. The Patents (Registration) Act – which facilitates protection in Tanzania mainland of industrial designs already protected in the UK – does not define the subject matter of industrial designs protection. The industrial design laws in force in the UK of Great Britain serve as a focal reference point insofar as delineation of the subject matter of industrial design protection in mainland Tanzania is concerned.

On its part, ZIPA contains a clear delineation of the subject matter of protection under design law. According to section 2 of ZIPA, elements of a product that qualify for protection as an industrial design in Tanzania Zanzibar are those related to 'a combination of lines or colours or any three-dimensional form, whether or not associated with lines or colours, provided that such composition or form gives special appearance to a product of industry or handicraft and can serve as a pattern for a product of industry or handicraft, and appeals to and is judged by the eye'.[670]

§3. Conditions of Protection

242. To obtain protection for industrial designs in Tanzania mainland, the proprietor has to first secure protection in the UK. This position is stipulated under section 76 of the Patents (Registration) Act[671] in the following manner:

> the registered proprietor of any design registered in the United Kingdom under the Patents and Designs Acts, 1907 to 1932, or any Act amending or substituted for those Acts shall enjoy in Tanzania the like privileges and rights as though the Certificate of Registration in the United Kingdom had been issued with an extension to Tanzania.

668. The ARIPO is a regional organization (which was mainly for English-speaking countries) established in 1976 in order to facilitate the coordination, harmonization and development of the IP activities affecting its member States. At present, the following are ARIPO Member States: Botswana, The Gambia, Ghana, Kenya, Lesotho, Malawi, Mozambique, Namibia, Sierra Leone, Liberia, Rwanda, São Tomé and Príncipe, Somalia, Sudan, Swaziland, Uganda, United Republic of Tanzania, Zambia and Zimbabwe. In line with Art. VI of the Lusaka Agreement, ARIPO has concluded a cooperation agreement with twelve non-Member States; namely, Angola, Algeria, Burundi, Egypt, Eritrea, Ethiopia, Libya, Mauritius, Nigeria, Seychelles, South Africa and Tunisia. Cf. http://aripo.org/about-aripo/membership-member-states (accessed: 1May 2022).

669. The Harare Protocol is in force in the United Republic of Tanzania since 1 Sep. 1999.

670. Section 2, ZIPA.

671. Cap. 217 RE 2002.

In view of the foregoing; the patent office of Tanzania does not carry out any formal or substantive examination of industrial designs that becomes effective in Tanzania by virtue of registration in the UK. As a matter of principle, production of a certificate of design registration issued by the Patents and Trademarks Office of the UK generally entitles its holder a right to enforce his corresponding industrial design rights in Tanzania. Section 76 of the Patents (Registration) Act[672] subjects protection in Tanzania of the UK designs to other provisions contained in the patent law. These 'other' provisions are presumably those relating to patents and utility models. It, therefore, seems that an industrial design protected in the UK cannot be protected in Tanzania if it conflicts with a right protected in the latter country under a patent or a utility certificate.

On its part, the design protection regime established under the ZIPA, requires – as prerequisites for protection – that an industrial design should be new and non-functional.[673] An outline of these two requirements follows herein below.

I. Non-functional Elements

243. It is an acceptable position of the law that the design protection, which the ZIPA offers 'does not extend to anything in an industrial design, which serves solely to obtain a technical result and to the extent that it leaves no freedom as regards arbitrary features of appearance'.[674] Certain conclusions are implicit in this rule. First, design law does not aim at granting monopoly over utilitarian features of an article of manufacture or products; this objective is realized via patent law. Second, design law concerns with external appearance of products or articles of manufacture; it grants to manufacturer exclusive rights to apply or embody a design in an article in connection with which the design is registered. Third, manufacturers other than the holder of design rights are free to manufacture products with respect to which design rights are registered, provided that design elements identical or closely resembling the registered design are not applied or embodied in the products. Fourth, conceptual separation between design elements and utilitarian aspects of an article of manufacture is a determining factor for the grant of design rights: if these elements are inseparable, the design elements are said to be functional and hence no exclusive rights thereof can be granted.

Exclusion from protection under design law of functional features safeguards the designer's creative freedom. This exclusion has a logical support: some attributes or aspects of the product in which design features are embedded must inevitably be reproduced in their exact form if the product is to perform its function. Such unalterable product's features take away the designer's freedom of art; the designer is not free to change them. For this reason, he cannot be held liable for reproducing

672. Cap. 217 RE 2002.

673. This particular piece of legislation follows a general pattern of design law; it does not enshrine a provision requiring the designer to claim design protection for design elements featuring on the whole article to which the design relates; hence, the designer is at liberty to limit his claim of design rights to a part of the article, which is not functional (cf. *Ocular Sciences Ltd v. Aspect Vision Care* [1997] RPC 289).

674. Cf. s. 29, ZIPA.

such features; the law regards functional features as insignificant product features whose reproduction does not affect the scope of design protection. A hypothetical scenario can put a flesh on this conclusion: imagine Carpenter A creates a wooden stool, which has four legs and successfully applies for design registration. The truth that most of the standard stools have four legs cannot be questioned. Consequently, no one can invoke the design rights subsisting in Carpenter A's stool to prohibit Carpenter B from creating a four legs stool, provided that the latter stool does not contain the design features of the former.

II. Novelty and Originality of a Design

244. One of the central requirements under the ZIPA in relation to designs registrable in Tanzania Zanzibar is that which makes a registration dependent on the novelty of the design sought to be registered.[675] According to ZIPA, an 'industrial design is new if it has not been disclosed to the public, anywhere in the world, by application in tangible form or by use or in any other way, prior to the filing date or, where applicable, the priority date of the application for registration'.[676]

One of the factors to be taken into account when assessing whether a particular design is new or original is the overall impression the article in which the design is applied or embodied produces: if on the basis of this impression the designs examining officer is of the view that the design sought to be registered is markedly different from other prior arts, he would register the design in issue. In assessing such impression, the examiner normally has to don the spectacles of a 'designer of ordinary skills' who is aware of the prior arts in the designs industry. The 'designer of ordinary skills' test makes sense; 'a [designer] who has experience of other similar articles will be reasonably discriminatory – able to appreciate enough detail to decide whether a design creates an overall impression'.[677]

§4. Formalities: Procedure for Obtaining Protection

245. In cases other than those concerning design protection under Copyright law of Tanzania whereby nothing else than creation and fixation of an artistic work is required to guarantee copyright protection for the artistic design elements of the work concerned, an application for design registration under the ZIPA is a stepping stone to the acquisition of industrial design protection in Tanzania Zanzibar. In this regard, the proprietor has to apply to the registrar in charge of the Industrial Property Office of Zanzibar (IPOZ) for the registration of the design concerned.[678]

675. Cf. s. 30, ZIPA. The novelty and originality requirements enshrined in the ZIPA are in full accord with the stipulation of Art. 25(1) of the TRIPS Agreement.
676. Cf. s. 30(2), ZIPA.
677. Cf. *Procter & Gamble Company v. Reckitt Benckiser (UK) Ltd* [2007] EWCA Civ 936, para. 23.
678. IPOZ is established under s. 115, ZIPA.

I. Conditions for Acceptance of Application

246. In order to be accepted by IPOZ, an application for design registration in Tanzania Zanzibar must be filed by a person entitled to make such an application. Section 31 read together with section 5 of the ZIPA, hints at two categories of persons in whom the right to file an application for the registration of a particular design in Tanzania Zanzibar is vested. These are: (i) the creator or the proprietor of the design; and (ii) the legal representative of the proprietor.

In certain circumstances, the IPOZ cannot accept an application for industrial design registration notwithstanding the fact that the applicant thereof legally qualifies to make such an application. The IPOZ accepts only applications that contain the following information: (i) particulars of the creator or the applicant (if the creator is not the applicant, in which case the applicant has to accompany his application with evidence sufficiently justifying his entitlement to the registration of the industrial design concerned); and (ii) request and particulars of the industrial design under application such as 'drawings, photographs or other adequate graphic representations of the article embodying the industrial design and an indication of the kind of products for which the industrial design is to be used';[679] and (iii) declaration of priority where one is claimed.

II. Examination of Application

247. The registrar has powers to register or not to register designs whose protection is sought in Tanzania Zanzibar. In so doing, the registrar is guided by the letters of the law.[680] Upon receiving an application for registration of a particular design, the law requires the registrar to cause that application to be examined for compliance with the conditions for acceptance of the application for designs registration outlined above in §4(I) of this chapter. The registrar must further carry out substantive examination to determine whether the design for which registration is sought meets the conditions of protection, of being new or original, outlined above in §3 of this chapter. The usual way to ascertain whether the design under application is new is the search which the Registrar does to see if the claimed industrial design is already available in the prior art.

In the event the application meets the conditions for design registration and protection in Tanzania under the ZIPA, the registrar will register the design in the register kept in the IPOZ. Prior to registering an industrial design in the register, the registrar has to advertise the design application in the Official *Gazette*. The registrar is also duty-bound to advertise an industrial property in the Official Gazette, once he grants registration thereof.[681]

679. Cf. s. 32, ZIPA.
680. Cf. s. 33, ZIPA.
681. Cf. s. 34, ZIPA.

§5. Ownership and Transfer: Assignment, Licences

I. Ownership

248. In relation to designs protection in Tanzania Zanzibar, Zimbabwe Investment and Development Agency provides for three scenarios of ownership of designs. The first scenario establishes the creator as the owner, whereas the second scenario refers to creation under contractual obligation either explicitly (e.g., by commission) or by implied terms (e.g., under contract of employment), whereby an industrial design created in the course of one's employment becomes the property of the employer, and the one created by an independent contractor becomes the property of the person who has commissioned the contractor to create the design concerned.[682]

II. Transfer of Rights

249. As the case is with other IP rights discussed in previous chapters of this monograph, industrial design rights registered and protected in Tanzania Zanzibar are capable of being transferred. Such a transfer can be realized through assignments and licences as well as through transmission or operation of law.[683]

§6. Scope of Exclusive Rights

250. Persons owning industrial designs registered and protected under ZIPA enjoy a right to 'prevent others from exploiting the registered industrial design in Zanzibar'. In particular, the proprietor is entitled to prohibit third persons from commercially making, selling or importing articles in which his registered industrial design is embodied.[684]

§7. Limitations of the Scope of Protection

I. The Principle of Exhaustion of Rights

251. According to ZIPA, the principle of exhaustion of patent rights serves as a limitation to the exclusive exploitation right protected in Tanzania Zanzibar that the owner of industrial designs is entitled to. ZIPA provides for the principle of international exhaustion. According to relevant provisions of the law, the rights under industrial designs do not cover 'acts in respect of articles which have been put on

682. Cf. s. 31 read together with s. 5, ZIPA.
683. Cf. s. 31 read together with s. 5(4), ZIPA.
684. Cf. s. 34, ZIPA.

the market in any territory or country by the owner of the (industrial design) or by any party authorized, consequently exhausting the owner's (rights subsisting in an industrial design)'.[685]

II. Term of Protection

252. The owner or possessor of an industrial design protected in the United Republic of Tanzania cannot enforce his exclusive rights thereof against third parties beyond the duration within which the rights are protected.[686] The time span of an industrial design protected in Tanzania is outlined below in §8 of this chapter.

§8. Duration of Design Protection

253. Industrial designs are protected in Tanzania Zanzibar under ZIPA for a maximum period of fifteen years of three cumulative terms of five years for each term. The initial term is granted immediately following positive examination of the industrial design sought to be registered and the term runs retrospectively 'from the filing date of the application for registration' of the design. Extension of the initial term of protection to the second term and/or the third term depends on the question whether the owner of a registered industrial design has timely applied for such an extension and paid the prescribed extension fee. Usually, an extension of design protection is supposed to be done before the term sought to be extended comes to an end. However, the law provides for a grace period of three months following the expiry of the current term within which the design proprietor can submit to the Industrial Property Office of Tanzania Zanzibar an admissible application for the extension of protection of his industrial design rights.[687]

The term of protection of industrial designs registered in the UK of Great Britain whose effectiveness extends automatically to the United Republic of Tanzania by virtue of section 76 of the Patents (Registration) Act applicable to mainland Tanzania, has to be determined according to English laws on industrial designs.

§9. Infringement and Remedies

I. Infringement

254. It constitutes infringement of rights in a design registered in Tanzania Zanzibar if a third party exercises any of the exclusive rights outlined above in §6 of

685. Cf. s. 34(3) read together with s. 12(4)(a)(i), ZIPA.
686. Cf. s. 34(5), ZIPA.
687. *Ibid.*

this chapter. Nevertheless, to constitute infringement such exploitation has to be of commercial nature and is done without the consent of the proprietor of the registered industrial design concerned.[688]

The Patents (Registration) Act in force in Tanzania mainland acknowledges the fact that industrial designs may be protected under copyright.[689] Thus, in order for the proprietor of the UK design rights to recover damages in respect of copyright infringement of his design rights effective in Tanzania by virtue of automatic extension to the territory of Tanzania on the basis of registration of those rights in the UK of Great Britain in accordance with section 76 of the Patents (Registration) Act, he must prove that the infringement was intentional. To achieve this end, the proprietor must show that the infringer was aware or had any reasonable means of making himself aware of the existence of the design rights in Tanzania. Even where the proprietor is unable to prove as above he will still be entitled to an injunctive relief prohibiting future copyright infringement of his design rights.[690]

The High Court of Tanzania is vested in jurisdiction to deal with action or legal proceedings appertaining infringement of industrial designs.[691]

II. Remedies

255. Any person whose interests have been prejudicially affected by a person purporting to enjoy industrial design protection in Tanzania either based on industrial designs rights protected in the UK – as extended to Tanzania under section 76 of the Patents (Registration) Act – or based on industrial designs protected in Tanzania Zanzibar under ZIPA,[692] may ask the court to declare that such protection does not exist in Tanzania. The grounds upon which this declaration can be made in relation to design rights registered in the UK include 'any of the grounds upon which United Kingdom registration might be cancelled under the law for the time being in force in the United Kingdom'.[693] Such a declaration may as well be made upon proof that the protected design was published 'in Tanzania prior to the date of registration of the design in the United Kingdom'.[694]

There are various remedies that can be awarded to a successful party in a suit concerning infringement of a right subsisting in an industrial design protected in the United Republic of Tanzania. Some of the possible remedies are damages, interdict and injunctions.[695]

688. Cf. s. 75, ZIPA.
689. Cf. s. 77, Patents (Registration) Act, Cap. 217 RE 2002.
690. *Ibid.*
691. Cf. s. 34(4), ZIPA.
692. Cf. ss 75 & 34(4), ZIPA.
693. Cf. s. 78, Patents (Registration) Act, Cap. 217 RE 2002.
694. *Ibid.*
695. Cf. ss 75 & 34(4), ZIPA.

§10. Overlapping and Relation to Other IP Rights

256. To the extent that the Tanzanian law governing industrial designs excludes functional aspects from industrial design protection the possibility of overlap with patent protection is excluded.

Given that the trademark law of the United Republic of Tanzania – apart from protecting traditional trademarks – also protects figurative marks such as patterns, ornamentation, shapes and configurations, it is also possible to protect these items under both industrial design law and trademark protection regime. However, protection of an industrial design as a trademark is only possible if the design concerned meets the protection requirements under the trademark law outlined in Chapter 4 of this chapter.

With respect to copyright law, the Patents (Registration) Act in force in mainland Tanzania enshrines a provision that hints at the possibility of protecting a design under both copyright law and design law,[696] provided that such a design fulfils the conditions for protection as an artistic work in which a copyright subsists as well as a design that can be applied industrially to articles of manufacture.

696. Cf. s. 77, Patents (Registration) Act, Cap. 217 RE 2002.

Chapter 6. Trade and Service Marks

§1. Sources: Legislation

257. The trade and service marks protection regime in place in the United Republic of Tanzania is based on two distinct pieces of principal legislation. One of these pieces of legislation is the Trade and Service Marks Act of 1986 (Act 12 of 1986) (TSMA). This legislation provides for protection of trade and service marks rights that are generally effective in Tanzania mainland. On the contrary, the ZIPA establishes a trade and service mark protection regime exclusively for Tanzania Zanzibar.

The TSMA traces its roots from the UK. It repealed Trade Marks Ordinance (Principle Legislation) Chapter 394 of the Laws of Tanzania of 1958, whose section 69 repealed the Trade Marks Ordinance Chapter 216 of 1922. The 1922 and 1958 Trade Mark Laws were respectively modelled on the Trade Mark Acts, 1905–1919 and the Trade Marks Act, 1938 of the UK. Prior to the 1986 TSMA, service marks could not be protected in Tanzania and registration of trademarks was dependent on a respective mark being registered in the UK.[697] The Trade and Service Marks Regulations, 2000 (TMRs)[698] complement and implement the substantive provisions of the TSMA.

The MMA (Act No. 20 of 1963) is another significant piece of legislation relevant for trade mark protection in mainland Tanzania. This principal legislation regulates issues concerning counterfeits of trademarks and trade descriptions. The Merchandise Marks Act Regulations, 2008[699] complement and implement provisions of the MMA.

ZIPA is a comprehensive piece of legislation covering protection of all major industrial property rights in Tanzania Zanzibar. Part III of ZIPA provides for protection of distinctive signs. Trade and service marks are a category of distinctive signs protectable under the provisions of ZIPA. ZIPA came into force on 29 July 2008; and effectively repealed and replaced the Trade Marks Decree, 1932 (Chapter 159 of the laws of Zanzibar). The Industrial Property Regulations of 2014[700] complement and implement provisions of ZIPA. The Regulations came into force on 17 April 2015.

There are various international, regional, bilateral and multilateral legal instruments on trade mark protection which, by virtue of the United Republic of Tanzania

697. Estaliano Mahingila, *Intellectual Property Landscape in Tanzania – The Emerging Role of the Business Registration and Licensing Agency (BRELA) in Assisting Small Medium Enterprises Use Intellectual Property*, A paper presented during the WIPO Workshop on IP for Business for Small Medium-Sized Enterprises (SMES) held on 10 and 11 May 2005, at Dar Es Salaam. Paper available in WIPO document reference No. WIPO/SMEs/DAR/05/.

698. These regulations were enacted on 3 Mar. 2000 and published in the Government Gazette as a Government Notice (GN) No. 40 of 2000.

699. Published in the Government Gazette on 20 Jun. 2008 as Government Notice (GN) No. 89 of 2008.

700. Published as *Legal Supplement (Part II) to the Zanzibar Government Gazette Vol. CXXIV No. 6558D of 17th April 2015.*

having assented to them, are applicable in both Tanzania mainland and Tanzania Zanzibar. The most relevant regional and/or international legal instrument include:

African Regional Intellectual Property Organization (ARIPO) – The Banjul Protocol on Marks, 1993 (BPM):[701] This Protocol, which facilitates regional trade and service marks registration in Tanzania, is complemented by the Regulations for Implementing the BPM (henceforth, the BPM Regulations). Provisions of the BPM form part of the Lusaka Agreement on the creation of an Industrial Property Organization for English-Speaking Africa of December 1976 (as amended). The Agreement empowers ARIPO to enact some Protocols that are necessary to define the functions and powers of ARIPO in specific fields of intellectual property rights, trade marks in particular. The central object of the BPM is to define legal competence of ARIPO in relation trademark registration and protection framework in ARIPO Member States, such as the United Republic of Tanzania.[702]

Paris Convention for the Protection of Industrial Property of 20 March 1883 (as amended and revised) (Paris Convention): The United Republic of Tanzania became party to the Paris Convention on 16 June 1963. Both the TSMA and ZIPA enshrine provisions referring to the Paris Convention. The delineation of the terms 'Convention' in Section 2 of the TSMA and 'Paris Convention' in Section 2 of ZIPA and the specific references these two pieces of legislation make to the Paris Convention's key trade mark principles such as the principle of priority right, attest to the good intention of the United Republic to domestic provisions of the Paris Convention. The Paris Convention's relevance to the protection of trade and service marks is evident mainly under Articles 1, 6, 7, 9 and 10 of the Paris Convention.

World Trade Organization (WTO) – Agreement on Trade-Related Aspects of Intellectual Property Rights (TRIPS Agreement) (1995): The Agreement came into force with regard to the United Republic of Tanzania on 1 January 1995. The relevance of the TRIPS Agreement to the protection of trade and service marks is evident mainly under Articles 15 to 21 of the Agreement.

701. Adopted by the Administrative Council at Banjul, The Gambia, on 19 Nov. 1993 and as amended from time to time.

702. Cf. the Lusaka Agreement on the creation of an Industrial Property Organization for English-Speaking Africa of December 1976, as amended by the administrative council of ARIPO on 10 Dec. 1982, 12 Dec. 1986 and 27 Nov. 1996, and as amended by the Council of Ministers on 13 Aug. 2004.

§2. Subject Matter of Protection

I. Signs Which May Serve as Trade Marks

258. To potentially qualify for registration and protection, as a trade or service mark, in Tanzania mainland, a sign must meet the relevant criteria. Section 2 of the TSMA describes the term 'trade or service mark' in the following manner:

> 'trade or service mark' means 'any visible sign used or proposed to be used upon, in connection with or in relation to goods or services for the purpose of distinguishing in the course of trade or business the goods or services of a person from those of another'.

One of the key terms used in the above quotation is the term 'visible sign'. Clarification of this term is required for a thorough understanding of the term 'trade or service mark'. Section 2 of the TSMA offers the following definition:

> 'Visible sign' means any sign which is capable of being reproduced graphically, such as a 'word, name, brand, device, heading, label, ticket, signature, letter number, relief, stamp, seal, vignette, emblem or any combination thereof'.

Section 2 of ZIPA uses the following explanation in relation to conditions applying to signs registrable as trade or service marks in Tanzania Zanzibar:

> 'Mark' means any sign susceptible of being specifically represented graphically that is capable of distinguishing goods ('trade mark') or services ('service mark') of one undertaking from those of other undertaking. A mark may, in particular, consist of words (including personal names), designs, letters, colors or combinations of colors, numerals or the shape of goods or their packaging, holograms, sounds and scents. Slogans, when they are not long enough to be protected by copyright, shall be protected as marks

Both TSMA and ZIPA protect, as a trade or service mark, any sign that possesses the capability of being portrayed graphically in the register of trade marks. However, the two pieces of legislation use different terms when referring to the manner of realizing such portrayal of the registrable trade mark. Whereas TSMA uses the noun 'reproduction' after the adjective 'graphic', the noun 'representation' supersedes the adjective 'graphic' under ZIPA. The difference, if any, between the terms 'graphic reproduction' and 'graphic representation' is more semantic and apparent than real. From a practical point of view, both terms have the same meaning. Regulation 19 of the TMRs clarifies this position by revealing the legislative intent behind the use of the term 'graphical reproduction' instead of the now more conventional term 'graphical representation' used in trade mark legislation of various jurisdictions such as Tanzania Zanzibar. Regulation 19, mentioned in the immediately preceding sentence, does not use the term 'graphical reproduction' appearing in TSMA; it employs the term 'graphical representation' in the following manner:

> Every application for the registration of a mark shall contain a durable graphic representation of the mark in the space provided on the application form for that purpose.

Therefore, one can safely endorse the view that, both TSMA and ZIPA incorporate the requirement of a registrable trade mark to be capable of graphical representation/reproduction.

Section 2 of both TSMA and ZIPA enshrine a list of signs that generally possess capability of graphical representation. That list is by no means exhaustive; it is open to any other signs which meet the thresholds for graphical representation/ reproduction.

The WIPO has commented on the categorization of signs that are capable of constituting a registrable trade mark as hereunder:

> It follows from the purpose of the trademark that virtually any sign that can serve to distinguish goods from other goods is capable of constituting a trademark. Trademark laws should not therefore attempt to draw up an exhaustive list of signs admitted for registration. If examples are given, they should be a practical illustration of what can be registered, without being exhaustive. If there are to be limitations, they should be based on practical considerations only, such as the need for a workable register and the need for publication of the registered trademark.[703]

In addition to fulfilling the requirements for graphical representation, a sign registrable as a trade or service mark must comply with the conditions of being distinctive. It must be noted that, a legally acceptable trade mark use is that which, as its effect, enables the mark to distinguish the goods or services in relation to which the mark's actual or intended use can be demonstrated from same goods or services connected in the course of trade with a person other than the rightful user of the aforesaid trade mark.

The position regarding attributes required of a sign that may serve as a trade mark under both TSMA and ZIPA fully complies with the minimum requirements a registrable sign has to meet under Article 15.1 of the Agreement on TRIPS. According to this provision of TRIPS, 'Any sign, or any combination of signs, capable of distinguishing the goods or services of one undertaking from those of other undertakings, shall be capable of constituting a trade mark.' Similarly, section 2 of both TSMA and ZIPA require a registrable sign to be capable of making it possible to distinguish the products or services of one company from those of other companies. As regards the definition of a sign capable of constituting a trade mark, TRIPS on one hand as well as both TSMA and ZIPA on the other, share a common attribute; namely, they all allow registration and protection of distinctive signs. It is indisputable that many signs are capable of distinguishing goods and services.[704] The threshold upon which this capability of a sign to distinguish goods or services is

703. WIPO IP Handbook, 2nd edn, Publication No. 489 (E), at p. 70.
704. W. Cornish & D. Llewelyn, *Intellectual Property: Patents, Copyrights, Trade Marks and Allied Rights* 696 (Sweet & Maxwell 6th ed. 2007).

judged is straightforwardly clear; the sign is assessed abstractly by considering the sign apart from the goods or services associated with that sign.[705] The distinctiveness requirement under section 2 of both TSMA and ZIPA on one hand, and under Article 15.1 of the Agreement on TRIPS on the other, only suggests signs or combination of signs, which are capable of registration, but which are not necessarily registrable as trade mark in the United Republic of Tanzania.[706] Therefore, both TSMA and ZIPA do not entail obligation to register a trade mark simply because a sign involved is distinctive. The trade mark authorities, in both Tanzania mainland and Tanzania Zanzibar, are not limited by the notion of distinctiveness when deciding on registrability of a sign as a trade mark. They are also entitled to take into account other factors included in the national law. It is pertinent to note that provisions of section 2 of both TSMA and ZIPA add to the distinctiveness requirement a condition qualifying a sign for registration as a trade mark if such a sign possesses the capability of being specifically represented/reproduced graphically.

The TRIPS Agreement does not stipulate the capability of a trade mark to be represented graphically as a condition of trade mark protection. However, a municipal legislation, such as TSMA and ZIPA, subjecting registration of a trade mark to the mark's capability of being represented graphically does not come into conflict with the provisions of the TRIPS Agreement; such a legislation is, acceptably, said to be above the minimum requirements for trade mark protection, which the TRIPS Agreement stipulates. Given that the requirement is contained in the national law, whose legal force is recognized under Article 6.1 of the Paris Convention,[707] the graphical representation requirement under Article 2 of both TSMA and ZIPA is justifiable under Article 15.2 of the TRIPS Agreement, according to which the distinctiveness requirement 'shall not be understood to prevent a Member State from denying registration of a trademark on other grounds, which do not derogate from the provisions of the Paris Convention (1967)'.

II. Categories of Trademarks

A. *Certification Marks*

259. The Standards Act, 2009 (Act No. 2 of 2009) and the Standards (Certification) Regulations of 2009[708] establish a scheme for certifying standards of products or services. Section 3 of the Standards Act establishes the Tanzania Bureau of Standards (TBS). The TBS is 'the custodian and an overseer of observance of standards in Tanzania'. In line with section 4 of the Standards Act, the mandate of the

705. I.M. Davies ed., *Sweet & Maxwell's European Trade Mark Litigation Handbook* 36 (Sweet & Maxwell 1998).

706. WTO, TRIPS Agreement – Art. 15 (Jurisprudence). https://www.wto.org/english/res_e/publications_e/ai17_e/trips_art15_jur.pdf (accessed: 12 May 2020).

707. According to Article 6.1 of the Paris Convention, the 'conditions for the filing and registration of trademarks shall be determined in each country of the Union by its domestic legislation'. Consequently, the BIPL is the main law that has to govern the registration and protection of trade marks in Tanzania.

708. Government Notice No. 406 published on 25 Dec. 2009.

TBS extends to approving, registering and controlling 'the use of standards mark in accordance with the provisions of (Standards) Act'. Any manufacturer whose products conform to the standards recognized by the TBS is eligible for a licence to use the TBS standards mark depicted below:

tbs

MARK APPLIED ON THE PRODUCT
WITH A NUMBER FOR THE
RELEVANT TANZANIA STANDARD
(TZS ....)

(TZS ....

The above 'tbs' Standards Mark of Quality is a registered trade mark, which can be licensed to manufacturers conforming to the rigorous quality auditing requirements of the standards mark licensing procedures. Where such a standards mark is applied on a product, it will be prima facie evidence of the fact 'that samples of the product are independently and routinely tested and certified by TBS against relevant Tanzania standards'.[709]

It is important to note that there is no provision in the TSMA that is specifically devoted to the protection of certification marks in mainland Tanzania. As long as a sign possesses qualities of a certification mark, the trademark office in Mainland Tanzania will find no justification to exclude such a mark from registration as such.

ZIPA provides for protection of certification marks in Tanzania Zanzibar. As employed under ZIPA, the term 'certification signs' refers to 'signs or combination of signs capable of designating any common characteristic, including quality, origin or methods of production, of goods and services and which are used under the control of the owner of the signs'.[710] Usually, a certification mark is used to certify standards of goods or services. A sign applied to products or used in relation to services, that meet certain prescribed standards in order to differentiate standards of those products or services conforming to the prescribed standards from products or services not meeting those standards, qualifies for registration and protection as a certification mark. In addition to the foregoing, there are two further conditions governing protection of certification marks in Tanzania Zanzibar: the owner of the mark – whose role is confined to a duty to exercise control over the marking of goods so that its certification mark is only applied to products that meet the prescribed standards – must not be the one who uses the mark insofar as the marking of goods or services is concerned.

A certain form of legal personality is required for one to qualify as an applicant for protection of a certification mark. It is intended that the applicant would be a registered association or a limited liability company controlling or intending to control conformity, to standards, of goods or services in relation to which the certification mark is used.

In order for a certification mark to be registered, an applicant must prove to the satisfaction of the office of the Registrar of trade marks that they are competent to

709. At http://www.tbs.go.tz/index.php/services/category/certification_services (accessed: 13 May 2020).

710. Cf. s. 2(1), para. 4, ZIPA.

certify the goods and services in respect of which the certification mark is used. The applicant's certification competence can be proved through the regulations drafted by them governing the use of their mark and standards appertaining goods and/or services in relation to which the certification mark is used. These rules and standards form part of the application for registration and must be submitted to the office of the Registrar of trade marks. It is necessary that the rules specify the conditions for the use of the mark, the circumstances in which the proprietor is to certify the goods or services and in respect of which characteristics of the goods or services or any other aspects the applicant will use the mark to certify the goods or services: It is on the basis of these rules that the registrar is able to draw an inference as to whether the applicant is competent as above.

The following conditions circumscribe the extent to which a certification mark enjoys protection in Zanzibar: (1) the registrant does not enjoy a right to exclude third parties from using the trade mark in relation to goods that have quality or characteristics of the goods in relation to which the certification mark is normally used to certify; (2) the proprietor of a certification mark is not allowed to use the mark to certify its goods or services: the proprietor's benefits in relation to the mark is mainly based on a fee chargeable for rendering certification services to users of the certification mark; and (3) so as a certification mark to qualify for registration, an applicant's competence to certify the goods and services in respect of which the certification mark is used must be properly established.[711]

ZIPA sets a time limit within which an interested party can challenge the validity of a certification mark protected in Tanzania Zanzibar. In this regard, one must institute invalidation proceedings within five years of the sign's registration; beyond this period the sign's validity becomes incontestable.[712] Factors that may render invalid a sign enjoying registration as a certification mark in Tanzania Zanzibar include where: (1) the proprietor of the certification mark applies it to his goods or uses it to market service he offers; and (2) the proprietor of the mark allows it to be used in a way that misleads or confuses marketers and the public at large insofar as the origin and quality (or other characteristic) of the products or services in relation to which the sign is used are concerned.[713]

B. Collective Marks

260. There is no specific provision under the TSMA providing for protection of collective marks in Tanzania mainland. Whether a trademark qualifies for registration and protection in Tanzania mainland as such, it all boils down to the question of whether such a mark meets the necessary conditions of trademark protection.

Section 51 of ZIPA, read together with Regulation 70 of the ZIPARs, establishes the legal protection of collective marks in Tanzania Zanzibar. A collective trade mark is constituted by a mark capable of distinguishing, in the course of trade,

711. Cf. s. 52, ZIPA.
712. Cf. s. 50(I)(b), ZIPA.
713. Cf. s. 52(3), ZIPA.

goods or services of persons who are members of any association from goods or services of persons who are not members thereof. In this sense, a sign that qualifies for registration as a collective mark under the ZIPA is that which belongs to a 'collectivity, such as a cooperative or an association or federation of industrialists, producers or merchants'.[714]Several categories of marks including geographical names or other indications of geographical origin may qualify for registration and protection as collective trade marks in Tanzania Zanzibar. Only an association can become a rightful proprietor of a collective trade or service mark hence a qualifying applicant for registration of such a trade mark.

A proprietor of a collective trademark has to discharge certain obligations so as to secure registration of the mark in Tanzania Zanzibar. First and foremost, the applicant has to state clearly in the application that the mark applied for is a collective mark. It is also a *sine qua non* that the applicant accompanies their application for registration of the collective mark with some rules prescribing the context in which the collective mark concerned is to be used. A trader acquires the right to apply the collective trade mark to the goods not only if these goods meet the standards prescribed in the rules governing the use of the collective mark, but also such a trader must belong to the association or cooperative. In the event the association owning the collective trade mark amends or modifies the rules governing the use of the mark, a legal obligation requiring the trade mark proprietor to inform the Registrar of trade marks about the modifications arises, since the association cannot use the amended rules to regulate the use of a collective trade mark, unless the registrar sanctions such use.

As regards the qualifications of the applicant for collective marks, the requirement that the applicant 'possesses an industrial or commercial establishment anywhere in a Member of the Paris Union or a Member of the World Trade Organization' – as is a case for other categories of trademarks – does not apply in respect of collective marks.[715] Moreover, the organization owning a collective mark has a right to use the mark involved. Any member of the association is entitled to use a registered collective trade mark belonging to the association as long as the goods or services in relation to which the mark is used meet the standards prescribed under the regulations governing that collective mark. Use of a collective mark by individual members of the association owning the mark constitutes use of the mark by that association; and such use is a sufficient proof for any purpose where the use of that mark is required under the law.

C. Well-known Trademarks

261. Legal protection of well-known trade or service marks is available in both Tanzania mainland and Tanzania Zanzibar. Although TSMA enshrines a relevant provision on well-known trade marks, it does not outline the meaning of the term

714. Cf. s. 2, para. 6, ZIPA.
715. Cf. s. 51, ZIPA.

'well-known trade mark'. However, ZIPA contains the relevant delineation. Accordingly, 'marks that are considered to be well known by the competent authority of the country where protection for the mark is sought' can enjoy protection as 'well-known marks'.[716]

To the extent that it does not provide for a specific definition of the term 'well-known mark', TSMA has adopted a position that is also common under both the Paris Convention and the TRIPS Agreement.[717] This lacuna is not without any significance: a trademark's 'well-known' status is a subjective and factually verifiable attribute. Basically, trademarks do enjoy legal protection mainly in two capacities; namely, as registered trademarks, and as unregistered trademarks. Protection of the latter being specifically availed under the law of passing off.[718] Indeed these multiple scenarios of trade mark protection liberalize the trade mark governance regime. On the contrary, however, they constrain the legislature in its attempt to devise a definition of a well-known trade mark embracing all scenarios under which protection of a well-known trade mark can be considered.

The regime for protection of well-known marks is founded on the principle established under Article 6*bis*(1) of the Paris Convention.[719] This Article stipulates as follows:

> The countries of the Union undertake, ex officio if their legislation so permits, or at the request of an interested party, to refuse or to cancel the registration, and to prohibit the use, of a trademark which constitutes a reproduction, an imitation, or a translation, liable to create confusion, of a mark considered by the competent authority of the country of registration or use to be well-known in that country as being already the mark of a person entitled to the benefits of this Convention and used for identical or similar goods. These provisions shall also apply when the essential part of the mark constitutes a reproduction of any such well-known mark or an imitation liable to create confusion therewith.

Article 6*bis*(1) of the Paris Convention does not operate in isolation; it has a link with, and is enforced by, other legal provisions. Notable in this regard is Article 16(2) of TRIPS Agreement. This provision extends protection of a well-known trade mark, within the context of Article 6*bis*(1) of the Paris Convention, to service marks.

Article 16(3) of TRIPS Agreement implements the regime for the protection of well-known marks enshrined in the Paris Convention; it stipulates that:

---

716. Section 2, TSMA.
717. Michael Blakeney, *The Protection of Well-known Trademarks*, Paper delivered at a WIPO seminar on IP at the University of Cairo in February 2003, retrieved from https://www.wipo.int/edocs/mdocs/arab/en/2003/ip_cai_1/pdf/wipo_ip_cai_1_03_8a.pdf (accessed: 16 Feb. 2022).
718. Section 30, TSMA. In relation to trade mark enforcement under the tort of passing off, *see also* Harms, L.T., *A Casebook on the Enforcement of Intellectual Property Rights* 47 (WIPO 2008).
719. The Paris Convention, to which reference is made in s. 35, is the Paris Convention on the Protection of Industrial Property of 20 Mar. 1883 as revised or amended from time to time (s. 2, TMA).

> Article 6*bis* of the Paris Convention (1967) shall apply, mutatis mutandis, to goods or services which are not similar to those in respect of which a trademark is registered, provided that use of that trademark in relation to those goods or services would indicate a connection between those goods or services and the owner of the registered trademark and provided that the interests of the owner of the registered trademark are likely to be damaged by such use.

The basic provision governing protection of well-known marks in Tanzania mainland is section 19(d) of TSMA. This provision extends negative rights to proprietors of well-known marks; it excludes from being accepted for registration and protection in Tanzania mainland 'trade or service marks which constitute reproductions in whole or in part, imitations, translations or transcriptions, liable to create confusion of trade or service marks ... which are well known in the country and belong to third parties'.

On the face value, section 19(d) of TSMA fully complies with the provisions of the Paris Convention and the TRIPs Agreement quoted above. Indeed, section 19(d) of TSMA extends protection to registered or unregistered trade or service marks, which are well known in Tanzania mainland, irrespective of whether the marks concerned are local or foreign marks. However, in terms of section 27 of TSMA, section 19(d) of TSMA seems to protect unregistered well-known trade or service marks only if they have been used, in relation to goods or services, in Tanzania mainland.

Section 46(2)(v) of ZIPA takes a centre stage in relation to the protection of well-known trade or service marks in Tanzania Zanzibar. It enshrines negative rights, by prohibiting registration as a trade or service mark of a sign, which is:

> ... identical with, or confusingly similar to, or constitutes translation of, a mark or trade name which is well known in Zanzibar for identical or similar goods or services of another enterprise, or if it is well-known and registered in Zanzibar for goods or services which are not identical or similar to those in respect of which registration is applied for, provided, in the latter case, that use of the mark in relation to those goods or services would indicate a connection between those goods or services and the owner of the well-known mark and that the interests of the owner of the well-known mark are likely to be damaged by such use.

§3. Conditions of Protection

262. An analysis of absolute or relative grounds for trademark refusal provides an answer to the question whether a particular trade or service mark meets the protection criteria. The TSMA describes these grounds under section 16, whereas the relevant provision under ZIPA is section 46.

I. Absolute Grounds

263. Absolute grounds for trade mark refusal are the legal justifications upon which registration of a sign as a trade or service mark may be refused based on the characteristics or attributes of that mark. The aim of these grounds is to exclude from registration various types of marks such as those which lack distinctiveness, those which are descriptive marks and those which are generic. Other marks to which absolute grounds for registration refusal apply include those which directly or indirectly make use of insignias of the State and of international and/or intergovernmental organizations, just to mention but a few. A brief discussion on these grounds follows hereunder.

A. *Lack of Distinctiveness*

264. Distinctiveness of a sign is one of the factors to consider when determining issues relating to the sign's registrability as a trade or service mark in Tanzania mainland or Tanzania Zanzibar. According to both the TSMA and ZIPA, any sign that lacks distinctiveness does not deserve an outright acceptance for registration. In stipulating this position, sections 16 and 46 of TSMA and ZIPA, respectively, subject registrability of a trade or service mark to the condition according to which such a mark must be capable of distinguishing the goods or services of one source, in respect of which it is registered or proposed to be registered from the goods or services of another origin either generally or where the trade mark is registered or proposed to be registered subject to limitations, in relation to use within those limitations. In other words, a validly registrable trade mark must possess capability to distinguish goods or services of one firm from those of other firms. The burden to prove that the mark is distinctive lies with the applicant for trade registration.

The threshold for distinctiveness under sections 16 and 46 of TSMA and ZIPA, respectively, is distinct from that, which a definition of a sign capable of functioning as a trade mark provided for under section 2 of both TMSA and ZIPA envisages. A sign could be excluded from registration, under section 16 of TSMA and section 46 of ZIPA, merely because it does not enable the public to associate it with a particular source of goods. Section 2 of both TSMA and ZIPA confirms a sign's distinctiveness based on abstract analysis of that sign. Thus, the trade mark law applicable in both Tanzania mainland and Tanzania Zanzibar would support a trade mark registrar's decision to accept for registration of a sign which is yet to acquire distinctiveness as regards particular goods or services, but whose use in trade would enable consumers associate such a sign with the relevant source of goods or services for which the mark is registered. In this sense, the distinctiveness of a trademark capable of registration and protection in the two independent trade mark jurisdictions of the United Republic of Tanzania is twofold in nature; namely, inherent distinctiveness and acquired distinctiveness or acquired secondary meaning. A mark that is inherently distinctive deserves outright protection by way of registration, unless there are some other grounds for denying such protection. Factors that the registrar of trade marks may take into account when determining whether a particular mark has acquired distinctiveness through use include the market share of the trade mark proprietor with regard to the relevant mark of the goods and services marketed or offered under the mark, duration of use made of the mark, the amount of resources used to market the goods and services in relation to which the mark is used and the extent to which the public is knowledgeable about the mark.[720] Acquired distinctiveness relates to a mark that initially lacked distinctiveness, but which, following the commercial use made of it, acquired a secondary meaning giving it the capability to distinguish goods and/or services of the trade mark proprietor from goods and services of other commercial origins.

B. Descriptive Marks

265. Descriptive marks cannot function as trade or service marks for lack of distinctiveness within the meaning of sections 19 and 46 of TSMA and ZIPA respectively. Regulation 16 of TMRs permits registration of trade or service containing words describing goods or services designated by that mark. However, the trade or service mark proprietor does not acquire exclusive right in the descriptive words by virtue of the registration of the mark. The trade mark law excludes descriptive marks from being monopolized as trade or service marks, given that these marks are incapable of distinguishing goods and services of the sign's proprietor from those of other undertakings. The TSMA prohibits monopolization of these signs or indications as a legal technique to protect public interests by ensuring that non-distinctive features remain free for exploitation by members of the public. The corollary to this position is the permission under section 34(ii) of TSMA pursuant to which a trademark proprietor's consent is not required for third parties to use a trade or service mark, when that use is a bona fide description of the character or quality of a third party's goods. In fact, a trade or service mark feature considered common to a particular trade cannot be monopolized, since this would deny a large section of the society an access to an essential tool or facility without which they cannot compete fairly in a particular trade. For instance, there could be good reasons for disallowing a monopoly in respect of descriptive word mark 'green' for any environmental conservation-related activity.[721] In a different scenario, the trade mark registrar may endorse a decision to register trade or service mark resulting from a combination of descriptive words; provided that such a mark creates an impression other than that the literal meaning of the word elements of the said combination produces.[722]

720. *Windsurfing Chiemsee Produktions-und Vertriebs GmbH v. Boots-und Segelzubehor Walter Huber and Franz Attenberger* [1999] ETMR 585.

721. F. Giola, *Alicante and the Harmonization of Intellectual Property Law in Europe*, 41(1) CML Rev. 975, 981 (2004).

722. Cf. CJEU, Case C-265/00, *Campina Melkunie BV v. Benelux-Merkenbureau* [2004] ECR I-01699.

C. Generic Marks

266. The term 'generic mark' generally refers to words or expressions that are commonly used by consumers and technical words or expressions from the field to which the goods and services belong. This term is also used in the context of trademark law to refer to a trademark which was once distinctive but in the course of time has turned out to be used as a name of the very goods it used to distinguish. By their nature, these categories of signs or indications are generic, in the sense that they are devoid of any distinctive character since they are 'accepted and recognized description of a class of goods or services'.[723]

Thus, a generic sign cannot be registered as a trademark if adduced, factual evidence shows that the use of the sign is well known and established not only in respect of the goods connected with the proprietor of the sign, but also with other identical goods not connected in trade with the proprietor.

Much the same a non-distinctive trade mark may acquire a secondary meaning and become distinctive of the goods in relation to which it is used, it is worth noticing that a distinctive trade mark may lose its distinctiveness and become generic if in the course of time it turns out to function as a name of the very goods whose commercial origin it used to identify and distinguish those goods from goods of other commercial sources.[724]

D. Shapes, Configurations and Colours

267. It is indisputable that the shape, configuration, colour of goods or the containers thereof may constitute a sign registrable under both TSMA and ZIPA. However, for these signs to be registrable, besides meeting the requirements of graphical representation and capability to distinguish, the legal exclusion under sections 19(b) and 46(2)(i) of TSMA and ZIPA respectively, must not be applicable to them. Section 19(b) of TSMA excludes from protection 'trade or service marks which consist solely of the shape, configuration or colour of the goods, or the containers thereof'. The legal exclusion under section 46(2)(i) of ZIPA applies if the shape, configuration or colour 'is incapable of distinguishing the goods or services of one enterprise from those of other enterprises'. Moreover, the second part of section 46(2)(i) of ZIPA adds that, 'the scent or other material characteristic of goods shall not be deemed capable of distinguishing the goods when they result normally from the common composition of those goods'. Thus, within context of section 46(2)(i) of ZIPA, a shape, configuration or colour of the goods are signs that are based on 'material characteristic of goods resulting from common composition of those goods', which, as such, lack distinctiveness and hence generally unregistrable.

723. Cf. R. Radhakrishnan & S. Alasubramanian, *Intellectual Property Rights: Text and Cases* 135 (Excel Books 2008).

724. J. Timothy, *What You Don't Know About Trademarks*, 6/2009 *WIPO Magazine* (November 2009), retrieved from https://www.wipo.int/wipo_magazine/en/2009/06/article_0010.html (accessed: 18 May 2020).

Both TSMA and ZIPA have one thing in common: a mark consisting of a shape, configuration or colour of the goods, or the containers thereof cannot be registered as trade or service marks, as they are broadly constituted by aesthetic appearance of the goods. While it is true that such an aesthetic appearance may be instrumental to enable a consumer reach a particular conclusion regarding their decision to buy or to refrain from buying the goods bearing the mark, still such aesthetic features are hardly protectable as a trade mark.[725] This is because these features may possess distinctiveness capability, which is not acceptable from trade mark law point of view. For instance, a shape or configuration which is well known by consumers not because of its capability to indicate the source of origin, but due to the attractiveness of that shape or configuration, cannot be protected as a trade mark; that shape or configuration serves to attain non-trade mark functions of making the product ornamental or of being part of the design of the product.

Sections 19(b) and 46(2)(i) of TSMA and ZIPA respectively concern certain signs, which, as a matter of principle, should not outright constitute trade or service marks. By having such an effect, these provisions appear to deviate from the universal underlying objective of the trademark protection regime, which is to virtually protect a sign as long as such sign is capable of distinguishing goods of one undertaking from those of other. In addition, there is a risk that the provisions of sections 19(b) and 46(2)(i) of TSMA and ZIPA respectively contravene Article 15(1) TRIPS pursuant to which any sign (including figurative elements) that is capable of identifying one's goods or services may be registrable.[726]

However the principle of 'acquired distinctiveness', stipulated in sections 16(3)(b) and 46(3) of TSMA and ZIPA respectively, resolves the conflict between the liberal position, under TRIPS agreement, that virtually permits registration of any sign and the trade mark registration stunt respectively introduced under sections 19(b) and 46(2)(i) of TSMA and ZIPA. It should be noted that the prohibition of registration of the signs mentioned in sections 19(b) and 46(2)(i) of TSMA and ZIPA respectively applies generally when trade mark registration is sought on the basis of inherent distinctiveness of the mark involved. Hence, no justification both in law and fact, for excluding from registration of those signs, when, following the use made of them in relation to goods or services, they possess acquired distinctiveness or secondary meaning.

E. Insignias of the State or Intergovernmental Organizations

268. Both Tanzania mainland and Tanzania Zanzibar maintain a legal regime for the protection of flags of countries, emblems and other insignias of the State or

---

725. The possibility for legal protection of these features exists under other branches of IP, design law in particular (Cf. I.M. Davies ed., *Sweet & Maxwell's European Trade Mark Litigation Handbook* 39 (Sweet & Maxwell 1998)).

726. Regarding the signs capable of being registered as trade or service marks in Tanzania, including shape marks *see* J. Jaconiah, *The Requirement for Registration and Protection of Non-Traditional Trade Marks in the European Union and in Tanzania*, 40 IIC 756–781 (2009).

Intergovernmental Organizations. According to sections 19(c) and 46(2)(iv) of TSMA and ZIPA the following trade or service marks may not be registered in the Republic of Tanzania:

> [Trade] or service marks which are identical with, or imitate the armorial bearings, flags and other emblems, initials, names, or abbreviations or initials of name or official sign or hallmark of any state or of any organisation created by an International Convention, unless authorized by the competent authority of that state or international organisation.[727]

In view of the foregoing, signs that are made of insignias of the State or intergovernmental organizations cannot be validly registered in the Republic of Tanzania except with appropriate consent of the State or the intergovernmental organization concerned.

Regulation 14 of the TMRs elaborates on how section 19(c) of the TSMA operates in practice. It stipulates that: 'Where a representation of the armorial bearing, insignia, orders of honour, decorations or flags of any State, city, borough, town, place, society, body corporate, institution or person appears, the registrar shall, if he so require, be furnished with a consent to the registration and use of such emblems from such official or other person as appears to the registrar to be entitled to give consent, and in default of such consent he may refuse to register the mark.'

Interpreted in the light of Regulation 13 of the TMRs,[728] section 19(c) of TSMA must be seen as excluding from registration and protection, as a trade or service mark, not only flags, armorial bearings and emblems, but also signs containing any word, letter or device indicating State patronage.

In line with the import of paragraph (c) of Article 6*ter* of the Paris Convention,[729] registration of a trade mark cannot be prohibited outright on State patronage allegations without further inquiry. In principle, if State patronage is alleged, the factor controlling a decision to deny a trade mark registration is the effect of the impression the use of the mark creates in the mind of the consuming public. It would be a straightforward case for refusing registration/protection of a mark applied for,

727. This is verbatim quotation of s. 19(c) of TSMA. Section 46(2)(iv) of ZIPA reflects provisions of s. 19(c) of TSMA.

728. Regulation 13 of the TMRs provide that: 'The following may not appear on a mark the registration of which is applied for – (a) representations of the armorial bearings of Tanzania or devices so nearly resembling it as to be likely to be mistaken for it; (b) representations of the national flag of Tanzania; (c) any words such as "the President", "Republic" or "Tanzania" or any letters or devices if used in such manner as to be likely to lead to persons to think that the applicant either has or recently has had the patronage or authorization from the Government of the Republic of Tanzania, whether or not such may be the case.'

729. According to 'the second sentence of Article 6*ter* (1)(c), it is permissible, in the case of the emblem of an international organisation, to allow registration of a mark if it is not of such a nature as to suggest to the public that a connection exists between the organisation concerned and armorial bearings, flags, emblems, abbreviations and names or if such registration is probably not of such a nature as to mislead the public as to an existence of a connection between the user and the organisation' (GCEU, Case T-127/02, at para. 63).

if the use of the mark would cause the public to be misled by thinking that a connection between the trade mark user and the intergovernmental or organ of the State exists.

F. Signs Declared as Prohibited under the Law

269. Regulation 12 of TMRs gives discretion to the registrar to refuse acceptance of a trade or service mark applied for if certain prohibited words appear upon that mark. In this regard, prohibited words include 'the words "Patent," "Patented," "Registered Design," "Copyright," "Entered at Stationers," "Hall," "To counterfeit this is a forgery" or words to like effect'. Generally, the registrar cannot endorse registration of a trade or service mark containing 'representations of the President or any colourable imitations thereof'.

Other words of similar effect as above are 'Red Cross, Red Crescent or Geneva Cross'. In this regard, any representation of the Geneva Cross or any other cross in red or of the Swiss Federal Cross in white on a red ground or in silver on a red ground or such representations in a similar colour or colours' can neither be registered as a trademark nor form part of a mark whose registration is sought in Tanzania. However, it flows from the general principle of trade mark law that a cross, which does not fall within the specifications mentioned above, deserves protection and registration as a trade mark. The applicant for such a mark must nevertheless assure the trade mark examiner that the cross device will not be used in red, since this mode of use of the device mark would create an impression that device mark is a 'Red Cross or Geneva Cross'.

G. Bad Faith Registrations

270. Trade mark laws of both Tanzania mainland and Tanzania Zanzibar prohibit registration of a trade or service mark in bad faith. The TSMA does not make a specific reference to the concept 'bad faith', but refers, in section 37, to registration of a trade or service mark obtained fraudulently as a ground for deregistration of the mark. Section 46(2)(vii) of ZIPA categorically prohibits registration of trade or service mark 'if the application has been made in bad faith'. The term 'mala fide' is another expression of 'bad faith'. The term 'bad faith' is the opposite of 'good faith' or 'bona fide'. It is instructive to note that, the terms 'mala fide', 'bona fide' and 'bad faith' are 'what are sometimes called 'chameleon words' and take their content from the colour from their surroundings'.[730] Indeed, these terms do generally take their meanings from the context in which they are used.

According to the judgment in *Gromax Plasticulture Ltd v. Don & Low Nonwovens Ltd*, the term 'bad faith' refers to 'dishonesty and some dealings which fall short of the standards of acceptable commercial behaviour observed by reasonable and

730. *Harrison v. Teton Valley Trading Co* [2004] EWCA Civ 1028 (27 Jul. 2004), para. 19, retrieved from: http://www.bailii.org/ew/cases/EWCA/Civ/2004/1028.html (accessed: 18 May 2020).

experienced men in the particular area being examined'.[731] One authority regards the term 'bad faith' as the opposite of the term 'good faith':

> ... [which involves], 'but not limited to actual or constructive fraud, or a design to mislead or deceive another, or any other sinister motive'. Conceptually, bad faith can be understood as a 'dishonest intention'. This means that bad faith may be interpreted as unfair practices involving lack of any honest intention on the part of the [trademark] applicant ... at the time of filing. Example: if it can be shown that the parties concerned had been in contact, for instance at an exhibition in the respective trade, and where then one party filed [a trademark] application ... consisting of the other party's brand, there would be reason to conclude bad faith.[732]

The concept of bad faith can also be discussed in connection with provisions of Article 6*septies* of the Paris Convention, which addresses agent's mark.[733] Section 27(2)(c) of TSMA implements the foregoing provision of the Paris Convention in Tanzania. According to this section, registration of trade or service mark can be refused if an agent or a representative, of a person owning a trade mark registration in another country, files an application for registration of that mark in his name in the country where he acts as the trade mark proprietor's agent or representative. Such an application for trade or service mark registration can be opposed on the 'bad faith' ground, unless the trade mark proprietor authorizes the agent or representative to pursue that cause. Short of such authorization, the trade mark proprietor's agent or representative must render acceptable justifications for seeking registration of the mark in his name.

The overall proposition regarding the foregoing position would be that in order to permit the conclusion that the applicant is acting in bad faith it is necessary to take into consideration all the relevant factors specific to the particular case which pertained at the time of filing the application for registration. The fact that the applicant knows or should know that a third party is using a mark abroad at the time of filing his application which is liable to be confused with the mark whose registration has been applied for is not sufficient, in itself, to permit the conclusion that the applicant is acting in bad faith within the meaning of that provision.[734]

731. Lindsay J. in *Gromax Plasticulture Ltd v. Don & Low Nonwovens Ltd* [1999] RPC 367 at 379.
732. The *Senso Di Donna's Trade Mark* Case C0006716979/1, [2001] ETMR 5, para. 17. *See also* in this regard the decision in *Lancôme Parfums et Beauté and Cie's Trade Mark* [2001] ETMR 89.
733. Article 6*septies* of the Paris Convention states that: 'If the agent or representative of the person who is the proprietor of a mark in one of the countries of the Union applies, without such proprietor's authorization, for the registration of the mark in his own name, in one or more countries of the Union, the proprietor shall be entitled to oppose the registration applied for or demand its cancellation or, if the law of the country so allows, the assignment in his favour of the said registration, unless such agent or representative justifies his action.'
734. Case C-529/07 *Chocoladefabriken Lindt & Sprüngli* [2009] ECR I-4893, paras 37 and 40–42; CJEU Case C-320/12 *Malaysia Dairy Industries Pte. Ltd v. Ankenævnet for Patenter og Varemærker*, para. 37.

II. Relative Grounds for Trademark Refusal

271. Relative grounds for trade mark refusal relates to factors that are outside the attributes of the sign sought to be registered as a trade mark. They are basically based on existing trade mark rights contradicting or conflicting with the right of the trade or service mark applicant to secure an exclusive monopoly in relation to that mark.

A. *Earlier Trade Mark Rights*

272. Within the ambit of the TSMA and ZIPA, a trademark cannot be registered if a third party successfully claims that he is the proprietor of a trademark and that the applicant has submitted to the trademark registrar an application for the registration of an identical or confusingly similar trademark.[735] Thus, earlier trade mark rights may constitute relative grounds for refusing registration of a particular sign as a trade or service mark in Tanzania. Both a pending application for trade mark registration and an earlier registered or unregistered trade mark legally recognized in Tanzania as such may be cited as relative grounds for trade mark refusal.

1. Registered Trade or Service Marks

273. Insofar as earlier registered trade or service marks as relative grounds for withholding registration of a competing trade mark are concerned, both section 20(1) of the TSMA and section 46(2)(vi) of ZIPA allow the proprietor thereof to oppose registration of a subsequent trade mark which is identical or similar to the earlier trade mark and the goods or services in relation to which registration of the subsequent mark is sought are identical or closely resemble those in respect of which the earlier mark is registered. The trade mark registrar can invoke his powers to reject application for trade mark registration based on an earlier registered trade mark only if he is convinced that allowing registration of the trade mark applied for would be likely to deceive or cause confusion, given the similarity or identity (whichever is relevant) of the marks concerned as well as of the similarity or identity of the goods and/or services to which both trade or service marks relate.

2. Well-Known Marks

274. The owner, of an earlier mark that is well known in Tanzania, is entitled to object registration of any identical or confusingly similar mark in two scenarios. First, such objection can base on section 19(d) of TSMA and section 46(2)(v) of ZIPA. These provisions prohibit registration of an infringing mark even where an application for registration of such a mark is sought for goods or services that are

735. Section 20(1), TSMA & s. 46(2)(vi), ZIPA.

different from those connected with the registered well-known trade mark. In this regard, prohibition of trade mark registration is only justifiable when the infringer's use of the mark conflicting with the well-known trade or service mark is 'likely to impair the distinctive character or acquired reputation of the trade mark' with the meaning of section 32(b)(b) of TSMA.[736] Second, a mark conflicting with a well-known trade or service mark as per Article 6*bis* of the Paris Convention would not be accepted for registration in Tanzania, if the registration thereof is sought for identical or similar goods with which the former trade mark is identified as a well-known trade or service mark in Tanzania. It is noteworthy that a mark can conflict with a well-known trade or service mark in the foregoing sense when such a sign constitutes, wholly or essentially, a reproduction, imitation or translation of the well-known trade or service mark.[737] Under this latter scenario, the onset of the ground for refusing registration of the conflicting mark is based on the likelihood of deception or confusion when such a mark is used in relation to goods or services that are identical or confusingly similar to those identified with the well-known trade or service mark.

3. Trade or Service Mark Applications

275. An application for trade mark registration that is pending before the office of the trade mark registrar can constitute earlier trade mark rights, which can block registration of another trade mark which is a subject of a trade mark application of a later filing date. A presumption in this regard is that the trade mark proprietor of the senior application has overriding rights over the proprietor of the trade mark with subsequent application date. As the case is with a registered trade mark serving as a relative ground, the earlier trade mark application is allowed to prevail over a trade mark contained in the junior application as a means to avoid consumer confusion. Such confusion is imminent when both marks are either identical or confusingly similar and are meant to be used in relation to identical or confusingly similar goods.[738]

4. Business Names; Company Names

276. Section 27(1)(b) of TSMA hints to the possibility of both earlier and junior applications for trade mark registration serving as relative grounds against each other. It is assumed that the earlier trade mark application will always prevail over the subsequent application. However, under section 27(1)(b), which recognizes unregistered rights such as business names or company names already in use in Tanzania, a junior application can serve as a ground for blocking registration of the trade mark contained in the earlier application if registration of such a mark would

736. *See also* s. 46(2)(v), ZPA, which in this context would be invoked to protect the interests of the proprietor of a registered well-known trade mark in Tanzania Zanzibar.
737. Section 19(d), TSMA and s. 46(2)(v), ZIPA.
738. Section 27(1)(a), TSMA & s. 46(2)(vi), ZIPA.

be a contravention of existing rights of the person making the later application. There are two scenarios, under the TSMA, whereby a junior application for trade mark registration may take precedence over a senior application. First, such would be the case if the trade mark which is the subject of the later application claims a priority right based on an earlier application filed, or an earlier trade mark registration granted, in a Paris Convention country or any other country.[739] Second, the later trade mark applicant may have unregistered trade mark rights, such as business names, company names or other protected titles of protected literary or artistic works, overriding the rights of the earlier applicant.

5. Unregistered Rights

277. Although unregistered trade mark rights are only enforceable through an action for unliquidated damages under the common-law tort of passing off,[740] they may be invoked to block an application for registration of a junior trade mark.[741] For an unregistered trade or service mark to constitute a relative ground for trademark refusal, fulfilment of certain preconditions is inevitable. For instance, it would be necessary that the proprietor of the unregistered trademark proves that his mark has been in genuine use prior to the date on which the person submitting an earlier application adopted the opposed trade mark. Where possible, it is equally important that the opponent submits to the office of the trade mark registrar evidence showing he has acquired clientele and that this clientele attaches a certain reputation to the unregistered trademark, which is a subject of the later application. It is worth noticing that if a proprietor of an unregistered trade mark files an application for registration of that trade mark, his trade mark acquires a formal recognition tracing back from the date he adopted the unregistered trade mark for his business.

B. Deceptive Use of a Trade Mark

278. Section 19(a) of TSMA excludes from registration and protection a sign that as a result of the manner in which it has been used, would be likely to cause deception or confusion.[742] In most cases, such deception or confusion relates to 'geographical or other origin, manufacturing process, characteristics or suitability for their purpose, of the goods or services concerned'. This includes, for instance, marks indicating that goods are made in Tanzania mainland or Tanzania Zanzibar while they are in fact made in another country. There are some good reasons to exclude deceptive signs from registration as trade or service marks: given that deceptive marks may claim the nature, the quality or geographical origin, which

739. Section 22, TSMA & S. 47(2), ZIPA. *See also* Art. 4 of the Paris Convention, which provides for the principle of priority.
740. Section 30, TSMA.
741. Section 27(2)(a), TSMA & s. 46(9), ZIPA.
742. Section 46(2)(iii) of ZIPA implements this position in Tanzania mainland.

they do not have, consumers may be misled and turn to the goods or services marketed under the deceptive mark with a certain level of expectation based on their previous experience relating to the claimed nature, quality or geographical origin.

C. Other Relative Grounds

279. According to section 19(a) of TSMA, a 'trade or service marks the use of which would be contrary to law or morality or which would be likely to deceive or cause confusion as to the nature, geographical or other origin, manufacturing process, characteristics or suitability for their purpose, of the goods or services concerned' cannot constitute a trade mark protectable in Tanzania.[743]

Section 19(a) of TSMA consists of two main elements; namely: (1) deceptive marks or marks which are likely to deceive/cause confusion; (2) contrary to law or morality.

1. Likely to Deceive or Cause Confusion

280. Consumers' perception is a key determinant of trade mark 'deception' or 'confusion' or the likelihood thereof within the ambit of section 19(a) of TSMA. There is a legal presumption that a particular trade mark is not used in a deceptive or confusing manner or in a way likely to lead to this undesired outcome if such a mark is used in the normal course of trade to identify the source of goods or services in relation to which it is registered and distinguish that source from other sources of other goods or services.

2. Contrary to Law or Morality

281. A trade mark is said to be contrary to law if there is any piece of legislation specifying the particular mark or the use thereof as being contrary to that legislation. In this regard, one may wish to make reference to the TMA, TMRs and other pieces of legislation, including those outlined above in §3(I)(F) of this chapter, stipulating conditions which trade or service marks must fulfil to comply with the legal requirements for registration or protection.

The term 'contrary to morality', as used in section 19(a) of TSMA, is often referred to by its Latin expression counterpart '*contra bonos mores*' – an expression that has been defined to mean 'against good morals: harmful to the moral welfare of the society'.[744] Thus any trade mark that in one way or the other is likely to come into conflict with public order or morality cannot be registered as a trade mark.

Put in a nutshell, public order or morality is the basis for the exclusion, under section 19(a) of TSMA, from registration and protection as trade or service marks of

743. Sections 46(2)(ii) and 46(2)(iii) of ZIPA corresponds to s. 19(a) of TSMA.
744. 'Contra bonos mores.' *Merriam-Webster.com Legal Dictionary*, Merriam-Webster, https://www.merriam-webster.com/legal/contra%20bonos%20mores. Accessed: 19 May 2020.

signs that are contrary to law or morality. In principle, contravention of public order and morality, as a ground for refusal of trademark registration, should exclusively result from the nature of the mark. The fact that the nature of the goods or services in relation to which the mark is applied contravenes public order or morality cannot constitute a ground for refusing an application for registration of such a mark as a trade mark. The obstacle to registration does not lie in the goods or services, but rather in the signs themselves or in their use. Hence, the Registrar of trade marks may rightly and correctly accept for registration of a mark, which by its nature is not obscene or otherwise immoral, but designates, for example, the commercial provision of services considered immoral or the distribution of prohibited substances.[745]

§4. Formalities: Procedure for Obtaining Protection, Establishing and Maintaining Trademarks

I. Trade Mark Application

282. Legal protection of trade and service marks in Tanzania does not accrue automatically. The proprietor must make a formal application for registration of the mark. There are different offices through which a trade mark applicant can file an application for trade mark registration that would lead to acquisition of exclusive trade mark rights that are effective in Tanzania. Two alternative routes of filing a trade mark application are available to the applicant; namely, national and regional routes. Protection, in Tanzania, of a trade or service mark via regional trade mark registration scheme is available under the regime established and managed by the ARIPO.

The United Republic of Tanzania does not subscribe to the international system of trade mark registration.[746] Consequently, local filing before the trademark office of Tanzania is required in respect of any foreign trade mark. Traditionally, two international treaties governed the international registration of marks, namely: (1) the Madrid Agreement Concerning the International Registration of Marks adopted in Madrid in April, 1891; and (2) the Protocol Relating to the Madrid Agreement adopted in Madrid on 27 June 1989 and came into force on 1 April 1996. However, as of now, all contracting parties to the Madrid Agreement have formally accepted to be bound by the Madrid Protocol. This milestone paved a way for a decision by the Madrid Union Assembly in October 2016 that made the protocol a controlling instrument insofar as international registration of marks under the auspices of WIPO is concerned. Following that decision, States wishing to be part of the Madrid Union for international protection of marks must, at least, accept to be bound by the

745. Cf. Nuno Pires de Carvalho, *The TRIPS Regime of Trademarks and Designs* 330 (Kluwer Law International BV 2nd ed. 2011).

746. World Trademark Review – Challenges of using Madrid Protocol in Africa, 28 January 2021, available at https://www.worldtrademarkreview.com/challenges-of-using-the-madrid-protocol-in-africa (accessed: 20 Jan. 2022).

Madrid Protocol. Prospective members of the Madrid Union may still become contracting parties to the Madrid Agreement provided they become signatories to the Madrid Protocol as well. This is because, there is no obligation on those States to be contracting parties to the Madrid Agreement, which has now become inoperative.

A. *The Applicant*

283. The general entitlement to file an application for trade mark registration before the trade mark office in Tanzania rests with the proprietor of the trade mark involved. Where a trade mark owner is an individual natural person, this very person has the legal power to submit a trade mark application, which, upon fulfilling the requirements of the law, the office of the Registrar of trade marks must accept.

As a matter of principle, an unincorporated business firm cannot enjoy an absolute right to apply for trade mark registration. Such a firm does not have independent legal personality other than that of the partners of the firm. This is opposed to a position applying to an incorporated company; such an entity enjoys a legal personality that is different from that of its directors. When taken as a basis for determining a rightful applicant for a trade mark registration, this distinction regarding legal personalities of incorporated and unincorporated business establishments would lead to different results. For instance, it would mean that one, or all individual partners, of a firm may file an acceptable trade mark application and hence, entitled to append their signature on the application form. Insofar as an incorporated business entity is concerned, a managing director of the company would have legal powers to sign an application for trade mark registration on behalf of the company owning the mark applied for.[747]

A trade mark proprietor has a right to appoint a representative or an agent. This is a person who steps into the shoes of the applicant. A representative or a trademark agent derives from the trademark proprietor powers to make trade mark filings or appear for hearings before the Registrar of trade marks. Section 65 of TSMA legitimatizes the practice of trade mark proprietors to appoint agents and the powers bestowed upon the agents to act on behalf of trade mark applicants. According to Regulation 11 of the TMRs, a person appointing an agent must inform the trade mark office about their decision to transact via a representative or an agent. To convey this information to the office, the appointing party has to fill in a TM/SM1 form and attach that form to their application for trademark registration. Alternatively, the trademark applicant may use any other document indicating that the agent has duly secured a power of attorney from the applicant in lieu of Form TM/SM1.

Regulation 11(3) of TMRs contains a list of persons who qualifies to be registered with the trade mark office as trade mark agents and therefore qualify, once appointed by a client, to file notice, request and make any other representations before the Trade Mark Office. The following persons can be entered into the register of Trade Marks Agents: any national of Tanzania, any person living or having commercial establishment in Tanzania, any person with a right of audience at the

747. Regulation 7, TMRs.

High Court of Tanzania, any business person who has been examined and approved by the Registrar of trade marks as being fit to serve as a trade mark agent, and any person who is a 'member of the Chartered Institute of Trade and Service marks Agents'.

B. Application Formalities

1. Filing of an Application

284. Trademark proprietors who are desirous of having their marks registered and protected in Tanzania have to lodge an application for trademark registration at the trade mark office. According to section 21 of TSMA, an application for trade mark registration must be made in a prescribed format and manner. In line with Regulation 17 of TMRs, which implements section 21 of TSMA, a trade mark applicant has to use Form TM/SM2 to file an application for trade or service mark registration. Such an application must bear the applicant's signature or a signature of the applicant's duly authorized agent as well as a date of signing the application form. On filing Form TM/SM2 the applicant must pay the amount of TZS 50,000 currently prescribed under the TMRs as a trade mark application fee.

Translation or transliteration is required in respect of any word or numeral contained in the application, unless such word or numeral is in roman characters.[748] Where this is the case, the applicant must state the fact that a translation or transliteration has been made to the required standards. One of the ways to satisfy the registrar insofar as the correctness of the translation or transliteration is concerned is for the applicant to prove that such a translation/transliteration has been done by a legally accredited professional. Likewise, a requirement for translation and endorsement of such translation arises in respect of any trade mark containing a word in a language other than Kiswahili or English. In line with the requirements under section 21(2) of TSMA and Regulation 20 of TMRs, if the translation or transliteration relates to the mark itself, the applicant or his duly appointed agent will have to file additional six representations of the mark using Form TM/SM3.

The general procedural formalities for applying for a trade or service mark registration as provided for under section 21 TSMA require a trade or service mark proprietor to apply for registration of their mark to the registrar. The application must be in writing and contain the following particulars: (1) the applicant's name and address as well as the description of his trade or business; (2) the class of the goods or services in respect of which the mark is used or intended to be used; (3) 'production of the trade or service mark' under application; and (4) a declaration indicating that he or 'his proposed registered user is using or proposes to use the trade or service mark within Tanzania'.

748. Regulation 25, TMRs.

2. Graphical Representation

285. Graphical representation of a trade mark applied for must accompany the application. This is achieved by affixing a representation of the mark in the relevant space on form TM/SM2. Thus, an acceptable representation of the mark, in line with Regulation 19 of TMRs, must not only be durable in nature, but also should fit in the space allocated in the application.

Where a trade mark applied for in constituted by a word, letter, numeral or combination thereof as a trade mark, reproduction of these types of marks in the space provided for in the From TM/SM2 constitutes sufficient representation of the mark. In instances in which the application for trade mark registration concerns a mark other than the foregoing, a special or particular way of representation may be required. In this case, the applicant has to accompany his application for trade mark registration with an annex to form TM/SM2 containing a representation of the mark involved. It is instructive to note that the Registrar of trade marks has inherent powers to instruct a trade mark applicant to file additional graphical representations of the mark complementing those already filed.

Regulation 23 of TMRs envisages circumstances wherein certain marks are incapable of being represented in a form that is suitable for graphic representation in the trade mark application form as above. Where this is the case, the traditional rule of graphical representation of the mark applied for is dispensed with so as to allow the trade mark applicant to include in his application a specimen or copy of the trade mark in such size and scale, which makes it convenient for the trade mark examiner to examine the trade mark applied for. It is also not uncommon for the trade mark registrar to require the trade mark applicant to furnish the registrar's office with a specimen or copy of any trade mark, which cannot be easily represented in the register of trade marks in the traditional manner.

The legal significance of graphical representation of a trade mark is that such a representation is the main, and possibly the only way one can claim 'special graphic features or colours, the use of small and capital letters and three-dimensional marks'.[749] It follows that the graphical representation required under section 2 of both TSMA and ZIPA is not limited to an actual reproduction of the mark in the trade mark register. Although this reproduction of the mark would constitute graphical representation for those signs which are visually perceptible, providing in the trade mark application some contours representing the signs and some description of the sign involved would constitute a sufficient graphical representation of marks that are not visually perceptible as long as the trade mark office and other interested parties would identify, from the representation and description, the sign claimed as a trade mark and the extent of the consequential monopoly thereof.[750] Indeed, the legal monopoly relating to a trade or service mark is not automatic; it is granted in response to an application for trade mark registration containing information sufficiently establishing what the sign is, which constitutes a trade or service mark

749. P.A.C.E. van der Kooij, *The Community Trade Mark Regulation: An Article by Article Guide* 60 (Sweet & Maxwell 2000).

750. *See* the opinion of Advocate-General Ruiz-Jarabo Colomer in Case C-273/00, *Ralph Sieckman* [2002] ECR I-11737.

involved. The clarity and preciseness of this information, which is mostly realizable through graphical representation of the sign, alerts marketers as to what they must refrain from doing in relation to a registered trade or service mark.

3. Classification of Goods and Services

286. An application for registration of a trade or service mark must contain a list of goods and services for which the registration of the mark is sought. Such a list has to be made in the order of the relevant classes of the international classification prepared in accordance with the NICE Agreement on International Classification of goods and services of 1957 in its most recent edition. The current version is the eleventh edition (as revised) of the NICE International Classification of Goods and Services, which consists of thirty-four goods classes and eleven service classes.[751]

Section 15 of the TSMA stipulates the requirement for classifying trade marks in terms of goods and services in relation to which the trade mark registration is sought. It stipulates that: 'Trade or service Marks shall be registered in respect of particular goods or services in one or more classes of International Classification'. The Registrar of Trade and Service Marks has a final say as regards the classes of goods or services individualized by the trade or service mark applied for.

The legal significance of trade mark classification is that a trade mark proprietor acquires exclusive rights to use his trade mark in relation to all goods and services for which the mark is registered under the specified class or classes of the NICE Agreement. Unless an exception applies, third parties are free to use a registered trade mark in relation to goods or services that are not covered by the class or classes of goods and services for which the proprietor's trade mark is registered.

C. *Foreign Trade Marks*

1. Priority Right

287. Trade and service mark law of Tanzania envisages circumstances whereby two or more commercially unrelated applicants may compete to register an identical or confusingly similar trade or service mark for identical or confusingly similar goods or services. If, according to circumstances of the case, one of the competing applicants has had their mark registered or an application for the mark's registration submitted in a foreign country that is bound by the Paris Convention,[752] the foreign registration or application will entitle the applicant to have his application for registration of the same mark in Tanzania considered first. This position reflects the right of priority of trade mark application enshrined in Article 4 of the Paris Convention.

---

751. At https://www.wipo.int/classifications/nice/en/ (accessed: 26 Jan. 2022).

752. That is the Paris Convention of 20 Mar. 1983 for the Protection of Industrial Property and any revisions thereof to which Tanzania is or may become party in future (cf. s. 2, para. 2, TSMA).

The United Republic of Tanzania, being a member of the Paris Convention, has international obligation to observe the principle of priority right stipulated under the Paris Convention and domesticated in Tanzania by section 22 of TSMA as implemented by Regulation 18 of the TMRs. The general import of these pieces of legislation is that a trademark proprietor who first files an application for trademark registration in a foreign country that is a member of the Paris Union (henceforth, the Convention country) enjoys a right to file an application for registration of the same mark in Tanzania and claim as a filing date of this application, the date on which the registration of the mark in the Convention country was granted or was applied for.

The right under reference is termed 'priority right' in the sense that, intervening events such as another trademark filing made by another person in Tanzania – after the person entitled to the priority right had filed the trademark application in the Convention country – does not affect the right of the latter person to file in Tanzania a trademark application corresponding to his application made in the Convention country. To be entitled to claim the right of priority in Tanzania, the trade mark applicant must submit to the office of the Registrar of trade and service marks an application thereof within a period of six months from the date the applicant or their authorized agents filed the trademark application in the Convention country. A trademark application first filed in the Convention country forms a basis for the claim of priority right in Tanzania irrespective of whether or not it has graduated into registration of the trade or service mark that is the subject of such an application.

It is worth noticing that the right of priority, provided for under TSMA, must be specifically claimed by the applicant for trademark registration using form TM/SM2. Regulation 18 of TMRs is more explicit on this; it requires the person claiming the priority right to state so specifically and provide details about the foreign application or registration that has given rise to the priority right. The relevant details in this regard include the date on which the earlier application for trade or service mark registration was made in the foreign country and the name of this foreign country involved. In case the earlier application referred to above is a regional or international application, the claimant must mention the name of the office where they filed the application. In certain instances, the person claiming the priority right may be required to furnish the office of the trade mark registrar with a certified copy of the earlier application. If that copy is in a language other than Kiswahili or English, the claimant will be required to furnish the office with office within three months following the date of filing of the trade or service mark application in Tanzania.

The date of the foreign application is assumed to be the date of the application for registration of the mark in Tanzania. Moreover, only one foreign trademark application is taken into account when determining entitlement to the right of priority. An applicant owning two foreign applications for registration of a single mark, can exercise the priority right in Tanzania based on the application date of the earlier foreign application alone.

The successful claim of a right of priority does not entitle the trade mark proprietor to institute trademark infringement proceedings in respect of any prior activities undertaken in Tanzania, which would have constituted infringement if those activities were perpetuated while the mark enjoyed legal protection in Tanzania. It is inferable under section 30 of TSMA that an infringer of a trade mark claiming priority in Tanzania as above, would only be responsible for the trade mark infringement and consequently be obliged to pay damages to the trade mark proprietor, only if the infringement occurs after the Tanzanian trade mark office has accepted the application for trade mark registration and the application had been advertised in the Patents and Trade Marks Journal.

It is instructive to note that priority right does not lead to automatic acceptance for registration in Tanzania of the mark to which the right relates: the application has to go through the normal examination procedure in the light of absolute and relative grounds for trademark refusal.

2. Telle-Quelle Principle

288. According to the telle-quelle principle, trade or service marks registered in a foreign country, in compliance with the laws of that country, qualify for registration and protection in the United Republic of Tanzania 'as they are'. This position is in line with the provisions of Article 6*quinques* of the Paris Convention. This article contains the *telle quelle* doctrine – a principle that requires Member States of the Paris Union, such as the Republic of Tanzania, to accept for registration 'as is' a trade mark duly registered in another Member State. In this regard, Article 6*quinques* (A)(1) of the Paris Convention puts it more lucidly that 'every trademark duly registered in the country of origin shall be accepted for filing and protected as is in the other countries of the Union, subject to the reservations indicated in this article'. The obligation placed on the trade mark offices of the United Republic of Tanzania to accept for registration a foreign trademark 'as is' relates to the form of the relevant trademark. Slight modifications made to the form of the foreign mark, but which does not affect the mark's identity and distinctive character, cannot constitute a ground for refusing acceptance for registration in Tanzania of that mark. Generally, the *telle-quelle* principle has been interpreted as preventing the Republic of Tanzania from rejecting an application for trade mark registration simply because its form (i.e., to say, the sign constituting the trade mark) does not comply with the requirements stipulated in the TSMA and not in the sense that the Republic of Tanzania is obliged to interpret the notion of a trademark in a manner which differs from the provisions of the TSMA and ZIPA. If, for example, a three-dimensional object as such is regarded and registered as a trademark in the country of origin but is not considered a trade mark in Tanzania, the Republic of Tanzania is not obliged to register and protect this subject.[753] With regard to the *telle-quelle* principle, Article 6*quinques* (A)(1) of the Paris Convention, stipulates that:

753. *See*Bodenhausen, G.H.C., *Guide to the Application of the Paris Convention for the Protection of Industrial Property* (United International Bureaux for the protection of intellectual Property (BIRPI) 1969). The Guide is available at https://www.wipo.int/publications/en/details.jsp?id=239 (accessed: 7 May 2022).

> Every trademark duly registered in the country of origin shall be accepted for filing and protected as is in the other countries of the Union, subject to the reservations indicated in this Article. Such countries may, before proceeding to final registration, require the production of a certificate of registration in the country of origin, issued by the competent authority. No authentication shall be required for this certificate.

The second part of the first sentence of Article 6*quinques* (a)(1) of the Paris Convention, which states 'subject to the reservations indicated in this Article' essentially, refers to the circumstances under which a trade mark registered in one country may be refused registration and protection in another country under Article 6*quinques* B of the Paris Convention. Consequently, the possibility for rejecting acceptance for registration of a foreign mark in Tanzania exists under three main circumstances; namely:

(1) if the mark 'is likely to infringe rights acquired by third parties in Tanzania';
(2) if the mark does not have any distinctive character or is composed exclusively of a sign or indication 'which can be used in business to designate the type, the quality, quantity, destination, value or place of origin of the products or the time of production, or which have become common in everyday language or in the bona fide and established practices of the trade in the country where protection is sought'.
(3) if the mark is 'contrary to public order or morality', in particular when it is 'of such a nature as to deceive the public'.

On perusing the relevant legislation governing trade and service marks protection in the United Republic of Tanzania, one notices that the pertinent pieces of legislation enshrine provisions outlining the scope of application in the United Republic of Tanzania of Article 6*quinques* B of the Paris Convention. Insofar as the legislation governing trade and service marks protection in Tanzania mainland is concerned, provisions of Article 6*quinques* B of the Paris Convention are reflected in the following provisions: (1) Section 16(1) of TSMA excluding from protection non-distinctive signs; and (2) Section 19(a) of TSMA excluding from registration and protection in Tanzania 'trade or service marks the use of which would be contrary to law or morality or which would be likely to deceive or cause confusion as to the nature, geographical or other origin, manufacturing process, characteristics or suitability for their purpose, of the goods or services concerned'. As regards the regime for trade and service marks protection in Tanzania Zanzibar, the provisions that corresponds with Article 6*quinques* B of the Paris Convention include the following: (1) Section 46(2)(i) of ZIPA that prohibits registration and protection as trade or services mark non-distinctive signs; (2) Section 46(2)(ii) of ZIPA excluding from protection signs which are 'contrary to public order or morality'; and (3) Section 46(6) of ZIPA outlawing registration of 'Words or expressions of common use by consumers and technical words or expressions that pertain to the field to which the goods and services belong' as the law deem these not to possess distinctive character.

In view of the foregoing, one may rightly conclude that a trade mark registered in a foreign country is not immune from scrutiny when the need for its registration in Tanzania arises. Hence, such a trade mark has to be subjected to the absolute and relative grounds for trademark refusal that might stand against the mark's acceptance for registration in Tanzania. *See* an outline of grounds provided above in §3 of this chapter that one may cite in objecting to or refusing registration of trade and service marks in the United Republic of Tanzania.

3. Well-known Unregistered Trade Marks

289. Foreign trade marks that are well known in the Republic of Tanzania enjoy special legal protection. It is arguable that proprietors of this category of marks can decide to apply for registration in Tanzania of the trade mark involved based on the right to exclude third parties from claiming the same mark in the Republic of Tanzania in line with sections 19(d) and 46(2)(v) of TSMA and ZIPA respectively.

D. Trade Mark Examination

290. Upon receipt of an application for trade or service mark registration in respect of which the trade mark proprietor has paid the corresponding application fees, the office of the trade mark registrar is duty-bound to examine the application and conduct trade mark search in the trade mark register in line with the provisions of Regulation 26 of TMRs. According to section 26 of TSMA, the objective of conducting trade mark examination is threefold; namely, to assess a trade or service mark for: (1) 'conformity with the formalities' stipulated in the TSMA and the TMRs (henceforth, formal examination); (2) its 'registrability … in accordance with the provisions of Part IV [of TSMA] and of the [relevant] regulations'(henceforth, substantive examination); and (3) determination of whether the trade and service mark is required to be associated in accordance with the provisions of section 41 [of TSMA].

1. Formal Examination

291. A trade or service mark application has to be examined in terms of the formalities required of a trade mark. In particular, the trade mark office conducts formal examination in order to make sure that the application complies with the filing formalities. An inquiry in this regard will be directed to the question whether the trade mark application form that the applicant has lodged with the registrar's office is duly signed and contains all required information. The trade mark office also pays special attention to the requirement of graphical representation or reproduction of the mark applied for to ensure that the relevant legal requirements have been complied with.

2. Substantive Examination

292. Substantive examination of a trade or service mark assesses registrability of the mark in terms of the substantive grounds for trade or service mark registration refusal outlined above in §3 of this chapter. In this regard, part of the enquiry will juxtapose the mark applied for with the distinctiveness criteria provided for under Article 16 of TSMA. Moreover, the examination enquiry has to address the question whether the trade mark applied for is not one of the categories of signs excluded from serving as trade or service marks under section 19 of TSMA. The prohibited signs, the list of which features above in §3 of this chapter, include deceptive or confusing marks, signs contravening law or morality, signs reproducing flags, emblems and other insignias of the State or of intergovernmental organizations as well as signs consisting of or imitating a well-known mark, just to mention but a few.

In assessing distinctiveness a trade or service mark, two issues, which the examining officer has to address, becomes paramount; namely: (1) whether a trade or service mark claims colour as its distinctive feature; and (2) whether a trade or service mark contains non-distinctive features that the proprietor must disclaim.

Marks Claiming Colours: there are three ways in which colours can enjoy protection under a trade mark protection regime; namely: 'a dependent or indirect protection of a colour or a colour combination, an independent or direct colour protection and an absolute or abstract protection of a colour or colour combination'.[754]

Section 17 of TSMA, which hints to the regime for protection of colour marks in Tanzania mainland, enshrines a rule requiring a trade or service mark to be registered subject to that mark being partially or wholly limited to a single colour or combination of colours. However, there is no obligation to make such limitation: Section 17(2) of TSMA allows a trade or service mark to be registered without such limitation to colours, in which event a presumption that registration of such a mark is sought in all colours will be endorsed. In the event the trade mark applicant limits his trade or service mark by specifying the relevant colour or colours, the colours will be taken into account to determine distinctiveness of the mark concerned. Hence, the limitation or non-limitation of colour or of colour combination has to be addressed as part of trade mark examination.

In view of the foregoing, the TSMA describes protection of colours in connection with a traditional trade or service mark as well as in connection with a product's get-up mark. The former reflects dependent or indirect protection whereby a colour is protected as a part of a word mark, device mark or any other traditional marks. The latter relates to independent or direct colour protection: it is independent and direct protection of colour simply because the colour is protected in relation to the product of that get-up and such a colour will be applied to the specified area of the product's get-up as a distinctive feature.

However, the TSMA neither stipulates nor prohibits protection of colour *per se* in the absolute sense, whereby abstract single colour or colour combination would

754. M.C. Caldarola, *Questions Relating to Abstract Colour Trade Marks: Recent Developments in Germany*, 25(6) E.I.P.R. 248-255, 248 (2003).

be claimed as independent trade or service mark. It can therefore be assumed that the registration stunt in relation to colour per se does not emanate from the preclusion from protectable subject matter; it rather results from the challenges of meeting the threshold for graphical representation of a colour mark.

Disclaimers: trade or service marks are protected as long as they are distinctive of goods or services for which they are registered. In line with this rule, the trade or service mark protection regime does not extend monopoly to trade mark proprietors in respect of descriptive features of a trade or service mark. These features must be freely available within the public domain. It takes an exception, to the rule that a trade or service mark can contain any distinctive features but a descriptive matter, to allow the proprietor to have a trade mark consisting of both distinctive and descriptive features registered. Where such proviso exists, this kind of mark can be registered only if the trade mark office is convinced that, given the information entered into the trade mark register relating to the specification of the mark, the public will be able to grasp the extent of the applicant's exclusive trade or service mark rights. In this regard, section 18 of TSMA, read together with Regulation 31 of TMRs, requires the applicant to make to disclaim all non-distinctive features of the mark applied for. Such a disclaimer must be in writing clearly stipulating that the proprietor of the mark does not wish to claim exclusive rights in respect of the non-distinctive features of the mark.

3. Examination Outcomes

293. If the examination results are such that no grounds for trade or service mark refusal exist, the registrar must accept the application for registration of the mark and make a corresponding advertisement in the Trade and Service Marks Journal in line with the provisions of section 26 of TSMA read together with Regulation 32 of TMRs. Apart from absolute acceptance of a trade mark as above, it also constitutes an acceptance that triggers advertisement of the trade mark in the Journal if the registrar has accepted the trade or service mark application subject to conditions or limitations, which do not require the applicant to respond or to react to them.

Should any grounds that stand against registration of the mark be spotted, the registrar cannot accept the application for the mark's registration. Instead, the registrar is required to send a written communication to the applicant informing them of the refusal to accept the mark for registration and outlining the applicant's rights in relation to such refusal. These rights include the applicant's right to submit a written statement disputing the grounds on which the registrar's decision to refuse acceptance of the application is based as well as the right to ask the registrar to convene a hearing, thus affording the applicant an opportunity to dispute, in person or through representation, the registrar's refusal to accept the application. If, during the hearing or through written submissions, the applicant convincingly disputes the grounds on which the registrar's refusal to accept the application for registration of the mark is based, the registrar may make a conditional acceptance of the application requiring the applicant to amend, modify or limit the application to the extent the registrar deems fit. The registrar may also advertise the application's conditional acceptance in the Trade and Service Marks Journal.

E. Opposition Proceedings

294. Section 27 of the TSMA allows members of the public to oppose an application for the registration of a mark that is advertised in the Trade and Services Mark Journal. The notice of opposition, which has to be lodged with the Office of the Registrar, must be made in a duplicate written form using form TM/SM5. In order for a trade mark opposition notice to be admissible, the opponent must file such a notice within sixty days following the advertisement of acceptance of the mark in the Trade Marks Journal. Usually, a notice of opposition may base on one or more relative and/or absolute grounds for trade or service mark refusal outlined above in §3 of this chapter. Mostly, the basis for opposing trade mark registration will be that the trade mark applied for is identical or confusingly similar to the trade mark belonging to the person opposing registration. Where this is the case, the opposition notice must state the registration number of the trade mark, if the trade mark already appears in the register of trade or service marks, as well as the number of the Trade Mark Journal in which the trade mark involved was advertised.

It is incumbent upon the Registrar of trade marks to send a duplicate of the opposition notice to the trade mark applicant. According to the relevant provisions governing opposition proceedings,[755] on receipt of the duplicate, the trade mark applicant has sixty days to show cause as to why the trade mark should be registered and the opposition should fail. Should the applicant admit some of, or all, the grounds of opposition, they should state so in their counterstatement. A duplicate of the counterstatement is then sent to the opponent. The opponent's response to the counterclaim and the trade mark applicant's rejoinder to the response to the counterclaim are made through statutory declarations of evidence.

It is important to note that the applicant is deemed to have abandoned his application if he does not respond to the notice of opposition and any statutory declarations the opponent makes. Likewise, the opponent is deemed to have abandoned the opposition if he fails to respond to the counter statement and to any other statutory declarations the trade mark applicant makes.

After the evidence-gathering phase, the registrar may invite the parties for a hearing. In this regard, the registrar has to give the trade mark applicant and the opponent at least thirty days' notice requiring them to appear before him for a hearing. Such appearance before the registrar is not a mandatory requirement; the registrar may proceed with the case if any of the parties do not appear. Usually, upon receiving the notice of hearing, the recipient of the notice has fifteen days within which to inform the registrar of their intention to attend the hearing. They do so by filling in and filing form TM/SM7. The party abdicating to inform the registrar as above cannot grab the opportunity to appear for a hearing before the registrar. The hearing phase is followed by the registrar making a decision on whether, and subject to what conditions or limitations, if any, registration is to be permitted. The registrar's decision in this regard is usually based on a thorough consideration of the evidence adduced by the parties.

Both the opposing party and the applicant, if aggrieved, may appeal to the High Court of Tanzania against the registrar's decision in relation to the opposition.

755. That is Regs 34–45 of TMRs.

A significant feature of the opposition proceedings must not skip one's attention: when the opposition process reaches a stage whereby the registrar is required to furnish the parties with a notice of hearing, such notice must be given within a period of three months. If the registrar does not abide by this time limit, any party to the opposition proceedings is at liberty to ask for court's intervention. In this regard, the party concerned has to file an appeal to the High Court of Tanzania, which will then control the opposition proceedings and make a corresponding judgment.

F. Grant of Registration

295. Following the registrar's acceptance of an application for registration of a trade or service mark, the applicant may legitimately expect that the subject matter of his application will finally be registered, 'unless the application has been accepted in error'.[756] It is instructive to note that the registrar will usually suspend a decision to register a trade or service mark if someone has opposed such registration. In case of pending trade mark opposition proceedings, the registrar can process and finally endorse registration of the trade or service mark applied for only if the lodged notice of opposition has been unsuccessful or withdrawn.

Where a trade mark applicant is successful to have a trade or service mark registered in his name, the trade mark office will be duty-bound to issue to the applicant a certificate evidencing the registration of the mark and the applicant's exclusive rights. The registrar does not act on his own issuing the certificate of registration: in pursuant to Regulation 46 of TMRs, the trade mark applicant has to file Form TM/SM8 asking the registrar to register the applicant's trade or service mark. Upon filing this form and paying the trade mark registration fee of TZS 60,000 the registrar will register the trade or service mark involved by entering into the register details about the trade mark such as the date of registration, goods or services in respect of which the trade mark is registered and disclaimers, if any. Personal particulars of the applicant, such as names, business/profession and the address for service must feature in the trade mark register as well. The registration certificate will also bear these particulars and a representation of the mark as it appears in the trade mark register. The authenticity of a certificate of trade or service mark registration is demonstrated by the seal of the Registrar of trade marks appearing on such a certificate. The registrar uses Form 02 to issues the certificate of trade mark registration.

The effective date of registration of a trade or service mark is the date on which the application for the mark's registration was submitted to the registrar. The effective date of a mark claiming priority right under the Paris Convention will be the date on which the application for registration of the mark was made in a foreign country.

756. Cf. s. 28(1)(b), TSMA.

G. Appeals and References to the High Court

296. Under Tanzanian Law, persons aggrieved by any decision of the Registrar of trademarks enjoy the right to lodge an appeal to the High Court of Tanzania.[757] Likewise, the trademark law of Tanzania bestows upon the registrar a right to make reference to the High Court of Tanzania for a decision appertaining to any complicated issues involving a point of law or which are of unusual importance. The registrar has a duty to notify all interested parties prior to making such a reference to the High Court. The registrar is similarly required to act in accordance with the court's decision or guidance concerning the issues that were the subject matter of reference to the High Court.[758] Should the trademark law of Tanzania avail the applicant for trademark registration with alternative options allowing them to lodge an application either with the High Court of Tanzania or with the office of the Registrar of trademarks and he opts to make such an application to the registrar; 'the registrar may, at any stage of the proceedings, refer the application to the court, or may after hearing the parties, determine the question between them, subject to appeal to the court'.[759]

Note that if the High Court is dealing with an interested party's request to have the register of trade and service marks altered or rectified,[760] the registrar has a standing to appear voluntarily or upon being summoned by the court so to appear. In any legal proceedings in which, given his freedom to appear or not to appear, the registrar may, instead of appearing before the High Court, decide to submit to the court a signed written statement. This statement is 'deemed to form part of the evidence in the proceeding'.[761] The statement may give the following: (1) an account of any proceedings before the registrar relating to the subject matter under deliberation before the court; or (2) the particulars of the grounds of any decision given by the registrar affecting the subject matter under deliberation as above; (3) an account of the Trade and Service Marks Office of Tanzania's (TSMO's) practice in relation to the subject matter of the proceedings before the court; or (4) the particulars of such other matters relevant to the subject matter of the proceedings as above, which are within his knowledge as registrar.

II. Regional Trade Marks

297. Founded in 1976 and headquartered in Harare, the ARIPO is one of institutions providing regional registration and management services *inter alia* with respect to industrial property rights (such as trademarks) in Africa. The United Republic of Tanzania has been an active member of ARIPO since when it signed

757. Cf. s. 48, TSMA.
758. Cf. s. 49, TSMA.
759. Cf. s. 55, TSMA.
760. Alteration or rectification of the register is for instance permitted under s. 36, TSMA, according to which any 'person aggrieved by the non-insertion in or omission from the register of any entry, or by any entry wrongly remaining in the register, may apply to the court' for an order 'expunging or varying the entry in the register as shall be deemed fit'.
761. Section 52(2), TSMA.

the Lusaka Agreement on the creation of ARIPO.[762] According to Article III of the Agreement, ARIPO aims *inter alia* to 'establish such common services or organs as may be necessary or desirable for the coordination, harmonization and development of intellectual property activities' affecting its members. With respect to trademarks, this objective is implemented by the Banjul Protocol on Marks (BPM) within the framework of the ARIPO adopted on 19 November 1993 in Banjul (Gambia) and the Protocol's implementing regulations.

The United Republic of Tanzania became party to the BPM on 1 September 1999. Neither the TSMA nor the TMRs domesticate provisions of the BPM in Tanzania. However, the practice shows that Tanzania fully participates in the regional trade or service mark protection scheme managed by ARIPO pursuant to the BPM provisions. Information found on ARIPO website is conclusive evidence of the fact that Tanzania is fully integrated in a regional multilateral trade mark protection system provided for under the BPM. The relevant part of the website[763] states that:

> Following the approval by both the Council of Ministers and the Administrative Council, the ARIPO Secretariat amended the Banjul Protocol to include the individual fee structure based on the Madrid System of WIPO. The sharing of fees between designated States and the Office will only apply to those designated States that choose to do so.
>
> To date, out of the 9 Member States party to the Banjul Protocol, only the United Republic of Tanzania has adopted the Banjul Protocol Individual Fee Structure based on New Rule 10.3 of the Protocol. Therefore, with effect from 1st January 2015, when lodging a new regional trade mark application designating the United Republic of Tanzania and in respect of the renewal of a regional application, applicants are obliged to lodge the national individual respective fees charged by the United Republic of Tanzania.

The regional trade mark system under the BPM permits an application filed before trademark office of any of ARIPO Member States or at ARIPO Head Office in Harare, Zimbabwe to be protected in more than one designated country.

A. *Filing of ARIPO Applications*

298. Section 1 of the BPM empowers ARIPO to register trade or service marks on behalf of contracting States such as Tanzania. In this regard, the trademarks registration system established under the BPM serves as a legal infrastructure enabling applicants to submit their applications for trade and/or service mark registration either directly to ARIPO or to the trademarks office of an ARIPO Member State

762. That is, the Agreement on the creation of the ARIPO (as adopted by the Diplomatic Conference for the adoption of an Agreement on the Creation of an Industrial Property Organization for English-Speaking Africa at Lusaka (Zambia) on 9 Dec. 1976, and amended by the Administrative Council of ARIPO on 10 Dec. 1982, 12 Dec. 1986 and 27 Nov. 1996, and as amended by the Council of Ministers on 13 Aug. 2004) [As in force from 13 Nov. 2004].
763. At https://www.aripo.org/the-united-republic-of-tanzania-adopts-the-individual-fee-structure-of-the-banjul-protocol-as-from-1st-january-2015/ (accessed: 20 May 2022).

such as trade mark office for the case of Tanzania. While legal representation in connection with an ARIPO application for trade or service mark registration submitted to the trade mark office by an applicant who is neither the national nor a habitual resident of Tanzania becomes mandatory, such a representation before ARIPO is not necessarily required if the applicant resides in one of ARIPO's Member States.[764]

For an ARIPO mark to enjoy legal protection in Tanzania, an ARIPO application for trademark registration must designate Tanzania as a country (or one of the countries) where the applicant desires protection of his trademark. When such designation is made, the trade mark office of Tanzania gets involved in the process leading to the grant of the mark's registration. In this regard, ARIPO receives an application directly from the applicant or from a national trademark office of a Member State (should the applicant channel his ARIPO application via the national office). Although a national IP office such as the trade mark office of Tanzania is empowered to receive regional applications for trade or service mark registration, the ultimate powers to register ARIPO trademark is exclusively vested with ARIPO; the national office (such as the trade mark office of Tanzania) only acts as an intermediary. The trade mark office of Tanzania is therefore required to transmit an ARIPO trademark application to ARIPO headquarters within a month from the date on which the application is received at the trade mark office of Tanzania.[765] In view of the precedent, which the ARIPO Board of Appeal laid down in *the matter of trademark application no. AP/M/2005/000303 FONES 4 U in the name of Langton Nyatsambo*,[766] a failure on the part of a national office such as the trade mark office of Tanzania to forward an ARIPO trademark application to ARIPO secretariat in Harare within a month of receipt of such an application does not mean that the secretariat cannot accept such an application after the substantive period. In this regard, the Board of Appeal was of the view that non-acceptance of such an application would be tantamount to punishing the applicant for a fault that he did not commit.

B. Establishment of Filing Date

299. One of the routine works of the ARIPO secretariat is to assign a filing date to each application for trade or service mark that meets the legal conditions for being assigned such a date. Article 3*bis* of the BPM regards as a trade or service mark application filing date the date on which a complete application for the mark's registration reaches the national trademark office such as the trade mark office of Tanzania or the ARIPO secretariat. To be complete, an application for trade or service mark registration has to contain an express or implied request for the mark's registration, particulars identifying the applicant and contact details of the trademark proprietor or his agent, including his email address (if any). To concretize an application for a trade or service mark registration, an applicant is also required to include in the application a 'clear reproduction of the mark' as well as a 'list of goods or services for which the registration is sought'. While the BPM mandates

764. Cf. s. 2(2), BPM.
765. Cf. s. 2(4), BPM.
766. *See* http://www.aripo.org/resources/board-of-appeals-cases (accessed: 25 Apr. 2017).

the ARIPO secretariat to record as a filing date a date on which a complete application is lodged before it, the law provides for two alternative approaches insofar as establishment of a filing date of an ARIPO trademark or service mark application filed at a national trademark office such as the trade mark office of Tanzania. The first approach, which is to record the date on which the TRADE MARK OFFICE received the application as the application's filing date,[767] is legally acceptable only if the trade mark office of Tanzania forwards such an application to ARIPO secretariat within thirty days of receipt of such an application: otherwise a filing date of such an application will be the date on which the application, which the trade mark office of Tanzania has forwarded, is actually received at ARIPO.[768]

C. Examination of ARIPO Applications

1. Formal Requirements

300. It falls within the mandate of ARIPO secretariat to examine all ARIPO applications for trade or service mark registration, for compliance with the formal requirements.[769] An admissible application should contain some particulars identifying the applicant such as the applicant's name, address and nationality or place of business as well as names of designated ARIPO Member States wherein the applicant wants his mark to enjoy protection.

It is a mandatory formal requirement that an application for ARIPO trade or service mark registration contains a list of goods or services (for which the applicant seeks registration) classified in accordance with the provisions of the Nice Agreement.[770] In the event the applicant classifies the goods or services incorrectly or if no such classification is made at all, the ARIPO secretariat may take over the role of rectifying the errors and omissions, provided that the applicant accepts to pay the fee for the classification services rendered by ARIPO.

Applicants for ARIPO trade or service marks are at liberty to claim exclusive rights in relation to any distinctive feature of a sign. In the event such a distinctive feature constituting a subject matter of ARIPO trademark application is a colour, an obligation, requiring the applicant not only mention the name of the colour and depict the main part of the colour involved, but also to categorically state that the application claims colour as a distinctive feature of the trade or service mark applied for, arises.

In case an ARIPO application for trade or service mark registration is in respect of a three-dimensional mark, the proprietor of the mark must include in the application a statement to this effect. The relevant provision of the BPM requires an applicant for registration of the three-dimensional mark to 'attach to the application

767. This approach assumes an ARIPO application filed at the national office (such as the TRADE MARK OFFICE) to have been received by ARIPO the same day it was received at the TRADE MARK OFFICE.

768. Cf. s. 3*bis*, BPM.

769. Cf. s. 5, BPM.

770. That is, the Nice Agreement Concerning the International Classification of Goods and Services for the Purposes of the Registration of Marks of 15 Jun. 1957, as revised.

a reproduction of the mark consisting of a two-dimensional graphic or photographic reproduction either of a single view of the mark or several different views of the mark'.[771]

The BPM incorporates a legal mechanism ensuring that ARIPO trade or service marks system is not a conduit for granting monopolies in words and other signs registrable as trade or service marks without such words and signs actually being used in relation to goods or services. In this regard, section 3(5) of the BPM requires a trade or service mark applicant to attach to the application for the mark's registration a declaration of actual use of the mark or an intention to use the mark in relation to goods or services. The law dispenses with this requirement if the applicant accompanies his application for registration of an ARIPO mark with a request to have another person registered as the mark's registered user. This latter alternative is more than a mere declaration; the ARIPO secretariat can allow registration of the mark only if, in addition to his intention to exploit the mark in relation to goods or services in respect of which registration is sought, the prospective registered user really accepts to be registered as the mark's user shortly after the mark is registered as ARIPO mark.

If, in the light of the examination results regarding an ARIPO trade or service mark application, the application does not meet the formal requirements for acceptance, the ARIPO secretariat may reject the application or accept the same subject to the condition requiring the applicant to complement the application with the missing formal elements. In case of rejection of the application, the applicant has a right to ask the ARIPO secretariat to reconsider its decision, so that an aggrieved party can appeal against such a rejection to the ARIPO Board of Appeal only if, even after reconsidering the matter, the ARIPO secretariat maintains its original decision.

Upon positive findings insofar as compliance with the ARIPO trade or service mark application's formal requirements is concerned, the ARIPO secretariat is required to forward the application to all designated contracting States, which in turn have to conduct substantive examination of the application in accordance with the domestic law on trade or service marks.

2. Substantive Examination

301. In case the trade mark office of Tanzania is one of the designated offices, it will be under obligation to examine an ARIPO application with a view to determining whether the trade or service mark, which is the subject matter of the application, qualifies for protection through registration in the Republic of Tanzania by virtue of the provisions of the TSMA and communicate its findings thereof to the ARIPO secretariat. In conducting such an examination, the trade mark office of Tanzania can take into account all absolute and relative grounds for trademark refusal outlined above in §4 of this chapter. The trade mark office of Tanzania is given a duration of a nine-month period to conclude the substantive examination and communicate to the secretariat the results thereof. This time limit runs from the date on

771. Section 3(4), BPM.

which ARIPO informs the trade mark office of Tanzania that an application in which the Republic of Tanzania is designated and which complies with the formal requirements of ARIPO trade and/or service mark applications has been accepted by the ARIPO secretariat.

In the event the trade mark office of Tanzania concludes that the ARIPO trade or service mark application does not fulfil the legal requirements for registration (and protection) pursuant to the provisions of the TSMA, ARIPO must be informed of this position,[772] in which event the latter will forthwith convey the same information to the trade or service mark proprietor. If aggrieved by the trade mark office's refusal to accept for protection an ARIPO mark, the proprietor has a right to directly challenge the decision before the appropriate national authorities in Tanzania. It is worthwhile to note that refusal by one designated State to protect an ARIPO mark affects protection of the mark in the refusing State: the ARIPO secretariat may issue the mark's proprietor with a certificate of registration having effects in other designated States whose law supports such protection of the mark. Similarly, if the trade mark office of Tanzania on its own motion or following an opposition by the applicant overrules its decision to deny protection of the ARIPO mark in the Republic of Tanzania, it has to immediately inform the ARIPO secretariat of that fact so that the latter can issue a certificate of registration of the mark effective in Tanzania.

D. Conversion of Applications

302. Within the ambit of section 5(4) of the BPM, an applicant for registration of an ARIPO mark enjoys a right to convert his ARIPO application into national applicant(s). This legal avenue is available to the applicant who, having exhausted all available remedies (i.e., reconsideration of his application by ARIPO secretariat and appeal against the secretariat's decision to the ARIPO Board of Appeal), still ARIPO authorities reject his application for non-compliance with formal requirements. The applicant has to be advised accordingly and – within a period of three months from the day ARIPO communicates rejection of the application to the applicant – decide whether he wishes to take advantage of the provisions of section 5 of the BPM, which bestows upon the applicant a right to request ARIPO that his application be treated as national application for trademark registration in any ARIPO contracting State which the application designates as a country wherein protection of the mark is sought. Should the Republic of Tanzania be one of the designated ARIPO contracting parties, provisions of the TSMA must exclusively apply to ARIPO trademark application that has been converted into a national application.

772. Note that, the trade mark office of Tanzania has to give reason and supporting documents indicating that the ARIPO mark does not qualify for protection in the Republic of Tanzania. Wherever applicable, the trade mark office of Tanzania may include in such notification all relative and absolute grounds that stand against protection of the ARIPO mark (cf. s. 6, BPM).

E. Publication, Registration and Opposition of ARIPO Mark

303. In case of the trade mark office of Tanzania's positive findings insofar as compliance with formal requirements by an ARIPO application is concerned, and also in case the nine-month period lapses before the trade mark office of Tanzania communicates its findings as above, ARIPO is mandated to accept the application.

If the period within which interested parties can oppose registration of an ARIPO mark expires without such an opposition having been, raised the ARIPO secretariat must register the trade or service mark concerned and declare that the protection of an ARIPO mark is effective in the Republic of Tanzania and in any other designated ARIPO Member State which is presumed under the law to have directly[773] or constructively[774] given ARIPO leeway to register the trademark contained in the ARIPO application. The secretariat is also required to register an ARIPO mark and make the same declaration as above if opposition proceedings against registration of the mark terminate in favour of the trade or service mark proprietor. It is important to note that an ARIPO mark protected in any of the Member States enjoys such protection in accordance with the national law. Thus, once an ARIPO mark is declared to be effective in Tanzania as a result of trade mark office of Tanzania's positive examination of the mark, the rights and obligations accruing to the trademark proprietor are determined in accordance with the TSMA.

The ARIPO secretariat has a duty to inform the public of the fact that it has accepted for registration an ARIPO application for trade or service mark. This duty entails making available to the public information about the trade or service mark applied for, as well as details regarding registration of the mark, once ARIPO registers the mark. Disclosure of information regarding acceptance of the mark by the secretariat gives interested parties an opportunity to oppose the registration of the ARIPO mark, whereas information concerning registration of the mark, creates an awareness of the fact that a particular mark is registered so that third parties may avoid infringing the same or institute legal proceedings seeking to nullify the registration if they have cogent reasons to argue that the mark ought not to have been registered due to one or more relative or absolute ground for trade or service mark refusal.

To realize the disclosure of information on the status of an ARIPO mark as above, the BPM requires the secretariat to publish an ARIPO mark it accepts in the ARIPO Marks Journal, providing an allowance of three-month duration prior to registering the mark so that interested members of the public may oppose acceptance of the said mark for registration. Note that, opposition proceedings against registration of ARIPO marks as well as any other proceeding in relation to the mark (such as trade or service mark infringement and nullification as well as requests for compulsory licences) are conducted at the national trademark offices of States (such as the trade

773. That is, if the trade mark office of Tanzania has examined the ARIPO trade and/or service mark application and confirms that the mark, which is a subject matter of the application, qualifies for registration and protection in the Republic of Tanzania.

774. That is, when a period of nine months elapses before the trade mark office of Tanzania submits to ARIPO its examination reports, in which event a presumption that the trademark under application has been accepted for registration and protection in the Republic of Tanzania.

mark office of Tanzania) designated in the ARIPO application for registration of a trade or service mark concerned and in accordance with the domestic law governing registration and protection of marks.

III. International Trade Marks

304. The basic legal structure underlying international registration of marks is provided for in two international legal instruments, namely the Madrid Agreement Concerning the International Registration of Marks[775] and the Madrid Protocol on Marks.[776] The United Republic of Tanzania is neither a contracting party to the Madrid Agreement nor to the Madrid Protocol. Hence, it is currently not possible for one to secure international trade mark registration in Tanzania based on the procedure governing international registration of marks under the Madrid System. Local filing of an application for trade or service mark registration is the only means by which a trade mark proprietor can obtain protection of international trade mark in the United Republic of Tanzania.

Acceptably, the Madrid Protocol has more beneficial features than the Agreement. It is notable from the text of the Agreement that the language applicable to international trade or service mark applications filed within the Agreement's framework is French only, whereas three languages – namely: French, English or Spanish – are acceptable under the protocol. Similarly, as the process leading to international registration of marks requires constant communication between contracting parties and the International Bureau at WIPO, contracting parties designated in an international application have at their disposal a period of at least eighteen months to decide whether to grant protection to international trademarks: under the Madrid Agreement only two-thirds of this period is acceptable. Moreover, under the Madrid Protocol regional organizations such as the European Union or ARIPO have a right to accede to the protocol, whereas this possibility is not available under the Madrid Agreement. It is also noteworthy that while only trade or service mark registration in the Member State constitutes a base for international trademark application under the Madrid Agreement, this is not the case under the protocol since either trademark registration or application for registration made in a contracting party may provide a legal basis for international trademark application.

The Republic of Algeria became the fifty-fifth country to accede to the Madrid Protocol on 31 October 2015. By its accession, Algeria became the last contracting party to the Madrid Agreement to allow provisions of the Madrid Protocol to govern applications for international registration in which this country is involved either as a designated State or as a country of origin. The fact that all parties to the Madrid Agreement are also parties to the Madrid Protocol made the Madrid Protocol a

775. This Agreement was enacted on 14 Apr. 1891 and it was last amended on 28 Sep. 1979. Text of the Madrid Agreement is available at http://www.wipo.int/wipolex/en/wipo_treaties/text.jsp?file_id=283529.
776. That is, the protocol relating to the Madrid Agreement concerning the international registration of marks adopted on 27 Jun. 1989 at Madrid and last amended on 12 Nov. 2007.

major instrument controlling international registration of marks and open for future accessions since its scope of membership extends to intergovernmental organization as well.

As a regional organization overseeing trade mark applications and registration on behalf of its Member States, ARIPO meets the general qualifications for becoming a contracting party to the Madrid. The Madrid system of international registration of marks would have indirect application in Tanzania by virtue of this country's membership to ARIPO. Nevertheless, ARIPO has not yet overcome the main huddle for becoming a contracting party to the Madrid Protocol. ARIPO Council of Ministers that met in Ghana in November 2011 permitted ARIPO to accede to the Madrid Protocol.[777] However, given that it currently has no legal powers to issue a unitary trademark right valid in all Member States; ARIPO has not fulfilled all the requirements for becoming a contracting party of the Madrid Protocol. Article 4 of the Madrid Protocol, which is the relevant provision in this regard stipulates that: 'any intergovernmental organization may also become party to this protocol where the following conditions are fulfilled: (i) at least one of the Member States of that organization is a party to the Paris Convention for the Protection of Industrial Property; (ii) that organization has a regional Office for the purposes of registering marks with effect in the territory of the organization'. While ARIPO fulfils most of the requirements under this provision, it lacks the legal capacity to register a trade or service mark that is effective in the whole territory of ARIPO contracting parties: ARIPO marks are only valid in the individual territories of the Member States.

§5. Ownership and Transfer (Assignment – Licences)

I. Ownership

305. Ownership of a particular trade or service mark protected in Tanzania is central for the determination of one's entitlement to exercise exclusive trade or service mark rights, to make trade or service mark transfer or to institute legal proceedings against any encroachment on the trade or service mark proprietor's exclusive rights. The TSMA does not provide for a universal clear formula on whose basis ownership of a particular trade or service mark can be determined. However, a trade or service mark proprietor is deemed to be the one who applied for registration and in whose name the mark is registered[778] as well as the one to whom the trade or service mark has been assigned or transmitted[779] – these two being differentiated from a registered user[780] who does not assume a title to the mark. However, the description under the TSMA regarding various categories of trade or service mark hints to the trade or service mark ownership modalities which

777. At http://www.wipo.int/edocs/mdocs/aspac/en/wipo_tm_tyo_12/wipo_tm_tyo_12_z.pdf (accessed: 28 May 2020).
778. Section 28(2), TSMA.
779. Section 40, TSMA.
780. Section 42, TSMA.

the TSMA envisages. Possible ownership modalities of trade or service marks registered under the TSMA may include ownership by individual natural person(s) and ownership by a body corporate. A trade or service mark can be owned by a single person, much the same as it can be the subject of joint ownership. A mark is owned jointly if whenever any of the joint owners who uses the mark is required to use it on behalf of all other joint owners; and the mark must only be used in relation to the goods with which all joint owners are connected in the course of trade or business. Generally, joint owners are not allowed to use the mark independent of each other.[781]

Different rules of ownership apply to certification and collective marks.[782]

II. Transfer

306. Ownership of a trade or service mark enjoying protection in Tanzania can change hands mainly through a transfer of such a mark.[783] Sections 40 and 42 of TSMA bestow to the trade or service mark proprietor a right to transfer their rights and/or title with respect to their protected trade or service mark. Such a transfer can be made temporarily, permanently, wholly or partially. Assignments, transmission and licences are the major means of transfer of rights in relation to a trade or service mark registered in Tanzania.

A. *Licences*

307. The term 'licence', as employed here, encompasses all circumstances wherein a person other than a trade mark proprietor gets permission from the proprietor to use the trade mark as a permitted user within the ambit of section 42 of TSMA. A trade or service mark licence is a temporary transfer of rights relating to that mark, which takes place upon free consent of the owner of the mark. Thus, licences are legally enforceable contractual arrangements allowing third parties to access, and exercise, the rights that only the trade or service mark proprietor would customarily exploit. Parties may determine the form a licence contract may assume. In view of the legal requirement that a person permitted to use the trade mark under the licence has to be registered as a user of the trade mark concerned, a licence contract concluded verbally would render the trade mark proprietor unable to prove a legal status of the permitted user. However, a contract reduced into a written form as a legal condition validating a trade or service mark licence would sufficiently constitute admissible evidence of the licensee's permission to use the mark.

In a manner virtually common to all categories of licences, a trade or service mark licensing contract may contain delimitations as to its scope, geographical area of effectiveness and the duration within which the licensee is allowed to enjoy the benefit associated with the licensed rights. Moreover, a licensing contract has to be

781. Section 24, TSMA.
782. *See* §2(II) of this chapter for an outline of ownership modalities regarding these marks.
783. Cf. Parts IX and X of TSMA.

free of ambiguity as to its scope. In particular, the text of a trade or service mark licensing contract must clarify the question of whether the licence issued is exclusive, non-exclusive or semi-exclusive. It suffices to note that, within the ambit of section 44 of TSM, a licence contract that does not take away the powers of the trade or service mark proprietor to grant licences to more than one licensee at a time is technically known as non-exclusive licence. In other words, a non-exclusive licence contract confers on two or many persons the right to exploit the licensed trade or service mark, whereas a licence that limits not only the powers of the trade or service mark proprietor to issue further licences but also the right to exploit the trade mark right during the pendency of the licence agreement is considered to be exclusive licence. Thus, an exclusive licence contract, bestows upon the licensee legal powers to exploit the licensed trade or service mark to the exclusion of all other persons, including the licensor. Although not stated clearly in the TSMA, parties are free to conclude a semi-exclusive licence extending to the licensee a right to exploit the trade or service mark to the exclusion of all other persons, except the right owner.

In view of the above, it is clear that a licence to use a registered trade mark does not have immediate binding effects on third parties, unless the licensee obtains a legal status of a permitted user of a trade mark. In certain circumstances, for this category of a contract to bind on third parties, the law requires ministerial approval. Section 45 of TSMA empowers the minister responsible for trade to make an order requiring 'licence contracts or certain categories of them, and amendments or renewals of such contracts' to first be approved by the office of the Registrar of trade or service mark. The economic development and the needs of the United Republic of Tanzania are the keys to the granting or denying such approval.

It is notable under section 42 of TSMA, read together with Regulation 76 of TMRs, that both the licensor and licensee play a significant role to ensure that a person to whom the trade mark proprietor has issued a licence to use the trade or service mark is duly recognized as such by the Registrar of trade and service marks. Both parties to the licence contract may apply for registration of a licensee as a permitted user: they do so using form TM/SM31 when lodging such an application. Section 43 of TSMA provides for information that has to feature in an application for registration of a person as a registered user. Relevant information, in this regard, includes personal details (i.e., the name and address) of the person proposed to be registered as a user of the proprietor's trade mark. Further required details include those regarding the relationship between the trade mark proprietor and the proposed trade mark user. Additionally, the goods or services in respect of which the proposed user is to be registered must to be specified.

Section 46 of TSMA outlines circumstances under which registration of a person as permitted user of a trade mark can be cancelled. Generally, the registrar is empowered to cancel registration of a permitted user as a response to an application to this effect made by both the registered user and the proprietor of the registered trade or service mark. Cancellation of registration of a permitted user is imminent if the trade mark proprietor or the permitted user misled the registrar to believe that the permitted user was entitled to such registration, while they were not. Moreover, in case of change of legal status of the trade mark such as where the trade mark is no longer registered serves as a legal ground for cancelling registration of a person as a trade mark user.

It is always in the interests of the trade mark proprietor to maintain reputation of his registered trade mark. Any agreement between the trade or service mark proprietor and the permitted user of the proprietor's mark would contain a clause ensuring that the proprietor retains powers to exercise effective control over the quality of the goods or services of the licensee, for which the mark is used. In this regard, the 'effective control' clause is included in a licence contract as a matter of volition. Sometimes, however, such a clause has to feature in the licence contract in order to fulfil a mandatory legal requirement, short of which the entire contract becomes null and void *ab initio*. Section 44(1) of TSMA reiterates this position in the following manner:

> A licence contract shall be invalid in the absence of relations or stipulations between the registered proprietor of the trade or service mark and the proposed registered user, ensuring effective control by the registered proprietor of the quality of the goods or services of the proposed registered user in relation to which the trade or service mark is to be used.

B. Assignments

308. An assignment of a trade or service mark is a permanent transfer of those rights; it entails a total change of ownership. Both registration of a trade or service mark and a pending application for registration of a trade mark are capable of being assigned under the TSMA.[784] Section 22 of TSMA provides a special scenario of assignment in relation to foreign trade marks; it recognizes the right, of a person entitled to have his trade mark registered in Tanzania by virtue of priority right, to assign that right.[785]

Section 2 of TSMA refers to the term 'assignment' as 'transfer by act of the parties concerned'. An assignment is done *inter vivos* through a voluntary agreement between the assignor and assignee. To be legally enforceable against third parties an assignment of a trade mark has to be registered in the trade mark register. Section 40(6) TSMA establishes the powers of the trade or service mark proprietor to assign the mark as follows:

> Subject to the provisions of this Act, the person for the time being entered in the Register as proprietor of a trade or service mark shall, subject to any rights appearing from the Register to be vested in any other person, have power to assign the trade or service mark and to give effectual receipts for any consideration for an assignment thereof.

784. Section 40, TSMA.
785. *See* §4(II)(A) of this chapter outlining the priority right.

Certain circumstances render a trade or service mark unassignable. The law categorizes as unacceptable, a trade mark assignment which, as its effects, causes consumer confusion or deception whenever the assignee uses the assigned trade mark. A serious case in favour of prohibiting trade or service mark assignment if the confusion or deception it causes relate to the 'nature, origin, manufacturing process, characteristics or suitability for their purpose, of the goods or services in relation to which the trade or service mark is intended to be used or is being used'.[786]

Two options are available to a trade mark proprietor contemplating to transfer his trade mark by way of assignment. He may assign the mark with or without goodwill. Trade mark assignment, which does not involve transfer of good will, is also known as trademark assignment in gross. The Oxford Online English Dictionary refers to the term 'goodwill' as the 'established reputation of a business regarded as a quantifiable asset and calculated as part of its value when it is sold'.[787] Indeed, the trademark goodwill is the 'inherent value of trademarks' reflected by the recognition of the mark concerned among consumers and 'the extra earning power that it generates'.[788] The legal implication of assigning trade or service mark with a goodwill is that the transferee will be required to maintain the same quality or standards of goods or services in relation to which the mark enjoys protection. While this legal option aims to protect the trust that the consuming public has in relation to quality of the goods or services marketed or offered under the mark, it also aims to prohibit the assignee of the mark from changing the list of goods and services for which the assignment contract permits him to use the mark. This in turn leads to avoidance of consumer confusion in the market and maintains legitimate expectations of the consumer insofar as it concerns making an informed selection of goods or services. On the contrary however, by providing for an option to assign a trade or service mark without goodwill, the Regulation 62 of TMRs essentially appreciates the fact that a trade or service mark can be a subject of trade by itself. Although trademark assignment in gross (i.e., without goodwill) may not avoid criticisms as it could be seen as conduit for trafficking in trademarks,[789] its endorsement under the law may be seen as a modernization of the trademark regime of Tanzania: such a regime recognizes the fact that trade or service marks are property rights and as such, legal transfer of the same should not be subjected to unnecessary restrictions. In this, it is commonplace that, depending on marketing strategies and capabilities an assignee may create goodwill far beyond that enjoyed by his predecessor in title.

Exclusive rights one acquires as a result of a trade or service mark are not automatically enforceable against third parties. Those rights are activated when particulars of the relevant assignment contract are entered into the register of trade marks

786. Section 40(2), TSMA.

787. At https://en.oxforddictionaries.com/definition/goodwill (accessed: 22 May 2020).

788. At http://www.franchiselawsolutions.com/blog/what-is-trademark-goodwill/ (accessed: 22 May 2020). *See also* Miriam D. Trudell & P.C. Sheridan Ross, *Issues to Consider in Assignments of U.S. Trademark Applications and Registrations*, 69(21) INTA Bulletin (15 Nov. 2014).

789. The term 'trafficking in trademarks' refers to the 'act of getting a trademark registered without any intention to use it in relation to any goods but to deal with the mark itself to gain monetary benefit by its sale' (cf. Kunal Ambasta, *Trademark Licensing and Trafficking in Trademarks: Does the Law Promote it?*, Indian J. Intell. Prop. Law 73, http://www.commonlii.org/in/journals/INJlIPLaw/2011/4.pdf (accessed: 22 May 2020)).

kept at the trade mark office. In other words, unless an assignment agreement is registered with the office of the registrar, it will only bind the assignee and the assignor.[790] Section 40 of the TMA provides for registration of trade mark assignments, which stipulates as follows:

> Where a person becomes entitled by assignment or transmission to a registered trade mark, he shall make application on the form prescribed to the registrar to register his title, and the registrar shall on receipt of the application and of proof of title to his satisfaction, register him as the proprietor of the trade mark and shall cause particulars of the assignment or transmission to be entered in the register.

The assignee of a trade mark desiring to have official recognition of his status as a new proprietor of the trade mark must file an application for registration of the assignment at the trade and service mark office. Forms TM/SM12 and TM/SM13 are used when applying for registration of a trade mark assignment. The former form becomes relevant when an application for registration of assignment is filed either by the assignee alone or both the assignee and the assignor as conjoint applicants. The latter form is only used when registering an assignment in line with what is already stipulated in the trade mark register. In most cases, this happens if the subject matter of the assignment is unregistered trade or service mark whose application for registration is pending before the trade mark office. In this case, the trade mark registrar will provisionally record particulars of the assignment in the register. Final official registration of that assignment can take place only if the pending trade mark application is successfully approved.[791]

For instance, this could be in relation to a trade mark applied for by a natural person with the intention to assign the same to a legal person. In case the registrar had recorded this fact in the register of trade marks, that legal person can apply for the registration of the corresponding assignment.

Rule 59 of TMRs specifies particulars that must feature in an application for registration of an assignment: some of these are the personal details of the assignee (i.e., name, address and nationality), as well as a proof of entitlement to an assignment. A claim to a trade mark proprietorship by virtue of a trade mark assignment must be evidenced by a written document the veracity of which may be verified through a statutory instrument made on Form TM/SM14.

In principle, an assignment of a trade mark relates to particular goods and services for which the trade mark is registered. Consequently, it is indisputable that a registered trade mark can be a subject of partial assignment or full assignment. Partial assignment leads to two or more persons being severally entitled to proprietorship of a single trade mark. Partial trade mark assignment becomes a reality if the assignment contract specifies and differentiates the goods or services, which each of the assignees is permitted to use the trade mark involved.

A trade mark assignment under the trade mark regime of Tanzania may as well be confined to certain localities of markets thus leading to more than one person

790. Section 40(5), TSMA.
791. Section 40(4), TSMA.

being entitled to the proprietorship of the trade mark not only with regard to specified goods or services, but also to identified places and markets.[792]

In case a single trade mark is a subject of more than one assignment, the duty of the Registrar to scrutinize the relevant agreements becomes onerous. In doing so, the registrar must observe the caveat that an application for registration of a trade mark assignment becomes inadmissible if transferring of the trade mark proprietorship in the manner envisaged under the assignment contract is likely to cause some hardship. In particular, the registrar must decline registration of a trade mark assignment, when the assignment involved is likely to cause consumer confusion or deception.

C. *Transmission*

309. Transmission is one of the legal means by which ownership of a trade or service mark can move from one person to another. The TSMA delineates the term 'transmission' as a 'transfer by operation of law, demolition on the personal representatives of a deceased person and any other mode of transfer not being an assignment'.[793] Both assignment and transmission have similar end effects; namely, to move trade mark ownership from one party (transferor) to the other (transferee). However, they do have a marked difference when analysed from their legal contexts with special reference to natural persons: whereas a trademark assignment is realized *inter vivos*, there is no possibility for both parties to be alive at the time when transmission of a trademark comes into effect. It suffices to note that a legal process culminating into transmission of a trademark can be exemplified by a scenario whereby the trademark passes onto another person through inheritance or when a company declared insolvent or taken over by another company is forced to have its tangible and intangible assets passing onto an insolvency administrator or to the taking-over company. Insofar transfer of trade mark through inheritance is concerned, a piece of legislation other than the TSMA would be more relevant as regards modalities of succession. As a matter of a general principle, succession can be testamentary where before their death the trade mark proprietor (i.e., testator) had made a testament (will) transferring the trade or service mark to the person named in the will. In case the trade or service mark owner dies intestate, that is to say without making a will, resort could be had to the law regulating inheritance and succession matters in Tanzania to determine the rightful successor.

The legality of transmission of a trade or service is subject to requirements similar to those applicable to trade or service mark assignment.[794] Such requirements include the condition that there should be no likelihood of consumer confusion or deception whatsoever caused by the transmission. Moreover, exclusive rights of the person entitled to a trade or service mark by virtue of the transmission only when particulars regarding transmission of a trade or service mark are entered into the register of trade marks.

792. Regulation 64, TMRs.
793. Section 2, para. 16, TSMA.
794. Section 40, TSMA.

§6. SCOPE OF EXCLUSIVE RIGHTS

310. A valid trade or service mark extends to its proprietor the 'exclusive rights to the use of a trade or service mark in relation to any goods including sale importation and offer for sale or importation'.[795] The proprietor is accordingly entitled to interdict third parties from using in the course of trade or business the proprietor's trade mark or any other sign which is identical to or nearly resembles the proprietor's mark provided that if unchecked, such use would deceive or confuse consumers as to the true source of the goods or services; or would have detrimental effect to the repute of the proprietor's mark. Section 32 of TSMA outlines circumstances of trade mark use, which the trade mark proprietor must authorize in order for a particular trade mark use by third parties to be legitimate.

I. Section 32(1)(a) of the TSMA

311. Section 32(1)(a) and (b) of TSMA provides for a systematic description of the scope of protection a trade mark receives in Tanzania. It stipulates that:

> (1) The exclusive right referred to in section 31 shall be deemed to be infringed by any person who, not being the proprietor of a trade mark or registered user thereof using by way of the permitted use, uses a sign either (a) identical with or so nearly resembling it as to be likely to deceive or cause confusion, in the course of trade or business, in relation to any goods in respect of which it is registered or in relation to any closely related goods and in such manner as to render the use of the sign likely to be either(i) as being used as a trade mark or business or company name, or (ii) in a case in which the use is upon the goods or in physical relation thereto, or in relation to services, or in an advertising circular or other advertisement issued to the public, as importing a reference to some person having the right either as proprietor or as a registered user to use the trade marks or to goods or services with which such a person as aforesaid is connected in the course of business or trade;

Trade mark infringement under section 32(1)(a) of TSMA is based on two main tests; namely: (1) the subject matter test; and (2) the effect of use test. The subject matter test relates to conditions regarding identity or similarity of the conflicting marks on one hand and of goods or services in relation to which the conflicting marks are used, on the other. On its part, the 'effect of use test' addresses conditions regarding the effects the use of the conflicting marks must produce or likely to produce, and the circumstances under which the conflicting trade marks must be used in order for such use to constitute trade mark infringement.

---

795. Section 31, TSMA.

A. *The Subject Matter Test*

1. Double-identity Rule

312. Confirmation of trade mark infringement under section 32(1)(a) of TSMA requires the trade mark proprietor to prove existence of double identity; namely, identity between the infringing mark and the protected mark as well as identity between the goods or services in respect of which the protected mark is registered and those in relation to which the third party has used (or uses) the infringing sign. It is instructive to note that an infringing sign may be regarded as identical with a protected trade mark if such a sign, when judged by the elements of features constituting it, is an exact copy of the infringed trade mark or where, viewed as a whole, the infringing sign differs from the proprietor's trade mark only in insignificant elements or features such that the difference may go unnoticed by an average consumer. Consequently, a proprietor of a trade mark protected in Tanzania is legally able to prohibit the use of an infringing sign within the meaning of section 32(1)(a) of the TSMA only if the infringing sign and the proprietor's trade mark corresponds in all aspects. In trade mark infringement cases that are based on double-identity rule as elaborated above are cases of strict liability.[796] Hence, the likelihood that the infringer's use of the trade mark causes consumer confusion or deception is presumed; the trade mark proprietor has no burden to prove the likelihood of consumer confusion or consumer deception. Therefore, one can argue that, pursuant to the foregoing double-identity rule of trade mark protection, counterfeit or piracy cases are much easier to curb.[797] It is instructive to note that, where an infringing sign copies a part of the protected trade mark, infringement proceedings regarding that scenario cannot be brought under the double-identity rule even if the trade mark proprietor manages to prove that the part reproduced in the infringing sign is the most prominent part of the infringed trade mark.[798]

2. Cases Not Covered under the Double-Ident Rule

313. A trade mark proprietor enjoys some powers to prohibit third parties from using a sign that infringes on his exclusive rights where such infringement is associated with the identity or similarity between the infringing sign and the registered trade mark and the use of the infringing sign in relation to goods or service which are similar to those the proprietor's trade mark is registered, provided as a result of such identity or similarity 'there exists the likelihood of deception or confusion'. Two main conclusions, regarding trade mark infringement not covered under the double-identity rule, can be drawn from the provisions of section 32(1)(a) of the TSMA. First, where the infringed trade mark enjoys protection in respect of some

796. R. Annand & H. Norman, *Blackstone's Guide to the Community Trade Mark* 162 (Blackstone Press 1998).

797. P.A.C.E. van der Kooij, *The Community Trade Mark Regulation: An Article by Article Guide* 33(Sweet & Maxwell 2000).

798. J. Philips, *Trade Mark Law: A Practical Anatomy* 314 (Oxford University Press 2003).

goods, such infringement may result from the unauthorized use of an identical sign in relation to similar goods; or of similar signs in relation to identical goods; or of similar sign in relation to similar goods. Second, a trade mark designating services would be infringed if the infringer uses an identical sign in relation to similar services; similar sign in relation to identical services; and a similar sign in relation to similar services.

B. The Effect of Use Test

1. Likelihood of Confusion or Deception

314. The subject matter test is necessary to found a claim for trade mark infringement. However, the test is not self-sufficient as it must be complemented by the effect resulting from the use of the infringing sign. The effect of use test takes into account the likelihood of confusion or deception, which the use of the infringing sign causes in the market for goods or services individualized by the protected trade or service mark.

Likelihood of confusion is central for determining whether some use made of a particular sign by unauthorized person is within the scope of the exclusive rights of a proprietor of a trade mark protected in Tanzania under section 32(1)(a) of TSMA. Likelihood of confusion constitutes the specific condition for finding trade mark infringement in cases not involving the double-identity rule.

Trade mark infringement cases that are based on double-identity rule as elaborated above are cases of strict liability.[799] Hence, the likelihood that the infringer's use of the trade mark causes consumer confusion or deception is presumed; the trade mark proprietor has no burden to prove the likelihood of consumer confusion or consumer deception. One can argue that, pursuant to the double-identity rule of trade mark protection, counterfeit or piracy cases are much easier to curb.[800] It is instructive to note that, where an infringing sign copies a part of the protected trade mark, infringement proceedings regarding that scenario cannot be brought under the double-identity rule even if the trade mark proprietor manages to prove that the part reproduced in the infringing sign is the most prominent part of the infringed trade mark.[801]

2. Manner of Trade Mark Use

315. Section 32(1)(a)(i) of TSMA considers as an infringement when, in addition to the subject matter test, the infringer uses the infringing sign as a 'trade mark or business or company name'.

---

799. R. Annand & H. Norman, *Blackstone's Guide to the Community Trade Mark* 162 (Blackstone Press 1998).
800. P.A.C.E. van der Kooij, *The Community Trade Mark Regulation: An Article by Article Guide* 33(Sweet & Maxwell 2000).
801. J. Philips, *Trade Mark Law: A Practical Anatomy* 314 (Oxford University Press 2003).

3. Other Modalities of Use of Infringing Sign

316. Section 32(1)(a)(ii) of TSMA identifies use of a trade mark, other than when the trade mark is used as a trade mark or business or company name as in the immediately preceding paragraph, which may lead to trade mark infringement. Such use relates to a 'case in which the use is upon the goods or in physical relation thereto, or in relation to services, or in an advertising circular or other advertisement issued to the public'. Where a trade mark is used as in the immediately preceding sentence, it will constitute a trade mark infringement if such use imports a 'reference to some person having the right either as proprietor or as a registered user to use the trade marks or to goods or services with which such a person as aforesaid is connected in the course of business or trade'.

II. Trade Mark with Reputation

317. Section 32(1)(b) of TSMA offers special protection to a trade mark registered in Tanzania; is stipulates that:

> The exclusive right … shall be deemed to be infringed by any person who, not being the proprietor of a trade mark or registered user thereof using by way of the permitted use, uses a sign … identical with or nearly resembling it in the course of trade or business in any manner likely to impair the distinctive character or acquired reputation of the trade mark.

The existence of reputation in relation to a registered trade mark is one of the elements that a trade mark proprietor must prove so as to avail himself of the protection against trade mark infringement, which section 32(1)(b) of TSMA provides for. Reputation must be in relation to goods and/or services. A trade mark is regarded to have reputation, when consumers place a particular value on the trade mark in order to make or avoid making repeat purchases.[802] The reputation of the mark must be appreciated in the Republic of Tanzania and, presumably, not later than the date of the purported infringement.[803]

The court may thus confirm reputation of a trade mark on the basis of any of the following factors, the existence of which the trade mark proprietor must prove:

> (a) The degree of inherent or acquired distinctiveness of the mark; (b) The duration and extent of use of the mark in connection with the goods or services with which the mark is used; (c) The duration and extent of advertising and publicity of the mark; (d) The geographical extent of the trading area in which the mark is used; (e) The channels of trade for the goods or services with which the mark is used; (f) The degree of recognition of the mark in trade areas and

802. *Ibid.*, 370.

803. D. Kitchin et al, *Kerly's Law of Trade Marks and Trade Names* 383 (Sweet & Maxwell 4th ed. 2005).

channels of trade used by the mark's owner; and(g) The nature and extent of use of the same or similar sign by third parties.[804]

It is noteworthy under section 34(1)(b) of the TMA that the proprietor of a trade mark with reputation may enjoy protection against two types of unauthorized trade mark use; namely: (i) the trade mark use, which is likely to impair the distinctive character of a proprietor's mark, (ii) the trade mark use, which is likely to impair the repute of the protected trade mark.

Impairment to the distinctive character or the repute of a registered trade mark signifies that the infringer's activities harm or injure the trade mark involved in such a way that the mark becomes 'less attractive (tarnishing) or less distinctive (blurring)'.[805] Indeed, the phrase 'impairment to the distinctive character or the repute of a registered trade mark' is an interchangeable reference to 'dilution', 'whittling away' or 'blurring'. This phrase becomes relevant when the ability of the registered trade mark to designate the trade mark proprietor as being the source of the goods or services in relation to which the trade mark is used is weakened. Such weakening of the trade mark's ability to distinguish goods and services becomes evident if the use of the infringing sign leads to dispersion of the identity and hold upon the public mind of the infringed trade mark. This then renders the infringed trade mark incapable of arousing, as opposed to the ability it used to possess, in the mind of the consuming public, immediate association of the registered trade mark and the goods and services for which the mark enjoys protection.[806]

Given the foregoing, it is tenable to argue that the legislative intent enshrined in section 34(1)(b) of the TSMA is to avoid detriment to the distinctive character or reputation of a registered trade mark, which can be a consequence of trade mark infringement. Essentially, section 34(1)(b) of the TSMA aims at curbing 'tarnishment' or 'degradation' of the distinctive character or reputation of a registered trade mark. The school of thought in this regard holds that, a detriment to the repute of an earlier mark 'is caused when the goods or services for which the identical or similar sign is used by the third party may be perceived by the public in such a way that the trade mark's power of attraction is reduced'.[807] This is particularly a case when, due to their characteristics or quality, the infringer's goods or services negatively impact on the image of the infringed trade mark.

In view of the foregoing, section 32(1)(b) of the TMA extends special protection to a registered trade mark by going beyond the conventional trade mark protection

804. R. Annand & H. Norman, *Blackstone's Guide to the Community Trade Mark* 183 (Blackstone Press 1998). *See also McDonald's Corporation v. Joburgers Drive-Inn Restaurant (Pty) Ltd and Another; McDonald's Corporation v. Dax Prop CC and Another; McDonald's Corporation v. Joburgers Drive-Inn Restaurant (Pty) Ltd and Dax Prop CC* 1997 (1) SA 1 (SCA).
805. D. Kitchin et al, *Kerly's Law of Trade Marks and Trade Names* 384 (Sweet & Maxwell 4th ed. 2005).
806. Case C-252/07, *Intel Corporation Inc. v. CPM United Kingdom Ltd* [2008] ECR I-08823, para. 29.
807. Case C-487/07, *L'Oréal SA v. Bellure* [2009] ECR I-05185, para. 40.

enshrined in the TRIPS Agreement:[808] The trade mark infringement rule enshrined under the section is not confined to the existence or likelihood of trade mark confusion or deception.[809]

§7. Limitation of the Scope of Trademark Protection

318. A trade mark registration does not extend to a proprietor a monopoly over a mark in all circumstances. Third parties may, for instance, use the very registered trade mark owned by an independent person without infringing it. Section 32(3) of TSMA is one of the provisions describing this possibility. An outline of this and other provisions that limit the exclusive rights of the trade mark proprietor follows herein below.

I. Bona Fide Use of a Trade Mark

319. Where unauthorized persons use a protected trade or service mark in a way that is considered bona fide for being consistent with fair practice underlying the relevant industry and commercial circle, the proprietor has no legal entitlement to prohibit such use of his trade mark. Three scenarios of unauthorized trade or service mark use are considered bona fide use, unless proved otherwise. These are (i) the use of one's own name or address, or the name or address for which a claim of right to use exists (ii) descriptive use of a trade mark and (iii) use of a trade mark to indicate the intended purpose of a product or service.

A. *Use of Names and Addresses*

320. Trademark law of Tanzania entitles any person to the use of 'his own name, or of the name of the geographical location of his business, or of the name of any of his predecessors in business' in relation to goods or services, even where another person owns a registered trademark similar to the third party's name.[810] This rule essentially signifies that a man is entitled to trade in his own name provided he does what is reasonable, necessary to distinguish his business from that of another person of the same name. However, such use of the name by the third party cannot be justified unless it is a bona fide use.

808. Article 16(1) of TRIPS limits trade mark protection to the same scope provided for under s. 32(1)(b) of the TSMA.
809. Case C-251/95, *Sabel BV v. Puma AG* [1997] ECR I-06191.
810. Section 34(i), TSMA.

B. Descriptive Use of a Trade Mark

321. It is lawful, under Tanzanian law, for marketers to describe the quality or characteristics of their goods using a trademark irrespective of whether the trademark owner has consented to the use.[811] This is, however, a rebuttable presumption: a person resorting to a descriptive use of the mark must ensure that the use does not influence the public to think that the goods under description come from the proprietor of the trade mark, or that there is any connection whatsoever between the goods under description and the proprietor of the trademark.[812]

C. Use of a Trade Mark to Indicate Intended Purpose

322. A registered trade mark does not empower its proprietor to prohibit an unauthorized persons from using it in the course of trade 'in relation to goods adapted to form part of, or to be accessory to, other goods in relation to which the trade mark has been registered if the use of the trade or service mark is reasonably necessary in order to indicated that the goods are so adapted'.[813]

Indicating the intended purpose of a product using a trade or service mark belonging to another person, becomes lawful when the third party's use of that trade mark is the only practical and reasonable means of furnishing the public with the relevant information insofar as that product's intended purpose is concerned.[814]

The question of whether informative use of a trademark by an unauthorized person infringes the exclusive rights of the proprietor of a registered trade mark would be paramount if, for instance, a person not authorized by the BMW company uses the famous BMW trade mark in advertisements to inform the public that he carries out the repair and maintenance of BMW cars or he has specialized, or is a specialist, in the sale or repair and maintenance of those cars. The BMW company would definitely object to such third party's use of the trademark, since the third party, who carries on a garage business, uses in course of trade the BMW's trade mark. Indeed, the court dealing with this case would, in the first place, determine whether the third party uses the BMW mark as a trade mark as such. The Court in Tanzania would find the third party to have used the mark in issue as trade or service mark that the mark was used as a mark.[815] However, infringement in this case would be upheld only if section 32(3)(b) of TSMA did not exempt the use complained of. In this regard, the justification for the court's holding in favour of the purported infringer would base on the acknowledgement of the reality that restricting a third party's

811. Sections. 32(3)(b) and 34(ii), TSMA.
812. Section 34(ii), TSMA.
813. Section 32(3)(b) of the TSMA.
814. *Gillette Company and Gillette Group Finland Oy v. LA-Laboratories Ltd Oy* [2005] ECR I-02337, para. 1 of the operative part.
815. *See* by analogy Case C-63/97 *BMW v. Ronald Karel Deenik* [1999] ECR I-00905, operative part at [2].

right to use a registered trade mark, when such use aims to communicate to the public that the third party carries out repair and maintenance of BMW cars, would remove all practical possibilities of communicating this fact to the consumers.[816]

In the above scenario, the third party's use of the BMW mark would not only be considered legitimate but also bona fide within the meaning of the proviso to section 32 of TSMA, especially if he acts consistent with fair practice in relation to the legitimate interests of the proprietor of the registered trade mark.

II. Principle of Exhaustion

323. The principle of exhaustion of trade mark rights is one of the tenets, usually employed to limit the scope of exclusive rights which a registered trade mark extends to its proprietor. For instance, a trademark proprietor is presumed to have exhausted his trademark rights once he or any other person permitted by him applies the trade mark to goods and place them on the market. Where the principle of exhaustion is applicable, a third party who buys goods on which the proprietor has consensually applied his trademark does not need any form of authorization from the trade mark proprietor to be able to engage in further commercialization of those goods.

The tenet of trade mark exhaustion is subject to two main limitations. First, this principle empowers the trade mark proprietor to prohibit use of his trade mark on products he has initially marketed as above if the trade mark which was put on the goods has been subsequently removed or obliterated by a person other than the trade mark proprietor or his duly authorized agent. Second, the principle is circumscribed in terms of a definite geographical market. This market may be a national market, a regional market, or a global market.

Exploitation of trademark rights in Tanzania is subject to the principle of national exhaustion. Pursuant to this principle, a trademark proprietor is not entitled to restrict third parties from further commercializing goods bearing the proprietor's trademark where the proprietor, or any other person with the proprietor's permission, had initially placed those goods on the market in the United Republic of Tanzania, unless the condition of the goods concerned has been impaired after the sale or offer for sale of those goods.[817] Therefore, the principle of exhaustion of trademark rights cannot be invoked to allow a third person to apply the proprietor's trademark 'upon the goods after they have suffered alteration as respects their state or condition, get-up or packaging'.[818]

According to section 32(3)(a) TSMA, a trademark proprietor is also presumed to have exhausted his trade mark rights once he or any other person with the proprietor's authorization applies the trademark to the goods. To rebut this presumption,

816. Opinion of Mr Advocate General Jacobs delivered on 2 Apr. 1998 in ECJ, Case C-63/97 *BMW v. Ronald Karel Deenik* [1999] ECR I-00905.

817. Cf. s. 32(3)(c), TSMA. For an analysis of different forms of trade mark exhaustion, *see* J. Jaconiah, *The Parallel Importation of Trademarked Goods in the Framework of the Economic Partnership Agreement Between the East African Community and the European Union*, 42(6) IIC 685–686 (2011).

818. Section 32(2)(a), TSMA.

the proprietor must rely on the provisions of section 32(2) of TSMA and prove the following: (1) the third party has altered or obliterated the trademark, which the proprietor has applied to the goods; or (2) the third party has applied another trademark to the goods in addition to the trademark, which the proprietor has applied to the goods; or (3) in addition to the proprietor's trademark, the third party has also added to the goods other matter in a written form and that the added matter are likely to injure the reputation of the trademark; or (4) in addition to the trademark, the proprietor has also applied to the goods other matter suggesting existence of business connection between the proprietor or a registered user of the mark and the goods; and that the third party has removed or obliterated the trademark without removing that other matter too.

The principle of trademark exhaustion applicable in Tanzania Zanzibar regards trade mark rights as exhausted if the relevant trademarked good is placed on a market anywhere in the world.[819] By allowing unauthorized third parties to deal in a trademarked good in different ways including by importing them, where the trade mark proprietor has placed those goods for the first time in a market outside Tanzania Zanzibar, section 49(4) of ZIPA the ZIPA postulates the tenet of international exhaustion of trademark rights. This form of trade mark exhaustion operates to restrict the trade mark proprietor's monopoly in relation to goods the proprietor (or another person approved by the proprietor) has put on the market in any country.[820]

It is important to note that, by establishing the principle of international trade mark exhaustion, section 49 of ZIPA plays a significant role of strengthening the single market between Tanzania mainland and Tanzania Zanzibar. International exhaustion of trade mark rights effectively takes away the possibility of a trade mark proprietor to partition the market of the United Republic of Tanzania into two separate markets. Under this principle, trademarked goods marketed in Tanzania mainland, are considered exhausted not only in the mainland, but also in Zanzibar. Consequently a trade mark proprietor owning a registered trade mark in Zanzibar is unable to limit further commercialization of his trademarked goods in one part of the United Republic of Tanzania having exploited the corresponding trade mark right in the other part of the United Republic of Tanzania. As good as it is, in fostering the interests of the united market of the United Republic of Tanzania, the principle of international exhaustion, which section 49 of ZIPA enshrines, is likely to come into conflict with the principle of national exhaustion applicable in Tanzania mainland under section 32(3) of TSMA. This conflict can arise in relation to a single trade mark registered and protected in both parts of the United Republic. In line with the principle of national exhaustion applicable in Tanzania mainland, the proprietor of the foregoing trade mark has the possibility to sale or supply trademarked goods to consumers or marketers in a country outside the United Republic and retain the right to prohibit further commercialization of those goods in Tanzania mainland. In view of the principle of international exhaustion, the trade mark

819. Section 49(4), ZIPA.
820. Ernst & Young (2019), Exhaustion of IP Rights – A feasibility study commissioned by the UK IP Office, retrieved from https://www.gov.uk/government/publications/exhaustion-of-intellectual-property-rights-a-feasibility-study?utm_source=c78de1a3-0edd-4793-9745-8fedfc8933a0&utm_medium=email&utm_campaign=govuk-notifications&utm_content=immediate (accessed: 25 May 2020).

proprietor's act of selling trademarked good abroad as in the immediately preceding sentence will exhaust the pertinent trade mark rights in Tanzania Zanzibar. It follows that although parallel importers can reimport those goods into the United Republic of Tanzania through the window of Tanzania Zanzibar, the legal powers of the proprietor to prohibit resale of those goods in Tanzania mainland is imbued with uncertainty. First, Tanzania Zanzibar being part of the single market of the United Republic of Tanzania, the principle of national exhaustion applicable in Tanzania mainland has the effect of denying the trade mark proprietor the legal power to prohibit resale of the trademarked goods covered under the foregoing scenario. Second, the trade mark proprietor may successfully prohibit resale of the goods concerned in Tanzania mainland by considering importation into Tanzania Zanzibar of the products the proprietor marketed abroad to be a contravention of the national exhaustion principle to which the proprietor's trade mark rights protected in Tanzania mainland is subjected.

III. Utilitarian Features of a Trade Mark

324. Trade mark law does not bestow to a trade mark proprietor a right to exclude other persons interested in using utilitarian features of a registered trade mark from doing so. Trade mark protection does not grant to trade mark proprietors exclusive rights in utilitarian features. The trade mark proprietor would be entitled to such right by virtue of other IP protection frameworks such as patent and design protection regimes, just to mention but a few.

Notable legal bases for limiting exclusive rights of the trade mark proprietor in respect of utilitarian features both in Tanzania mainland and Tanzania Zanzibar are sections 19(b) and 46(2)(i) of TSMA and ZIPA respectively. Section 19(b) of TSMA excludes from protection 'trade or service marks which consist solely of the shape, configuration or colour of the goods, or the containers thereof'. The legal exclusion under section 46(2)(i) of ZIPA applies if the shape, configuration or colour 'is incapable of distinguishing the goods or services of one enterprise from those of other enterprises'. In view of the foregoing, both TSMA and ZIPA have one thing in common: a mark consisting of a shape, configuration or colour of the goods, or the containers thereof cannot be registered as trade or service marks, as they are broadly constituted by aesthetic appearance of the goods. While it is true that such an aesthetic appearance may be instrumental to enable a consumer reach a particular conclusion regarding their decision to buy or to refrain from buying the goods bearing the mark, still such aesthetic features are hardly protectable as a trade mark.[821] This is because these features may possess distinctiveness capability, which is not acceptable from trade mark law point of view. For instance, a shape or configuration which is well known by consumers not because of its capability to indicate the source of

821. The possibility for legal protection of these features exists under other branches of IP, design law in particular (Cf. I.M. Davies ed., *Sweet & Maxwell's European Trade Mark Litigation Handbook* 39 (Sweet & Maxwell 1998)).

origin, but due to the attractiveness of that shape or configuration, cannot be protected as a trade mark; that shape or configuration serves to attain non-trade mark functions of making the product ornamental or of being part of the design of the product.

IV. Honest Concurrent Use of a Trade Mark

325. As a limitation to the scope of the trademark proprietor's exclusive rights described above in §6 of this chapter, the TMA provides for exceptional circumstances warranting the Registrar of trade marks to approve coexistence in the trademark register and concurrent use in Tanzania of two or more identical or confusingly similar trade or service marks.[822] The conditions for such coexistence are met if two persons, with no commercial connection, adopt and use in identical trade or service marks in relation to identical or confusingly similar goods or services. The adoption and the use of the mark must nevertheless be concurrent and in an honest manner. However, in allowing coexistence of trademarks the trade registrar may set out some conditions and limitations to be observed by the concurrent users of the trademarks. This is particularly the case if the concurrent use of the trademark is likely to defeat the key objective underlying the regime for trademark protection; namely, to avoid likelihood of consumer deception and confusion in the marketplace.

V. Use of Another Registered Trade Mark

326. A proprietor of a trade or service mark registered in Tanzania does not derive from such a mark a right to exclude others from using another registered trade mark that is 'identical or nearly resemble' the trade mark purported to be infringed.[823] Section 50(1) of the TMA is one of the provisions justifying this limitation to the trade mark proprietor's exclusive rights. It provides that '… the fact that a person is registered as the proprietor of the trade mark shall be *prima facie* evidence of the validity of the original registration of the mark and of all subsequent assignments and transmissions thereof'.

In view of the above, it is up to a trade mark proprietor, who thinks that his trade mark rights are unjustifiably limited by the use of another conflicting trade mark, to institute legal proceedings. After assessing all the circumstances that surround the case, the court may decide to maintain coexistence in the register of trade marks of both marks or invalidate one of the two marks.

---

822. Section 20(2) of TSMA.
823. Section 32(4), TSMA.

VI. Earlier Rights

327. Section 33 of the TSMA limits the extent a trade mark proprietor may enjoy his exclusive trade mark rights. It outlines circumstances under which a proprietor, say WR, of a trade or service mark registered in Tanzania and/or a proprietor, say XJJ, of a trade mark protected in Tanzania by virtue of the Paris Convention have no legal power to prohibit another person, say GBH, from using a trade mark that is identical to any of the trade marks mentioned above. There are key conditions that each of the persons mentioned in the immediately preceding sentence must fulfil for the provisions of section 33 of TSMA to apply.

In its more specific terms, section 33(i) of TSMA provides that:

> Nothing in this Act shall entitle the proprietor or a registered user of registered trade or service mark to interfere with or restrain the use by any person of a trade or service mark identical with or nearly resembling it, in relation to goods or services in relation to which that person or a predecessor in title of his Bona fide use of name or description has continuously used that trade or service mark from the date anterior … to the use of the first mentioned trade or service mark in relation to those goods or services by the proprietor or his predecessor in title.

The scenario under section 33(i) of the TSMA becomes applicable if: (1) GBH is the owner of an earlier trade mark rights claimable based on the fact that GBH or his predecessor in title has made a continuous and bona fide use of the trade mark. (2) GBH uses a trade mark that is same as the one belonging to WR. (3) GBH must have been using that trade mark for goods or services that are same as those for which WR's trade mark is registered. (4) The date on which GBH made first genuine use of that trade mark predates that on which WR used his trade mark for the first time; or the date on which GBH made first genuine use of that trade mark predates that on which WR's trade mark was registered. (5) WR's trade mark must be registered at the time when he attempts to prohibit GBH from using the trade mark.

On its part, section 33(ii) of TSMA stipulates that:

> Section 33(ii) provides that 'Nothing in this Act shall entitle the proprietor or a registered user of registered trade or service mark to interfere with or restrain the use by any person of a trade or service mark identical with or nearly resembling it, in relation to goods or services in relation to which that person or a predecessor in title of his Bona fide use of name or description has continuously used that trade or service mark from the date anterior … to the registration of the first mentioned trade or service mark in respect of those goods or services in the name of the proprietor or his predecessor in title, whichever is the earlier, or to object (on such use being proved) to that person being put on the register for that identical or nearly resembling trade or service mark in respect of those goods or services under section 20(2) [of TSMA]'.

For the scenario under section 33(ii) of the TSMA to apply, the following must be proved: (1) XJJ's trade mark must be registered in Tanzania (2) GBH must be using a trade mark which constitutes, or the essential parts of which constitute, a reproduction, imitation or translation XJJ's trade mark. (3) GBH must have been using that trade mark for goods or services that are same as those XJJ seeks to prohibit GBH from using the trade mark. (4) the date on which GBH made first genuine use of that trade mark in respect of those goods or services must be a date that predates the date on which XXJ's trade mark became entitled to protection in Tanzania.

In both two scenarios under section 33 of TSMA, neither WR nor XJJ may successfully prohibit registration of GBH's trade mark. Section 33(ii) makes reference to section 20(2) of TSMA as an enabling provision in this regard. Provisions of the latter Section allow GBH's trade mark rights to coexist alongside WR's and XJJ's trade mark rights.

§8. USE REQUIREMENTS

328. The TSMA enshrines a legal technique that is meant to avoid the trade and service marks protection regime operational in Tanzania being used as a means of granting monopoly in words and other signs without such words and signs actually being used in relation to goods or services. To this end, the TSMA[824] obliges the proprietor of a registered trade or service mark to genuinely use the trade mark.

A trade mark may qualify for registration, under the trade mark law of Tanzania,[825] on the basis of prior use made of the mark or on demonstration of intention to use the mark once the applicant secures registration thereof. Trade mark use is not only an issue at the time of applying for registration of trade mark, but also in the period following such registration.

There is no express provision under the TSMA which places the trade mark proprietor under the obligation to genuinely use a trade or service mark registered in Tanzania. However, such a duty is implied under section 35(1)(b) of TSMA. According to this provision, a trade mark proprietor has got a grace period of at least five years during which the risk of deregistration of a trade or service mark on a non-use ground is non-existent. Such risk exists from the sixth year of the trade mark's registration. The trade mark proprietor's failure to observe the duty to put the trade mark to genuine use for a consecutive period of three years becomes a legal basis for deregistration of the mark, when part of such period falls within the above grace period and another part extends to the sixth year of registration. The first sentence of section 35 of TSMA is more explicit on this; it provides that:

> A registered trade or service mark shall be removed from the register in respect of any of the goods or services in respect of which it is registered … on the ground that up to one month prior to the filing of the application a continuous period of three years or longer had elapsed during which the registered proprietor did not use the trade or service mark in relation to those goods or services … .

824. Section 35, TSMA.
825. Section 16(3), TSMA.

The implication of the above-quoted provision on trade mark governance is that, a person, who is able to prove that a period of consecutive three years and one month has elapsed without the mark being put to genuine use, has a leeway to ask for deregistration of such a trade mark. However, it is important to note that, according to section 35(1)(a) of the TSMA, an application for deregistration of a trade mark made on the non-use basis cannot succeed if circumstances beyond the trade mark proprietor's control rendered it impossible for one to engage in genuine use of the trade mark. The Corona Virus (COVID-19) pandemic outbreak presents a real life example in this regard, as this outbreak has made businesses close down. Any person who is unable to put his registered trade mark to genuine use during this pandemic would successfully plead the COVID-19 outbreak as a justification thereof.

Certain conclusions may be drawn from the provisions of section 35(1) of TSMA. First, the person requesting deregistration of a trade mark on non-use ground as above, has an option to submit such an application to the High Court of Tanzania or to the office of the Registrar of trade marks. Hence, section 55 of the TSMA, which regulates proceedings before the registrar's office and gives the applicant an option to submit his application for trade mark deregistration either before the court or the registrar, applies. Second, absence of genuine use of a trade mark, may lead to total or partial deregistration of the trade mark involved. In this regard, total deregistration of a trademark becomes eminent if the proprietor of the mark does not put the mark to genuine use in relation to all goods or services for which the mark enjoys protection. Partial deregistration does not affect the validity of the trademark in relation to classes of goods and services for which the mark was genuinely used; it happens where deregistration of the mark is confined only to classes of goods and services in relation to which the mark was not used. Third, the absence of genuine trade mark use referred to in section 35 of TSMA does not automatically invalidate registration. In this regard, the High Court of Tanzania or the office of the Registrar of trade mark does not act on its own motion; an interested party must apply for trade mark deregistration. Likewise, the specification of time in section 35 of TSMA, requiring a period of up to one month following the consecutive period of three years of non-use of the trade mark involved, to have lapsed as a condition for filing an admissible application for deregistration of a trade mark on non-use grounds implies an obligation on the part of the party applying for such deregistration to give notice to the trade mark proprietor of the former's intention to apply to the court for the deregistration order, should the latter not be able to genuinely use the trademark following such a notice. Fourth, the law does not require the trademark proprietor to use the mark personally so as to conform to the user requirement; use of the trademark by persons authorized by the trademark proprietor such as licensees, constitutes a constructive trade mark use by the trademark proprietor within the ambit of section 42 of TSMA.

Section 35(2) and various other provisions of TSMA outline several circumstances under which a trade mark use, include the use which is relevant for maintaining trade mark protection in the Tanzania, may be confirmed. The following chart outlines different acceptable modalities of trade mark use:

Corresponding Provision	*Modality of Trade Mark Use*	*Relevance of Trade Mark Use*
S. 35(2)(a), TSMA	Use of whole of a registered trade mark constitutes the use of any other trade mark belonging to the same person and registered as part of the said first trade mark.	Relevant to any scenario requiring proof of trade mark use
S. 35(2)(d), TSMA	Use of one associated or substantially identical trade mark tantamount to use of another belonging to the same person.	Relevant to any scenario requiring proof of trade mark use
S. 42(2), TSMA	Use of a trade mark by a registered user constitutes use of such a mark by the trade mark proprietor.	Relevant to any scenario requiring proof of trade mark use for any purpose including for maintaining trade mark registration
S. 35(2)(c), TSMA	Use of a trade mark in relation to goods to be exported from the United Republic of Tanzania.	Relevant to any scenario requiring proof of trade mark use for any purpose
S. 35(2)(b), TSMA	Use of a trade mark in relation to some goods, constitutes trade mark use for all goods and services in respect of which the trade mark enjoys protection in Tanzania	Relevant to any scenario requiring proof of trade mark use for any purpose

§9. Duration of Protection: Renewal – Termination

I. Term of Protection and Renewal

329. The initial term of protection of trade and service mark registered in Tanzania lasts for a consecutive period of seven calendar years. This period that runs from the date of filing, at the trade mark office, of the application for the registration of the trademark.[826] With regard to a trade mark that has been a subject of an earlier application for registration in a country that belongs to the Paris Convention, the law slightly adjusts the foregoing formula of calculating the initial term of trade

826. Section 28, TSMA.

mark protection in order to cover a special scenario pertaining to a trade mark application claiming a right of priority under section 22 of TSMA. In this regard, the initial term of protection of that trade mark dates back to the date on which the original application was lodged in a foreign Paris Convention country.

Upon application made through form TM/SM9 accompanied by the appropriate renewal fees, section 29 of the TSMA, read together with Regulation 51 of the TMRs, extends to the Registrar of trade marks powers to grant extension of the initial term to subsequent consecutive terms of trademark protection of ten years each. A trade mark proprietor can keep on renewing a registered trade or service mark as long as that mark still functions as a trade mark. In this regard, a possibility exists that a trade mark can enjoy legal protection for indefinite period of time.

The possibility for extending a term of trade mark protection only exists in respect of trade marks that cannot be deregistered on non-use basis as outlined above in §8 of this chapter. Thus, the trade mark proprietor must accompany his application for trade mark renewal with evidence indicating that at least in the last three consecutive years immediately preceding the protection term sought to be renewed, such a trade or service mark has been genuinely used in respect of goods or services for which it is registered. Where such use has not taken place, the trade mark registration can still be renewed, but subject to the trade mark proprietor justifying such non-use especially if 'special circumstances prevented use of the trade or service mark'.[827]

The timing for an application for the renewal of a term of trade mark protection is very important and must be observed if the trade mark proprietor is to continue owning the trade mark involved. Regulation 52 of the TMRs prescribes six months shortly before the end of the protection term sought to be renewed as a period within which a trade mark registered in Tanzania can be renewed. During this period, the trade mark office will remind the trade mark proprietor of the impending expiration of the term of protection and ask him to pay a renewal fee for extending registration of the trade or service mark involved to another term of protection. Following communication of the first reminder to the trade mark proprietor, the trade mark office will send a second reminder if the period left to the expiration of the trade mark registration term sought to be renewed is between one month and two weeks; and provided the trade mark proprietor has not paid the trade mark renewal fee notwithstanding the first reminder. In the event the term that the trade mark proprietor is supposed to renew expires before such renewal has actually been effectuated, the law gives the trade mark proprietor a grace period of one month within which the renewal fee may still be paid and accepted by the trade mark office. Any attempts to renew registration of a trade mark after the grace period will not be taken lightly by the trade mark office. Expiration of the one month grace period entitles the trade mark office to deregister the trade mark concerned and make a permanent record in the register of trade marks to that effect. The fact that a trade or service mark has been removed from the trade mark register must be published in the Trade and Service Marks Journal. It is important to note that, a deregistered

827. Section 29, TSMA.

trade or service mark can still be restored if the trade mark proprietor justifies the failure to renew the trade mark in time and if the trade mark office deems it fit to restore such registration.

It is worthy noticing that a trade or service mark deregistered on non-renewal grounds may still serve as a relative ground for trade mark refusal against future application for registration of an identical or similar trade marks. Unless the trade mark office rules that there would be no consumer confusion or deception if a trade mark that is identical or similar to the deregistered trade mark is registered, an application for such a mark cannot be accepted in Tanzania within a period of one year immediately succeeding the removal from the trade mark register of the deregistered mark.[828]

II. Termination of Protection

330. There are three main circumstances under which legal protection of a trade mark registered in the Republic of Tanzania may come to an end; namely: (a) when the trade mark is revoked; (b) when the trade mark is invalidated; (c) when the trade mark proprietor request cancellation of registration of the trade mark.

A. Revocation of the Trade Mark

331. A registered trade mark can be revoked on various grounds include upon the proprietor's failure to observe conditions for which such registration was granted. Section 38 of TSMA attests to this position in the following manner:

> The Registrar shall, make such order, as he shall deem fit for expunging or varying registration of a trade or service mark on the ground of any contravention of or failure to observe a condition entered on the register in relation thereto.

If the trade mark proprietor has not made a genuine use of the trade mark, protection of the trade mark involved can be terminated on the non-use ground. In this regard, §8 of this chapter outlines circumstances under which trade mark protection may cease, when such a trade mark has not been used for a certain statutory period.

Trade mark protection may come to an end on the applicant's failure to renew the relevant term of protection in line with the provisions of section 29 of TSMA read together with Regulation 51 of TMRs.

828. Section 29(5), TSMA.

B. Invalidity

332. Protection of a registered trade mark comes to an end if the court invalidates such a trade mark. Section 36 of the TSMA is more relevant in this regard; it provides that:

> Any person aggrieved ... by any entry wrongly remaining on the Register, or by any error or defect in any entry in the Register, may apply to the court or at the option of the applicant ..., to the Registrar, and the court or the Registrar shall make such order for making, expunging or varying the entry as shall be deemed fit.

Scenarios under which this provision may be applicable include if the Office of the Registrar granted registration of the trade mark concerned in oversight of the absolute and relative grounds, which would have been successfully invoked to block registration of such a trade mark, but for the said oversight.[829]

Invalidation of trade or service mark rights is also eminent in case of fraudulently obtained registration, renewal of registration, assignment or transmission of trade or service mark. Where fraud is a fact in issue as in the immediately preceding sentence, the registrar is himself entitled to apply to the High Court for an order 'expunging or varying the entry in the register as may be deemed fit'.[830] The High Court of Tanzania has powers to invalidate trade and service mark rights if the registration of the said rights was obtained by fraud or was granted in foresight of some absolute grounds for trade and service marks refusal.[831]

It is instructive to note that the validity of a trade or service mark registered in the United Republic of Tanzania generally becomes incontestable after seven years from the date of registration of the mark concerned. However, such incontestability defence does not apply if fraud in relation to the process that led to registration of the mark or any of the absolute grounds for trade or service mark refusal is the ground for challenging the mark's validity.

C. Volition of the Trade Mark Proprietor

333. A proprietor of a registered trade mark may, if he wishes, ask the registrar for cancellation of registration of the trade mark. The removal of such a trade mark from the register of trade mark will effectively serve as a confirmation of the cancellation asked for.

829. For an outline of absolute and relative grounds for trade mark refusal refer to §3 of this chapter.
830. Cf. s. 37, TSMA.
831. Cf. s. 50, TSMA. Absolute grounds for trade and service marks refusal are outlined above in §3 of this chapter.

§10. Infringement and Remedies

334. Proprietors of a trade or a service mark enjoying protection, by virtue of the mark's registration, in Tanzania have a legal right to sue third parties for actual or perceived infringement.[832] In most cases, the trade mark proprietor exercises the foregoing right on his own volition. However he may, sometimes, do so as an obligation to cater to the interests of a registered user of that trade mark. Registered users of a trade or a service mark are also entitled, under section 42(3) of TSMA, to institute legal actions against infringers of the rights accruing to them by virtue of their statuses. The registered user's entitlement, in this regard, arises only if the trade mark proprietor, when requested by the registered user, refuses or negligently fails to sue the infringers. Usually, a presumption of such refusal or negligent failure on the part of the proprietor exists if the registered user having informed the proprietor of the infringement, and having asked him to sue infringers, the latter does not take any action in that regard. In addition to their powers to inflict criminal penalties to infringers, the judicial authorities in Tanzania may, in relation to trade or service mark infringement, award civil remedies as well.

I. Infringement

335. The scope of exclusive rights which a trademark proprietor enjoys in Tanzania by virtue of registration of his mark defines the circumstances in which a trade mark is considered to be infringed under TSMA. Unauthorized exploitation of a trade or a service mark constitutes infringement of exclusive rights which the proprietor of the mark enjoys.[833] In fact, section 32(1) of TSMA clarifies that the exclusive trade or service mark rights are infringed by any person who, not having the legal authority to use the proprietor's mark, uses such a trade or a service mark or any other sign nearly resembling it to market goods or services that are identical or confusingly similar to the goods or the services for which the mark purported to be infringed enjoys protection in Tanzania.

A claimant in a trade or a service mark infringement suit must prove one or a combination of any of the following elements so as to be successful: (a) that the defendant uses in trade a sign which is identical with the claimant's mark; or (b) that the defendant uses in trade a sign which is similar to the claimant's mark; or (c) that the defendant uses in trade a mark which is identical with the claimant's mark for goods or services that are similar to those for which the claimant's mark is used; or (d) that the defendant uses in trade a mark which is similar to the claimant's mark for goods or services that are similar to those for which the claimant's mark is used; or (e) the defendant uses in trade a mark which is identical with the claimant's mark for goods or services that are identical with those for which the claimant's mark is

832. Section 30, TSMA.

833. *See* §6 of this chapter, which outlines the scope of exclusive rights of the trade or service mark proprietor.

used; or (f) that the defendant uses in trade a mark which is similar to the claimant's mark for goods or services that are identical with those for which the claimant's mark is used.

In addition to proving existence of one or more of the above grounds, the claimant must as well prove that the use of the defendant's mark in any of the above circumstances is likely to cause consumer confusion or deception. As a matter of law, where consumer deception or confusion is attributable to similarity between the protected and infringing marks, the claimant has to adduce evidence of actual, or likelihood of, confusion or deception. In case the infringement concerns trade or service marks which are identical and whose exploitation is in respect of identical goods, the claimant does not bear the obligation to prove the likelihood of confusion or deception. In that case, there exists a legal presumption that the use of the mark is likely to confuse or deceive consumers.

It is worthwhile to note that determination of infringement of a trade mark with reputation registered in Tanzania follows a different rule concerning similarity or identity of goods and services. The requirement that the infringing mark be used for goods or services that are similar or identical to those in respect of which the trade mark with reputation is used does not apply as a key condition for proving infringement of the mark: section 32(1)(b) of TSMA protects a registered trade mark with reputation against any commercial exploitation whatsoever made of an identical or a confusingly similar mark irrespective of the classes of goods and services.[834] Indeed, such protection is available to the proprietor of a trade mark with reputation even where, given the circumstances in which the infringing sign is used, no consumer confusion or deception is likely to ensue, provided such use of the infringing sign is calculated or likely to 'impair the distinctive character or acquired reputation of the trade mark'.

II. Remedies

336. In case of infringement, the High Court is empowered to grant injunctions, award damages and other court orders according to circumstances of case.[835]

A. *Interdicts*

337. An interdict is a negative injunction, also known as a cease and desist order. An injunction is a 'judicial order restraining a person from beginning or continuing an action threatening or invading the legal right of another, or compelling a person to carry out a certain act, e.g., to make restitution to an injured party'.[836] Two kinds of injunctions can be deduced from the foregoing definition; namely positive injunctions and interdicts (or negative injunctions). A positive injunction is an order issued

834. *See* §2(I)(C), which outlines the legal regime for protection of a trade mark with reputation in Tanzania on the basis of the mark's defensive registration.
835. Cf. s. 30, TSMA.
836. At https://en.oxforddictionaries.com/definition/injunction (accessed: 27 May 2020).

by a judicial or quasi-judicial authority to compel a person to whom it is directed to perform certain acts, which the issuing authority deems appropriate to prohibit or remedy infringement of exclusive rights of a trade or service mark proprietor.

The High Court of Tanzania enjoys powers, under section 30 of TSMA, to grant an interdict stopping or prohibiting a purported trade or service mark infringer from carrying out actual or perceived infringement. As its legal effects, this kind of injunction directs a person to whom it is served to stop doing the complained activity with immediate effect. In other words, an interdict, 'effectively places an injunction on the person or entity that prohibits the named activity as suspicious or illegal'.[837]

B. Damages

338. In any legal proceedings concerning trade or service mark infringement, Section 30 of TSMA vests the High Court of Tanzania with powers to award damages to a successful party. Naturally, the award of damages aims to redress economic loss quantifiable in monetary terms. An infringer of a trade or service mark against whom the High Court decrees an order to pay damages has to compensate the damage resulting from his infringement activities by paying a sum of money to the trade or the service mark proprietor.

Judicial authorities competent to resolve disputes concerning infringement of trade or service mark rights are usually confronted with a question regarding the modality of calculation of damages. Based on conventionally accepted methods, courts in Tanzania have a leeway to consider any of the following factors when devising appropriate damages, which the defendant is liable to pay to the holder of trade or service mark: (i) reasonable royalty; (ii) infringer's profits; and (iii) trade or service mark owner's lost profits.

Reasonable royalty is a hypothetical amount of money the trade or service mark proprietor would have charged the defendant had the latter negotiated for a licence to exploit the trade or service mark invention. Calculation of damages – in trade or service mark infringement cases – based on reasonable royalty is advisable in case business 'operating reality of the claimant is not definitive' and/or the manner in which the defendant exploits the exclusive rights concerned does not severely damage economic interests of the owner thereof.[838]

Infringer's profits as a method of damages calculation is appropriate in the circumstances whereby the infringer exploits the trade or service mark more efficiently thus making more earnings than the trade or service mark proprietor would have done.[839]

---

837. At https://legaldictionary.net/cease-and-desist-order/ (accessed: 27 May 2020).

838. Norman V. Siebrasse & Alexander J. Stack et al, *Damages Calculations in Intellectual Property Cases in Canada* 4 (Cole & Partners 12 Jul. 2015), https://www.researchgate.net/publication/265239875_DAMAGES_CALCULATIONS_IN_INTELLECTUAL_PROPERTY_CASES_IN_CANADA (accessed: 27 May 2020).

839. Roger D. Blair & Thomas F. Cotter, *An Economic Analysis of Damages Rules in Intellectual Property Law*, 39(5) William & Mary L. Rev. Art. 4 1590 (1998).

The High Court of Tanzania has to accommodate a certain degree of flexibility when calculating damages on the basis of the trade mark proprietor's lost profits. The court is therefore entitled to consider several factors that are relevant for determining the appropriate amount of damages. Flagrancy of the infringement or the magnitude of the loss suffered by the trade or service mark proprietor as a result of the infringement of his trade or service mark is one of the factors courts analyse. Courts must also consider market and operating realities prevailing at the time of infringement of the trade or service mark for they are essential for deciding questions regarding the extent of damage a victim of trade or service mark infringement might have suffered.

C. Reasonable Royalty

339. When seeking compensation for trade mark infringement, the trade mark proprietor has an option under section 30 of the TMA, to prefer the award of reasonable royalty to damages. Where such a relief is available to the trade mark proprietor, it takes into account an amount of fee a fictitious licensee would have paid for the licence for the duration of infringement. The trade mark proprietor is entitled to reasonable royalty for infringement taking place after acceptance for registration of the trade mark involved, provided if the infringement details became material after registration of the said trade mark would constitute trade mark infringement as well.

D. Other Deterrent Measures

340. Following confirmation of infringement, the High Court may order corrective measures other than damages to be enforced against the infringing items. In this regard, the court may order destruction and/or removal from commercial channels of infringing goods as well as removal of unlawfully fixed trademark.

III. Criminal Offences and Penalties

A. Criminal Offences

341. The TSMA regards the following as trade and service mark offences punishable under Tanzanian law:

(1) Making or causing to be made a 'false entry in the register', or 'writing falsely purporting to be a copy of an entry in the register', or producing or tendering 'in evidence any such writing, knowing the entry or writing to be false'.[840]

840. Cf. s. 56, TSMA.

(2) Presenting the following: (i) unregistered service or trademark as a registered mark; (ii) a part of a registered trade or service mark as an independent registered mark; or (iii) a registered trade or service mark as being registered for goods or services A, B and E, while the mark is registered for goods or services C, D and F; or (iv) a registered trade or service mark as extending to the proprietor some exclusive rights, whereas given the limitation entered in the register in relation to the mark, the proprietor is not entitled to enjoy those exclusive rights.[841]

(3) Using 'in Tanzania in relation to a trade or service mark of the word "registered" or the symbol R, or of any other word or symbol referring whether expressly or impliedly', to the fact that a trade or service mark is registered, while it is not.[842] Note that the use of the symbol or word as in the immediately preceding sentence does not constitute an offence if the following conditions are met: (i) 'that word or symbol is used in physical association with other words delineated in characters at least as large as those in which the word or symbol is delineated' and the word or the symbol only serves to indicate that the words in physical association of which the symbol or the word is used is actually a valid trade or service mark registered and protected in a foreign country;[843] or (ii) if the word or the symbol is used in relation to a trade or service mark under the law of a foreign country and in relation to goods or services to be exported to that foreign country.[844]

(4) Intentional making or submitting a written or oral false statement or representation in order to do the following: (i) deceive the registrar or any other TSMO official in execution of the provisions of the TSMA; or (ii) procure or influence the doing or omission of anything in relation to the TSMA or any matter under the TSMA.[845]

B. Penalties

342. The offence of falsely representing a trade or service mark as a registered mark outlined in item 2 above is punishable by a fine of TZS 50,000 or; by a term of imprisonment up to seven years or by 'both such fine and imprisonment'.[846] Persons found guilty of committing any of offences outlined in items 1, 3 and 4 above are liable to pay up to TZS 10,000, or up to three years imprisonment term, or 'to both such fine and such imprisonment'.[847]

841. Cf. s. 57(1), TSMA.
842. Cf. s. 57(2), TSMA.
843. Cf. s. 57(2)(a) and (b), TSMA.
844. Cf. s. 57(2)(c), TSMA.
845. Cf. s. 58(2), TSMA.
846. Cf. s. 57(1), TSMA.
847. Cf. s. 59, TSMA.

§11. Overlapping and Relation to Other IP Rights

343. Items that can be a subject matter of trademark protection in the United Republic of Tanzania may also enjoy protection under other categories of IP rights such as designs law, business or trade names law and Copyright law. Shapes of goods generally constitute a registrable trademark if – in addition to possessing the capability to distinguish goods and/or services marketed under them – they meet the formal registration requirements such as those relating to graphical representation/ reproduction and are not excluded from protection under trademark law.[848] Given that the subject matter of design protection are visible design features embedded in a finished article of manufacture, it is possible that a shape of a particular product may enjoy protection under both trademarks protection regime (once it becomes distinctive) and under design law if its visible features fulfil the requirements for designs protection. Registration of a sign as both a trademark and industrial design is more meaningful if both the design and the trademark belong to one proprietor. Otherwise, the proprietor of an industrial design may base on their industrial design rights to oppose registration of a trademark that is similar or identical to the industrial design and vice versa. The list of items that can enjoy protection under more than one IP category is not exhaustive and my include audio or sound mark. This kind of a sign can enjoy protection under both trademark protection regime and copyright law if the relevant conditions regarding the latter are fulfilled, key of which is originality of the musical work that makes up the sound mark. Other signs

848. Note that shapes, which consist exclusively of the shape of goods, which is necessary to obtain a technical result, or which results from the nature of the goods or which gives substantial value to the goods do not enjoy protection under trademark law.

that may potentially serve trademark functions such as logos or slogans can also be protected under copyright law thus affording those items double protection. Last but not least, trademarks and trade names are both corporate identifiers; it is common to have a sign protected both as a trademark and a trade name.

Chapter 7. Plant Variety Protection

§1. Sources: Legislation

344. The legal regime for the protection of plant varieties in the United Republic of Tanzania is established under Plant Breeders' Rights Act No. 9 of 2012 (hereinafter PBRA) that is in force in Tanzania mainland, and Plant Breeders Act No. 1 of 2014, of the laws of Zanzibar. Provisions of the latter legislation are substantially similar to those contained in the PBRA. Both the foregoing legislations coexist in harmony. In view of the provisions of section 21(3) PBRA, applications for the grant of plant breeders' rights lodged at the office responsible for granting plant breeders' rights in Tanzania Zanzibar is deemed to be an application for the same variety filed with the Registrar of plant varieties in Tanzania mainland. Section 28(7) PBRA provides for the same harmonizing effect by stipulating that any 'grant of breeder's right made by the authority responsible for granting breeders' rights in Zanzibar shall have the same effect as the grant of breeder's right of the same variety made by the registrar'. The position under sections 21(3) and 28(7) of PBRA is reciprocated in Tanzania Zanzibar by the provisions of section 22(3) of Plant Breeders Act No. 1 of 2014, of the laws of Zanzibar, stipulating that:

> The Minister shall enter into bilateral agreement with relevant Minister of Tanzania Mainland regulating the following-: (a) any application filed with Registrar of Plant Breeders' Right of Tanzania Mainland to be recognized as an application, for the same variety, filed [at the office of] the Registrar [of plant varieties in Zanzibar]; (b) a grant of breeder's right made by the Registrar of Tanzania Mainland to be recognized as the grant made by the Registrar; (c) distribution of fees for registration of plant breeder's right.

345. The PBRA, which repealed and replaced the Protection of new Plant Varieties (Plant Breeders' Rights) Act No. 22 of 2002,[849] came into force on 1 March 2013 following its publication in the Gazette of the United Republic of Tanzania No. 9 Vol. 94 of 1 March, 2013. According to its long title, the PBRA provides 'for the grant and protection of plant breeders' rights, for establishment of Plant Breeders' Rights Office and for related matters'.

346. The Plant Breeders' Rights protection regime, which the PBRA establishes, is largely modelled on the International Convention for the Protection of

849. In line with its long title, the chief object of the repealed Act was the establishment of a registry of Plant Breeder's Rights; promotion of plant breeding and facilitation of agricultural advancements through the grant and regulation of Plant Breeder's Rights and for matters connected therewith.

New Varieties of Plants (UPOV) of 1961 as last revised in 1991,[850] although the United Republic of Tanzania has not yet formally accepted to be bound by this Convention.[851]

347. The United Republic of Tanzania is party to International Treaty on Plant Genetic Resources for Food and Agriculture of 2001, adopted on 3 November 2001 at Rome and entered into force on 29 June 2004. This Treaty which, insofar as it applies to the United Republic of Tanzania, became effective on 29 July 2004, contains provisions for protection of plant varieties.

At regional level, the Arusha Protocol for the Protection of New Varieties of Plants within the Framework of the ARIPO adopted by a Diplomatic Conference of ARIPO at Arusha, Tanzania on 6 July 2015 is pertinent to the legal regime for the protection of plant breeders' rights in the United Republic of Tanzania.[852] It is instructive to note that provisions of the PBRA are in harmony with provisions of the Arusha Protocol, notwithstanding the fact that the PBRA came into existence three years prior to the enactment of the Arusha Protocol. The Administrative Council of ARIPO, which met in Lilongwe, Malawi on 22 November 2017, adopted the Regulations for Implementing the Arusha Protocol for the Protection of New Varieties of Plants within the Framework of ARIPO. Indeed, the establishment of the ARIPO framework for the protection of plant breeder's rights is a manifestation of ARIPO's concerted effort to pool together human and financial resources for the efficient administration of plant breeder's rights and related matter.[853]

The United Republic of Tanzania and other Member States of ARIPO are contracting parties to the WTO Agreement whose Annex 1C contains the Agreement on TRIPS. Both the PBRA and the Arusha Protocol are sui generis legislation, which were enacted as a response to provisions of Article 27(3)(b) of TRIPS Agreement.

Generally, Article 27(3)(b) of TRIPS Agreement approves legal position, adopted by the WTO Member States, prohibiting the grant of patents in respect of 'plants and animals other than microorganisms, and essentially biological processes for the production of plants or animals other than non-biological and microbiological processes'. The article also places WTO Member States, such as the United Republic of Tanzania, under obligation to 'provide for the protection of plant varieties either by patents or by an effective sui generis system or by any combination thereof'. It important to note that the main conundrum underlying the provisions of TRIPS

850. Cf. P. Ngwediagi, *Establishment of Plant Breeders' Rights System in Tanzania: Achievements and Challenges – A Case study under the Ministry of Agriculture Food Security and Cooperatives, Tanzania*; paper available http://www.wipo.int/wipolex/en/text.jsp?file_id=216639 (accessed 1 Jul. 2020).
851. The International Seed Federation (ISF) proposes the modelling of national legislation of individual WTO Member States on the provisions of the 1991 Act of the UPOV Convention.
852. The protocol was signed on the day of adoption by four countries namely; The Gambia, Ghana, Mozambique and Sao Tome & Principe. The United Republic of Tanzania signed the Protocol subsequently on 28 Sep. 2015.
853. Cf. the recitals to the Arusha Protocol.

Agreement is that the WTO has neither guided its Member States 'as to what constitutes 'effective', nor what a sui generis system should entail at minimum' within the ambit of Article 27(3)(b) of TRIPS.[854]

§2. Subject Matter of Protection

348. Generally, the PBRA provides for protection of plant varieties. The term 'variety' as applied under the PBRA refers to a 'plant grouping within a single botanical taxon of the lowest known rank, which grouping, irrespective of whether the conditions for the grant of a breeder's right are fully met, can be- (a) defined by the expression of the characteristics resulting from a given genotype or combination of genotypes; (b) distinguished from any other plant grouping by the expression of at least one of the said characteristics; and (c) considered as a unit with regard to its suitability for being propagated unchanged'.[855]

349. Section 12 of the PBRA provides for protection of breeders' rights in relation to 'all plants genera and species'. The terms 'genera' and 'species' are technical terms, hence the need to expound their meaning in a much simplified perspective. **According to the Encyclopaedia Britannica, the term genus or genera (in plural form)**, is a 'biological classification ranking between family and species, consisting of structurally or phylogenetically related species or a single isolated species exhibiting unusual differentiation (monotypic genus). The genus name is the first word of a binomial scientific name (the species name is the second word) and is always capitalized'.[856] It follows that, the genus refers to the plant's generic name, whereas species denominate the plant's specific name. The National Association of Gardening subscribes to this distinction by making the following observation:

> A genus is a group of related plants. The similarity among members of a genus may or may not be obvious. But taxonomists have determined that, due to certain features, these plants are related and thus classify them in the same genus. Genus names are often derived from Latin or Greek words, mythological figures, or plant characteristics.

350. The species name is the basic unit of classification. It describes one kind of plant within the genus, and is almost always an adjective. By itself, the species name is meaningless. For example, *Digitalis purpurea* is the botanical name for foxglove, while *Echinacea purpurea* is the name for purple coneflower. The species name, *purpurea*, indicates only that some part of the plant is purple; by itself it gives no clue to the identity of the plant.[857]

---

854. At http://www.wipo.int/wipolex/en/text.jsp?file_id=216639 (accessed 1 Jul. 2020).
855. Section 2, PBRA.
856. At https://www.britannica.com/science/genus-taxon (accessed: 17 Feb. 2022).
857. National Association of Gardening (1999), 'Terminology: genus and species', retrieved from https://garden.org/courseweb/course1/week3/page3.htm (accessed: 17 Feb. 2022).

§3. CONDITIONS OF PROTECTION

351. To obtain legal protection of plant breeders' rights in Tanzania in relation to a new plant variety, the breeder has to submit an application in that respect to the Registrar of Plant Breeders' Rights. It is worth noticing that only persons possessing a status specified under the PBRA are entitled to file an admissible application for plant breeders' rights. In this regard, a plant breeders' rights applicant must qualify as a breeder within the ambit of section 2 of the PBRA. The term 'breeder' is used under the PBRA as reference to the following persons: '(a) a person who bred or discovered and developed a variety; (b) a person who is the employer of the person who bred or discovered and developed a variety or who has commissioned the employer's work; or (c) a successor in title of a person mentioned in paragraph (a) or (b) as the case may be'. Admissibility of an application for plant breeders' right is dependent on such an application being in conformity with two sets of rules. First, the plant variety, which is a subject matter of the application, must be genera or species. Second, the variety must fulfil four requirements stipulated under section 13 PBRA; namely, novelty, distinctness, uniformity and stability. These requirements are expounded below.

I. Novelty

352. Plant Breeder's Rights in Tanzania are a granted in respect of a plant variety that is new. Acts of selling or disposing of the harvested or propagating material of the variety to others done by or with the consent of the breeder are the factors that may generally kill the novelty of the variety in respect of which plant breeders' rights are claimed. Under certain circumstances, a breeder may still enjoy a grace period within which to submit his application for registration of a plant variety even after he has perpetuated the acts mentioned in the immediately preceding sentence. Section 14 of the PBRA outlines this grace period based on a response to the question whether the above-mentioned acts were carried out within Tanzania or abroad. If the selling or disposing of the variety was done in Tanzania, the breeder must apply for protection within a year from the day of such selling or disposal. In relation to the selling or disposing of the variety made abroad the breeder has a grace period of four years within which he may apply for the plant breeder's rights in respect of the varieties involved. It is instructive to note that two years are added to make a total of six years' grace period if the varieties sold or disposed of abroad are tree or vines.

There are circumstances whereby the acts of selling or disposing of the variety, do not affect the novelty of the plant variety for which the applicant seeks protection of plant breeders' rights in Tanzania. Thus, in line with the provisions of section 14(2) of the PBRA the following acts do not affect a novelty of a plant variety:

(a) trials of the variety not involving sale or disposal off to others for purposes of exploitation of the variety;
(b) sale or disposal off to others without the consent of the breeder;

(c) sale or disposal of to any person that forms part of an agreement for the transfer of rights to the successor in title;
(d) sale or disposal off to any person that forms part of an agreement under which a person multiplies propagating material of the variety concerned on behalf of the breeder, provided that: (i) the property in the multiplied material reverts to the breeder; (ii) the multiplied materials is not used for the production of another variety;
(e) sale or disposal off to any person that forms part of an agreement under which a person undertakes field tests or laboratory trials, or small-scale processing trials with a view of evaluating the variety;
(f) sale or disposal off to any person that forms part of the fulfilment of a statutory or administrative obligation concerning biological security or the entry of varieties in an official catalogue of varieties admitted to trade;
(g) sale or disposal of to any person of harvested material which is a by-product or a surplus product of the creation of the variety or of the activities referred to in paragraphs (e) and (f) provided that the said material is sold or disposed of without variety identification for the purposes of consumption; and
(h) disposal off to any person due to or in consequence of the fact that the breeder had displayed the variety at an official or officially recognized exhibition.

II. Distinctness

353. A plant variety meets the requirements of distinctness 'if it is clearly distinguishable from any other variety whose existence is common knowledge at the time of the filing of the application for the granting of Plant Breeders' Rights or for the entering of another variety in the official register of varieties in any country'.[858] According to section 15(2) PBRA, 'the filing of an application for the granting of breeder's right or for the entering of another variety in the official register of varieties in any country, shall be deemed to render that other variety a matter of a common knowledge from the date of the application', unless the application does not 'lead to the granting of breeder's right or to the entering of the said other variety in the official register of varieties'. In other words, a plant variety is excluded from plant breeder's right protection for want of distinctness if it is identical to another variety that has been a subject of a successful application for the grant of plant breeder's right irrespective of whether such an application has been made in Tanzania or abroad.

354. There, the distinctness and novelty requirements have marked differences: whereas distinctness requirement is not met if the plant variety for which plant breeder's rights are sought is anticipated by prior registration of the same variety in Tanzania or abroad, a plant variety is not new if it has been deliberately made available to the public by the proprietor, especially for non-exempted commercial purposes as outlined in section 14 PBRA.

858. Section 15(1), PBRA.

III. Uniformity

355. Section 16 PBRA provides for the requirement of uniformity of a plant variety in respect of which plant breeders' rights are claimed. The adjective of the term 'uniformity' is 'uniform'. According to the Oxford online dictionary, this adjective signifies the following: 'Remaining the same in all cases and at all times; unchanging in form or character'. The PBRA deems a plant variety to meet the uniformity requirement if, 'subject to the variation that may be expected from the particular features of its propagation, it is sufficiently uniform in its relevant characteristics'.

IV. Stability

356. With respect to the stability requirement, section 17 PBRA states that a 'variety shall be deemed to be stable, where its relevant characteristics remain unchanged after repeated propagation or in the case of a particular cycle of propagation, at the end of each cycle'.

§4. Formalities: Procedure for Grant and Obtaining Protection

357. As a strategy to realize objectives of the Plant Variety Protection Regime in Tanzania, the PBRA sets out Plant Breeders' Rights Fund, a government office within the Ministry of Agriculture to serve as the Plant Breeders' Rights Registry and a Plant Breeders' Rights Advisory Committee.[859]

358. The Plant Breeders' Rights registry is manned by a ministerial appointee designated as registrar. In executing his duties, the registrar may direct his deputies and other officers working in the registry, who are also appointed by the minister responsible for agriculture, to carry out some duties, which section 5 PBRA imposes on the registrar. The registrar's duties include: (1) granting Plant Breeders' Rights; (2) maintaining a register and providing information on Plant Breeders' Rights issued in Tanzania; (3) facilitating transfer and licensing of Plant Breeders' Rights; and (4) collaborating with domestic and foreign authorities dealing with Plant Breeders' Rights matters. In relation to his duty to maintain an official Plant Breeders' Rights register, the registrar is *inter alia* required to enter into the register the following: (1) species and denomination of varieties; (2) the complete name and address of the original breeder, any other holder of plant breeders' right, and each person to whom such right has been transferred or assigned; (3) the date of inception of the Plant Breeders' Rights; and (4) all other matters which may affect the validity or ownership of Plant Breeders' rights.

359. Plant Breeders' Rights Advisory Committee is a standing committee established under the PBRA to carry out the following duties: (1) advise the minister for

859. Cf. Parts II and X, PBRA.

agriculture on efficient protection of Plant Breeders' Rights in Tanzania; and (2) advise the registrar on the grant of Plant Breeders' Rights based on the committee's expert consideration on the Plant Breeders' Rights application reports and on the registrar's tests results, both reports being submitted to the committee by the registrar. To carry out these functions, the Committee enjoys powers to establish its own procedural rules, to advise the registrar on specific and general matters, and to summon applicants and other interested parties for hearing prior to the approval of Plant Breeders' Rights applications. The importance of the Plant Breeders' Advisory Committee can be seen through the lens of its composition: The Committee is composed of ministerial appointees as follows: a chairman of the Committee representing the Ministry of Agriculture, and the Registrar of Plant Breeder's Rights who acts as the Committee's secretary. Moreover, section 9(2) PBRA identifies some other institutions or authorities each of which is represented in the Committee by one member. These are plant breeders' association, seed traders' association, seed growers' association, farmers' association, one university or training institute dealing with plant breeding, government agency or authority responsible for registration of IP rights, the office responsible for granting plant breeders' rights in Tanzania Zanzibar, and the office of the Attorney General.

In addition to its primary duties stipulated under section 10 PBRA, the Plant Breeders' Advisory Committee also manages Plant Breeders' Rights Development Fund by serving as the Fund Committee with the Registrar of Plant Breeder's Rights heading the secretariat of the Committee.

360. Plant Breeders' Rights Development Fund is provided for under section 46 PBRA. Provisions of this section empower the minister responsible for agriculture to establish the fund after consultation with the minister for finance. The fund accommodates some money obtained from 'Plant Breeders' Rights registration, maintenance and licence fees determined by the minister for the purpose' as well as 'any donations or grants from government or individuals'. The fund serves as a financing source for several activities such as the following: (1) 'development and promotion of the plant breeders' rights'; (2) 'training of plant breeders on matters concerned with plant breeders' rights'; (3) 'establishment and maintenance of the variety collections and data base'; and (4) 'such other activities relating to administration of the (PBRA)'.

I. Applications for Plant Breeders' Rights

361. The right to apply for a Plant Breeders' Rights is exercisable by an individual breeder of a new variety. In the light of the delineation of the term 'breeder' provided for in section 2, both the breeder, their assignee or agent as well as the successor in title to the breeder or the assignee have a standing to apply for plant breeders' rights in Tanzania. A person qualifying as the applicant's agent has to be 'a person who is duly authorized by the applicant or holder (of the plant variety) to act, on behalf of the applicant or holder'.[860] With regard to varieties developed by the government, the law bestows this right upon the minister responsible for agriculture.

362. Section 19 PBRA enshrines a mandatory admissibility requirement of an application for Plant Breeders' Rights. The section requires the application to contain the following: (i) the name and address of the applicant. Should the applicant be an assignee or successor in title to the breeder, they must then legally prove his status. In this regard, the applicant must provide satisfactory explanation to the registrar of Plant Breeders' Rights, which may be supported by an assignment deed or evidence of succession. In addition to including their name in the application, the assignee or successor in title to the breeder must also indicate in the application the name and address of the person who has bred the new plant variety in respect of which the Plant Breeders' Rights are being sought; (ii) the denomination, along with other description of the characteristics and properties of the new variety; (iii) samples of propagating material, the quantity of which may be determined by the Registrar of Plant Breeders' Rights.

363. NAME OF THE VARIETY. As noted in the immediately preceding paragraph, a new plant variety must be given a name. The PBRA uses the term 'denomination' as a reference to the plant variety's name. This name which designates the variety is proposed at the time of application by the applicant for Plant Breeders' Rights and it can only be used in relation to the variety after the registrar has approved such denomination. The law prohibits reference to a plant variety by a name other than the one approved by the Registrar of Plant Breeders' Rights. This prohibition applies irrespective of whether the variety still enjoys protection in Tanzania. Note that the variety name is used generically. Therefore, the breeder is not entitled to exclude third parties from using the name when referring to the same plant variety. Indeed, it is a mandatory legal requirement to use such a name in any commercial transaction involving the relevant plant variety. However, it is not unlawful for a trader to use a trade name and a trade mark alongside with the plant variety denomination when selling such a variety, or any harvested or propagating material thereof, provided the plant variety denomination remains visibly legible at all times.

Section 20 PBRA prescribes conditions subject to which a plant variety denomination can qualify for registration in Tanzania. In order to be approved for registration by the registrar, a denomination of a plant variety must, by its nature, be capable of enabling members of the public to identify the variety involved. Indeed, a plant variety's denomination cannot be approved by the registrar if the use of such denomination is likely to cause confusion or mislead the public in relation to the 'characteristics, value or identity of the variety or the identity of the breeder'. Such confusion or misleading would be imminent if the denomination is similar or identical to another name of a plant variety already protected in Tanzania. Thus, the registrar cannot register a denomination of a plant variety, unless such a denomination

860. *See* the definition of the term 'agent' in s. 2 PBRA.

is 'different from every denomination which designates, in the territory of any member of international organisation dealing with plant breeders' rights matters to which Tanzania is a party, an existing variety of the same plant species or of a closely related species'. As a general rule, a registrable plant variety denomination 'may not consist solely of figures except where this is an established practice for designating varieties'.

364. APPLICATION'S EFFECTIVE DATE. A date on which an application for plant breeders' rights in Tanzania becomes effective constitutes a significant milestone insofar as such an application is concerned. According to section 21 PBRA, an application for Plant Breeder' Rights becomes effective on the date the registrar receives the application. Submission of an incomplete application file does not make the application effective on the submission date: The application is then deemed received by the registrar on the date the application file is complete.

365. PRIORITY RIGHT. The PBRA entitles an applicant for the Plant Breeders' Rights to a right of priority based on an application for Plant Breeders' Rights made abroad. This is provided for under section 22 PBRA as follows:

> Any breeder who has duly filed an application for the protection of a variety in one of the members of an international organization dealing with plant breeders' rights matters which Tanzania is a party shall enjoy a right of priority for a maximum period of twelve months. This period shall be computed from the date of filing the first application. The day of filing shall not be included in the latter period.

366. The general import of section 22 PBRA is that a breeder or discoverer of a new plant variety who first files an application for the grant of plant breeders' rights in a foreign country enjoys a right to file an application for the grant of the same mark in Tanzania and be able to claim as a filing date of this application, the date on which the application for plant breeders' rights made in the foreign country was granted or was applied for. The principle of reciprocity guides the Registrar of plant varieties in determining whether a particular foreign application may give rise to priority right. In this regard, the principle of reciprocity is met if the foreign country in which an application for plant breeders' rights on which the priority right is founded has cooperation with the United Republic of Tanzania in relation to plant varieties protection. It is such cooperation which operationalizes the principle of reciprocity, since applications for the grant of plant breeders' right first made in Tanzania would also support the claim for priority right in the foreign country with which the Republic of Tanzania has concluded the relevant cooperation agreement.

367. The right under reference is termed 'priority right' in the sense that, intervening events such as another application for the grant of plant breeders' rights made by another person in Tanzania – after the person entitled to the priority right had filed the plant breeders' rights application in a country other than the United Republic of Tanzania – do not affect the right of the latter person to file in Tanzania an application for plant breeders' rights in respect of the same plant variety, which is the subject matter of the foreign application. In order to benefit from the priority right, the applicant for breeders' rights must specifically claim that right in Tanzania within the period of twelve months subsequent to the date of filing of the basic application serving as the basis for claiming the priority right.

Section 22(3) PBRA is more explicit on the conditions underlying the principle of priority; it requires the person claiming the priority right to state specifically that the application claims the priority right and provide details about the foreign application or registration that has given rise to the priority right. The relevant details in this regard include 'samples or other evidence indicating that the variety which is the subject matter of both applications is the same'. Further information required to support the claim to priority right include the date on which the earlier application for trade or service mark registration was made in the foreign country and the name of this foreign country involved. The person claiming the priority right may be required to furnish the office of the plant varieties Registrar with a certified copy of the earlier application made in the foreign country. If that copy is in a language other than Kiswahili or English, the claimant will be required to furnish the office with official translation of the document. The person claiming priority right in relation to an application for the grant of plant breeders' right in Tanzania as above has a minimum period of three months to submit to the Registrar of plant varieties the documents proving the applicant's entitlement to the priority right.

On being successful in their claim for priority right, the plant breeders' applicant will have their application assigned as its filing date in Tanzania the date on which the applicant filed the corresponding application in the foreign country.

368. AMMENDMENT TO THE APPLICATION. It is not uncommon for an application for the grant of plant breeders' rights, which has been duly lodged before the Registrar of Plant varieties, to be amended in line with the provisions of section 23 PBRA. There is a risk of such amendments affecting the effective date of the application involved. To avoid such a risk, the applicant must confine the amendments to matters other than those likely to 'affect the variety which is the subject of the application'. However, where an application is amended after the registrar had published a notice of such application in the *Gazette*, the applicant bears the responsibility of paying the cost of republication. It is worth noticing in this regard that the Registrar of Plant Breeders' Rights is required, under section 24 PBRA, to notify by a notice published in the *Gazette* or 'in a newspaper of vast circulation' of every filed application that relates to a variety that satisfies the requirements of the law. The contents of this notice include: (i) the applicant's name and address; (ii) the application's effective date; and (iii) the proposed name of the variety.

369. OPPOSITION. Interested individuals and government agencies may respond to the registrar's notice publishable as above by lodging an opposition against the matters specified in the notice. The objection is admissible if made within two months after the date on which the registrar publishes the notice. Where it is in the government's interests to lodge an objection, this task will be carried out by the minister responsible for agriculture. It is a requirement of the law that a person lodging a notice of objection specifies the reasons for the objection and supports these reasons by including in the objection a statement of the facts he alleges.

Moreover, the registrar may require the person lodging an objection notice to support the objection 'by an affidavit or other proof'.

An objection notice must cite one or more grounds supporting the objection. According to section 25 PBRA, legally acceptable grounds of objection are those alleging: '(a) that the applicant is not entitled to file the application; (b) that the application contains a material misrepresentation; (c) that the contents of the application do not comply with this Act or the Regulations'.

370. In view of the foregoing, an objection against an application for the grant of plant breeders' rights would be successful if it puts forth the following grounds of objection: (i) that application does not contain a clear description of the variety in respect of which the grant of plant breeders' rights is sought; (ii) that the application does not contain all particulars that must usually feature in an application for Plant Breeders' Rights as required under section 19 PBRA; or that the variety has not been given a denomination pursuant to section 20 PBRA; or that the applicant is not one of the persons entitled to lodge an application for Plant Breeder's Rights in Tanzania within the meaning under paragraph 4 of section 2 PBRA; (iii) that the variety described in the application does not meet the novelty requirements under section 14 PBRA, and that no legal presumption may be cast under sections 15, 16 and 17 PBRA respectively that the variety meets the distinctness, uniformity and stability requirements; (iv) that the subject of the application is not a genus or a specie, hence disqualified from protection under section 12 PBRA; (v) that there are grounds to deny approval and registration of the proposed denomination of the variety should be rejected or modified; (vi) that the variety has been reproduced by the repeated use of the reproductive material of another variety for which Plant Breeders' Rights have been granted to or applied for by a person other than the applicant, without licence or permission or in violation thereof; (vii) that any claim of priority based on an application for, or grant of Plant Breeders' Rights under the law of another country is not valid or does not relate to the variety of the current application.

The registrar is duty-bound to inform the applicant of the fact that an objection notice has been filed against their application. In this regard, the registrar is required to furnish the applicant with a copy of the objection notice and all documents supporting the objection within two weeks from the filing date of the objection. The registrar's notification to the applicant as above, affords the latter an opportunity to respond to the allegations put forth by the person objecting. Should the applicant be an agency of the government, the right to respond to the objection notice may be exercised by the minister responsible for agriculture; otherwise the applicant enjoys this right in his individual capacity. The response to an objection notice takes the form of a written statement. The applicant has to submit this statement to the registrar, copying the same to the same to the objector, within a month from the date on which the latter informs the former of the objection notice. In exceptional circumstances, the registrar may permit the applicant to submit his statement within a period longer than the one stated in the immediately preceding sentence.[861]

861. Cf. s. 27, PBRA.

371. GRANT OF PLANT BREEDER'S RIGHTS. After the expiry of the deadline within which an objection notice against an application for Plant Breeders' Rights and a statement of reply thereof may be filed under section 27 PBRA, the registrar goes on to evaluate the application. He does this based on the particulars contained in the application, counter statements, if any, and the results of any tests and trials of the variety.

372. It is important to note that the registrar has an obligation to register a plant variety and grant the applicant with a certificate of registration of plant breeders' right in relation to the variety, provided the registrar is satisfied as regards the following: (i) the application conforms to the requirements of PBRA and there is no any factor that would disentitle the applicant to file the application; (ii) the variety is a new variety; (iii) there are no grounds for objection; and (iv) the application has not been objected, and if it has, the objection does not state an impediment to the availability of Plant Breeder's Rights for the variety. Likewise, following the registration of a plant variety and the grant of the certificate of the plant breeders' right thereof, the registrar has to additionally 'publish a notice of the grant of breeder's right and the approved denomination in the Gazette'.[862]

373. If the registrar is of the opinion that an application does not qualify for the grant of Plant Breeders' Rights, he has to reject the application and provide the applicant with a statement containing reasons for the refusal.

II. Appeals Against Registrar's Decisions

374. Decisions and rulings, which the Registrar of plant breeders' rights makes are not immune from being challenged in higher authorities such as the Appeals Board. In this regard, it is instructive to note that section 43 PBRA empowers the minister responsible for agricultural matters to appoint an Appeals Board to which all grievances pertaining to decisions made by the registrar may be directed. Pursuant to its mandates in this regard, the Appeals Board may 'confirm, set aside or vary any decision or action of the registrar; and may order the registrar to carry out the decision of the Appeals Board'.[863] In the course of exercising the above powers, the Appeals Board may investigate the complaint before it, hear the appeal or 'make a decision based on written submissions'. The Appeals Board is required to justify its decision on any appeals by giving reasons in writings and furnish the appellant, the registrar and any other interested party with copies therefore. Usually, the Board's decision is final.

862. Section 28, PBRA.
863. Section 45, PBRA.

§5. OWNERSHIP AND TRANSFER: ASSIGNMENT – LICENCES

I. Ownership

375. Modalities of ownership of plant breeder's rights can be surmised from section 2 PBRA, which defines the term 'applicant' to mean 'the breeder entitled to file an application for the grant of a breeder's right in accordance with the definition of "breeder" provided for in (Section 2 PBRA)'. This section lists the following persons who are competent to submit to the Registrar of plant varieties a legally admissible application for the grant of plant breeder's rights: '(a) a person who bred or discovered and developed a variety; (b) a person who is the employer of the person who bred or discovered and developed a variety or who has commissioned the employer's work; or (c) a successor in title of a person mentioned in paragraph'. It follows that the applicant for plant breeders' rights whose name features in the certificate of registration becomes the ultimate owner of the plant breeders' rights.

II. Transfer

376. Section 40 PBRA provides for transfer of plant breeders' rights. Transfer is legal transaction whose effect moves the plant breeders' rights from the proprietor to other persons either on permanent or temporary basis. The terms 'assignment' and 'transmission' are commonly used under the PBRA to refer to the former mode of transfer, whereas in relation to the latter mode the applicable term is 'licence'. In lieu of the term 'licence', the PBRA uses the term 'authorization'. Etymologically, the two terms referred in the immediately preceding sentence are synonymous.

A. Assignments

377. Plant Breeders' Rights may be assigned. The PBRA does not provide for an operational definition of the term 'assignment' as used in the context of plant breeder's rights protection regime of Tanzania. However, from its customary meaning, the term refers to a legal process whereby the holder of plant breeder's rights agrees – (in most cases) on prospect of financial consideration – to transfer to another person his title regarding all or part of the exclusive rights he enjoys in relation to a particular plant variety. Such a transfer is made on a permanent basis. As a matter of principle, the assignee is required to ask the registrar to register the assignee's title or interest in the Plant Breeders' Rights. The registrar may register the title or interest mentioned in the immediately preceding sentence only if he is satisfied as to the existence of such a title or interest.

378. The parties to an assignment agreement have a duty to keep secret all information concerning the assignment. Any disclosure thereof constitutes a criminal offence, unless it is a disclosure, which section 51 PBRA permits. In this regard, the law regards as lawful any disclosure of assignment made to the following persons:

'(a) the minister, the Appeals Board, the registrar or any other person for the purposes of carrying out his duties or the performance of his functions under this Act; (b) a police officer for the purposes of an investigation or inquiry relating to the enforcement of the provisions of this Act; or (c) any other person when required to do so by any court or under any written law' .[864]

B. Transmission

379. Both assignment and transmission transfer plant breeders' rights permanently. Whereas assignment results from voluntary contractual arrangements between living persons, an assignment of breeders' rights comes into effect by virtue of succession following the death of the proprietor of the rights involved. In case of transmission of plant breeders' rights, section 42 PBRA requires the recipient to notify the Registrar of the transmission. Upon such notification, the registrar must make the change of ownership in the Register of plant breeders' rights.

C. Licences

380. The proprietor of Plant Breeder's Rights (i.e., licensor) protected in the United Republic of Tanzania enjoys the right to issue licences authorizing third parties (i.e., licensees) to carry out some activities the undertaking of which in relation to a protected plant breeders' rights without such permission contravenes the proprietor's exclusive rights outlined below in §6 of this chapter. The PBRA does not contain any categorization of licences of plant breeders' rights registered in Tanzania. Generally, three types of licences are perceivable; namely: (1) sole licence, which only allows the licensee to exploit the protected breeders' rights to the exclusion of anyone else including the proprietor; (2) exclusive licence, entitling both the licensee and licensor to exploit the rights covered under the registration certificate of the plant breeders' rights but, which does not allow the licensor to issue to other persons further licences; and (3) non-exclusive licence, which not only allows both the licensee and licensor to exploit the protected breeders' rights, but also entitles the licensor to the right to issue further licences.

381. A licence contract concerning Plant Breeder's Rights is governed by its terms. It is commonplace for such a contract to address the following: the quantity of propagating material covered by the licence and the price thereof. The licence may also contain information pertaining to the royalties payable by the licensee, the scope and duration of the licence, any limitation on the licensees' ability to transfer all or any part of his rights under the licence, or to enter into sub-licence arrangements and enforcement measure in the event of parties' failure to fulfil their contractual obligations.

864. Section 51, PBRA.

382. The law obliges the licensee to notify the registrar of the existence of a licence agreement and furnish the latter with a copy of the licence concerned within a period of up to fifty-nine days from the date on which the licence becomes effective. Should there be no reasons to doubt the validity of a licence; the registrar is required to register the licence. Such registration serves as evidence of the licensee's title or interest in the Plant Breeders' Rights.

383. It is a condition under the law that the contents of a licence be generally kept confidential. Access to particulars of a licence by third parties is only possible if and to the extent the parties to the licence agreement have jointly agreed to waive the confidentiality requirement.

§6. Scope of Exclusive Rights

384. Section 30 PBRA reserves to the proprietor of a registered plant breeders' rights the doings or authorization of the doings of several acts, which when carried out 'in respect of the propagating material of the protected variety' by unauthorized parties the said third parties will be liable for infringing plant breeders' rights. The relevant acts include: (i) 'production or reproduction (multiplication)' of the propagating material or harvested material of the protected variety; (ii) 'conditioning for the purpose of propagation' of the propagating material or harvested material of the protected variety; (iii) 'offering for sale' the propagating material of the protected variety; (iv) 'selling or marketing' the propagating material or harvested material of the protected variety; (v) 'exporting' the propagating material or harvested material of the protected variety; (vi) 'importing' the propagating material or harvested material of the protected variety; and (vii) stocking the propagating material or harvested material of the protected variety for production or reproduction (multiplication), conditioning for the purpose of propagation, offering for sale, selling or marketing, exporting, or importing. It is instructive to note that, insofar as the foregoing exclusive rights of the plant breeder relate to harvested material those exclusive rights extends to 'entire plants and parts of plants obtained through the unauthorized use of propagating material of the protected variety'. Likewise, the exclusive rights of the holder of the plant breeders' right entitle them to the right to control 'products made directly from harvested material of the protected variety … through the unauthorized use of the said harvested material'. However, the law permits the holder of the Plant Breeder's Rights protectable in the second phase who 'has not had a reasonable opportunity to exercise his right in relation to the propagating material' to 'assert the same rights with respect to harvested material obtained through the unauthorized use of the propagating material of the variety, and the products from it'.

385. Section 30(5) PBRA widens the scope of the exclusive rights of the holder of Plant Breeder's Rights by specifying the varieties, other than the holder's protected variety, to which the holder may assert exclusive rights outlined above. These varieties are grouped into three categories, as follows: (i) 'varieties whose production required the repeated use of the protected variety'; (ii) varieties, which are not clearly distinguishable from the protected variety; and (iii) varieties that are essentially derived from the protected variety where the protected variety is not itself essentially derived from another variety.

386. Section 30(6) PBRA casts irrebuttable presumption in favour of the fact that a variety is essentially derived from another variety if the following conditions are met: (i) the variety 'is predominantly derived from the initial variety, or from a variety that is itself predominantly derived from the initial variety, while retaining the expression of the essential characteristics that result from the genotype or combination of the genotypes of the initial variety'; (ii) the variety 'is clearly distinguishable from the initial variety'; (iii) apart from the difference emanating from the act of derivation, the variety 'conforms to the initial variety in the expression of the essential characteristics that result from the genotype or combination of genotypes of the initial variety'.

§7. Limitations of the Scope of Protection

I. Exceptions to Plant Breeders' Rights

387. Section 31 PBRA limits the exclusive rights of the holder of Plant Breeder's Rights. The section gives third parties a green light to perpetuate some acts, which would customarily constitute infringement when committed in relation to a protected variety. These acts include the following: (i) 'acts done privately for non-commercial purposes'; (ii) 'acts done for experimental purposes'; (iii) 'acts done for the purpose of breeding varieties' provided that the varieties so bred meet the following conditions: (a) they are not regarded as essential derivatives of the protected variety; and if they are so regarded, the protected variety is itself essentially derived from another variety; or (b) they are clearly distinguishable from the protected variety; or (c) they are varieties whose production did not require the repeated use of the protected variety; and (iv) they are 'acts done by farmers with the purposes of propagating, on their own holdings, the product of the harvest, which they have obtained by planting the protected variety' or any other variety to which a Plant Breeder's Rights apply by virtue of section 30(5)(a) or (b) PBRA.

II. Compulsory Licences

388. A compulsory licence limits the scope of the exclusive rights exercisable by the holder of plant breeders' right. Imposition of this limitation is permitted under section 41(2) PBRA: any person may request the registrar to grant him a compulsory licence. Admissible requests for compulsory licences are usually justified when the holder of Plant Breeder's Rights either unreasonably refuses to grant a licence to the person petitioning for a compulsory licence or imposes unreasonable conditions for the grant of such a licence. In the circumstances, by granting a request for a compulsory licence, the registrar plays a key role of safeguarding the public interest. Indeed, a compulsory licence is granted to further public interests such as the availability to the public at reasonable prices of the propagating material of the variety concerned while affording the holder of Plant Breeders' Rights an opportunity to derive a reasonable advantage from the material. Consequently, 'the person to whom the compulsory (licence relating to breeders' rights) is granted shall pay the holder of the breeder's right an equitable remuneration' in line with the provisions of section 41(2) PBRA.

III. Exhaustion of Breeders' Rights

389. The PBRA provides for the principle of exhaustion by prohibiting reliance on plant breeders' rights to assert exclusive rights over the doings or authorization of the doings of certain acts in relation to the specified material of the protected variety when such material are made a subject of sale or marketing in the United Republic of Tanzania. Section 32(1) PBRA is more specific in this regard; it provides that:

> The breeder's right shall not extend to acts concerning any material of the protected variety or of a variety covered by the provisions of section 30(5), which has been sold or otherwise marketed by the breeder or with his consent in the territory of the United Republic of Tanzania or any material derived from the said material …

390. The term 'material' within the ambit of the foregoing quotation and the provisions of section 30(5) PBRA is a key to unlocking the full understanding of the scope of the principle of exhaustion enshrined under section 32(1) PBRA. The word 'material' as it relates to a variety within the context of section 32(1) PBRA refers to three items; namely: (i) 'propagating material of any kind'; (ii) 'harvested material, including entire plants and parts of plants'; and (iii) 'any product made directly from the harvested material'.[865] The above-quoted provision of section 32(1) PBRA makes reference to a variety covered by section 30(5) PBRA – a provision that widens the scope of the exclusive rights of the holder of Plant Breeder's Rights: it specifies the varieties, other than the holder's protected variety, to which the holder may assert exclusive plant breeders' rights. These varieties are grouped into three categories, as follows: (i) 'varieties whose production required the repeated use of the protected variety'; (ii) varieties, which are not clearly distinguishable from the protected variety; and (iii) varieties that are essentially derived from the protected variety where the protected variety is not itself essentially derived from another variety.

391. Generally, exhaustion of breeders' rights within the ambit of section 32(1) PBRA takes place if the material listed in the immediately preceding paragraph in relation to which the relevant plant variety is protected are sold[866] or marketed in

865. Section 32(2) PBRA.
866. Section 2 PBRA defines the term 'sell' to mean 'to offer, advertise, keep, expose, transmit, convey, deliver or prepare for sale or exchange or dispose off for any consideration or transmit, convey or deliver in pursuance of the sale'.

the United Republic of Tanzania. This position implements in Tanzania the principle of national exhaustion of the relevant plant breeders' rights. Consequently, the marketing of the said material relating to a protected plant variety outside the territory of the United Republic of Tanzania will not entitle third parties to carry out in the United Republic of Tanzania acts that they would otherwise need no authorization if the sale or the marketing of the material was done in Tanzania. The justification for this conclusion is that the sale or the marketing in a foreign country of material of a protected plant variety will not trigger exhaustion of the pertinent breeders' rights in Tanzania.

392. It is worth noticing that the principle of exhaustion does not apply in relation to certain acts that unauthorized third persons carry out in relation to material of a protected a plant variety covered by plant breeders' rights. In this regard, section 31(1) PBRA specifies the following acts as not giving rise to exhaustion of plant breeders' rights: (i) acts involving 'further propagation of the variety in question'; or (b) acts involving 'an export of material of the variety, which enables the propagation of the variety, into a country which does not protect varieties of the plant genus or species to which the variety belongs, except where the exported material is for final consumption purposes'.

§8. Duration of Protection

393. The duration of protection of Plant Breeder's Rights granted under the PBRA depends on whether the varieties concerned are trees, vines or are other types of varieties. The law allows initial term of protection of twenty-five years with respect to trees and vines, whereas varieties other than trees and vines enjoy a twenty-year term of protection. Upon the holder's request, the initial term of protection may be extended for a further five-year term irrespective of whether the variety concerned are trees or vines. However, the request for extension must be made to the registrar six months before the expiration of the relevant initial term of protection.

394. Plant Breeders' Rights can be terminated before its term of protection comes to an end. Such termination of rights can be realized through nullification, cancellation or surrender.

I. Nullification

395. The Registrar of Plant Breeder's Rights may nullify a plant breeders' right in circumstances outlined under section 36 PBRA. Plant Breeder's Rights may be nullified under any of the following grounds: (i) the information on the basis of which the registrar accepted the application for and granted the Plant Breeder's Rights concerned was incorrect, hence such rights would not have been granted should the registrar had been given or known the correct information; (ii) the applicant was not entitled to be granted the Plant Breeder's Rights in view of the fact that another applicant enjoyed a priority right to the grant of the rights in the same variety;[867] (iii) the registrar granted the certificate of registration of plant breeders' rights in foresight of the absolute grounds for refusal of such issuance of the certificate. These grounds are those, which sections 14, 15, 16 and 17 PBRA state; namely, the requirement that a registrable plant breeders' rights should be in relation to variety that is new, distinct, uniform and stable.

II. Cancellation

396. Section 37 PBRA empowers the registrar to cancel Plant Breeder's Rights protected in Tanzania if the proprietor fails to furnish the registrar with the information, documents or material that the office of the registrar considers essential for establishing that the proprietor of the plant breeders' rights has maintained the rights involved. Likewise, cancellation of plant breeders' right is imminent if the proprietor fails to pay the statutory fees required for maintaining the existing Plant Breeders' rights. Moreover, the plant breeders' rights proprietor cannot succeed in challenging cancellation of those rights if the reason for such cancellation is the proprietor's failure to propose a denomination of the plant variety involved the registrar having deregistered the denomination that the proprietor had initially assigned to the plant variety.

III. Surrender of Plant Breeders' Rights

397. Holders of Plant Breeders' Rights protected in Tanzania may surrender their respective rights in line with the provisions of section 39 PBRA. In this regard, any holder who wants to exercise this right must furnish the registrar with a notice of his intention. It is a mandatory requirement that the registrar must deregister the surrendered plant breeders' rights within one month of receipt of the notice of surrender and publish in the *Gazette* a notice of termination of the plant breeders' rights involved.

§9. Infringement and Remedies

398. In case of infringement of their rights, holders of breeders' rights enjoying protection in Tanzania are entitled to both civil and criminal remedies. It constitutes infringement of breeders' rights if a person who is not authorized by the holder of breeders' rights carries in relation to material of a protected variety acts the doings of which is reserved to the proprietor of the breeders' rights. In the event of infringement, the holder may institute a suit asking the court to grant him an appropriate

867. However, nullification of rights in this latter scenario may be effected only if the Plant Breeder's Rights are transferred to the person to whom the rights should have been granted first (s. 36, PBRA).

remedy. The court may remedy the infringement by granting 'an injunction or damages or both' as the circumstances of the case may reasonably dictate. Likewise, the court may award the holder of breeders' right the cost of the suit.

The PBRA provides for certain acts which constitutes criminal offences in relation to matters appertaining protection and governance of breeders' rights. The following table depicts the relevant offences and the corresponding penalties.

	Offence[868]	*Penalty*
1	Making or entering false information in the Register of breeders' rights.	Up to TZS 10million or up to one year imprisonment term; or to both fine and imprisonment
2	Making a written false statement purporting to be a 'copy of an entry in the Register or of a document lodged with the Registrar of breeders' rights.	Up to TZS 10million or up to one year imprisonment term; or to both fine and imprisonment
3	Tendering or producing a 'false entry of copy as evidence'.	Up to TZS 10million or up to one year imprisonment term; or to both fine and imprisonment
4	Submitting a false document or making a 'false statement or representation to the Registrar in regard to any action described under [the PBRA]'.	Up to TZS 10 million or up to one year imprisonment term; or to both fine and imprisonment
5	Obstructing or hindering the 'Registrar or any officer in the exercise of his powers or the carrying out of his functions under this Act'.	Up to TZS 10 million or up to one year imprisonment term; or to both fine and imprisonment
6	Failing to appear at any proceedings under [the PBRA] without lawful excuse for such appearance and having been duly summoned to appear.	Up to TZS 10 million or up to one year imprisonment term; or to both fine and imprisonment
7	Having appeared as a witness at any proceedings under [the PBRA], refusing unlawfully 'to be sworn or to make affirmation or to produce any document or answer any question which he may be lawfully required to produce or answer'	Up to TZS 10 million or up to one year imprisonment term; or to both fine and imprisonment

868. Liability for the offences listed in this table is subject to the prosecutor proving the proprietor's intent to commit the crime.

	Offence[868]	*Penalty*
8	Offering for sale or marketing propagating material of a variety protected under the PBRA without using the correct denomination of the variety concerned.	Up to TZS 10 million or up to one year imprisonment term; or to both fine and imprisonment
9	Providing false information in any application or making any false statement in evidence	Up to TZS 10 million or up to one year imprisonment term; or to both fine and imprisonment
10	Violating breeder's right recognized as such under the PBRA.	Up to TZS 10 million or up to one year imprisonment term; or to both fine and imprisonment
11	Disclosing secret information relating to plant breeders' rights.	Up to TZS 5 million or up to one year imprisonment term; or to both fine and imprisonment.

Chapter 8. Integrated Circuit Layout-Designs

§1. Sources: Legislation

399. The legislature of the United Republic of Tanzania has not yet enacted a piece of legislation that would create a regime for integrated circuit layout-designs protection regime effective in the whole United Republic. This is notwithstanding the fact that Tanzania has a latent obligation to implement in the municipal legal system rules underlying international regime for the protection of integrated circuit layout-designs contained in the TRIPS Agreement[869] and the Paris Convention.[870]

The ZIPA establishes a legal framework for integrated circuit layout-designs protection in Tanzania Zanzibar. The discourse in this chapter is by and large based on the provisions of ZIPA.

§2. Subject Matter of Protection

400. The ZIPA provides for the protection of integrated circuit layout-designs under Chapter IV entitled 'layout-designs (topographies) of integrated circuits'. In this regard, ZIPA offers to protect design elements in the layout of integrated circuits. Both 'layout-design' and 'integrated circuit' are technical terms, which deserve delineation especially when applied in the legal context. Thus, the term 'integrated circuit' means a 'product, in its final form or an intermediate form, in which the elements, at least one of which is an active element, and some or all of the interconnections are integrally formed in or on a piece of material and which is intended to perform an electronic function'. Following the delineation under the ZIPA, the term 'layout-design' is 'synonymous with "topography" and means the three-dimensional disposition, however expressed, of the elements, at least one of which is an active element, and of some or all of the interconnections of an integrated circuit, or such a three-dimensional disposition prepared for an integrated circuit intended for manufacture'.[871]

§3. Conditions of Protection

401. Protection of integrated circuit layout-designs (hereinafter 'IC layout-design') in Tanzania is obtained through registration of the designs. To qualify for the registration, an IC layout-design has to be original and new. These requirements are outlined herein below.

869. The TRIPS Agreement has been binding on the United Republic of Tanzania since 1 Jan. 1995.
870. Tanzania is, since 16 Jun. 1963, bound by the Paris Convention of 20 Mar. 1883 as last revised in 1967.
871. Cf. s. 2, ZIPA.

I. Originality

402. Originality of an IC layout-design is one of the conditions for registration and hence protection in Tanzania of a particular layout-design of an integrated circuit. To fulfil the originality requirement under the Tanzanian law, an IC layout-design has to result from 'its creator's own intellectual effort and (should not be) commonplace among creators of layout-designs and manufacturers of integrated circuits at the time of its creation'.[872] Similarly, a 'layout-design consisting of a combination of elements and interconnections that are commonplace' may be registered and protected in Tanzania, provided that such combination and interconnections are attributable to the creator's own ingenuity.[873]

II. Novelty

403. Protection by way of registration of an IC layout-design in Tanzania is subject to the novelty requirement. In keeping with this protection condition, a layout-design can be registered only if 'it has not been exploited commercially anywhere in the world' and in case it has been so exploited, it may qualify for registration for protection only if the duration of such prior exploitation must be a period of up to two years.[874]

§4. Formalities: Procedure for Obtaining Protection

404. A person who is desirous of getting protection of an IC layout-design in Tanzania Zanzibar has to lodge an application for registration of the design with the IPOZ. To qualify to submit an acceptable application, the applicant must be the creator (i.e., the owner) of the layout-design or an assignee of the design or a person legally representing the interests of the assignee or owner of the design in respect of which registration is sought in Tanzania Zanzibar.[875]

The ZIPA provides for formalities with which an application for the registration of an IC layout-design must comply. In line with the required formalities, a statement indicating that that the applicant requests for the registration of his IC layout-design and the applicant's personal particulars such as his names, residential address, place of business establishment, nationality and entitlement to make an application for the IC layout-design concerned must form part and parcel of the application package. In case the applicant is an agent of the creator or owner of the IC layout-design, he cannot submit an admissible application for registration of the layout-design, unless he accompanies it with the power of attorney allowing him to assume the step into the shoes of the owner of the IC layout-design concerned. Other information that must necessarily feature in the application include a concise

872. Cf. s. 38(1), ZIPA.
873. Cf. s. 38(2), ZIPA.
874. Cf. s. 37, ZIPA.
875. Cf. ss 39 & 5, ZIPA.

description of the layout-design and any supporting data such as a copy or drawing of the layout-design and information elaborating on the function, which the integrated circuit concerned can perform. Moreover, it is a requirement under the law that the applicant specify in his application the date on which commercial exploitation of the layout-design first took place anywhere in the world, and where no such exploitation has so far taken place, provide a statement to that fact.[876]

Further to the foregoing, an application for registration of an IC layout-design in Tanzania must be accompanied by a prescribed fee. Any application for registration of an IC layout-design that does comply with the requirement stated in the immediately preceding sentence is treated by the registrar's office as not having been filed. The applicant is, however, notified of that fact so that he may pay the prescribed fee as a condition for application to be accepted as having been duly filed with the registrar's office.

Once an application for registration of an IC layout-design is filed in a manner conformable to the stipulation of the law, the registrar has to accept it. If the registrar is of the opinion that the application does not conform to the formal requirements, he will bestow upon the applicant an opportunity to update the application for conformity with the required formalities, as a condition subject to which the former is prepared to accept the application. In case the applicant wishes to retain the date on which he submitted his application as the filing date of the application, he has to rectify the defects spotted in his application by the Registrar within a period of two months. Any rectifications done outside of this timeframe will render the application concerned being assigned as its filing date the date on which the applicant corrected the defects in the application.

An application for an IC layout-design registration submitted in compliance with the formal requirements outlined above is not subjected to substantive examination as a condition for registration. The registrar is required to register in the register of layout-designs each and every IC layout-design in respect of which an application for registration has been duly filed.[877] The law requires the registrar to cause a notice regarding the fact that an IC layout-design has been registered in the register of layout-designs to be published in the Official Gazette. Such a publication serves duo interconnected purposes; namely, to inform the public existence of such a registration so that they can avoid infringement and to also check whether the registered IC layout-design infringes on prior rights.

876. It is instructive to note that information concerning prior commercial exploitation of an IC layout-design is of paramount importance, especially when it comes to determining the commencement date of protection. In this regard, if an IC layout-design is commercially exploited prior to the date of application for registration, registration of such an IC layout-design with the IPOZ will have a retrospective effect to that date provided that the application for IC layout-design registration was lodged within two years succeeding the date of first commercial exploitation of the design (cf. s. 41, ZIPA).

877. The register of layout-designs normally contains the following information: names and address of the proprietor; number of registration, title and filing date of the application for an IC layout-design registration, etc., (cf. s. 43(2), ZIPA).

§5. OWNERSHIP AND TRANSFER (ASSIGNMENT: LICENCES)

I. Ownership

405. ZIPA rovides for three scenarios of ownership in relation to layout-designs. The first scenario establishes the creator as the owner alone or jointly with other co-creators. The second scenario refers creation under contractual obligation either explicitly (e.g., by commission) or by implied terms (e.g., under a contract of employment), whereby a layout-design created in the course of one's employment becomes the property of the employer, and the one created by an independent contractor becomes the property of the person who has commissioned the contractor to create the layout-design concerned. The third refers to ownership acquired through transfer of legal rights in the layout-design.[878]

II. Transfer

406. The ZIPA bestows upon the owner of a layout-design a right to transfer his title in the design temporarily, permanently, wholly or in part. Temporary transfer of rights in a layout-design may be realized through the grant of licence.[879] Being a legal means through which third parties can access and exercise the rights usually enjoyable by the proprietor of a layout-design without infringing upon those rights, a licence in respect of a layout-design can be either exclusive or non-exclusive. A licence contract that does not prohibit the proprietor to grant further licences to more than one licensee is technically known as exclusive licence, whereas a licence that limits the powers of the proprietor to issue further licences is considered to be exclusive licence.

Permanent transfer of layout-design can be realized in Tanzania as a result of assignment of ownership – which is usually concluded between living persons (i.e., *inter partes*) – and transfer by succession either on the basis of a will or on grounds of law in case of intestate succession.[880]

§6. SCOPE OF EXCLUSIVE RIGHTS

407. The Tanzanian law on the protection of IC layout-designs does not grant positive rights to the owner of a registered IC layout-design; it rather extends to him some negative rights entitling him to prohibit third parties from carrying out certain commercial activities in relation to his layout-design. It is thus within the ambit of exclusive rights of the proprietor of a layout-design registered in Tanzania Zanzibar to reproduce the whole or any part of the layout-design. Consequently, the proprietor enjoys right to import, sell and distribute in Tanzania for commercial purposes the layout-design, an IC layout-design, which incorporates the layout-design' as

878. Cf. ss 39 & 5, ZIPA.
879. Cf. s. 20, ICLD Act.
880. Cf. s. 39, ZIPA.

well as an article which incorporates an integrated circuit, which incorporates unlawfully reproduced registered layout-design. It falls within the proprietor's power to authorize any commercial exploitation of his registered layout-design as above.[881]

§7. LIMITATIONS OF THE SCOPE OF PROTECTION

I. Principle of Exhaustion

408. The exclusive rights of the proprietor outlined above in §6 of this chapter cannot be invoked to exclude third parties from importing into the United Republic of Tanzania, sell and distribute a layout-design or a circuit incorporating layout-design, which has been initially put on the market anywhere in the world by the proprietor or any other person authorized by the proprietor of the layout-design. In this regard, section 40 of the ZIPA employs the principle of international exhaustion.

II. Compulsory Licence

409. Compulsory licence is a permission issued to a third party to use a registered layout-design against the will of the proprietor. The application for the compulsory licence can be approved by the Registrar of layout-designs, other administrative authority such as the minister responsible for industrial property matters as well as judicial authority only if the applicant proves that the layout-design will be used to further public non-commercial ends or to remedy an anticompetitive practice.[882] Note that application for compulsory licence is regarded as a last resort attempt to complement unsuccessful efforts made by the applicant to apply for a voluntary licence. Thus, the applicant for a layout-design must satisfy the authority responsible for granting compulsory licences in Tanzania that the owner of the layout-design is not willing to grant the applicant a voluntary licence and that no reasonable justification for the proprietor's denial to issue the licence exists.

III. Other Limitations

410. The right of the proprietor of layout-design to reproduce or to authorize reproduction of the design cannot be invoked to prohibit third parties from reproducing a registered layout-design, if such reproduction is done for private purposes. This applies also to reproduction of a registered layout-design, which is done for the purpose of evaluating and analysing design as well as reproduction done for the purpose and in the course of research and teaching. Note further that, a third party may analyse and evaluate a registered layout-design and on the basis of such evaluation and analysis create an original layout-design and incorporate such a design in

881. Cf. s. 40, ZIPA.
882. Cf. s. 45(2), ZIPA.

an integrated circuit and consequently enjoy exclusive layout-design rights without interference by the owner of the layout-design on whose basis the evaluation and analysis that led to the creation of the third party's original layout-design was made.[883]

§8. Duration of Protection

411. Protection of layout-designs in Tanzania lasts for ten calendar years calculated from the date of first commercial exploitation of the layout-design, if the layout-design concerned was exploited commercially prior to its registration anywhere in the world. In relation to a layout-design, which was not commercially exploited as above, the term of protection runs from the date of commencement of protection of the layout-design concerned.[884] Once the ten-year duration comes to an end, it is not possible to extend legal protection of the layout-design in Tanzania: thereafter, third parties do not need any authorization for any commercial activities involving the layout-design whose term of protection has come to an end.

§9. Infringement and Remedies

412. It constitutes infringement of rights in a layout-design registered in Tanzania if a third party exercises any of the exclusive rights outlined above in §6 of this chapter without authorization from the proprietor of the layout-design.[885]

The Tanzanian law on the protection of layout-designs provides for various remedies that can be awarded to a successful party in layout-designs infringement suits. These remedies include damages, injunctions, attachment, the rendering of account, the delivery of infringing copies or articles used or intended to be used for making infringing copies and Anton Piller orders.[886]

883. Cf. s. 40, ZIPA.

884. Cf. s. 41(2), ZIPA. The formula for calculating an effective date of registration of a layout-design is outlined under s. 41(1) of ZIPA. In this regard, protection of an IC layout-design, which was commercially exploited prior to the date of application for registration commences retrospectively from the date on which the layout-design was first put to commercial use by the owner, provided that an application for registration of such an IC layout-design was lodged within two years succeeding the date of first commercial exploitation of the design. Protection of a layout-design, which was not put to commercial prior use commences on the filing date of the application for registration thereof.

885. Cf. s. 77(1), ZIPA.

886. Cf. ss 77(2) & 89, ZIPA.

Chapter 9. Trade Secrets

§1. Sources: Legislation

413. The ZIPA, 2008 provides for trade secrets[887] protection in one territorial part of the United Republic of Tanzania; namely, Tanzania Zanzibar. There is no effective piece of legislation that has a specific object of protecting trade secrets in Mainland Tanzania, which is the other geographical part of the United Republic of Tanzania. This leaves the general legal protection of trade secrets in this territory to be based on the common-law principles regulating breach of confidence and the law governing contractual relations.

In the advent of the Agreement on TRIPS of 15 April 1994 (henceforth, the TRIPS Agreement), trade secrets have gained a special status entitling it to legal protection under unfair competition regime established under the Paris Convention for the Protection of Industrial Property of 20 March 1883 as revised and amended (henceforth, the Paris Convention).[888] The United Republic of Tanzania being one of the signatories to both the TRIPS Agreement and the Paris Convention has an obligation to put in place an unfair competition regime that addresses not only general unfair competition issues but also specific cases of trade secrets protection.

§2. The Protection of Trade Secrets

414. The obligation to establish a municipal regime for the protection of trade secrets, which the United Republic of Tanzania as a WTO Member State has to discharge, is founded on Article 39 of the TRIPS Agreement. In view of the opening provisions of this article, the United Republic of Tanzania has a duty to protect trade secrets based on unfair competition rules that are enshrined in Article 10*bis* of the Paris Convention. When fully implemented, provisions of Article 39 of the TRIPS Agreement bestow upon natural and artificial persons a right to enjoin any unlawful access to, or unauthorized use and/or disclosure of secret commercial information. It is important to note that unlawful disclosure or acquisition of secret commercial information within the ambit of Article 39 of the TRIPS Agreement is that which is done in a 'manner contrary to honest commercial practices'. According to the TRIPS Agreement, the term 'a manner contrary to honest commercial practices' encompasses the following:

> at least practices such as breach of contract, breach of confidence and inducement to breach, and includes the acquisition of undisclosed information by third parties who knew, or were grossly negligent in failing to know, that such practices were involved in the acquisition.[889]

887. The WIPO defines trade secret as any 'confidential business information which provides an enterprise a competitive edge' such as 'manufacturing or industrial secrets and commercial secrets' (http://www.wipo.int/sme/en/ip_business/trade_secrets/trade_secrets.htm (accessed: 18 Dec. 2015)).

888. Cf. Art. 39, TRIPS Agreement.

889. Article 39(2), TRIPS Agreement.

There is no specific piece of legislation that implements Article 39 of the TRIPS Agreements in mainland Tanzania. However, common-law principles on breach of confidence and the law governing contractual obligations can be invoked to support an action against unlawful access, exploitation and disclosure of trade secrets in mainland Tanzania.

The ZIPA, 2008 provides for protection of trade secrets in Tanzania Zanzibar. One of ZIPA's provisions with direct relevance to Article 39 of the TRIPS Agreement is section 72, which provides that:

> Any act or practice, in the course of industrial or commercial activities, that results in the disclosure, acquisition or use by others of secret information without the consent of the person lawfully in control of that information … and in a manner contrary to honest commercial practices shall constitute an act of unfair competition.[890]

The term a 'manner contrary to honest commercial practices' as employed in the foregoing quotation has the meaning ascribed to it under section 67 of ZIPA as hereunder:

> An act or practice that is contrary to honest practices, [for the purposes of ZIPA], shall mean at least practices such as breach of contract, breach of confidence and inducement to breach, and includes the acquisition of undisclosed information by third parties who knew, or were grossly negligent in failing to know, that such practices were involved in the acquisition.[891]

An actionable 'disclosure, acquisition or use of secret information' under the ZIPA must be perpetuated without the consent of the proprietor of the trade secret concerned. The absence of such consent is presumed in cases of 'industrial or commercial espionage', the 'breach of confidence', failure to observe contractual obligations and 'inducement to commit any of the (foregoing) acts'.[892] However, it is important to note that knowledge on the part of the acquirer of the trade secret that his acquisition of the secret results from any of the acts mentioned in the immediately preceding sentence is indispensable to hold one liable for trade secrets infringement. The law endorses a constructive knowledge of such acquisition if the infringer ought to have known that his acts constitute infringement of trade secret, but for gross negligence on his part.[893]

To successfully institute an action for trade secrets infringements under section 72 of the ZIPA, it is imperative that the plaintiff proves three requirements stipulated under the TRIPS Agreement. First, that the trade secret 'is secret in the sense that it is not, as a body or in the precise configuration and assembly of its components, generally known among or readily accessible to persons within the circles that normally deal with the kind of information in question'. Second, that the trade

890. Cf. s. 72(1), ZIPA.
891. Cf. s. 67(1)(b), ZIPA.
892. Cf. s. 72(2), ZIPA.
893. Cf. 72(2), ZIPA.

secret 'has commercial value because it is secret'. Third, that the trade secret has been subject to reasonable steps under the circumstances by the rightful holder to keep it secret.[894]

894. Cf. s. 72(3), ZIPA & Art. 39(2), TRIPS Agreement.

Chapter 10. Geographical Indications

§1. Sources: Legislation

415. The ZIPA provides for registration and protection of geographical indications (GIs) in Tanzania Zanzibar. There is no piece of legislation that specifically protects GIs by way of registration in Tanzania mainland. A jurisdiction, such as Tanzania mainland, that does not have a specific legislation for the protection of GIs may, in addition to resorting to trade mark laws, protect GIs based on laws governing trade practices. In this regard, the relevant laws include those regulating trade descriptions, consumer protection and laws on protection against unfair competition.[895] Consequently, pieces of domestic legislation that can be invoked to protect GIs in mainland Tanzania include the following: (1) the MMA enacted to address trade descriptions, labelling and counterfeiting cases;[896] (2) The TSMA, 1986 that came into force in October 1994; and (3) the Fair Competition Act, 2003 (Act No. 2/2003).[897] In their generality, these pieces of legislation stipulate negative rights, which proprietors or lawful users of GIs may invoke to prohibit third parties from exploiting the GIs involved. Principles that are relevant for protection of GIs and which are contained in the pieces of legislations mentioned above are founded on GIs protection standards promulgated in various international legal instruments on IP matters, to which the United Republic of Tanzania is a contracting party. One of these instruments is the Paris Convention for the Protection of Industrial Property of 20 March 1883 as revised and amended (henceforth, the Paris Convention). Some of the subject matters protectable under the Paris Convention are indications of source and appellations of origin,[898] with specific protection being offered against unfair competition behaviours relating to the foregoing subject matter of protection.[899]

The Agreement on TRIPS of 15 April 1994 is a multilateral agreement, which stipulates minimum provisions for the protection of various IP rights including GIs.[900] The United Republic of Tanzania is a contracting party to the Agreement on TRIPS.[901] The main obligation the TRIPS Agreement imposes on WTO Member

895. Dev Gangjee, *Relocating Geographical Indications*, available at http://ssrn.com/abstract=1863350.
896. This piece of legislation remained dormant for more than forty years; it just became operational in 2005 following its commencement notice published in the Government Gazette on 15 Apr. 2005. This law was last amended in 2007 by the Written Laws (Miscellaneous Amendments) (No. 19) Act, 2007.
897. Act No. 2/2003 of the Law Tanzania regulates *inter alia* unfair trade practices and applies to mainland Tanzania alone.
898. Article 1.2, PC.
899. Article 10*bis*.
900. Cf. Lennart Schüßler, *Protecting 'Single-Origin Coffee' Within the Global Coffee Market: The Role of Geographical Indications and Trademarks*, 10(1) Estey Centre J.Int'l L. & Trade Pol'y 149-185, at 153 (2009), available at https://ideas.repec.org/a/ags/ecjilt/48799.html (accessed: 17 Feb. 2022).
901. Other prominent international legal instruments for the protection of GIs – which the United Republic of Tanzania has neither ratified nor accessed – are: (1) the Madrid Agreement for the Repression of False or Deceptive Indications of Source on Goods of 14 Apr. 1891; and (2) the Lisbon Agreement for the Protection of Appellations of origin and their International Registration of 1958.

States, such as the United Republic of Tanzania, is the duty to establish a legal regime for the protection of GIs – a duty that is inherent under Article 22(2) TRIPS. Indeed the aim of this provision is to harmonize the national regimes for the protection of GIs. However, the achievement of this objective is imbued with uncertainty: the wording of Article 22(2) TRIPS effectively bestows upon each WTO Member State a leeway to protect GIs in a manner that best suits the local circumstances. Thus, a country, such as the United Republic of Tanzania, which does not have a law specifically providing for GIs protection, may nevertheless comply with the obligation under Article 22(2) TRIPS, even where the legal basis for the envisaged GIs protection regime is implied under pieces of legislation that are non-specific to GIs protection.[902]

§2. Subject Matter of Protection

416. A GI is a sign which connects a product (or service) to a particular specific place such as a country, a region, or a locality. International instruments and national legislation employ different terminologies when referring to this category of a sign. For instance, the Paris Convention uses 'indications of source' and 'appellations of origin'. The former term refers to: any expression or sign used to indicate that a product or service originates in a country, a region or a specific place. The latter refers to a 'geographical name of a country, a region or a specific place' that serves to 'designate a product originating therein the characteristic qualities of which are due exclusively or essentially to the geographical environment, including natural or human factors'.[903]

Contrary to what the Paris Convention does, the Agreement on TRIPS does not refer to 'indication of source' and 'appellation of origin'; it refers to GI as one of the subject matters of protection under it. Article 22.1 of TRIPS defines the term 'geographical indication' in the following manner:

> Geographical indications are, for the purposes of [TRIPS] Agreement, indications which identify a good as originating in the territory of a Member, or a region or locality in that territory, where a given quality, reputation or other characteristic of the good is essentially attributable to its geographical origin.

The ZIPA, 2008 makes a specific identification of GIs as one of the subject matters of IP protection and delineates the term 'geographical indication' in the manner that does not substantially differ from the definition of the same term provided for under Article 22.1 of the TRIPS Agreement.[904] However, the scope of the definition

902. G. Mengistie & M. Blakeney, *Geographical Indications and the Scramble for Africa*, 25.2 Afr. J. Int'l & Comp. L. 199–220 at 201 (2017), retrieved from: www.euppublishing.com/ajicl (accessed: 29 Jun. 2020).
903. Cf. WIPO, IP Handbook, 2nd edn, WIPO Publication No. 489 (E), 2004, p. 120. www.wipo.int/edocs/pubdocs/en/intproperty/489/wipo_pub_489.pdf.
904. Cf. Art. 2, para. 12, ZIPA.

of the term 'geographical indication' under both the ZIPA and the TRIPS Agreement should particularly be noted for the inherent slight difference. Whereas pursuant to the definition under the former piece of legislation GIs that may be protected in Tanzania Zanzibar are those recognized as such in any country in the world, the definition under the latter recognizes as protectable subject matters only GIs that are available in countries that are members of the WTO. In this regard, the GIs protection regime, which the ZIPA stipulates is commendable for being generous when judged by the minimum standards that the TRIPS Agreement promulgates.

A close examination of the statutory delineations of the terms 'indication of source', 'appellation of origin' (employed under the Paris Convention) and 'geographical indication' (applied under the TRIPS Agreement – and as further reproduced in the ZIPA, 2005), may lead to several conclusions. Due to its broadest context, the term 'indication of source' covers as well the terms 'geographical indication' and 'appellation of origin'. The central protection condition in relation to indications of source only necessitates that the products, which the indication of source identifies originate in a particular geographical location. Given its narrow scope of application, not all indications of source, which the Paris Convention covers can be accommodated under the term 'Geographical Indication' provided for under the TRIPS Agreement. A clear case buttressing this contention involves indications of source whose exploitation with respect to products does not convey a suggestion of some quality, reputation or some other characteristics that are particularly notable insofar as those relevant products are concerned. At a comparative level, GIs covers many items than those, which the term 'appellations of origin' can legally extend protection to. As a result of the broad meaning assigned to the former term, it is on firm ground to reason that all appellations of origin are GIs, but not all GIs are appellations of origin. To serve as a GI, it is a *sine qua non* that the products' reputation, quality or other characteristics be solely attributed to the geographical origin of the products concerned.

Tete goat from Mozambique is one of several examples of African products that may qualify for GI protection. Indeed, the goats from the Mozambican region of Tete have been proved as having unique sweetness and juicy flavour attributable to baobab fruits and dry grasses on which the goats feed during the country's dry season, which lasts longer than other seasons of the year. The environment in which the Tete goat are grazed is peculiar to the Tete region, hence the quality and reputation of the Tete goat meat is essentially due to the natural environment of the Tete region. The fact that there is a clear link between the quality of the Tete goat meat and the place of rearing of these goats, has led to the certification of Mozambican's Tete Goat as a first GI to be registered in a country that is a Member State of ARIPO.[905]

Like Mozambique and other African countries, the United Republic of Tanzania is also uniquely endowed with many products whose qualities and reputation is attributable to their place of origin, thus making them potential candidates for GI

905. ARIPO MAGAZINE: Vol. 8, No.2, April–June 2018, p. 7, retrieved from https://www.aripo.org/wp-content/uploads/2018/11/ARIPO_Mag_Vol.8_No.2.pdf (accessed: 29 Jun. 2020).

protection. These include 'rice from Kyela-Mbeya; cloves from Zanzibar; and coffee, Aloe Vera and sugar from the plains below Mt. Kilimanjaro'.[906] Other products include the Uyui honey from Uyui district, Tanzania.[907]

It is instructive to note that, in addition to an already prevailing legal protection gap resulting from the absence of a specific piece of legislation on GIs protection in Tanzania mainland, some of the potential GI products, such as the Uyui honey, do not have reputation that would make this honey distinct from honey available in other regions of Tanzania. Indeed, this is a stumbling block, which prohibits potential GIs from attracting specific legal protection in Tanzania mainland on the basis of their geographical origins. Concerted efforts are required to brand all potential GI products: it is only through such branding legal protection of the relevant GIs would have a meaningful impact on both GI users and the consumers of the GI products.

A good example that the government of the United Republic of Tanzania should emulate is the Zanzibar cloves branding project that, assisted by the WIPO, the International Trade Centre (ITC) has undertaken to promote the cloves cultivated in Zanzibar. A report outlining this project states in part as follows:

> Since late 2012 ITC has worked with the major stakeholders on the island to create a new and distinctive brand for cloves and spice based products from Zanzibar, capitalising on the heritage, culture and positive associations of the origin. A series of creative branding workshops were held with public and private sector stakeholders, engaging more than 100 people in the process. By ensuring commitment to the objectives behind the branding: that higher grade organic spices should be planted, nurtured and certified and that the profits of the project should be shared between farmers and other local actors involved in the transformation of the spices, commitment was achieved to a programme that will take several years to fully accomplish. The 'Exotic, organic and original' spice brand builds on the unique characteristics of Zanzibar's people and environment as well as the authentic history of cloves and spices in Zanzibar.[908]

---

906. Policy Brief, Protection of Quality Products with Geographical Indication in Tanzania, retrieved from https://efdinitiative.org/sites/default/files/publications/policy_brief_tanzania.pdf (accessed: 1 Mar. 2022).
907. A.E.G. Mwakaje, A.S. Bosselmann, L. Hansted, G. Nyunza & F. Maganga (2018) Using geographical indications for signalling quality and reducing transaction costs of marketing Uyui honey from Tanzania, Forests, Trees and Livelihoods, 27:2, 118-138, DOI: 10.1080/14728028.2018.1445040; retrieved from https://www.tandfonline.com/doi/full/10.1080/14728028.2018.1445040 (accessed: 1 Mar. 2022).
908. Branding Zanzibar cloves and revitalizing the island's spice sector and image, retrieved from http://www.intracen.org/uploadedFiles/intracenorg/Content/Redesign/News/Did_you_know/Case%20study%20on%20Zanzibar%20spices%20(v010).pdf.

§3. The GIs Protection

417. Article 22.2 of the TRIPS Agreement incorporates some global protection standards of GIs. It stipulates that:

> In respect of geographical indications, Members shall provide the legal means for interested parties to prevent:
>
> (a) the use of the designation or presentation of a good that indicates or suggests that the good in question originates in a geographical area other than the true place of origin in a manner which misleads the public as to the geographical origin of the good;
> (b) any use which constitutes an act of unfair competition within the meaning of Article 10*bis* of the Paris Convention (1967).

The TRIPS Agreement additionally decrees in its Article 22.3 that:

> A Member shall, ex officio if its legislation so permits or at the request of an interested party, refuse or invalidate the registration of a trademark which contains or consists of a geographical indication with respect to goods not originating in the territory indicated, if use of the indication in the trademark for such goods in that Member is of such a nature as to mislead the public as to the true place of origin.

It is to be noted that in addition to Article 10*bis* of the Paris Convention that addresses unfair trade behaviours, Article 10.1 of the Convention also requires Member States, such as the United Republic of Tanzania, to offer protection against 'direct or indirect use of a false indication of the source of goods'. Article 22.2 of the TRIPS agreement has recognized Article 10*bis* of the Paris Convention as a legal provision that can be invoked to justify protection of GIs. Unfair competition behaviours that Article 10*bis* of the Paris Convention outlaws, particularly because they are acts 'of competition contrary to honest practices in industrial or commercial matters', include the following:

> 1. all acts of such a nature as to create confusion by any means whatever, with the establishment, the goods, the industrial or commercial activities, of a competitor; 2. False allegations in course of trade of such a nature as to discredit the establishment, the goods or the industrial or commercial activities, of a competitor; 3. Indications or allegations the use of which in the course of trade is liable to mislead the public as to the nature, the manufacturing process, the characteristics, the suitability for their purpose, or the quality, of the goods.

The extent to which the United Republic of Tanzania has domesticated the TRIPS Agreement and the Paris Convention provisions outlined above is a moot point in this chapter. It is instructive to note that the United Republic has resorted to three main modalities of GIs protection; namely: (1) sui generis protection; (2) protection of GIs based on trademark law; and (3) regulatory regime that is centred on business practices.

I. Sui Generis Protection of GIs

418. 'Sui Generis' is a Latin term that means 'of its own kind'. *Evans Sikinyi* characterizes this term in the following manner:

> a sui generis is a system designed to address the needs of a particular issue. This could mean a system entirely separate and different from the current IP system. The term is sometimes used to refer to new IP, or IP-like, rights.[909]

The sui generis system for the protection of GIs is non-existent in Mainland Tanzania. However, this system exists in Tanzania Zanzibar under the ZIPA. The ZIPA, whose Chapter II contains provisions that are solely devoted to the protection of GIs, defines the term 'Geographical Indication' as an 'indication that identifies a good as originating in the territory of a country, or a region or locality in the territory, where a given quality, reputation or other characteristic of the good is essentially attributed to its geographical origin'.[910]

It is notable under the ZIPA that 'indications which do not correspond to the (above) definition' are not protectable as GIs in Tanzania Zanzibar. Other indications, which the ZIPA excludes from protection as GIs include the following: (1) indications, which contravene public order or morality; (2) 'GIs which are not or cease to be protected in their country of origin, or which have fallen into disuse in that country'; (3) 'indications with respect to goods that are identical with the term customary in common language as the common name for such goods in Zanzibar';[911] and (4) a 'geographical indication which, although literary true as to the territory, region or locality in which the goods originate, falsely represents to the public that the goods originate in another territory'.[912]

419. The GIs protection regime obtaining in Tanzania Zanzibar under the ZIPA covers both registered and unregistered GIs. However, a registered geographical indication enjoys a stable protection than unregistered indications. One of the advantages enjoyed in respect of a registered GI is the presumption of validity of such an indication. This implies that in legal proceedings concerning unregistered GI, the issue whether or not the geographical indication under dispute is constituted by a protectable subject matter has to be resolved first.

909. *See* Evans Sikinyi, *Plant Variety Protection [Plant Breeder's Rights] in Kenya*, in *Intellectual Property Rights in Kenya* 73 (Moni Wekesa & Ben Sihanya eds, Konrad Adenauer Stiftung 2009).
910. Cf. s. 2, para. 13, ZIPA.
911. Cf. s. 59, ZIPA.
912. Cf. s. 58, ZIPA.

Where registration of a Geographical Indication in Tanzania Zanzibar is desired, such registration does not happen automatically.[913] In most cases, the applicant for GI registration had to draft and send the relevant application to the Registrar of Industrial Property (henceforward, the registrar). Key information that must accompany an application for GI registration in Tanzania Zanzibar include specifications regarding the name, address, nationality of the natural person or legal entity filing the application and the capacity in which the applicant is applying for registration. Moreover, the applicant has to specify the geographical indication for which registration is sought, the geographical area, which the geographical indication covers and the goods for which such an indication applies. The law also requires the applicant to include in the application for a GI registration a description of the quality, reputation or other characteristic of the goods for which the geographical indication is used.

It is worth noticing that the admissibility of an application for GI registration is subject to the payment of the application fee as prescribed under the law.[914]

Section 60 of the ZIPA bestows upon natural persons, legal entities as well as any competent authority a right to make an application to the registrar for registration of a GI. According to section 2 of ZIPA, the competent authority having the right to lodge an application for registration of a particular GI in Tanzania Zanzibar is the minister responsible for industrial property matters in Zanzibar. It is a *sine qua non* that – to be able to fully claim the entitlement to file an application for GI registration in Tanzania Zanzibar – the qualified applicant, other than the competent authority, must be carrying on an activity as producer[915] in the specified geographical area with respect to the goods[916] particularized in the application.[917]

In his capacity as a guardian of groups of persons entitled to a particular GI, the registrar may – on his own motion or upon being moved by the persons concerned – register the GI. In essence, the registrar assumes this responsibility if the persons entitled to make such an application are unable to exhaust that right due to disorganization among them. It is instructive to note that even in these circumstances, the registrar has to file for, obtain and enforce the registration. Once the persons with initial entitlement to make such an application are formally organized, the registrar will cease to act as a guardian, and cede all rights and obligations in respect of the GI to the entitled persons.[918]

Upon receiving an application for GI registration, the registrar is duty-bound to carry out substantive examination in order to find out whether the grounds for

913. However, the registrar may initiate the registration process in exceptional circumstances described in s. 60(3), ZIPA.
914. Section 61, ZIPA.
915. ZIPA delineates the term 'producer' to mean: (i) any producer of agricultural products or any other person exploiting natural products; and (ii) any manufacturer of handcraft, or industry (cf. s. 56(a), ZIPA).
916. The term 'good' is employed under the ZIPA as a reference to any 'natural or agricultural product or any product of handcraft or industry' (cf. s. 56(a), ZIPA).
917. Cf. s. 60(2), ZIPA.
918. Cf. s. 60(3), ZIPA.

refusal of GIs protection that would disqualify such an indication from being registered exist.[919] The ZIPA does not contain any provision requiring the registrar to publish an application for GI registration. However, in case of an opposition against the sign's registration, the registrar is under obligation to publish such an opposition notice in the Official Gazette giving the applicant an allowance of ninety days within which to send to the registrar a counterstatement outlining the grounds supporting his application for the registration of the GI involved. The law obliges the registrar to furnish the objector with a copy of the applicant's counterstatement.

A successful application for GI registration culminates in the grant of the certificate of GI registration. However, the issuance such a certificate is preceded by one of two events; namely, unsuccessful opposition proceedings, and – in case of an unopposed application – the expiration of the duration within which an opposition notice can be legally lodged.[920]

ZIPA bestows an entitlement to use a GI validly registered in Tanzania Zanzibar upon a specific class of persons. According to the legal position enshrined under section 63 of the ZIPA '[only] producers carrying on their activity in the geographical area specified in the Register … [enjoy] the right to use a registered [GI], in the course of trade, with respect to products specified in the Register, provided that such products possess the quality, reputation or other characteristic specified in the Register'.

Granting that the interest of justice necessitates invalidation or rectification of a GI's register, the ZIPA bestows powers upon the HCZ to make a corresponding decision. The procedure leading to such invalidation or rectification obliges the registrar upon receiving a notice for invalidation or rectification to serve the same to the 'person who filed the application for registration or his successor in title'. Moreover, such a notice may be communicated to all persons enjoying a right to use the GI concerned. Such a communication is done through a notice published in the Official Gazette.[921] Indeed invalidation of a registered GI is imminent in case an interested party or the minister responsible for industrial property matters convinces the HCZ that the GI was registered in foresight of the grounds for refusal of registration.[922] Factors that would warrant rectification of the GI's register include a proof that the 'geographical area specified in the registration does not correspond to the geographical indication, or that the indication of the products for which the geographical indication is used or the indication of the quality, reputation or other characteristic of such products is missing'.[923]

Moreover, persons or groups of producers or consumers interested in a particular registered or unregistered GI possess a right to commence legal proceedings before the HCZ requesting the court to prohibit the following manner of exploitation of GIs:

919. These grounds are outlined in para. 418 above.
920. Cf. s. 62, ZIPA.
921. Section 64(2), ZIPA.
922. These grounds are outlined in para. 418 above.
923. Cf. s. 64, ZIPA.

(a) the use of any means in the designation or presentation of goods that indicates or suggests that the goods in question originates in a geographical area other than the true place of origin in a manner that misleads the public as to the geographical origin of the goods;
(b) any use which constitutes an act of unfair competition within the meaning of Article 10 of the Paris convention; or
(c) use of a geographical indication identifying any goods not originating in the place indicated by the geographical indication in question.[924]

II. Trademark Law

420. As an alternative approach to a sui generis protection of GIs, the legislature may incorporate in a trademark law two categories of provisions, namely: (1) those which prohibit geographical indication from registration and/or use by unauthorized third parties as a trademark; and (2) those providing for the protection of GIs as registered certification or collective marks. Two principal legislations – namely, the TSMA, 1986 and the ZIPA, 2008 – govern trademark matters in the United Republic of Tanzania.[925] As provided in the first sentence of this paragraph, a scrutiny on the extent to which these pieces of legislation provide for the protection of geographical indications necessitates an analysis of: (1) provisions regulating certification and/or collective marks; and (2) provisions prohibiting registration of geographical indication as a trademark.

A. *Certification Marks*

421. As opposed to ZIPA, which expressly enshrines provisions on the protection of certification signs in Tanzania Zanzibar, the TSMA does not contain a provision that can be invoked to protect this category of marks in mainland Tanzania. The term 'certification signs' is applied under the ZIPA as a reference to 'signs or combination of signs capable of designating any common characteristic, including quality, origin or methods of production, of goods and services and which are used under the control of the owner of the signs'.[926] Thus, where a sign is applied to products that meet certain prescribed standards only so as to differentiate those products from other products, it may qualify for registration and protection as a certification mark provided that two additional conditions are met: the owner of the mark – whose role is confined to a duty to exercise control over the marking of goods so that his certification mark is only applied to products that meet the prescribed standards – must not be the one who uses the mark insofar as the marking

924. Cf. s. 57, ZIPA.
925. The TSMA, which is the main source of trademark jurisprudence in mainland Tanzania was enacted in 1986 and became effective in October 1994. On its part, the ZIPA was passed in 2008 to serve as a point of reference when it comes to the regulation of trademark matters in Tanzania island (i.e., Zanzibar) and came into force towards the end of the same year.
926. Cf. s. 2(1), para. 4, ZIPA.

of his goods or services is concerned.[927] In view of the fact that a certification mark applied to goods serves as a guarantee that the goods are of certain origin, quality, characteristics, etc., a name of a geographical location that qualifies for protection as a geographical indication within the meaning of Article 22.1. TRIPS[928] may also meet the requirement for registration as a certification mark under section 52 of the ZIPA.

It is to be noted that individual natural and legal persons enjoy a right to apply to the Registrar of Trade Marks for the registration of a GI designated as a certification trademark. One of the conditions underlying the admissibility of an application for registration of a GI as a certification mark requires the applicant to accompany the application with the rules that govern the use of his certification mark.[929] The following conditions form part and parcel of the package for the protection of a GI as a certification mark: (1) the registrant does not enjoy a right to exclude third parties from using the geographical indication in relation to goods that have quality or characteristics of the goods in relation to which the geographical indication as a certification mark is normally used to certify; (2) the person in whose name the geographical indication is registered as certification mark is not allowed to use the certification mark to certify his goods or services: his benefit in relation to the mark only comes through a fee he collects for the certification services he renders to other persons; (3) in order a geographical indication to be registered as a certification mark, an applicant's competence to certify the goods and services in respect of which the certification mark is used must be properly established.[930]

When it comes to invalidating a geographical indication protected as a certification mark in Tanzania Zanzibar, the person instituting proceedings thereof must take this stance within five years of the sign's registration; beyond this period the sign's validity becomes incontestable.[931] Factors that may render invalid a geographical sign enjoying registration as a certification mark in Zanzibar include where: (1) the proprietor of the certification mark applies it to his goods or uses it to market service he offers; (2) the proprietor of the mark allows it to be used in a way that misleads or confuses marketers and the public at large insofar as the origin and quality (or other characteristic) of the products or services in relation to which the sign is used are concerned.[932]

---

927. *See* the ALRAESA Journal, vol. 1 Apr., 2011, p. 91.
928. Article 22.1 reads as follows:

> Geographical indications are, for the purposes of this Agreement [i.e., TRIPS], indications which identify a good as originating in the territory of a Member, or a region or locality in that territory, where a given quality, reputation or other characteristic of the good is essentially attributed to its geographical origin.

929. Cf. s. 52(1), ZIPA.
930. Cf. s. 52, ZIPA.
931. Cf. s. 50(I)(b), ZIPA.
932. Cf. s. 52(3), ZIPA.

B. Collective Mark

422. A response to the question whether or not rules governing protection of collective marks may be cited as an alternative to a sui generis system of GIs protection in the United Republic of Tanzania is partly affirmative and partly negative. Whereas under the law governing trademark matters in Tanzania Zanzibar collective marks are afforded legal protection, this is not the case under the TSMA, which controls the trademark protection regime in mainland Tanzania. A sign that qualifies for registration as a collective mark under the ZIPA is that which belongs to a 'collectivity, such as a cooperative or an association or federation of industrialists, producers or merchants'.[933] Protection by way of registration of a collective mark in Tanzania Zanzibar is preconditioned on the applicant thereof discharging certain obligations. For instance, the applicant has to 'designate the (collective) mark (in respect of which registration is sought) as a collective mark'. It is also a *sine qua non* that an application for registration of a collective mark is accompanied by rules prescribing the context in which the collective mark concerned is to be used.

As regards the qualifications of the applicant for collective marks, the requirement that the applicant 'possesses an industrial or commercial establishment anywhere in a Member of the Paris Union or a Member of the World Trade Organization' – as is a case for other categories of trademarks – does not apply in respect of collective marks.[934]

C. Prohibition of Registration of Geographical Indication as a Trade Mark

423. One of the qualifications a sign should possess as a precondition for its registration as a trademark is distinctiveness. The trademark legislations of both mainland Tanzania and Tanzania Zanzibar enshrine the distinctiveness requirement as a cornerstone of the trademarks protection regime obtaining in the United Republic of Tanzania.[935] In most cases, enforcement of this requirement will stand against registration of GIs as a trademark, thus providing an indirect protection to the GIs concerned. The justification for this conclusion lies in the fact that geographical indications are mostly regarded to lack distinctive character in the trade mark sense; they tend to be descriptive of the goods or services offered under them. In this regard, it is an understanding that a descriptive sign is incapable of distinguishing goods and services of the sign's proprietor from those of other undertakings. GIs are constituted by a descriptive term, which normally makes a direct reference to the character or quality of the goods or services it purports to market; and hence unqualified for protection as a trademark.[936]

933. Cf. s. 2, para. 6, ZIPA.
934. Cf. s. 51, ZIPA.
935. Cf. s. 16, TSMA & s. 46, ZIPA respectively.
936. In some cases however, a geographical indication may acquire a secondary meaning such that it qualifies for registration as a trademark. Given its acquired distinctiveness, such a geographical indication is capable of functioning as a badge of origin and hence registrable as a trademark.

In addition to the above, both the TSMA and ZIPA contain a provision, which prohibits registration of a mark the exploitation of which is likely to cause deception or confusion insofar as geographical origin of a product is concerned.[937] While this provision indirectly serves the interests of persons who exploits a GI in relation to goods or services they offer, the direct beneficiary of this provision are 'consumers of the goods or services offered under' the GI.[938]

Another indirect protection of GIs through exclusion from registration of a GI as a trademark is reflected in the provisions which requires the Registrar of trademark matters to grant a trademark registration only if he is satisfied that such registration does not interfere with one's bona fide use of his name or of the name of the geographical location of his business.[939]

III. Laws Regulating Business Practices

A. *Unfair Competition Law*

424. The incorporation of Article 10*bis* in the Paris Convention during the revisions that were made to the Convention in 1900 at Brussels made unfair competition law an integral part of IP law, and served as an assurance that protection against unfair trade practices is the viable means to supplement IP protection, especially when unfair trade behaviour is perpetuated in relation to an unregistered IP right such as geographical indications.[940]

425. Competition rules that essentially reflect the provisions of Article 10*bis* of the Paris Convention, and which can be invoked to protect geographical indications in the United Republic of Tanzania are contained in two principal legislations enacted by the legislature of Tanzania Zanzibar and that of Tanzania Mainland. These are the ZIPA of 2008 and the Fair Competition Act (FCA) in force in mainland Tanzania.[941] Section 57 of the ZIPA links the sui generis GIs protection regime obtaining in Tanzania Zanzibar with the unfair competition regime established under Article 10*bis* of the Paris Convention. It provides that:

> any interested person and any interested group of producers or consumers may institute proceedings in the [HCZ] to prevent, in respect of geographical indications, (a)… (b) any use which constitutes an act of unfair competition within the meaning of Article 10 of the Paris Convention; or (c)…[942]

937. Cf. s. 19, TSMA & s. 46, ZIPA.
938. WIPO, Standing Committee on the Law of Trademarks, Industrial Designs and Geographical Indications: Study on the Protection of Country Names, 2013 (Document No. SCT/29/5 REV.), p. 6 at para. 33.
939. Cf. s. 34, TSMA & s. 46, ZIPA.
940. Cf. M. Wekesa & B. Sihanya eds, *Intellectual Property in Kenya* 228–229 (Konrad Adenauer Stiftung 2009).
941. The FCA is only applicable to mainland Tanzania (cf. s. 6, FCA).
942. Cf. s. 57(b), ZIPA.

426. Similarly, several provisions of the FCA may justifiably be applied inasmuch as the protection of GIs in mainland Tanzania is concerned. In its part III addressing misleading and deceptive conduct, the FCA commences with a general stipulation, according to which 'no person shall, in trade, engage in conduct that is misleading or deceptive or is likely to mislead or deceive'.[943] In the same vein, section 16 of the FCA, which addresses issues concerning misleading or false representations, provides *inter alia* that 'no person shall, make a false or misleading representation concerning the place of origin of goods, in connection with supply or possible supply of goods or services or in connection with the promotion by any means of the supply or use of goods or services'.[944] These provisions can support a cause of action against a person who uses a GI in a misleading or deceptive manner. A hypothetical case can provide a better elaboration in this regard: Suppose that JOHNSON sells coffee. He claims that the coffee is produced in location X – a geographical area that is endowed with good soils and climatic condition that support growth of high quality coffee – whereby a traditional method peculiar to inhabitants of this area is employed in processing the said coffee. For instance, the coffee beans are dried through a flavoured smoke produced by burning tree leaves (available in location X only) and thereafter the coffee beans are put in a sack and soaked in a river whose water injects into the beans a stinging nettle flavour, a process subsequent to which the beans are traditionally ground using special stones that enrich the resultant coffee with iron substances. JOHNSON would act in contravention of the provisions of sections 15 and 16 of the FCA if his claim is untrue and the truth of the matter turns out that the coffee he sells is grown and processed in location Z using a method other than the one JOHNSON claims.

427. Chapter III of the ZIPA provides for a regime of protection against unfair competition, which can be invoked to address unfair commercial practices committed in Tanzania Zanzibar including the one which the hypothetical case in the immediately preceding paragraph describes. Section 70 is one of the provisions of ZIPA that serves as a cornerstone of the regulation of unfair competition practices in industrial and commercial matters. It is beyond argument that a trader, who seeks to trade on the marketing power of a particular sign that is used in trade, reaps unfair advantage if he makes the consumer to be deceived or misled that the trader's goods are the ones usually traded under or connected with the sign whose quality characteristic is well-known to them. It is on this understanding that section 70 of the FCA regards one of the factors that may cause 'unfair competition' to be any 'act or practice, in the course of industrial or commercial activities, that misleads or is likely to mislead the public with respect to an enterprise or its activities, in particular, the products or services offered by such enterprise'. The section defines the term 'misleading' in an approach that hints at the fact that an act of unfair competition directed at a protected GI falls within the ambit of the provisions of section 70 of the FCA. According to the provisions of this section:

943. Section 15, FCA.
944. Cf. s. 16, FCA.

> Misleading may [*inter alia*] arise out of advertising or promotion and may, in particular, occur with respect to (i) the manufacturing process; (ii) the suitability of a product or service for a particular purpose; (iii) the quality or quantity or other characteristics of products or services; (iv) the geographical origin of products or services.

B. The Tort of Passing Off

428. Passing off is a common-law action for unliquidated damages. A right to institute an action for this particular tort is bestowed upon a plaintiff who reasonably claims that the defendant – actively or passively – misrepresents facts regarding goods he trades in such that consumers are led to believe that the goods do not originate from the defendant but from the plaintiff or that the defendant's goods are – in one way or the other – associated or connected with the plaintiff. The case of *Erven Warnick B.V. & another appellant v. J. Townend & Sons (Hull) Ltd. & Anor* [1979] AC 732[945] gave *Lord Diplock* an opportunity to ingeniously devise five elements of the tort of passing off; namely:

> (1) misrepresentation (2) made by a trader in the course of trade, (3) to prospective customers of his or ultimate consumers of goods or services supplied by him, (4) which is calculated to injure the business or goodwill of another trader (in the sense that this is a reasonably foreseeable consequence) and (5) which causes actual damage to a business or goodwill of the trader by whom the action is brought or (in a quia timet action) will probably do so.

On the contrary *Lord Oliver* – in *Rekitt and Colman Products Ltd v. Borden Inc & Ors* [1990] UKHL 12[946] – summarized the tort of passing off in one brief sentence stating that 'no man may pass off his goods as those of another', and went on to reduce the five elements of the tort of passing off outlined by *Lord Diplock*[947] into three elements as follows:

> First, he must [the plaintiff] establish a goodwill or reputation attached to the goods or services which he supplies in the mind of the purchasing public by

945. The material facts of this case as summarized by *Lord Fraser* reveal that:

> The first appellants manufacture in the Netherlands the alcoholic beverage called *advocaat* and import it into England where they sell it through the second appellants. Both appellants are now members of the Allied Breweries Group, and for the purposes of this appeal, they can be regarded as one company. In this action they ask for injunction against the respondents... from selling or offering for sale any product under the name of '*advocaat*' unless it basically consists of spirit and eggs, and does not include wine, and UR-Tanzania, from representing that a mixture of wine and eggs is *advocaat*. The court granted an injunction.

946. The case is also cited as: [1990] 1 WLR 491, [1990] RPC 341, [1990] 1 All ER 873. URL: http://www.bailii.org/uk/cases/UKHL/1990/12.html (accessed: 16 Dec. 2015).
947. Cf. *Erven Warnick B.V. & another appellant v. J. Townend & Sons* (Hull) Ltd. & Anor [1979] AC 732.

> association with the identifying 'get-up' (whether it consists simply of a brand name or a trade description, or the individual features of labelling or packaging) under which his particular goods or services are offered to the public, such that the get-up is recognised by the public as distinctive specifically of the plaintiff's goods or services. Secondly, he must demonstrate a misrepresentation by the defendant to the public (whether or not intentional) leading or likely to lead the public to believe that goods or services offered by him are the goods or services of the plaintiff....[948] Thirdly, he must demonstrate that he suffers or, in a *quia timet* action, that he is likely to suffer damage by reason of the erroneous belief engendered by the defendant's misrepresentation that the source of the defendant's goods or services is the same as the source of those offered by the plaintiff.

429. Two categories of the tort of passing off; namely, 'classic passing off' and 'extended passing off' clarify circumstances, which may give rise to an action for GI's infringement under this tort in the United Republic of Tanzania.[949] The classic passing off deals with clear cases of unfair trade practices perpetuated with respect to a geographical indication, which is customarily capable of serving as a badge of origin insofar as the goods marketed under it are concerned. Under this form of passing off, a person represents his own goods as goods belonging to another person that is not connected with him in business.[950] A typical example falling under the classic case of passing off would be where a geographical term that has acquired a secondary meaning and hence distinctive for the goods marketed under it is being used by a third part claiming that the goods he markets under the geographical name are the same (in terms of origin, quality and other characteristics) as those marketed under the term while the contrary is true.

Section 30 of the TSMA provides for a possibility of a trademark proprietor to seek remedies under the classic passing off and thus serving as an enabling legal provision for the protection of GIs in Tanzania. It stipulates as hereunder:

> No person shall be entitled to institute any proceedings to prevent or to recover damages for the infringement of an unregistered trade or service mark, but nothing in [the TSMA] shall be deemed to affect rights of action against any person for passing off goods or services as the goods or services of another person, or the remedies in respect thereof.

---

948. In relation to this element, Lord Oliver goes on to aver: the public is aware of the plaintiff's identity as the manufacturer of supplier of the goods or services is immaterial, as long as they are identified with a particular source, which is in fact the plaintiff. For example, if the public is accustomed to rely upon a particular brand name in purchasing goods of a particular description, it matters not at all that there is a little or no public awareness of the identity of the proprietor of the brand name.
949. Cf. L.T.C. Harms, *The Enforcement of Intellectual Property Rights: A Case Book* 239–240 (WIPO 3rd ed. 2012), www.wipo.int/edocs/pubdocs/en/intproperty/791/wipo_pub_791.pdf (accessed: 30 Jun. 2020).
950. *See* the opening paragraph in Lord Diplock's judgment in *Erven Warnick B.V. & another appellant v. J. Townend & Sons* (Hull) Ltd. & Anor [1979] AC 732, where he draws the attention of the House of Lords to the two categories of the tort of passing off. 9.

On the contrary, the extended passing off applies to geographical terms, which are purely descriptive of the goods marketed under them – a factor that excludes them from being protected under classic passing off. The crux of the matter is that a descriptive geographical term does not serve as a badge of origin of goods, but tends to refer to the quality and other attributes of the goods in connection with which it is used. In the circumstances, the extended passing off can be invoked to curb unfair trade practices that cannot be stopped or remedied based on the classic tort of passing off. For instance, trader B who uses a descriptive geographical term in relation to honey that is normally produced in location X where he resides, while the said term customarily describes characteristic and quality of honey produced in location Y, the classic tort of passing off cannot be invoked to prohibit the said trader from using the geographical name because he is not using it as a badge of origin, but as a description of the honey he markets. In this regard, the goodwill[951] relating to the geographical indication concerned does not stem from the distinctiveness of the GI, but results from the reputation of the products.[952]

The foregoing factual scenario reflects the position laid down in *J. Bollinger v. Costa Brava Wine Co. Ltd.* [1960] Ch. 262: the plaintiff in this case was a businessman established in Champagne – an area located in France – where the wine he was trading in was produced and the grapes from which the wine was made was grown. The plaintiff's wine took the name of the place where it was produced and consumers knew it as a champagne wine with a high reputation. Following such a reputation, which was gained as a result of intensive advertisement, members of the public ordering the champagne wine expected to get wine produced in champagne using grapes grown in this area. The plaintiff sought to prohibit the defendants who were selling wine under the name 'Spanish champagne', whereby the said wine was not produced in champagne and the grapes were not grown there.[953] In granting the injunction against the defendants, *Danckwerts J.* pointed out as follows:

> There seem to be no reason why such [permission to engage in an intentional act that adversely affects proprietary interests of another person] should be given to a person, competing in trade, who seeks to attach to his product a name or description with which it has no natural association so as to make use of the reputation and goodwill which has been gained by a product genuinely indicated by the name or description. In my view, it ought not to matter that the persons truly entitled to describe their goods by the name and description are a class producing goods in a certain locality, and not merely one individual. The description is part of their goodwill and a right of property. I do not believe that the law of passing off, which arose to prevent unfair trading, is so limited in scope.[954]

---

951. The term 'good will' was defined by Lord Macnaghten – in *Inland Revenue Commissioners v. Muller & Co.'s Margarine Ltd.* [1901] A.C. 217, 223–224 – in the following manner: 'It is the benefit and advantage of the good name, reputation and connection of business. It is the attractive force which brings in custom.'
952. It is instructive to note that the right to use the geographical indication in a manner describing characteristic qualities of the goods extends to a class of persons.
953. *J. Bollinger v. Costa Brava Wine Co. Ltd.* [1960] Ch. 262, 273.
954. *J. Bollinger v. Costa Brava Wine Co. Ltd.* [1960] Ch. 262, at 283–284.

In conjunction with the above quotation, the insightful position regarding extended passing off summarized by *Harms* is also worth quoting:

> To succeed in extended passing off the plaintiff's goodwill must be damaged by the defendant's incorrect application of the term.
>
> Traders cannot use extended passing off to prevent rivals from applying the descriptive term correctly because this would not damage their goodwill.
>
> Extended passing off differs from classic passing off in two key respects. First, a misrepresentation of origin is not required (as) it protects traders as a class rather than as individuals. Second, it protects descriptive terms. This does not give monopoly rights in the descriptive term because only incorrect application of the term can be prevented.[955]

C. The Merchandise Marks Act

430. The MMA (as amended) provides for 'marking of goods, and for matters incidental thereto'.[956] This legislation is relevant to the protection of geographical indication in the sense that it controls labelling of goods and the use of trade descriptions so that correct information regarding origins, quality, mode of production, composition, etc., of goods accompanies the marketing of the goods concerned. The Act generally requires, as a condition for selling in Tanzania goods imported into or made in Tanzania, that the goods concerned be accompanied by indication of origin.[957] The Act further prohibits the use of false trade descriptions.[958]

955. Cf. footnote 245 in: L.T.C. Harms, *The Enforcement of Intellectual Property Rights: A Case Book* 341 (WIPO 3rd ed. 2012). According to the mentioned footnote, Harms borrowed the quoted information from Katherine Saunders '*Choccosu isee – the new "extended" passing of*' [2001] VUWLRev 13.

956. Cf. The long title to the Merchandise Marks Act.

957. Cf. ss 8 & 9, ZAMMA.

958. Cf. s. 6, ZAMMA.

Selected Bibliography

Mahingila, E. 'Intellectual Property Landscape in Tanzania – The Emerging Role of the Business Registration and Licensing Agency (BRELA) in Assisting Small Medium Enterprises Use Intellectual Property'. A paper presented during the WIPO Workshop on Intellectual Property for Business for Small Medium-Sized Enterprises (SMES) held on 10 and 11 May 2005, at Dar Es Salaam. Paper available in 'WIPO document reference No. WIPO/SMEs/DAR/05/'.

Olsson, H. 'Role of Copyright and Neighbouring Rights in Development'. *Lesotho Law Journal* Vol. 4(1) (1988): 51

Jaconiah, J. 'The Parallel Importation of Trademarked Goods in the Framework of the Economic Partnership Agreement Between the East African Community and the European Union'. *IIC* Vol. 42(6) (2011): 685–686.

Jaconiah, J. 'The Requirement for Registration and Protection of Non-traditional Trade Marks in the European Union and in Tanzania'. *IIC* Vol. 40(7) (2009): 756 et seq.

Mrema, A.N. *Recent Legislative Changes in Trademark Law in Tanzania.* A speech delivered at INTA conference (URL: http://www.mkono.com/pdf/Inta%20paper%202009-Final%20doc.pdf (accessed on 16 December 2015)).

Ngwediagi, P. 'Establishment of Plant Breeders' Rights System in Tanzania: Achievements and Challenges'. A Case Study under the Ministry of Agriculture Food Security and Cooperatives, Tanzania; paper available at http://www.wipo.int/wipolex/en/text.jsp?file_id=216639.

Rwezaura, B.A. 'Legal Protection of Intellectual Property in Tanzania'. *Lesotho Law Journal* Vol. 4(1) (1988): 240.

Selected Bibliography

Selected Bibliography

Index

The numbers here refer to paragraph numbers.

Index

www.ingramcontent.com/pod-product-compliance
Ingram Content Group UK Ltd.
Pitfield, Milton Keynes, MK11 3LW, UK
UKHW020137290926
15471UKWH00003B/540

9 789403 548210